Emerson's epistemology

Emerson's epistemology

THE ARGUMENT OF THE ESSAYS

DAVID VAN LEER

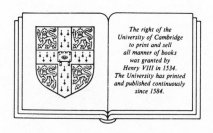

The right of the
University of Cambridge
to print and sell
all manner of books
was granted by
Henry VIII in 1534.
The University has printed
and published continuously
since 1584.

CAMBRIDGE UNIVERSITY PRESS

CAMBRIDGE

LONDON   NEW YORK   NEW ROCHELLE

MELBOURNE   SYDNEY

Published by the Press Syndicate of the University of Cambridge
The Pitt Building, Trumpington Street, Cambridge CB2 1RP
32 East 57th Street, New York, NY 10022, USA
10 Stamford Road, Oakleigh, Melbourne 3166, Australia

© Cambridge University Press 1986

First published 1986

Printed in the United States of America

Library of Congress Cataloging-in-Publication Data
Van Leer, David, 1949–
Emerson's epistemology.
Bibliography: p.
Includes index.
1. Emerson, Ralph Waldo, 1803–1882–Philosophy.
2. Philosophy in literature.   3. Idealism in
literature.   4. Idealism, American.   I. Title.
PS1642.P5V36   1986   814'.3   86-925

British Library Cataloguing in Publication Data
Van Leer, David
Emerson's epistemology: the argument of
the essays.
1. Emerson, Ralph Waldo – Criticism
and interpretation
I. Title
191   PS1638
ISBN 0 521 30820 8

To
MICHAEL J. COLACURCIO
πάνυ γε

Contents

Preface: Toward an "Age of Swedenborg"

There are many stories to be told of the American Renaissance. All share the same rough outline. The middle three decades of the nineteenth century were a turning point in American history. America entered the period buoyed up politically by the prestige of 1812 (and 1776 before that) and emotionally by the sense of an international destiny rising with the economy, expanding with the frontier. In the final third of the century, however, Americans felt disillusioned by the twin shames of civil war and reconstruction. This transition from youthful confidence to mature bewilderment – from Benjamin Franklin to Henry Adams – is prefigured in, even epitomized by, the literary activity of the antebellum decades. In the arts as well as in politics, it was an age of revolution.

The fundamental character of this literary renaissance, however, is less clear. Some scholars have looked at the general preoccupation with progress, politics, or the hypostatized self. Others have focused more narrowly on a single representative topic: the frontier, Adamic innocence, linguistic theory, or historiography. Aesthetic questions have seemed especially revealing. All readers have noted the general tendency to symbolic or stylistic dislocation. Some have detailed the age's preference for particular literary genres – old ones like typology, autobiography, and romance, or new ones like the essay and the catalogue. I study the commitment to philosophical idealism.

My choice is not innocent. Introducing his own account of the age's aesthetic theory, F. O. Matthiessen imagined that at least two other books remained to be written. One, "The Age of Fourier," would take utopian socialism as a synecdoche for all the radical movements of the period. This book has since appeared in many forms, from historical surveys of the age's "ferments" to more critically sensitive analyses of America's declaration of cultural independence. The other book, however, has been treated less frequently. Matthiessen's "Age of Swedenborg" – this title borrowed directly from Emerson – was to examine the philosophies of the period, especially the way idealism promised potential divinity to man through its recognition that the soul makes its own world. The notion of a broadly defined "American idealism" is, of course, a cliché. Yet few works have attempted to delineate precisely the influence of philosophical idealism on any of the major American texts.

Some of the reasons for this omission are obvious. No one denies the relevance of idealism in the nineteenth century. Idealism was *the* great topic of "modern" philosophy – at least until existentialism more "recently" declared the joint deaths of God and metaphysics. Yet it is a topic of notorious, even self-conscious, difficulty. Although we know that American writers responded directly to Descartes, Locke, and Hume, the very name of Kant (not to mention Fichte, Schelling, and Hegel) seems enough to have scared away all but the most foolhardy Americans. To think of German philosophy in the Age of Jackson smacks of hubris; and Matthiessen emphasized the modesty of American thought by naming in his title only the low idealism of Swedenborg rather than the high idealism of Kant (though Emerson had himself equated Transcendentalism with both). Furthermore the very popularity of metaphysics, the veritable chowder of idealisms characteristic of mid-century discourse, argues against the sincerity, maturity, and finally intelligence of these presumptive (not to say presumptuous) philosophers. If – it is claimed – "idealism" might mean in the nineteenth century anything from optimism to the phenomenality of experience, then it did not really mean much at all.

There is a kind of cogency to these objections, especially if we define philosophy very narrowly, America very broadly. But suppose we invert that emphasis and consider philosophy rather more loosely than the Kantians would wish. Then the story becomes accessible to both the nineteenth century and our sense of it. A generally Hegelian account readily suggests itself: with Emerson and Poe in hot pursuit of an ideal Absolute; Hawthorne and Melville grimly prophesying the fatal consequences of such overreaching; and Thoreau and Whitman trying to synthesize the two positions into an idealist phenomenalism that will celebrate spirit without vilifying nature or the body.

Yet such a story, though in some ways an adequate "Age," is distressingly broad. One might restrict the focus further and – borrowing again from Emerson – tell only of the solipsistic "Apocalypse of the Mind" toward which idealism tended. But even that topic does not

allow the required attention to detail. To take seriously American idealism – to read Kant and Fichte into the record, however casually – we
must demonstrate in our authors the kind of intellectual care and precision that would provide a congenial environment for the finer distinctions of systematic philosophy. If idealism in mid-century America
means no more than the attraction to a whomping Truth, then German
metaphysics is an unwarranted intrusion into our literary history, and
the authors (or this critic) are guilty of unforgivable pretentiousness.

One natural solution is to narrow the focus even further and examine
only a single aspect of the "Apocalypse" – the initial flirtation with
idealism in Emerson. Or so it seemed to me as I worked out in rejected
drafts the logic of the critical history just summarized. Having started
with a Matthiessenian history of everything, I thus found myself at its
end studying only one author, and only one aspect of his work at that.
There is, of course, reason to think Emerson the natural place to begin
a history of philosophical idealism. After a period of fluctuating fortunes, Emerson's stock has steadily risen since the early 1950s. Celebrated as the exemplary bard and prophet – as the father of modern
poetry and the chief formulator of the American myth – Emerson has
almost replaced Melville and Whitman as the seminal figure in American culture. Moreover, in the work of Harold Bloom and others, Emerson is beginning to equal (or even to supplant) Wordsworth and
Blake as the crucial transitional figure between Milton and Nietzsche in
the development of a modern transcontinental consciousness.

This very importance, however, may re-create all over again the
problem of scope. For at least part of Emerson's authority derives from
the sheer range of his concerns and the massiveness of his writing.
There is within Emerson as wide a variety of interests and approaches
as within the period as a whole. Like the American Renaissance itself,
Emerson may be studied for his epistemology, his ethical theory, his
aesthetics, his language theory, and even (as recent work has shown) his
politics. Emphasizing the first, then, may seem as arbitrary as my initial
choice to select him over the other Renaissance writers. And my focus
on philosophy just admits that I cannot talk about everything in so
encyclopedic an author.

Yet not entirely. For although any scholar might wish to write Matthiessen's third book, my focus on Emerson's epistemology registers a
more specific, even personal approach. And, in some sense, I feel less
comfortable as a self-proclaimed Emersonian than as an intellectual historian of the Renaissance. Emersonians are always pointing out the
marks of true Emersonianism in the ability to respond to some representative passage or essential virtue. I am, however, rarely attracted to
this aspect of Emerson. The moments I prize are not the stylish odes to

beauty and the over-soul, but the gnarled passages of almost meta-physical wit. And if my Emerson has a literary antecedent, it is less Wordsworth or Carlyle than Donne and Herbert.

I do not, then, so much respond to Emerson as stand perplexed and fascinated before his works. Although interested in the famous passages since my student days, the more I looked at those confusing statements about "original relations" or "foolish consistency," the more the words seemed to unravel before my eyes. Now in part all I was experiencing, of course, was the general indeterminacy of language. Yet it is hard not to feel that the problem was more specific. Emerson's meaning often feels wrong in interesting ways: if longings are really the issue, surely what we "want" is not an original relation to the universe but a natural relation to nature. Moreover the tensions and echoes within and be-tween the essays appear to be Emerson's way of controlling the ambig-uous shifts in his logic. It is hard, quite simply, not to hear in the "lively stones" of "Circles" a recollection of the stones flung in *Nature* and an anticipation of the "bleak rocks" of "Experience."

Finally neither a mystic nor a transcendentalist, I generally feel adrift in discussions of Emerson's characteristic topics – correspondence, com-pensation, the over-soul, the eternal now. Here the problem is largely one of vocabulary. Those who speak of Emerson's ideas address them wholly on his own terms, so that at some level all critics of Transcenden-talism transcendentalize. Although such a sympathetic reading is not wrong – is even generous – it automatically excludes outsiders like me. We listen to analyses of big and little Selves, knowing all the while that the concept of an over-soul is largely exploded, or at least vilified. It seemed valuable, then, to try to translate Emerson's private vocabulary into the more public one of traditional philosophy. The effect may finally be to convince readers that the professional terminology is even more arcane than Emerson's own. But at least it will allow Emerson, Des-cartes, Kant, and Wittgenstein to share thoughts about "transcendental idealism" in a way that they cannot share them about "compensation."

One result of this project of translation is that I am far less drawn than most critics to the psychological drama of Emerson's intellectual life. As David Robinson has recently observed, in their revaluation "both Whicher and Bishop run the risk of portraying Emerson as a man whose philosophy was no more than the compensating reflection of his personal inadequacies and disappointments." When coupled with the more general Bloomian notion that literature grows out of authors' anxious confrontations with previous literature, this psychological bias has encouraged critics to read past Emerson's ideas to the intellectual energy behind them. One understands the motive here; and Whicher, Bishop, and Bloom have in their dramatizations of Emerson's anxieties overturned the old objection about his facile optimism. Although I find such accounts convincing, however, I do not feel (as they implicitly do) that Emerson's meaning is all that clear. And as they read through to the why of Emerson's statements, I find myself all too often stuck on the preliminary question of what.

For a similar reason, I tend to be less concerned than most with identifying the sources of Emerson's ideas. The notebooks and letters are not only fascinating in themselves, but offer in many cases livelier accounts of the ideas than their final versions in the essays. As a result, the journals have tended in recent criticism to steal the spotlight from the published works. One critic has gone so far as to read ten pages of the journals for continuities and juxtapositions, as if these pages constituted a kind of natural unity – an unconscious essay. Another has declared the essays mere "epiphenomena" produced along the way. And the day is surely not far off when someone will identify the *JMN* as Emerson's true masterpiece, the great *roman-fleuve* of American Romanticism.

This tendency troubles me for two reasons. I no longer know exactly what we mean by authorial intention. But to the extent that contemporary theory convinces me that an "author" is not a biological entity but the limit function of a text, it seems that overinvestment in the journals commits the intentional fallacy in its most elementary form – the biographical one. If the author is a logical presupposition of a text, he cannot therefore exist apart from a text. To search for the "author" of "Self-Reliance" in some proto-textual notebook, then, is probably to confuse the (irrelevant) historical Emerson with the intending writer of a specific essay.

More generally, however, I fear that, whatever their epistemic status, the journals as sources for empirical evidence simply prove too much. Virtually anything can be found somewhere in those sixteen volumes. But the organization and argument essential to thought are excluded, by definition, from any such "notebook." The emphases (or generic lack of them) are so different that the journals almost seem to have different thoughts than the essays. Although Swedenborgian correspondence is still treated in the journals at least as late as 1837, for example, the concept does not play a significant philosophical role in the published works after the fourth chapter of *Nature*. To overvalue the journals – and thus implicitly to deny the meaning of the editorial selection Emerson so clearly exercised in publication – may rob him of one of his most important techniques for artistic control.

Thus not only do I find myself increasingly drawn to a philosophical sophistication Emerson is thought not to possess, but tend to look for it in a structural control he also lacks. As my subtitle implies, even the most aphoristic ideas cannot function as discrete units but only as part of a larger context, loosely called an "argument." Emerson's masterful style is evident on virtually every page he wrote – in every journal entry, letter, sermon, lecture, and essay. But attention to style as such can be misleading. It implies that some styles are so pleasing in themselves that they need not mean much of anything; and after Matthiessen we remember Emerson's phrase about "pot and kettle" far more than the Swedenborgian linguistic theory it underwrites.

I am not sure how I feel about this implication in general (though I would not want to defend the propositional logic of *The House of Life*). But whether or not a purely stylistic discourse is possible, I do not feel Emerson's prose to be one. It is difficult to prove conclusively that the essays are structured. The organizing potential of the mind means that an enterprising critic can always find a kind of order. But it seems equally foolish to overreact and assume disorganization. For such an argument, even if true, has a pernicious effect. It is hard, as one critic has wittily complained, to remember the source of any specific passage, and one does spend too much time leafing through texts in search of a page reference for a sentence one has quoted all one's life. But critics too often discover in Emerson's presumed disorder a dangerous license. The sense that in the essays anything can be anywhere liberates their own accounts, until the only thing less linear than an Emerson essay is a reading of one.

My response, then, is simply to treat the essays as if they were both philosophical and organized. After a theoretical introduction discussing some of the reasons why we tend to distrust Emerson's philosophy, I examine the major writings of the 1830s and 1840s, focusing especially on four works – *Nature*, the Divinity School "Address," "Self-Reliance," and "Experience." The approach is not empirical but hypothetical. In the absence of evidence one way or the other, I simply assume that the essays can be read seriously in terms of their philosophical content, and by such philosophical readings show the individual works to be more carefully structured than many have assumed.

I am not unaware of the potential for self-parody in such an approach. By reading so meticulously a small number of texts, I surely illustrate what one critic has called the "failure of tact." And what friendly readers may find indefatigable will strike others as merely relentless. Nor is it untrue that my Emerson displays a little too clearly my own penchant for Jacobean combat. Still I know no other way of taking care than to take pains. Nor does the fear of monstrous progeny seem a sufficient argument against procreation. For, finally, my hypothetical account means only to disprove the claim that Emerson cannot be read seriously as a philosopher. Whether he should so be read, I leave for others to decide.

Acknowledgments

The moment of public acknowledgment, for most a simple pleasure, is for me one of Protestant anxiety. I can no more fully confess my debts than my sins. I have always known myself original only in my errors; now even this claim seems hubris. Nevertheless the attempt may stand for something, and though all omissions are unintentional, the inclusions are real enough.

Work on this volume has been supported by grants from the National Endowment for the Humanities, the American Council of Learned Societies, the Huntington Library, and the Surdna Foundation at Princeton, to which I am most grateful; as I am to Princeton University for its generous leave policy for junior faculty. The dissertation form of the manuscript was awarded Cornell's Messenger-Chalmers Prize in intellectual history and its Guilford Prize in English. I thank both prize committees for financial and moral support in those most uncertain early stages of writing. I also thank the staffs of the Houghton, New York Public, and Cornell libraries for their aid. Special mention must be made of the staff and readers of the Henry E. Huntington Library, whose knowledge and good fellowship so facilitated the writing of the final draft.

I have been particularly lucky to have profited from the expert readings of a number of friends and scholars, many of whom have suffered through more drafts of this work than I can admit without embarrassment. Hans Aarsleff, Martha Banta, Sacvan Bercovitch, Jean Frantz Blackall, Alfred Bush, Edward Davidson, Robert Elias, Emory Elliott, Allan Moore Emery, Sander Gilman, William Howarth, James H. Kavanagh, Bruce Kuklick, David Levin, Thomas McFarland, Lee Clark

Mitchell, Kenneth Myers, Valerie Smith, and David M. Wyatt have all offered excellent criticisms, as did Michelle Parham Preston, who helped in the final stages of preparation. I am especially grateful for the help of Jonathan Bennett, Alan Donagan, David Fate Norton, Richard Rorty, Ernest Lee Tuveson, and John W. Yolton on some of the finer philosophical points. In all cases, of course, these generous readers are not to be held responsible for my subsequent misunderstanding or misuse of their insights.

The tradition of Emerson scholarship is a particularly long and venerable one, as I hope to have indicated in my notes. A special mention, however, must be made of Stephen E. Whicher, particularly since some of my argument seems to challenge the tendencies, though not the conclusions, of his work. It would be impossible to have studied in his library, poring over his books and marginalia, without admitting him as my intellectual grandfather (with his friend and colleague the taciturn Jonathan Bishop as something of an unwitting step-uncle). For whatever reasons, Whicher seems not to have called forth from his fellow Emersonians the customary degree of effusiveness. His "memorial" in the preface to EL.II is downright curt, and it is sometimes claimed that the manner of his death compromised his intellectual achievement. But at least for those of us who know him only through his work as critic and editor, Whicher remains the *sine qua non* of Emerson studies. And if his name figures less in my notes than those of more recent scholars, let it stand here in grateful acknowledgment of his triumphant contribution, never surpassed and scarcely equaled.

In the case of Michael J. Colacurcio, acknowledgment runs the risk of redundancy, and my dedication merely belabors the obvious. The idea for this project was originally his, and at times I fear he has seen it through more drafts than I. If I have not always been gracious (let alone grateful) in light of this debt, that is, as they say, my problem. For whether the ur-myth is Oedipus or Kronos, the simple truth is that only a coward would wish Socrates silent.

Years ago, at the start of my studies, a table of friends toasted my work "because the world can never have enough idealism." They, of course, got it wrong – what I meant by idealism and where I stood on it. But I appreciated the sentiment. As I have that of the family and friends who subsequently listened, corrected, and even brought me back to earth with their indifference. They will, I trust, understand their anonymity here. The publication of such names is almost an insult, and these debts, though the greatest of all, must be answered in other places, other ways.

A note on the editions cited

References to Emerson's writings are indicated parenthetically in the text by abbreviated title, volume, and page number. References not immediately identified are included in the next parenthetic citation. The following standard abbreviations are used.

CEC   *The Correspondence of Emerson and Carlyle.* Ed. Joseph Slater. New York: Columbia University Press, 1964.

CW   *The Collected Works of Ralph Waldo Emerson.* Ed. Robert Spiller, Alfred Ferguson, et al. 3 vols. to date. Cambridge, Mass.: Harvard University Press, 1971- .

EL   *The Early Lectures of Ralph Waldo Emerson.* Ed. Stephen Whicher, Robert Spiller, and Wallace E. Williams. 3 vols. Cambridge, Mass.: Harvard University Press, 1959-72.

J   *The Journals of Ralph Waldo Emerson.* Ed. Edward Waldo Emerson and Waldo Emerson Forbes. 10 vols. Boston and New York: Houghton Mifflin Co., 1909-14.

JMN   *The Journals and Miscellaneous Notebooks of Ralph Waldo Emerson.* Ed. William Gilman et al. 16 vols. Cambridge, Mass.: Harvard University Press, 1960-82.

L   *The Letters of Ralph Waldo Emerson.* Ed. Ralph L. Rusk. 6 vols. New York: Columbia University Press, 1939.

W   *The Complete Works of Ralph Waldo Emerson.* Centenary Edition. Ed. Edward Waldo Emerson. 12 vols. Boston and New York: Houghton Mifflin Co., 1903-04.

YES   *Young Emerson Speaks: Unpublished Discourses on Many Subjects.* Ed. Arthur Cushman McGiffert, Jr. Boston: Houghton Mifflin Co., 1938.

References to philosophical texts cite wherever possible both chapter and section headings and the page number in the most accessible modern edition. Detailed explanations are contained in the first reference to each work.

1

Emerson as philosopher

The life of the writer in America is, we are repeatedly told, a life of the mind. For no period is this truer than for the American Renaissance. Whether owing to the peculiarly ideological origins of New England or to a more general lack of cultural density, the classic American authors were more preoccupied than their English counterparts with the metaphysical implications of their fictions.[1] And of these writers, none (with the possible exception of Poe) aspired so relentlessly to the mantle of philosopher as did Ralph Waldo Emerson.

Yet, curiously enough, we rarely look at Emerson's thought at all. It might seem that a book on Emerson's philosophy would have been one of our first critical projects. There has surely been enough work on individual concepts, on his notion of correspondence or the soul, on his ideas about history or evolution or race. But Emerson's philosophy narrowly defined – his confrontation with certain traditional nineteenth-century questions about ethics and especially epistemology – has not really received much attention. And studies that start with an interest in Emerson's thought tend to be deflected into more biographical, even psychological, accounts of his "tragic sense."[2]

In part, of course, the omission is simply an expression of self-contempt. We hate our heroes and measure our maturity in the distance traveled from our teachers. And in part the problem resulted inevitably from the way we chose to tell the story. Answering those questions that seemed most pressing naturally meant putting aside other interesting issues. Our failure to return to those other questions suggests (if not Frostian negligence) at least a kind of intellectual lag. Initially we were afraid to examine too closely ideas whose thinness might tell not only

1

against their author but by extension against all subsequent American culture. Although now convinced that we may admire Emerson without shame, we have not quite realized that we therefore need no longer condescend to his once suspect ideas.

But the problem may lie deeper than the vagaries of the scholarly tradition, and the specific topic of Emerson's thought may be especially hard to reopen. For in constructing our argument about Emerson in certain ways, we have unconsciously accepted some basic principles that, though harmless enough in context, do have wider implications for the nature of thought. It is these unstated assumptions about the history of philosophy and the ways ideas work, and not anything we know about the man and his writings, that make it difficult to recover the lost topic of Emerson's epistemology. And some of the most influential criticism of Emerson rests, ironically, in work that, whatever we think of its findings, has taught us unwittingly to accept these assumptions. Only by examining the intellectual presuppositions of this work, then, will we be able to discover those invisible deterrents which, before the fact, make any particular argument for Emerson's philosophical sophistication unlikely, if not simply impossible.

I

The problem is not quite that of most intellectual history. Often historians complain that there is no empirical evidence for an author's concern with the idea under examination, that the historian of ideas imposes on the text an intellectual preoccupation (and coherence) more his own than that of the author he studies.[3] Such a claim cannot be made of Emerson. In the middle of his career, he defined his philosophy – Transcendentalism – in a lecture that he subsequently published.

> The first thing we have to say respecting what are called *new views* here in New England, at the present time, is, that they are not new, but the very oldest of thoughts cast into the mould of these new times. . . . What is popularly called Transcendentalism among us, is Idealism; Idealism as it appears in 1842. . . . It is well known to most of my audience, that the Idealism of the present day acquired the name of Transcendental, from the use of that term by Immanuel Kant, of Konisberg, who replied to the skeptical philosophy of Locke, which insisted that there was nothing in the intellect which was not previously in the experience of the senses, by showing that there was a very important class of ideas, or imperative forms, which did not come by experience, but through which experience was acquired; that these were intuitions of the mind itself; and he denomi-

nated them *Transcendental* forms. The extraordinary profoundness
and precision of that man's thinking have given vogue to his nomen-
clature, in Europe and America, to that extent, that whatever belongs
to the class of intuitive thought, is popularly called at the present day
Transcendental. (CW.I.201, 206-7)

It would be hard to imagine a more direct statement of purpose, one so
fully addressing all objections about explicitness or intention. Not only
does Emerson use philosophical terminology, but he announces overtly
his interest in epistemological concepts and their centrality to his
Transcendentalism.[4]

Not everyone, of course, aspires to a mantle he can wear. Nor does
Emerson's interest prove his sophistication or even coherence. Finally,
the test will be simply whether or not individual works bear up under
philosophical analysis. Yet, in fact, some scholars have attempted to
show the failure of Emerson's thought more generally by two related
attacks: one on his knowledge of the history of philosophy; the other
on the superficiality (even the immorality) of his use of ideas. And
before examining the specifics of Emerson's philosophy, we must address these two issues, for what they tell us about both Emerson's
thought and the history of ideas in general.

The first attack – on Emerson's insufficient knowledge of philosophy
in general and German idealism in particular – builds from an analysis of
Emerson's known sources.[5] Although Emerson knew German, there is
no evidence of his having read Kant in the original.[6] More likely
sources are the secondhand accounts in various books and periodicals.
Since these summaries by Drummond, Stewart, de Staël, Cousin, Carlyle, and Coleridge are highly biased, however, they could not – it is
argued – have offered a sophisticated understanding of Kant's transcendental idealism.[7]

Furthermore – it is claimed – Emerson's text shows little direct engagement with the specifics of Kantianism. Kant's name is rarely mentioned and his terminology largely avoided. Those terms that are present seem mere window dressing and are often misused. Emerson
bungles one of Kant's most famous terminological distinctions – between the epistemological conditions necessary for knowledge (which
Kant calls "transcendental") and the organizing mental principles that
are inaccessible to experience (which he calls "transcendent").[8] Worse,
Emerson's casual use of the distinction between Reason and Understanding seems to collapse into a more general contrast between faith
and reason. At one point he even attributes to Plato the explicitly
Kantian definition of philosophy as the attempt to find an unconditioned ground for the conditional.[9]

In general, then, Emerson is said to have misunderstood the purpose, even the tone, of the Kantian project. For him, transcendental idealism served mainly to protect traditional Christian beliefs against the implicit atheism of British empiricism. By these lights, Kant was only a bigger stick to beat Locke with, leaving the rest of the philosophical world more or less unchanged. By emphasizing Kant's intuitionism, Emerson reduced the Kantian notion of subjectivity to a psychological subjectivism, and Reason became just a more aggressive version of the "common sense" of Thomas Reid and Dugald Stewart.[10]

Emerson – it is claimed – lost many of the essentials of Kantianism in this moralization of idealism. He devalued Kant's special emphasis on epistemology and the problem of knowledge and abandoned the whole notion of a systematic philosophy, an architectonic. And the dialectic method that has been called Kant's greatest legacy to subsequent philosophy was more or less ignored. In Emerson's hands, Kant the great systematic dialectician became merely one more mystic validating faith by a special, quirky definition of the necessary conditions of experience.[11]

These objections, however, may in fact be less damning than they appear. Some are simply too severe, applying to Emerson standards stricter than those used to measure the greatest philosophers. Emerson's reluctance to name Kant is justifiable in light of his contemporaries' hostility to "foreign" influences – a simple recognition of the wisdom in certain situations of keeping silent about one's sources.[12] Similarly the conflation of Kant and Plato proves only that when reading Coleridge's *The Friend*, Emerson did not have a certain passage from the first *Critique* immediately in mind.[13] That he learned his Kant from allegedly flawed sources is equally inconclusive. Recent scholarship has tended to rate more highly the philosophical acumen of the French eclectics who taught Emerson.[14] But, more simply, a careful reader like Emerson might have seen through the deficiencies of his sources to the essentials of the philosophy they propound. Kant himself knew his progenitors largely at second hand, through summaries, yet no one has felt this to prove ipso facto his ignorance of Leibniz and Hume.[15]

More generally, the attack rests on Emerson's failure to support a particular interpretation of German idealism. But not all modern readers in fact agree on the essential characteristics of Kantianism.[16] Many of the passages that Emerson supposedly misunderstood are still hotly debated, and what have been attacked as Emerson's "mistakes" might more charitably be read as his interpretations. The very distinction between "transcendental" and "transcendent" that is supposed to prove Emerson's inability to understand Kantian terminology has itself come under attack. Such noted neo-Kantians as P. F. Strawson and

Jonathan Bennett have claimed that Kant himself was inconsistent in his use of the two terms.[17]

Nor is Emerson's indifference to Kant's systematizing necessarily a flaw. Kant's architectonics embarrass many contemporary readers, and all commentators admit that the structure of the first *Critique* is undermined by the disproportionate lengths of some of the supposedly equivalent sections.[18] Nor is Kant's dialectical method universally applauded. Though clearly an important historical influence on Hegel and his followers, the second half of the *Critique* now seems commonplace, even wrong. The famous Antinomies interest more than they convince, and one commentator even apologizes for bothering to write on the Dialectic at all.[19]

Similarly defensible is Emerson's treatment of Kant as a psychological subjectivist. Many critics are puzzled by the passages in which Kant differentiates his own transcendental idealism from the "dogmatic" psychologism of "the good Berkeley," and not all are convinced that Kant successfully defends himself against the charge of solipsism. For at least one reader, Kant's central mistake in the Analytic is this very conflation of logical and psychological necessity.[20] Finally, if Emerson was taught by Cousin to reduce Kant to the role of "great analyst," he is supported in this conclusion by most contemporary philosophers, who rate the Aesthetics and especially the Analytic as Kant's greatest achievements.[21]

Somewhat more problematic is the true center of the attack on Emerson's philosophical ignorance: his misuse of the Kantian distinction between the Reason and the Understanding. Largely absent in the first half of the *Critique,* Reason is introduced in the Dialectic to show how the misuse of its ideas leads to the illusions of traditional metaphysics. The concept is important in Kant, and Emerson treats it more enthusiastically than accurately. His failure to restrict himself, as Kant had insisted, to the purely negative use of Reason as a limit accounts for his conflation of "transcendent" and "transcendental." Moreover, his tendency to reify Reason as an absolute ego surfaces in the more significant error, in "The Transcendentalist," of claiming that the categories are really "intuitions of the mind."[22]

Yet though these mistakes strongly qualify Emerson's understanding of Kant, they do not demonstrate his total inadequacy to philosophy. As Emerson never uses the distinction in a central argument, his errors rarely affect his own more general point.[23] Moreover, the error is not unique to Emerson but is in fact implicit in most post-Kantian philosophy, whose history largely chronicles the unsuccessful attempts to prevent Reason from betraying the whole system to absolute idealism. Johann Gottlieb Fichte, Kant's disciple, attempted to correct what he felt to be an inconsistency in Kant's notion of causality by evolving the intuitions of experience directly from the initial premise of an Absolute Ego.[24] This revision, moreover, merely extended to its logical conclusion Kant's own troublesome notions in the first *Critique* about the "regulative" use of the Ideas and in the second about the "constitutive" and "immanent" character of the postulates of pure practical Reason.[25]

The point is not to pile up paragraphs from the two *Critiques* as proof that Emerson was adequate to Kant. Even less is it to build up Emerson by tearing Kant down. But it is time to confess that we may have misstated the problem. Not only do we at times apply to Emerson standards so harsh that most philosophers would be found wanting. More important, some of our conclusions about Emerson's thought are built on such problematic notions of the meaning of sources, Kant, and even philosophy that they cannot demonstrate anything at all. The empirical evidence both for and against Emerson's knowledge is circumstantial. But more simply, even if we could agree on which texts Emerson knew and how sophisticated an account of Kant was contained in each, we would still have come no closer to answering the essential question. For what we want to know is not Emerson's "familiarity" with Kantian concepts, or even his "knowledge" of them, but only his "understanding" of those concepts. And for questions of understanding, any study of the genesis of thought is irrelevant. There is no way of proving the two facts that would be most revealing – that Emerson did not read a text or that he did understand it. It is fully possible that Emerson could have read every Kantian text, known every Kantian term, and yet still not have understood a word of it. (Indeed, the history of philosophy is full of philosophers claiming that some other thinker has not understood the real implications of Kantian idealism. Even Kant himself has regularly been accused of being insufficiently Kantian.)[26] Moreover, it is equally possible – though perhaps less likely – that Emerson could, in total ignorance of Kant, have understood (even figured out for himself) some of the basic truths of what we now label Kantianism.

The study of Emerson's sources, then, is not so much a dead issue as a lost cause: a project that even under ideal circumstances could not address the real issue of Emerson's philosophical understanding. The misdirection of source studies, however, is itself only a specific version of a more general problem. Not only do we not know whether Kant influenced Emerson, but we do not even know why we would want to make such a claim, what we think it will get us. Whatever their intention, all such studies are implicitly negative. To say that Emerson learned his Kant indirectly from Cousin, or that his notion of the categorical imperative developed not from Kant but from Price, explicitly

attempts to delineate the actual lines of philosophical inheritance without commenting on the intellectual sophistication of that inheritance.
Implicitly, however, such claims tend to discredit Emerson's thought
by trivializing its source. Price and Cousin are effectively code names
for second-rate philosophy, and Emerson is covertly attacked by what
announces itself as a neutral, empirical study of historical influence.[27]

The implicitly debunking emphasis of most influence studies does
not measure the critic's skepticism or mean-spiritedness so much as his
real (and honest) uncertainty about what a positive influence would
mean.[28] If "Emerson's influence by Price" tends to mean "only by Price
and not by someone really smart like Kant," then what would a truly
Kantian influence prove? Surely not in which book Emerson learned a
fact, for that is – as we have seen – intellectually irrelevant. And probably not that the idea understood was *exclusively* Kant's, for the whole
notion of the history of philosophy suggests that few ideas are exclusively anyone's. Even the explanation of Kantianism as a complex of
related ideas – each alone common enough, but uniquely Kantian in
their interrelation – does not help much, and leads to awkward questions about how many of Kant's concepts are needed to make an argument truly Kantian.

The basic confusion about evidences and influences underlying the
attacks on Emerson's philosophical knowledge can be summarized in
terms of two related myths. The first myth – of genesis or genealogy –
insists that the way an idea is learned (and especially the sources from
which it derives) determines its validity. The second myth – of availability – argues more subtly that "any plausible account of what the agent
meant must necessarily fall under, and make use of, the range of descriptions which the agent himself could at least in principle have applied to describe and classify what he was doing."[29] Although such
attention to historical context is necessary, the emphasis on availability
tends to turn restrictive, denying both an individual's ability to extend
the range of description and an idea's attempt to address issues more
universal than those of its local historical moment. Behind both the
myth of genesis and the myth of availability, then, lies an unexamined
assumption about the ways in which ideas are true, and especially about
their relation to their history. By one account, history is a story that
really happened. However problematic the notion of "really happening," it does seem fair to claim that certain empirical procedures will
convince us of the truth of a historical interpretation by showing its
usefulness in explaining certain verifiable facts and events. Yet these
empirical procedures work less well on ideas, which are not quite
events and do not always address a verifiable reality. And although
ideas have a history, that history is rarely a sufficient or even an inter-

esting account of their value. It is thus hard to imagine what it would mean to say that an idea was true but still unthinkable *in principle*.

For finally, unlike history, an idea is true not because it "really happened" but because it is "really believed." And the establishment of that truth requires not the demonstration of its occurrence, or even the proof that once, like Camelot, it was believed in. Instead an idea is true if and only if it seems an adequate solution to a specific set of problems – if it can in some sense still be believed. By this definition a "history of ideas" is not merely a debased kind of history; it is a literal oxymoron, inherently self-contradictory. For the methods by which we believe ideas are so independent of those by which we prove events that the coupling of the two seems counterproductive. One might almost say that we study as history only what we have first failed to believe as truth: that only the idea that seems intellectually unjustifiable on its own terms requires the further justification offered by historical contextualization.

II

Behind the attack on Emerson's ignorance of philosophy, then, lies a complex of notions about sources and influences founded on the assumption that ideas are events and can be studied empirically like any other historical occurrence. Yet this attempted historicization of ideas has supported an even more general, and therefore more effective, attack on Emerson's ideas. This second argument – against the superficiality and immorality of Emerson's ideas – subsumes the academic objections about his sources under a more sweeping charge of immaturity. And here the question is less the relation of ideas to an ongoing intellectual tradition than their effect on political and social actualities.[30]

The most general (and famous) form of this objection is the attack on Emerson's optimism and his related inability to deal with evil. In an early formulation by Henry James, Jr., Emerson's eyes were "thickly bandaged" to the problem of evil. "He had no great sense of wrong, . . . no sense of the dark, the foul, the base."[31] It is in response to such objections that more sympathetic scholars constructed the arguments for Emerson's awareness of evil. His optimism was not temperamental, but an emotional discipline in the face of real pain, and the very elegiac tone that earlier critics rejected as facile was shown to presuppose the impossibility of realizing the glory we imagine.[32]

Although these arguments are convincing and have entirely destroyed the specific charges, however, they may not address the fundamental issue but only a symptom of it. One wonders if the objection really deserves answering: optimism is, after all, neither inherently good nor bad, and visions of evil are themselves notoriously prone to

seem with time nothing more than cosmic whines. Moreover, the substitution of psychology for philosophy refocuses the argument in potentially dangerous ways: to show that Emerson knew evil in his life is
not quite to answer the objection that his ideas never address that
knowledge. But most important, the knowledge of evil demonstrated
may not really be the same as that declared absent. Many of the attacks
on Emerson's optimism relate his naiveté to that of his Puritan
ancestors.[33] These attacks imply (though rarely state explicitly) that the
kind of knowledge missing is absent in the Puritans as well. Yet it is
only a very special definition of optimism and ignorance of evil that
will apply equally well to the "gloomy" Puritans and the "sunny"
Emerson.[34]

Although Santayana's definition of Emerson's "genteelity" set the
tone, the most explicit version of the argument is Parkes's claim that
both the Puritans and Emerson fail the "pragmatic test." Conceding
that an idea is not merely "a plan of action," Parkes nevertheless sup-
poses that "all ideas have practical consequences and that the best
method of evaluating ideas is to explore these consequences."[35] Similar
considerations underlie Winters's protest that Emerson is neither a true
mystic like Very nor a "practical" Calvinist like those Hawthorne
studies.[36] And even Matthiessen's far more restrained impatience focuses on Emerson's failure to effect the "dynamic extension" of his
theoretical democracy into the political and economic arenas.[37] The objections against facile optimism and ignorance of evil, then, really state
that, whatever Emerson and the Puritans thought, their ideas did not
have the effect of promoting a good society – either in Matthiessen's or
Parkes's proto-Marxist sense or in Santayana's and Winters's more general sense of rational confrontation with practical reality.

To this implicit attack the arguments for Emerson's tragic sense offer
no direct response.[38] As an indirect answer, analyses of Emerson's psychological honesty argue that ambivalence and even confusion have
something like good social effects. These critics simply suggest that
there are other ways of making society good. The defense of Emerson's
psychological honesty becomes a defense of individualism, and in one
sense Bloom stands as an inverted Winters, praising as antinomian and
strong what Winters rejected as unreasonable and obscurantist.[39] A
more general response claims that ideas can have other goals than the
production of a better society. Just as it is pointless to object that the
second *Critique* does not offer much in the way of personal consolation,
one cannot fairly complain if Emerson talks about other things than
evil. And the project shifts to show Emerson forging an American
poetics or mythos to which social reality is not inimical but simply
irrelevant.[40]

Although such responses widen the range of ways to talk about Emerson, however, they implicitly condone more of the initial attack than they realize. For just as the source studies contained implicit assumptions about how ideas operate, the social studies have an unstated model for the effect of ideas on history. Santayana tells us that "reality eluded [Emerson]," and we in response have worked to enumerate those realities he did grasp.[41] Even readings like Feidelson's that deemphasize social context still place Emerson within a broader American tradition – usually at its head. But as modern theory teaches us, there is another answer to Santayana. We can simply yawn and say "so what?" Or, more aggressively, cheer that in finding reality elusive Emerson alone among his generation refused to buy into a delusive metaphysics of presence.[42]

The problem is, perhaps, somewhat harder to define with actions than with events. For effects seem more completely built into things than causes. Even the pragmatic definition of truth as "what works" seems to imply efficaciousness.[43] Yet one wonders if such a focus on effects does not encourage a third false notion – what might be called the myth of consequentiality. The demonstration that Emerson's ideas are the natural ones for a man in his position – that in fact we ourselves have felt such feelings (even thought such ideas) under similar circumstances – is not really an answer to the objection that these ideas are false. Moreover, any attempt to characterize these ideas too fully in terms of their consequences tends to equate them with their consequences and thus to obscure a meaning that may be more nearly directed at other issues. But most simply, notions of causality and inevitability do not necessarily apply to ideas. One can think something without thinking its consequences; one can, in some general sense, "have" an idea without also having the related political, social, and even intellectual effects. Inconsistency may be a weakness, but it is not a logical impossibility. And the power of choice is such that one can always, as it were, draw a line between the falling of the intellectual apple and its hitting the ground.

This myth of consequentiality might seem the opposite of the historicist myths of the source studies. In one case critics argue backward, characterizing an idea in terms of its sources; in the other, they look forward, characterizing it in terms of its consequences. The one tends to overdetermine the question by placing the idea too exclusively in a historical tradition, the other to blur it by removing it from its specific moment to talk more generally of future results or even hypothetical ones. Yet in fact the two errors both treat ideas as if they were like "happenings." And though focusing on different aspects of historical continuity – on causes in the one case and responsibility in the other –

they share the same desire to relocate ideas from the atemporal realm of intellect to one more empirically analyzable.

The methodology in both cases is basically that of science and its lawfulness, a positivism in which history is more fully implicated than most humanist disciplines.[44] Yet it is unclear – *pace* Kant – that science is the best model for discussing how ideas work. At the very least, these emphases misrepresent the continuity of intellectual discussion by treating ideas in isolation. No one, in fact, has ever had a unit idea, any more than he has experienced a Humean sense datum. Ideas are specific answers to specific questions: their more immediate context is not their historical moment but the intellectual conversation within which they take place. And terms like "true" and "believable" do not reintroduce the banished empiricism, but more pragmatically identify within that ongoing conversation workable solutions to askable questions.

Although such an ahistorical notion of context as conversation may seem inelegant as a theory, it is fairly commonplace as a practice. Historians of philosophy have tacitly acknowledged the relative autonomy of ideas – the intention of philosophers to address timeless (not to say perennial) questions. Kant's "influence," when mentioned at all, means the ways in which his ideas are repeated and reformulated by subsequent thinkers, and not their tendency to support a particular form of Prussian militarism. Nor does a psychobiography of Locke or Wittgenstein seem an especially useful way of understanding their achievements.[45] Yet the most famous exemplar of (even spokesman for) this notion of ideological separation – the possibility of two truths related but distinct – is, of course, Hume. As part of a larger skeptical project, he explicitly argued for the discontinuity between an idea and its implications, the compatibility of thinking one way in the study and acting another way at the dinner table.[46]

We need not, however, accept the philosophers' own model for how their truth should be treated. For we have at least two other examples of an ahistorical approach to meaning. The simpler one is that of mathematical truth. Axioms are not, of course, true in any Platonic sense. Nor need they even be synthetic a prioris as Kant thought them. Nevertheless, their value seems largely distinct from the history of their development or of their consequences. And whatever we finally decide about the status of the system within which they operate, it is generally felt that they should first be examined within that system. Similarly atemporal, according to some theorists, is literature itself. The relation of texts to their historical production is at present a hotly debated topic. Equally uncertain is the status, or even existence, of a single system called literature and what its "history" might be.[47] Yet putting aside questions of justification, we can probably agree that literature – like mathematics – can be read in a vacuum, apart from its historical context, as texts largely talking to other texts about literary issues only loosely connected to an extratextual reality.

The point, finally, is that philosophy – like literature and mathematics, but unlike history – can be evaluated in terms of its internal consistency without reference to an external reality. And in analyzing this internal meaning, issues of truth and believability become paramount. The difference is, of course, one of proportion. Truth and believability are not so much irrelevant in the interpretation of events and actions as they are unproblematic: we will "believe" in the "truth" of any historical event of whose occurrence we can be convinced. In philosophy, however, evidence and belief are less causally related. We can always refrain from believing in a convincing argument or even believe in an idea for which we are certain that no compelling demonstration exists. This potential for bracketing does not necessarily imply that the essential nature of an idea, axiom, or literary work is distinct from its origin or effects.[48] But it does at the very least suggest that an ahistorical description of the idea might be a useful preliminary to other considerations.

III

It may seem odd, even perverse, to elevate the work of Winters and Wellek over more central statements by Whicher, Bishop, Porte, and Packer. Yet whatever the actual state of Emerson scholarship (and its literal history), it is nevertheless true that the approach to ideas most clearly embodied in the work of these two seminal critics is in fact implied in (or at least compatible with) all subsequent criticism. Both attacks on Emerson assume that ideas exist most interestingly in the world – whether as historical events or as sociopolitical consequences. The usual defense shows that the sources are more reputable than Wellek states, the consequences less unreasonable than Winters insists. Such answers, however, do not challenge the basic assumption, but only tend to reinforce it by dramatizing the psychological situation that led Emerson to think these thoughts – what we might call the "life of the mind" fallacy.

My response, instead, is to insist at least at first on the relative autonomy of ideas. Ideas do not exist solely within the world, and a biological account of their "lives" may fundamentally misrepresent their role in an ongoing intellectual debate. In this philosophical conversation, the crucial issue is not history or psychology but believability – not how or why Emerson could think such things but what questions did he mean to answer. The initial context of the essays thus becomes not nineteenth-century America but epistemology. And the project, to define the specifics of the problem of knowledge as the nineteenth century understood (or might have understood) it.

This focus on philosophy is in one sense purely personal – a decision arbitrarily to limit analysis to one fundamental, though not all-encompassing, topic. Other topics – Emerson's theism or mysticism, or even kinds of philosophy other than epistemology – remain for other studies. Moreover, it is still possible to ask why Emerson chose the aggressively intellectual, even abstract and cold, formulations he did. And to trace these philosophical and stylistic preferences back to biographical sources. Similarly, to claim that Emerson is intelligible is not to deny that some of his conclusions have dangerous social implications. Nor does the demonstration that he made no obvious mistakes prove that he did not make subtle ones, or at least lend his prestige to the errors of his disciples. Certainly his inability to purify his philosophical essays of pragmatic, epigrammatic advice suggests that his epistemology tends to flirt with a conservative political ethos.

Thus, in one sense, whatever we decide about Emerson's philosophy, the objections about his psychological immaturity and antisocial character may remain the same. Or almost the same. For it is one thing to claim Emerson's irrationality and another to show how his thoughts on one topic may be misapplied elsewhere. Although critics may not have been wrong in their evaluation of Emerson's tragic sense or his antinomianism, they have been ungenerous. Perhaps according to some very strict sense of historical determinism he is responsible for the sins of America, just as in the very long view all thought is a footnote to Plato. But in our eagerness to identify the great American misstep, we may obscure the truth of many observations along the way. So before rejecting him totally, perhaps we can be charitable enough to admit that even on the road to annihilation Emerson got many things right.

Epistemology, then, will not supplant aesthetic, psychological, or social readings, but only preface them. Even as a preliminary, however, such a use of philosophy seems suspect, perhaps even self-contradictory. My approach may appear simultaneously to deemphasize the privileged status of philosophical discussions and to shore Emerson up with that privilege. The problem rests in part with our undue reverence for philosophy. Humanists like to imagine that philosophy is the purest and most ennobling intellectual endeavor. Yet in fact that dignity has come increasingly into question. Recent philosophers suggest that we understand less than we think about the nature of philosophy as a professional discipline. Philosophical writing is far more diverse than the single term "philosophy" implies. And, at the very least, the notion of philosophy as the foundation of all other disciplines can no longer be accepted without reservation.

My approach, in part, applies this skepticism to the special problem of Emerson's philosophy. It would be pleasant to say in the end that Emerson actually "knew" Kant, or at least understood the contemporary philosophical debate more thoroughly than is usually thought. Perhaps the specificity of some echoes will be sufficient to convince readers of a real historical connection. Yet such an argument should probably be resisted as narrowly academic (or, in Emerson's term, "operose"). I doubt that even the best evidence could prove that Emerson "did" philosophy in quite that way; he never sounds enough like Kant (or Nietzsche or Derrida). But more important, I deny that philosophy is a certain way of doing things, with an especially strict period of apprenticeship. Emerson's disservice to Kant is presumably no worse than Kant's misuse of Berkeley or Locke's of Descartes. Reinterpretation (not to say misprision) is the name of the philosophical game – or at least more the goal than "getting Kant right." And although it is important to note misrepresentations as they occur (in Fichte or Strawson as well as in Emerson), it is foolish to read all revisions as failures before determining if they provide any new answers.

The claim that Emerson is as much a philosopher as Locke, Hume, or Kant, then, in one sense simply applies the general deconstruction of philosophy to a specific case, using Emerson's presumed lack of seriousness to challenge the notion of philosophical seriousness in general. The assertion that Emerson is an epistemologist, however, seems to move in another direction – to reprofessionalize both philosophy and Emerson in the very ways that current theory criticizes. The contradiction is again merely apparent – a legacy of our respect for the topic and its greatest practitioner, Kant. Although respectful of its individual insights, most modern philosophers are uncertain about the overall achievement of the epistemological tradition, and it scarcely needs the deconstructive fury of a Rorty or a Derrida to see the simpler point that in the twentieth century to call someone an epistemologist may not be a compliment at all. In labeling Emerson an epistemologist, then, I do not flatter him but merely attempt to identify his specific formulations as part of a larger set of traditional problems about the nature of knowledge.

It might seem that any definition of Emerson's philosophy as unsystematic epistemology is oxymoronic. Epistemology may not be the sort of thing one can do outside of a Prussian architectonic, and to toy with epistemological issues may trivialize the whole pursuit, like playing checkers with a set of chessmen. Yet such an objection may confuse the different kinds of difficulty present in epistemological studies. The first – a preoccupation with system and thoroughness especially characteristic of the post-Kantian tradition – is not essential to the more general epistemological project of deriving a model of reality from the nature of mind. The second – a complex of special problems and even terminology shared by all epistemologists from Descartes on – is.

The twin difficulties of epistemology are mirrored in the dual aspect of Kant and my use of him. Part of Kant's project was to treat philosophical issues with the kind of mathematical precision usually reserved for the natural sciences, especially physics. This quasi-scientific dimension is entirely absent in Emerson, and to this extent Kantian epistemology is wildly irrelevant to the study of Emerson. Yet recent philosophers have recast this scientific, Enlightenment Kant as a more modern propositional logician, redefining his question about the possibility of synthetic a priori knowledge as a more general examination of the logical conditions necessary for the possibility of knowledge of any sort. It is from this redefinition of Kant as logician of knowledge that my own sense of Emerson's Kantianism derives. Emerson belongs to a general tradition of epistemologists, then, insofar as his works examine how an understanding of the nature and structure of knowledge reveals the character of reality as man experiences it. And, to this extent, "Kant" in this study means little more than "ways of being smart about epistemology in the nineteenth century."[49] A Kantian influence on Emerson thus becomes merely a claim for the identifiability of Emerson's high-level use of some metaphysical concepts – not so much an influence *from* Kant or even, narrowly defined, an "influence" at all. Biographical considerations drop out. As does any notion of causality. Or the attempt to deduce from this influence a history of the "idea" of transcendental idealism and to follow its migration from Konigsberg to Concord. All that remains is the claim that, whether learned from Price and Cousin or even intuited from the mind of God, there are thoughts in Emerson as sophisticated as the finest contemporary epistemology – that in fact do appear (whether uniquely or only significantly) in the work of our greatest epistemologist, Kant. And although it is probably fruitless to modernize these concerns in order to bring them in line with some current conception of philosophical value – some postanalytic "argument of the philosophers" – it is still useful and reassuring to see that, however idiosyncratic his vocabulary, his concerns can be related to (even translated into) the terminology of traditional epistemology.

Idealism has a venerable history. It underwrites classical philosophy's superimposition of stability on a world of flux, and, more immediately, the Church Fathers' appropriation of this pagan idiom to provide a metaphysics for their own theological otherworldliness. But only in the rationalist preoccupation with the clear and distinct ideas of mathematical certainty did the philosophy take on the uncertain, finally skeptical, tone that characterizes modernity. For Descartes redefined idealism, previously the doctrine of a supernatural world of permanence, in terms of subjectivity; and philosophical inquiry shifted from ontology to epistemology, the being outside to the ideas within.

Descartes did not, of course, plan to introduce a new skepticism, and subjectivity seemed at first the cornerstone of rationality. But, as the British empiricists soon demonstrated, subjectivity guarantees the existence of nothing but itself. The first external to go was the material world – which, until the Cartesian "proof," rested secure in the commonsense belief in the testimony of experience. If the reality within the mind is defined as logically prior, however, it becomes difficult to determine precisely the nature of what is without. Yet, as Kant showed, this doubting of matter is finally less important than man's relation to his own self-awareness. Answering Hume's denial of "self" as a distinct entity, Kant recognized that self-consciousness is the necessary condition for all experience (even Hume's doubt), the implicit "I think" that permits thought in the first place. But Kant's failure to specify the objective, existential status of this unifying consciousness – his tendency occasionally to treat noumenality as more than a negative or limit concept – led to the nineteenth century's arguments over the relation of the consciousness of the individual person to that of a purportedly transcendent ego.

This general philosophical context defines Emerson's own epistemological study. The concept central to his work is the self-evidence of truth – the notion that reality cannot be thought of in terms of things accurately representing other things, but must be treated holistically as something that simply hangs together on its own terms. Throughout his essays, he is careful to distinguish between levels of discourse, to make sure that he uses only the vocabulary appropriate to the kind of epistemological examination being conducted. As corollaries to his general premise, he argues variously for the transcendentality of arguments (that certain concepts are so buried within other concepts that they cannot be logically separated); the autonomy of virtue (that goodness is not an external standard but a self-fulfilling condition); and the epistemological privacy of the self.

Such definitions will not accord with many more traditional approaches to Kant, epistemology, or philosophy, especially those that emphasize the systematic, logical dimensions of philosophical discourse. Emerson's accustomed mode was rarely logical or argumentative – although, as one critic admits, Emerson could employ such methods when he wished.[50] His mind worked at different levels and intensities, with the result that not all his statements are equally well thought out. He was fascinated by a set of interrelated epistemological questions to which he regularly returned. But even those problems that interested him most deeply were not always fully treated, and often the discussion of one issue did not adequately recognize the implications for other related problems.[51] Whether or not this lack of rigor reduces his philosophy to a patchwork – and whether or not a patchwork can be philosophy – however, are merely generic questions, whose solution adds little to our understanding of Emerson's specific methods. For the point is less to establish Emerson's academic credentials as a thinker than to understand the full implications of his philosophical manner as a literary style.

Authors are more often damned than pardoned for writing well. Emerson's renowned success with sentences is often read backward to prove his ineptness with larger forms. But the insinuation that the ability to write sentences implies the inability to build arguments is simply the revenge of the elephantine stylist. Any style has a philosophical point, just as any life has a metaphysic. But, more simply, Emerson's unsystematic style is particularly appropriate to his critical (not to say deconstructive) attitude toward epistemology. And although he never attacks metaphysics directly, as do more recent philosophers, it is not inappropriate that his aphoristic style so influenced the more radical iconoclasm of Nietzsche.[52]

To see Emerson's philosophy as a style, however, is not to reduce it to its style. For to conflate the philosophy and the poetry by collapsing the first into the second would be to lose track of the specific issues at stake. Not only would the meaning of a passage evaporate into its cadences, but the very admission that poetry might be something different from philosophy concedes the argument to Emerson's critics without a battle. It sets up a false opposition between thought and expression that proves before the fact the very elevation of what Emerson wrote to require his desertion of the lower scientific sphere of understanding. And makes his rhetorical moves – his interesting transitions, juxtapositions, and paradoxes – not the tools of his argument but its undoing.[53]

To claim that Emerson was a philosopher with a structured argument about epistemological issues, then, is not a denial of his poetry but a further characterization of it. It is frequently said that Emerson stands as the first in a tradition of stylistic dislocation or antinomianism.[54] I would add simply that such dislocation is a function of his philosophical topic and that any apparent displacement results from his oft-repeated recognition that "the mind is its own place." Thus, finally, epistemology is best seen as not a philosophical discipline but a literary genre. Like the lyric or the epic, epistemology tends to deal with certain questions (about the logical structure of the mind) while avoiding other topics (like history or society). And, in part, my account works to invert the implications of the philosophical and aesthetic vocabularies both: to use philosophical language about "transcendental apperceptions" and "empirical realisms" as if it were metaphoric, even poetic; and to treat literary terms like "juxtaposition," "paradox," and "pun" as if these were Emerson's philosophical terms of art. For, finally, Emerson as epistemologist is simply the man who had intellectual reasons for saying all the things we have always found so curious and challenging. And the argument of his essays is less a contribution to the history of ideas than it is the sustained romance of (and with) the literary figures we call ideas.[55]

2

The structure of nature

Nature is surely an important work. It has been convenient to date the official beginning of Transcendentalism from the book's publication late in 1836 or to see in it a New (American) Testament to supersede the Old Testament of Marsh's edition of Coleridge.[1] Yet despite this historical significance, the essay does not speak to us as it did to Emerson's contemporaries. The very care with which Emerson structures his argument seems simultaneously unsuccessful and inauthentic. The anger of the Divinity School "Address," the exuberance of "The American Scholar" or "Self-Reliance," the melancholy of "Circles" or "Experience": these are the more congenial tones for modern readers. And *Nature,* though admired for its moments, is rejected on the whole as stiff, overelaborate, and finally even irrelevant.[2]

This reaction is not entirely unjustified. *Nature* is unusual. Like most first books, it tries to solve too many problems, satisfy too wide an audience. Close reasoning may not have been the best method of winning over the conservative New England establishment; many Unitarians saw an adolescent pride showing all too clearly through the tattered cloak of philosophical humility. Nor were Emerson's friends unanimous about the form of their credo; at least one Transcendentalist tempered his praise by reading Emerson one last lesson on the Phenomenal and the Noumenal.[3] In any case, his rather casual approach to structure and logic favored a shorter, less linear presentation, and in general he seems more comfortable in the essays and lectures than he does in this "little book."

Yet Emerson's later, more mature triumphs should not blind us to the achievement of this early piece. For if Emerson was uncertain about his audience, he was clearer about his project. In *Nature* Emerson set himself the preliminary but necessary task of facing directly the question of experience and its relation to the individual mind.[4] Though not perhaps philosophical in method, the essay is so in motive. The general situation imagined and the answers offered are all recognizable versions of German thought. His interest is not scholarly: there is no careful exposition of current epistemological theories; nor can we best defend the essay by a detailed study of the intellectual voyage from Konigsberg to Concord. Instead we must let the essay work out its own definitions in its own rhetorical modes.

The results may be surprising. Considered on their own terms, the book's philosophical statements are remarkably careful, even true. But more important, they are integral to the rhetoric, style, and literary achievement of the work. In *Nature* more than in any other of Emerson's essays, meaning resides neither in content nor in form but in the subtle interplay between the two. What seems artificial is an attempt to woo the reader, even to trick him, into affirmations he might normally deem foolish. And philosophical idealism becomes more than a way of gluing together two separate essays. It is both means and end – the structural principle from which the essay grows and the epistemological revelation toward which it proceeds.

I

Halfway through *Nature* the argument pauses, apparently to consider a side issue. "A noble doubt perpetually suggests itself, whether this end [of discipline] be not the Final Cause of the Universe; and whether nature outwardly exists" (CW.I.29).[5] The question, of course, is hardly peripheral, and the casual tone only underlines the drama of this sudden recourse to idealism. Idealism is not a naive doctrine. No one ever stumbled onto the unobvious conclusion that the world might not exist. Nor did anyone ever intuit phenomenality. Instead idealism is a radical answer to a specific problem, embraced only when the unnaturalness of the solution is compensated for by certain practical advantages. The question, then, is not so much how Emerson painted himself into an idealist's corner but to what dilemma he offered idealism as a response.

The answer seems easy enough. After an abstract "Introduction," Emerson gives – in a chapter itself entitled "Nature" – an example of the kind of relationship he wishes to celebrate. "Crossing a bare common, in snow puddles, at twilight, under a clouded sky, without having in my thoughts any occurrence of special good fortune, I have enjoyed a perfect exhilaration. Almost I fear to think how glad I am" (p. 10).

Presumably this affirmation of human adequacy and consanguinity with nature is one more Transcendentalist revolt against corpse-cold liberal Christianity and the empiricist associationism that underwrote it.[6] Most Transcendentalists felt that their reading in British empiricism from Locke to Hartley allowed no convincing account for human virtue or even thoughts. Unable to evolve soul from sense or ideas from vibrating nerve endings, they were left only with Humean compatibilism and skepticism. It is such doubts that Emerson's experience is meant to answer, and his "glad," like the "joy" of the English romantics, becomes a technical term for the "perfect exhilaration" or "wild delight" man can feel.[7]

Yet Emerson's answer is disturbingly imprecise on the key issue of the ground for our delight. Granted that all men feel this way (or can imagine that they might), have they any knowledge of the cause or source of this feeling? On this point the hopeful first chapter is vague and even unencouraging. The assurances about consanguinity are everywhere matched by reminders that the objective world is ultimately unknowable. The very stars that make the atmosphere transparent with design awaken man's reverence only because of their inaccessibility. That all nature makes "a kindred impression" measures less man's equal reverence for the world than his equal distance from it: in his inability to get at objects in themselves, the natural world might as well be as far from him as the stars.

Even the "gladness" that defines his exhilaration shares in the ambiguity. Nature says that, since man is a part of me, I will ignore his selfish preoccupation and let him join in my happiness: "he is my creature, and maugre all his impertinent griefs, he shall be glad with me" (p. 9). But nature does not merely permit man's joy; she must suffer it. His gladness "with" her becomes less a celebration between equals than a condescending approval, man's godlike announcement of his pleasure with creation. Man "fears" his gladness not because it is so great but because it is so exclusively (perhaps delusively) his: "I am so full of gladness that I could never be this glad again," but also "I am so full that there can be no gladness left for anything outside of me." This very boundlessness calls into question the foundations of his emotion.[8]

These tensions, only hinted at in the chapter's ambiguous vocabulary, emerge overtly in the work's most notorious passage – the metaphor of the transparent eyeball.

> In the woods too, a man casts off his years. . . . In the woods, we return to reason and faith. . . . Standing on the bare ground, – my head bathed by the blithe air, and uplifted into infinite space, – all mean egotism vanishes. I become a transparent eye-ball. I am nothing.

I see all. The currents of the Universal Being circulate through me; I am part or particle of God. The name of the nearest friend sounds then foreign and accidental. To be brothers, to be acquaintances, – master or servant, is then a trifle and a disturbance. I am the lover of uncontained and immortal beauty. (P. 10)

Although the description is clearly presented as a second "natural experience," parallel to the bare common exhilaration, critics are right to challenge the "too" that factitiously equates the passages.

The problem is not primarily tonal: this moment is not less experienced than the other, nor is the language indecorously colloquial.[9] We recoil not merely because no one ever was a transparent eyeball or because "eye-*ball*" is a silly word. Worse than unreal or embarrassing, the image is intellectually incoherent. Clearly, something very close to power is promised as the "currents of the Universal Being circulate through me." Yet as "part or particle" of God, I have no access to an immensity that in the first half of the sentence seemed wholly within myself. The very notion of transparency is purgative: everything passes through and nothing is retained.[10] Even the claims for omniscience are confusing. A truly transparent eyeball would have no opaque retina on which to focus the image, and a cynic might claim that all Emerson's lens could really do would be to turn the world upside down.

The apparent incoherence of the image is not a miscalculation but an intentional dramatization of the kinds of tensions felt throughout the chapter.[11] And in this sense the second experience does proceed naturally from the first. What was merely paradoxical in the yoking of "glad" and "fear" becomes terrifying in the notion of blind transparency. Yet it is this ominous note that best characterizes the paragraph. People and community are pushed away in favor of the uncontained, the immortal, and the wild. With the memory of inhuman transparency still fresh, we worry whether the tranquility of this empty landscape is not dearly purchased. The final tableau of man's beholding "somewhat as beautiful as his own nature" may depict the unity of experience (p. 10). But the "his own" rings a little too possessive, and man's alleged union with nature seems more the subject's enslavement of the object.

The tensions within this introductory first chapter are duplicated in its troubled relation to the essay's true "Introduction," which stands to "Nature" much as the experience of the transparent eyeball does to that of the snow puddle.[12] Although in neither case is there a direct contradiction, in both the paired experiences and the paired introductions it is difficult to see the purpose of the pairing. The contrast between the two chapters is not simply that between theory and practice. The introduction is aggressively philosophical in its division of reality into the ME and the NOT ME. But "Nature" is not all that descriptive in its analysis of possible experiences, and the eyeball, at least, is more theoretical than physical. The real contrast lies in the kinds of questions they seem to ask. "Nature" examines a nonempirical feeling of adequacy and consanguinity and, without quite demonstrating the reality of that feeling, nevertheless speaks convincingly about some of the epistemological and psychological consequences of the felt unity. The "Introduction" entirely ignores the question of experience and addresses instead the possibility of a "theory" of nature. If the first chapter of *Nature* implicitly wonders "why do I feel as I do," the introduction explicitly asks "to what end is nature?" (p. 7).

This second question is, of course, wrongheaded. Badly (or at least unfairly) formulated, it does not permit the answer that strikes us as most likely – "to no particular end whatever." This teleological bias is not even consistent with Emerson's own definition of nature. The question assumes that nature serves as some sort of means. But, in fact, the world in this introduction is remarkably self-sufficient, as independent and subtly tyrannical as the observer-naturalist of the first chapter. There does at first seem to be some real exchange between man and nature: the order of things awakens in our minds questions that the order then answers. Yet the conversation soon short-circuits. Nature "already" describes its design, answering questions *before* they are asked, solving in hieroglyphic all inquiries man "would put" but that, in fact, he does not (p. 7).[13]

This subtle triumph of nature is clearest in the final paragraph, which defines the basic philosophical distinction of the book.

> Philosophically considered, the universe is composed of Nature and the Soul. Strictly speaking, therefore, all that is separate from us, all which Philosophy distinguishes as the NOT ME, that is, both nature and art, all other men and my own body, must be ranked under this name, NATURE. In enumerating the values of nature and casting up their sum, I shall use the word in both senses; – in its common and in its philosophical import. In inquiries so general as our present one, the inaccuracy is not material; no confusion of thought will occur. (P. 8)

The world is composed roughly of nature and the soul; all that is separate from us, the NOT ME, can be termed "Nature." Now, of course, "nature" more generally refers to matter wholly untouched by human hands, whereas "art" is reserved for those aspects of the NOT ME on which man has had an immediate influence. But, Emerson admits in a move as crippling as it is casual, these operations of the human will are "so insignificant, a little chipping, baking, patching, and washing, that in an impression so grand as that of the world on the human mind, they do not vary the result" (p. 8). Given the immensity of the world, the ME simply cannot do enough to affect noticeably external "impressions." Such an argument effectively denies any real power to man or his ME and makes the NOT ME so monstrous that it is impossible to imagine it as a means at all.[14]

The first two sections of Nature, then, are really at odds with one another. The introduction pretends to ask the purpose of nature but actually depicts a world of stuff so "grand" that it is largely intransigent, indifferent to the minor influences man might have upon it. A parallel tyranny is depicted in the experiential first chapter, "Nature," where man's feeling of relationship to the natural world collapses into a subjectivism so total that the world becomes wholly phenomenal. In both cases, the questions ironically yield the very responses they are meant to forestall: the pursuit of a "theory" of nature convinces only that matter is essentially inscrutable; the examination of real natural facts demonstrates that perception itself is the sole datum of experience. The obvious incompatibility of these two answers suggests that the formulations are themselves faulty and that the real issue lies in some unstated presupposition common to both.[15]

We might best think of these chapters as presenting two traditional ways of dealing with Cartesian dualism. Their intellectual allegiances need not be identified very precisely: the first is generally abstract, even philosophical; the second personal, even emotional. Certain schools would be more closely associated with one chapter than with the other. Teleologists (especially physicotheologians) and empiricists in general would prefer the first for the prominence given to the external world of sensation. The second would appeal more to moralists, sentimental philosophers, Romantics, and (by definition) idealists. The point, however, is that Emerson is attracted to yet unconvinced by both. His own question is less whether the dualism collapses into the tyranny of the NOT ME, as in the introduction, or into that of the Mind, as in the first chapter, than whether man can be sure of any kind of relation at all. He sees that the radical monisms of both the materialists and the spiritualists assume an interrelation that need not exist. In the famous journal phrase, Emerson longs for unity but everywhere beholds mere doubleness.[16]

Taken together, then, these two chapters question not the kind of relation between Descartes's two realms but the very possibility of a relation itself. This emphasis becomes clear near the end of the first chapter in the famous paragraph arguing for the "occult relation" between man and nature.

> The greatest delight which the fields and woods minister, is the suggestion of an occult relation between man and the vegetable. I am not alone and unacknowledged. They nod to me and I to them. The waving of the boughs in the storm, is new to me and old. It takes me by surprise, and yet is not unknown. Its effect is like that of a higher thought or a better emotion coming over me, when I deemed I was thinking justly or doing rightly. (P. 10)

What seems an embarrassing instance of the pathetic fallacy is not really a simple case of nature's reflecting man. Emerson's interest lies primarily with the incomprehensibility of the relation; otherwise "organic" and not "occult" would have been the more appropriate term.[17] The friendly waving of the boughs seems familiar, but also strange and "new." And in his conclusion that "it takes me by surprise, and yet is not unknown," he reformulates Leibniz's famous answer to materialism.

Leibniz accepted the empiricists' belief that nothing was in the mind that was not first in the senses.[18] So Emerson acknowledges the givenness of sensation in his notion of "surprise," an element downplayed, virtually ignored, in the two experiences of the previous paragraph. The otherness of this newness and surprise insists, as the transparent eyeball passage did not, that sensation is in some sense autonomous and obdurate. Yet at the same time, experience is truly ours – if not to create at least to describe and define. Leibniz rejected mere sensationalism by claiming that the one thing not first in the senses is the mind itself. Similarly, Emerson argues that, however surprising, the message is not entirely unknown. For the moment he leaves unclear the exact nature of the knowledge – whether it is merely some Platonic, even Wordsworthian, memory or whether its source is more integral to the experience. The important point is only that it exists and is mysterious.

The opening of the chapter's final paragraph summarizes these conclusions: "the power to produce this delight, does not reside in nature, but in man, or in a harmony of both" (p. 10).[19] It is not entirely convincing. The "in man, or in . . . both" construction wobbles on the very point that seems most important – the relation that, however "occult," will yet save man from the rampant subjectivism of the transparent eyeball. And the chapter ends with a solemn but undermotivated warning about nature's severity. Nevertheless, the more general point has been made. The penultimate paragraph – with its transition from occult relation to familiar surprise (and even beyond to some vaguely defined higher moral thought) – encapsulates the argument to follow. And the crucial question – not about nature's use or man's exhilaration, but about the grounds for a belief in any relation whatsoever – has been fairly posed.

II

As a possible (even traditional) means of bridging the gap between mind and matter, idealism is a plausible response to the antinomies of Nature's first two sections. The question then becomes whether the specific kind of idealism introduced in the sixth chapter is philosophically viable. Given that the noble doubt is in some sense relevant to the problem of interrelation, is it also serious? Do we quite simply want to dignify the doctrine of the noble doubt with the name of "idealism" at all?

"Idealism" is a broad term, meaning anything from a vague exuberance and optimism – the possession of "ideals" – to the encyclopedic taxonomies of Hegelianism. For nineteenth-century America, however, it took basically four forms.[20] Two were the legacy of classical thought. As a general mystical doctrine compounded from various traditions – Pythagorean, Gnostic, and Oriental, as well as certain Judeo-Christian heresies – idealism attested only to the primacy and unity of spirit, the famous "All" linking Emerson, Goethe, and Melville.[21] Platonic idealism, encountered directly in the dialogues or indirectly in English Romanticism, posited an immutable ideal world behind or above the world of experience, which was itself only a reflection of this permanence. Believing in the purity of a preexistent knowledge, Platonism emphasized memory as a road back to truth and childlike innocence as a converting influence.

Cartesian dualism encouraged more narrowly epistemological reformulations of the traditional problem. Proceeding from the empiricist insistence on the primacy of the senses, Berkeleian idealism argued that to the extent that sensible objects are really "ideas" (or things perceived by sense), they can only be said to exist within the process of perception, that is, within the mind. Transcendental or Kantian idealism – as a critique of all these formulations, especially Berkeley's – insisted that the problem is best treated as an examination of the limits of human knowledge: certain only of the nature of possible experience, man is unable to comment, positively or negatively, on the reality of any supersensible cause. The problem of contemporary philosophical idealism concerns largely the last two strains. And to question the seriousness of Emerson's philosophy in Nature is really to ask, given the obvious presence of all four strains throughout the book, whether we can identify in this sixth chapter an informed use of either Berkeley or Kant.

The casualness and abruptness of the introduction of the noble doubt might seem to argue against the passage's sophistication (or even importance). Yet if we for the moment ignore the tone and attend instead to the shape and even the language of the argument, Emerson's analysis becomes surprisingly precise. The sixth chapter divides roughly into three sections: the brief but philosophically crucial introduction of skeptical idealism; a long discussion of how culture teaches this doubt; and a fervent denial of what might seem to be some of the churlish implications of such idealism. Although this overall structure is not itself Kantian, the specific arguments made within the chapter are clearly so. And the theory of the noble doubt rehearses – without the names – the history of recent epistemological thought and especially Kant's inversion of it with the Copernican revolution of transcendental idealism.

A newfound intellectual rigor is evident from the very first sentence. Nature's lessons about the meaning of the world are said to be "unspeakable but intelligible and practicable" (p. 29). The adjectives make no literal sense. Whether it means "ineffable" or "objectionable," "unspeakable" is the wrong word for lessons that would disturb few liberal thinkers and might easily be found in the physicotheology of Paley or the Bridgewater Treatises. The word is used not in its everyday sense, however, but as a term of art. There are evidently things that can be spoken, things that can be thought, and things that can only be done.[22] The contrast is presumably the same as Kant's between what can be known as a true object of sensation and what can only be thought. In fact, Emerson's use of the Kantian "practicable" to define the third group unobtrusively but resolutely declares his intellectual allegiances.

What follows is a paragraph of self-conscious terminology, whose purpose seems as much to identify itself as philosophy as to make an especially difficult point.

> A noble doubt perpetually suggests itself, whether this end be not the Final Cause of the Universe; and whether nature outwardly exists. It is a sufficient account of that Appearance we call the World, that God will teach a human mind, and so makes it the receiver of a certain number of congruent sensations, which we call sun and moon, man and woman, house and trade. In my utter impotence to test the authenticity of the report of my senses, to know whether the impressions they make on me correspond with outlying objects, what difference does it make, whether Orion is up there in heaven, or some god paints the image in the firmament of the soul? The relations of parts and the end of the whole remaining the same, what is the difference, whether land and sea interact, and worlds revolve and intermingle without number or end, – deep yawning under deep, and galaxy balancing galaxy, throughout absolute space, or, whether, without relations of time and space, the same appearances are inscribed in the constant faith of man? (P. 29)

Forsaking the rudimentary dichotomy of ME and NOT ME, the paragraph abounds in "ends," "final causes," "appearances," "worlds," "impressions," "sensations," "sufficiencies," and "congruencies," most of them solemnly capitalized. The argument is simple enough. The single-mindedness of nature's lessons as rehearsed in Chapters Two through Five makes us doubt whether nature exists for any other purpose – whether in fact nature exists substantively apart from this pedagogic project. The logic is dubious, resting on a confusion of means and ends. Even if we concede that absolutely all parts of nature are indeed means to our discipline, it does not necessarily follow that our education is their end. But the announced concern to determine the end of nature is, for the moment at least, secondary. Later in the paragraph, Emerson implicitly admits his indifference to teleology by paradoxically coupling two kinds of "ends" in the same sentence. It does not matter, we are told, whether or not worlds intermingle "without number or end" so long as the "end of the whole" remains the same.

The apparently cavalier tone should not obscure the paragraph's real interest. The analysis of the noble doubt is serious, though not perhaps on the points we think it should be. Emerson accurately lays out the various possible positions, identifying each by characteristic terminology. He glances at empiricism in general, through an allusion to Hume's "impressions," and summarizes Berkeley's idealist notion of a reality "imprinted" on the senses by Spirit, in the slightly satiric image of "some god paint[ing] the image in the firmament of the soul."[23] German philosophy is represented by its subjectivization of the "relations of time and space," and Fichtean absolute idealism, recalled in the vision of the world as a mere posit "inscribed in the constant faith of man."[24] And the stable world view against which both idealisms react is clearly Newtonian, as the reference to "absolute space" indicates.[25]

But the familiar vocabulary does more than identify the philosophical context. It indicates how Emerson hopes to move beyond traditional distinctions and even to transcend his own earlier formulations. Here the use of "correspond" is central. A key concept throughout Emerson's career, correspondence refers earlier in the essay simply to Swedenborg's primitive notion of a literal parallelism between the two worlds of matter and spirit.[26] In the tortured logic of the chapter on "Language," the derivation of spiritual terminology from natural phenomena implies the emblematic character of nature itself. Now, however, this "radical correspondence between visible things and human thoughts" is turned upside down, and doubt about correspondence extends to the very representational dimension of sensory experience (p. 19). Unable to discover an objective standard against which to measure sensations, man cannot "know whether the impressions they make on me correspond with outlying objects." Swedenborgian lexicons become irrelevant. No longer can lions signify rage and lambs innocence, for it is uncertain if white, woolly, and bleating even mean real sheep anymore. In discarding Swedenborg, Emerson has moved from the periphery to the center of the philosophical debate: the representational power of sensation is the central assumption of philosophy since Descartes, and the correspondence theory of truth its chief pre-Kantian expression.[27]

If in one sense Emerson has upped the metaphysical ante, however, he has in another declared the game null and void. Although the noble doubt is only hypothetical, it is nevertheless a self-fulfilling prophecy.[28] The basic thrust of the paragraph is to claim disinterest in the question of the phenomenality of nature. Yet the reasons for this indifference shift subtly in the paragraph's concluding sentences. The first argues pragmatically that the question of absolute reality is irrelevant. "Whether nature enjoy a substantial existence without, or is only in the apocalypse of the mind, it is alike useful and alike venerable to me." It does not matter whether nature is real or only my projection, for in either case it works for me as if it were real. The second sentence, though apparently restating the first, actually concludes the opposite. "Be it what it may, it is ideal to me, so long as I cannot try the accuracy of my senses." Whereas the first argues that nature is real to me in its use, the second claims that it is ideal to me in its effect. The ideality is in fact more immediate than the reality. Usefulness and venerability only intimate reality; sensory unverifiability is identically idealism. Nature is not "real" in some ways and "ideal" in others, but always ideal, however much usefulness and venerability seem to imply an independent reality. And a paragraph that hypothetically outlines two forms of idealism ends necessarily committed to a third.

The shift marks the chapter's essentially Kantian orientation. As metaphysical idealists, both Berkeley and Fichte wanted to conclude something about the absolute nature of reality from their understanding of the problematic aspects of sensation.[29] Kant, on the other hand, was an idealist only "transcendentally." Once it was granted that mind and matter were both appearance – intuitions of a sensory apparatus that could reveal nothing about absolute noumenal reality – then man was free, even obliged, to admit the empirical reality of both.[30] The dual ending to Emerson's paragraph, then, merely repeats the Kantian argument to answer Berkeley and Fichte. In the absence of an objective sensory standard, nature is transcendentally ideal. Yet once we grant that, we must also admit that within the system of sensation, nature is to me useful and venerable, that is, empirically real.

Emerson's quite specific "transcendental idealism" leads, appropriately enough, to the problem of natural stability. Material annihilation posed no problem for Berkeley or Fichte. After bigger game in the reification of the Absolute Ego, Fichte was willing simply to let the world go.[31] Berkeley, though entirely more sober, was equally undistressed by the world's evanescence.[32] Chimeras and the real world are both only ideas in our minds, though God condescends to ensure the greater reality of the latter. This distinction, Berkeley explained, might seem "harsh," but it is not really so; if in some sense we eat, drink, and wear ideas, the poverty resides not in our world but only in our vocabulary.[33]

For Kant, however, the denial of the world was more dangerous. Like Fichte and especially Berkeley, he did not think he really denied anything. "This ideality of space and time leaves, however, the certainty of empirical knowledge unaffected, for we are equally sure of it, whether these forms necessarily inhere in things in themselves or only in our intuition of them."[34] But unlike the other two, he worried that empirical reality could be willfully degraded. If Berkeley feared that his system was too harsh, Kant feared that his was too lax. Without Berkeley's autonomous God arbitrarily upholding the difference between things and fancies, Kant's system had to establish stability from within itself. And in this context, the possibility that man could declare appearance to be entirely illusory was a real threat.[35]

Like Kant, Emerson sees idealism's challenge to the possibility of experience. Immediately after affirming transcendental idealism, he turns to attack those who would exploit this potential. "The frivolous make themselves merry with the Ideal theory, as if its consequences were burlesque; as if it affected the stability of nature. It surely does not" (p. 29). God does not jest with us by allowing gaps of "inconsequence" in the causal sequence.[36] But since Emerson's epistemological point is not inherently theistic, such a Berkeleian appeal to absolute authority is not possible.[37] Emerson therefore claims less absolutely that "any distrust of the permanence of laws, would paralyze the faculties of man. Their permanence is sacredly respected, and his faith therein is perfect" (pp. 29-30).

This second, lesser claim is absolutely Kantian (and absolutely correct). In a section entitled "Refutation of Idealism," Kant attacks the frivolous argument that the existence of objects in space is either indemonstrable or, worse, logically impossible. He contends that, in fact, empirical self-consciousness requires the existence of objects in space. Empirical self-consciousness, defined as consciousness of one's existence in time, presupposes some external means of determining time, which is itself imperceptible.[38] The possibility of such a determinant assumes that there is something permanent outside of me. Therefore (pace Descartes and Berkeley) the consciousness of self is necessarily bound up with the existence of things.

Whatever we think of this argument as a refutation of Berkeley, its general point about the interrelatedness of the concepts of time, self, experience, and world is undeniable.[39] Self-consciousness demands the possibility of experience (of something). And for an experience to be definable, to be distinguishable from a chaos of random sense data, it must take place against a backdrop of relative permanence. The very notion of change embedded in experience implies an enduring framework within which that change can be recorded. Without this basic stability, nothing whatever would be experienced, and we as empirical – or even as transcendental – selves could not be said to be. An experience of pure self-consciousness without reference to a relatively stable "other" is simply inconceivable.[40]

It is this Kantian context that Emerson evokes with his own insistence on the stability of nature. Emerson had, of course, always had some sense of the moral necessity of permanence. As early as 1822, he worried in his journals whether nature was eternal, or at least sufficiently long-lived to allow for teleology. Even compensation, he saw, required time for things to work out (JMN.I.80-81).[41] But in *Nature* such traditional moral observations were recast in epistemological terms. What is threatened is less man's morality than his "faculties." "The wheels and springs of man are all set to the hypothesis of the permanence of nature. We are not built like a ship to be tossed, but like a house to stand." Permanence is not absolute, but hypothetical, not a description of reality but of the way man is "built," the pattern to which his wheels and springs are set. (Both the ship and house metaphors have celebrated Kantian equivalents.)[42] Stability is not true, but a "structure," one of the necessary presuppositions of our ability to experience anything. And so long as we are concerned with the experienced rather than the noumenally real – what Emerson rather misleadingly called the "active" rather than the "reflective" – nature logically cannot be seen as "short-lived or mutable."[43]

Once we understand that nature's permanence is not merely desirable but epistemologically necessary, bound up in the very possibility of experience, some of the oddities of the chapter's first paragraph disappear. Epistemological necessity explains the paragraph's unusual preoccupation with time, why man's faith must be "constant" and the noble doubt suggested "perpetually." The denial of the absolute reality of the world can take place only within a system of relative permanence and stability. Otherwise change would not only be traumatic; it would be literally unintelligible, even unperceivable. The central statement of the hypothetical doubt explicitly takes place under this condition of internal congruency. The world can – indeed, in absolute terms, must – be called mere appearance, but only so long as the relation of parts stays the same, the end of the whole the same. Or in terms of the once troubling pun, the stability of the end of the whole makes worlds without end unnecessary; the permanence of the internal relation of parts makes absolute relations of time and space operose.

Emerson's witty choice of the constellation Orion to represent reality dramatizes the extent to which the question of the absolute must be answered from within the subjective realm and not apart from it. Perhaps a certain seven stars do exist up there in a real heaven. But the geometric pattern they seem to form is daily changing as the stars fly from each other at varying velocities. And the imagined correspondence between this temporary configuration and a fictional character is so tenuous as to undermine thoroughly any claim to real Orions "up there." The point quite simply is that reality is only the name given to the most stable tokens in the game of experience, and its "stars" are, in absolute terms, no more independent of subjective perceptions than is a mythological figure.[44]

Only within the context of this prior assumption of relative permanence and stability can we fully understand Emerson's announced indifference to questions of ultimate reality. Here again the German antecedents are suggestive. In part, Emerson's unwillingness to choose between nature and mind seems to reflect Fichte's claim that all metaphysics starts with either one or the other, and that the choice is largely a matter of individual temperament, personal preference.[45] But, in fact, Emerson does not really feel free to choose between the two. As the last sentences of the paragraph make clear, idealism is inevitable. Unlike Fichte's, then, Emerson's indifference is more narrowly epistemological, a mark of the lack of semantic difference between two apparent options. Having argued from Reason's urge for unity to the regulative use of the ideas of pure Reason, Kant announces his own "complete indifference" to whether the unity perceived is of God's design or nature's laws.[46] His point is not that he does not care to answer, but that any attempt to do so would be circular. Having derived God and nature from the observation of unity, it would be logically inconsistent to turn around and deduce that unity from nature and God. Similarly, Emerson's use of the observed unity of discipline to posit the relative existence or stability of man and nature rules out any subsequent attempt to say whether it is really man or really nature that accounts for that unified disciplinary end.

The point may become clearer if we recall Kant's distinction between the regulative and the constitutive. The distinction is not always maintained. At times the inapplicability of the regulative principles to possible experience seems to imply their qualitative difference, a function of their special character as noumena and not of their infinity, their being simply "too long" or "too many."[47] At its best, however, the distinction claims only that within certain contexts it is impossible to distinguish between the hypothetical and the real. Although acting as if it will rain tomorrow is not the same as believing it will rain, acting as if the world were infinite is the same as believing it so.[48] Certain statements can only be construed as imperatives, and indifference measures not a personal reaction to a situation but a logical (almost grammatical) property of it.

Emerson asserts, then, that relations and ends are valid topics for discussion only within the system of our subjective perceptions. Any question about how these internal elements relate outside in reality asks not what is (perhaps absolutely but ultimately indeterminately) "out there," but only what would happen within the system if I acted as if such relations actually existed. Emerson's "indifference" – his refusal to choose between constellation and apocalypse – registers not boredom but intellectual precision. The notion of a second-level, transcendent "world" or "mind" grounding our sensations can only be of practical value. Believing so may be helpful in certain situations. But in the absence of any objective standard to test sensation, these transcendent "ideas" cannot be called true knowledge. In terms of what can be objectively known (rather than subjectively thought), we cannot differentiate between a hypothetical acting "as if" and a literal belief in a noumenal reality, between Orion as absolute existence and Orion as mental apocalypse. According to our inescapably subjective perceptual apparatus, the notions are indistinguishably useful and venerable.[49]

The narrowly epistemological bias of Emerson's idealism, though implicit throughout the first part of the chapter, is really clear only in the third and final section. After a straightforward analysis of how culture – as motion, poetry, science, and religion – undermines our conviction of the reality of the external world, Emerson returns to the more theoretic tone of the opening paragraphs. First, he reaffirms his love of the nature he seems to have annihilated.

> But I own there is something ungrateful in expanding too curiously the particulars of the general proposition, that all culture tends to imbue us with idealism. I have no hostility to nature, but a child's love to it. I expand and live in the warm day like corn and melons. Let us speak her fair. I do not wish to fling stones at my beautiful mother, nor soil my gentle nest. (Pp. 35-36)

The particulars by which we are taught the general proposition of idealism should not be overemphasized. For, as he repeatedly implies, idealism is only a general truth or conceptual scheme and leaves the particulars more or less untouched. As he claimed earlier, the effect of

culture is "not to shake our faith in the stability of particular phenomena" but only "to lead us to regard nature [as a whole] as a phenomenon" (p. 30). The numbers are indicative: phenomena are stable,
though the overall phenomenon is not.

Denying hostility, Emerson claims to "expand and live in the warm
day like corn and melons." Whether powerful or silly as existential
report, the sentence contains an accurate epistemological observation.
In a strict transcendental context the world is less demonstrable than
consciousness: we can describe the structure of our sensations more
confidently than we can their foundations in the noumenal world. At
the level of particulars, however, all objects are equally knowable: the
empirical self or "I" occupies the same epistemological space as vege-
tables, grows in the same "warm day."[50] Nature, as our quaint name
for a collection of normal haveable experiences, is perfectly stable and
inviolable, no more phenomenal than any particular stone we might
throw at her. Here, as before, Emerson merely warns against conflating
transcendental idealism, in which all is equally phenomenal, with empirical realism, in which all is equally permanent. And the notion of
flinging real stones at a phenomenal mother becomes simply the comic
counterpart of the earlier confusion about whether a mythological character could be really "up there" in the sky. Recalling the special terminology he defined at the chapter's start, he concludes that whatever is
true transcendentally, we must, within the empiricist frame of reference, simply "speak" her fair.

The defense of his love for nature in her place leads to one final attempt
to define that place. The passage is puzzling, for more traditional affirmations of man's relation slide into intimations of his dominion.

> I only wish to indicate the true position of nature in regard to man,
> wherein to establish man, all right education tends; as the ground
> which to attain is the object of human life, that is, of man's connexion
> with nature. (P. 36)

The first phrase is careful enough. The inevitability of subjectivity is
implied by the suppressed perceptual metaphor of "regard," though the
passive construction minimizes the suggestion of human control implicit in the earlier formulation – man's being taught "to regard nature
as phenomenon." The inversion of the next phrase (and the awkward
comma), however, encourages misreading. The point is simply that all
education attempts to give man the right sense of his relation to nature.
But metaphors of relation are confused with metaphors of position, and
"establish" suggests not merely that man is "put" in his place but that
the place is an exalted one. The third phrase continues the subtle elevation of man in the triplicate pun of "ground." The primary, neutral

meaning of place does not obscure the implied glorification of man, whose "attained" ground is an elevation, or the devaluation of nature, whose ground is mere dirt. The final phrase, however, implicitly denies the grander implications of the sentence by defining the object of human life as the connection of man to nature. Here there is no implication of man's priority or dominion, but only the vaguely transcendental claim that certain concepts naturally come together.[51]

That a generally Kantian notion of connectedness is the real focus becomes clearer in the chapter's last paragraph, which offers one final definition of idealism. Characterizing idealism as advantageous, Emerson says that "it is, in fact, the view which Reason, both speculative and practical, that is, philosophy and virtue, take" (p. 36). The subdivision of Reason, with the appropriately Kantian names, is Emerson's most explicit clue to the context in which he would have us read the chapter. We will eventually have to worry his rough equation of practical Reason and virtue. But, for the moment, it is enough to consider what he says about epistemology and pure Reason.

As always, he begins with the phenomenality of the world from the point of view of thought. Then the definition turns distressingly theological, even Berkeleian.

> Idealism sees the world in God. It beholds the whole circle of persons and things, of actions and events, of country and religion, not as painfully accumulated, atom after atom, act after act, in an aged creeping Past, but as one vast picture, which God paints on the instant eternity, for the contemplation of the soul. (P. 36)

The Berkeleian overtones – the world in God or painted by Him – are misleading.[52] God and His act of painting are purely metaphorical, uninteresting (and probably imperceptible) in themselves. Nor is the soul a worthy object of examination. In the second half of the paragraph it serves mostly as a grammatical placeholder, the occasion to watch, much as idealism itself had been in the first half the opportunity to behold. The real focus is the unity of reality. Experience is a "whole circle," distinct from any potential dissection spatially into atoms or temporally into creeping acts. Instead it is "one vast picture," notable less for being vast or pictorial than for being simply unified, "one." The epitome of this holism is God's "instant eternity." This concept, paradoxical to the point of ineffability, is not to be analyzed or even experienced, but to be contemplated, and recalls the extent to which the "structure" of knowledge has been, from its beginning in permanence, one of belief and faith.[53]

Transcendental idealism, then, provides Emerson with a carefully circumscribed kind of power. The fact of subjectivity allows him, without denying the stability of experience, instantly to draw a circle around it, to subordinate sensation to the logical priority of consciousness. The claim seems fairly conservative compared to the more flamboyant metaphysics of Berkeley or Fichte. Very little can be said objectively of this consciousness except that it is unified, one. To someone uncertain about his feelings of universal consanguinity, of relationship of any kind, this oneness may be sufficient. For the moment, however, it is less important to define where he went with his philosophy than where he started. Whatever reservations we might have about the implications of the noble doubt, it is philosophically sophisticated. And however fanciful the metaphysical house he finally erected, its foundations were securely laid in precise epistemological observations.

III

The precise epistemological terminology of the chapter on "Idealism," however, proves very little about the philosophical sophistication of the book as a whole. After all, though nothing is known definitively about the order of composition, many critics assume the sixth chapter to be a last-minute addition.[54] The journals and letters focus largely on a "book about Nature" and suggest that the final work is really a combination of two separate essays – one on "Nature" and the other on "Spirit."[55] Scarcely a month before the book's release, Emerson was still complaining about the "one crack in it not easy to be soldered or welded" (L.II.32).

But we should resist assuming prematurely that the sixth chapter is Emerson's awkward attempt to bridge that gap and the doctrine of idealism only partly assimilated to the purpose of the essay as a whole. The first mention of the project in the journals begins with the statement "That the mind is its own place" (JMN.III.315-16). In one sense, then, idealism was a part of the argument from the first, and Emerson's definition of the mind as a "place" rather than a thing suggests his care from the beginning when treating epistemology.[56] If we bracket as inconclusive, then, the external evidence for the growth of Emerson's ideas, the question becomes whether or not we can discover in the work itself evidence for the importance of idealism to the final argument of the essay. More simply, given that idealism is intelligently expounded, can we show it to be integral as well?

First, we must recall the overall structure of the work. The "Introduction" and the first chapter, "Nature," are paired introductions, announcing the explicit project of determining the "end" of nature, but also demonstrating the implicit and more fundamental problem of establishing any kind of relationship between the inevitable dualism of ME and NOT ME. The subsequent four chapters treat the preliminary question of nature's purpose. As the first, "lower" half of the argument, they present various increasingly elevated aspects of nature's function, starting at the base level of commodity and progressing through beauty and language to discipline.[57] This last, which "includes the preceding uses, as parts of itself," is the most significant (p. 23). "Thus is the unspeakable but intelligible and practicable meaning of the world conveyed to man, the immortal pupil, in every object of sense. To this one end of Discipline, all parts of nature conspire" (p. 29).

Yet, in fact, the logic of the chapter on "Discipline" is self-defeating. The announced topic is the unlimited meaning of nature's lessons. "Space, time, society, labor, climate, food, locomotion, the animals, the mechanical forces, give us sincerest lessons, day by day, whose meaning is unlimited." The properties of matter teach to the Understanding the intellectual truths of, say, solidity, inertia, or divisibility. Reason then transfers these lessons into "its own world of thought, by perceiving the analogy that marries Mind and Matter" (p. 23). The limitlessness of the meaning, however, leads the Understanding to look elsewhere for a determinate truth, and unlimited meaning turns into simple meaninglessness. The laws of physics are apprehended so "calmly and genially" that they explicate not the experienced world but self-existence, the "privilege to BE!" (p. 25).

The very list of disciplinary facts is suspicious: if labor, climate, food, locomotion, animals, and mechanical forces are one kind of property, space and time, which head the list, are another. At best they teach the trivial lesson of differences, that "things are not huddled and lumped, but sundered and individual" (p. 24). More simply, however, they seem to exist only to disappear into Reason's "own world" of thought, carrying nature with them. As man perceives the beauty of nature shining within his breast, his greater refinement becomes her loss. And in an evaporation that anticipates the disappearance both of Orion in Chapter Six and of disagreeable appearances on the book's final page, "Time and Space relations vanish as laws are known" (p. 25).

This devaluation of the material world and concomitant glorification of the individual is especially evident in the final lessons of the Understanding – those of the Will and of power. Before the child learns to accept God's sovereignty – to proclaim " 'thy will be done' " – he is taught how "he can reduce under his will, not only particular events, but great classes, nay the whole series of events, and so conform all facts to his character." Nature is so "thoroughly mediate," so useful and made to serve, that "the world becomes, at last, only a realized will, – the double of the man" (p. 25). The limitations of this lesson of power are clear enough. The lesson ends when Reason teaches man to discover God's will in his own (and the argument moves directly from this ultimate lesson of the Understanding to the more elevated moral ones of Reason). But the transcendence of the purely personal may not be so automatic as the argument implies. Emerson's refusal to capitalize the pronoun when referring to God is ominous, and the conflation of wills – thy, his, and "a realized" – may not allow a subsequent acceptance of a divine omnipotence independent of human power.

A similar problem plagues the higher lessons of morality.

> All things are moral. . . . every animal function from the sponge up to Hercules, shall hint or thunder to man the laws of right and wrong, and echo the Ten Commandments. . . . This ethical character so penetrates the bone and marrow of nature, as to seem the end for which it was made. . . . In God, every end is converted into a new means. Thus the use of Commodity, regarded by itself, is mean and squalid. But it is to the mind an education in the great doctrine of Use, namely, that a thing is good only so far as it serves; . . . every natural process is but a version of a moral sentence. The moral law lies at the centre of nature and radiates to the circumference. It is the pith and marrow of every substance, every relation, and every process. All things with which we deal, preach to us. What is a farm but a mute gospel? (Pp. 25-26)

The very "completeness" with which Reason discovers moral lessons within itself makes the mental world seem realer than the morality. The various uses of nature combine to teach the "great doctrine of Use"; the moral sentences, the single moral law. This universal ethical character of nature – that "all things with which we deal, preach to us" – tends to be more startling for its universality than for its ethical content. At first, the content seems as real as the form, and animal functions thunder the laws of right and wrong, echo the Ten Commandments. But in the relentless conversion of old ends into new means, the radical identity of all organizations reduces moral influences to an "amount" of truth, and the farm, though gospel like the rest of experience, turns mute. The way in which "the endless variety of things" makes a "unique, an identical impression" proves merely the fact of unity – "the Unity of Nature, – the Unity in Variety." And just as time and space had vanished in the laws of the Understanding, so time, as the more spiritual, vanishes again here in "the perfection of the whole" (p. 27).

If this rage for unity blurs the essay's moral point, however, it clarifies the logical progression of the essay. The movement beyond discipline as the single end of nature to unity as its single condition is so inevitable that we wonder if unity has not been the true goal of the lower argument all along. The noble doubt that forms the transition to the higher argument of the final three chapters actually responds more to the unity of nature than to her discipline. Man doubts the world's independent existence less because she teaches him than because she is so completely accounted for by this single end. It is not the particular role she plays but the completeness, the "sufficiency," with which she plays it that initiates his doubt. Presumably any single function, if a sufficient account, would make her seem equally phenomenal.

But to say this is seriously to undermine the structure of the lower argument. If mere unity is the real end, then the steps by which man discovers that unity are more or less irrelevant. The ends of commodity, beauty, language, and discipline need not appear in that order, nor need they even be the sole ends of nature. Any number of any kind in any order will suffice if the final step is merely to compress all particulars into an ineffable unity, which can in turn be swallowed by the noble doubt of a voracious ego.

The logic of the lower argument, then, works in two directions at once. The announced (and somewhat artificial) examination of the ends of nature is gradually supplanted by an implied demonstration of her unity. By misdirecting our attention with an exploration of the function of nature, Emerson convinces us all the more dramatically of her uniformity. In this light, the irritating, overelaborate structure of Chapters Two through Five serves an effective rhetorical purpose. Were the announced proof of the centrality of discipline really the heart of the argument, critics would be right to protest. The chapters do not flow into one another, and commodity, beauty, and language do not lead irresistibly to the conclusion that nature is a teacher.[58] But as unity and not discipline is the real point, the divisions are constructed to collapse. Emerson himself hints that he does not take the lower argument very seriously, stating that although all uses of nature "admit of being thrown into" one of his four classes, the subdivisions are more or less arbitrary (p. 11). The final telescoping of these chapters under the single rubric of discipline just dramatizes the inevitable integration of parts that he hopes the reader will himself come to perform. Awkwardness is itself a rhetorical strategy, and the case for unity succeeds as (even because) the argument for discipline fails. Our very superiority to the essay's structure forces us to admit that, yes, indeed, they are all the same thing after all, and we unwittingly prove Emerson's point for him.

The lower argument is not built to stand, and the noble doubt, so far from being an imposition, is that necessary final turn that, by collapsing everything back into one, makes sense of the artificial superstructure. But idealism is more than the logical outcome of the lower argument for unity. For throughout these initial chapters, intimations of the mind's priority appear in discussion of the individual ends, and the noble doubt is everywhere anticipated in the tendency of nature to transcend – and thereby challenge – its own reality. The first use of "commodity" is the least idealist, which perhaps accounts for the indecent haste with which Emerson treats this "low" service. Yet even here nature is surprisingly dependent on man. She is, in her ministry to him, not only the material but also the process and result. The efficiency of nature's cycles, with nary a grain falling on barren ground, is simply too optimistic, and we suspect that nature is the "result" of her ministry to man more because man is doing the watching than because all seeds bear fruit.

The idealism implicit in the unsettling superficiality of the first use of nature becomes explicit in the later uses. Throughout the chapter on "Beauty," Emerson plays with the possibility that beauty is projected onto the world rather than perceived in it. The division of the chapter, after the general introduction, into the three levels of beauty – formal, spiritual, and intellectual – scarcely masks the extent to which mind is the determining factor in each. Although beauty may rest in "the constitution of all things," its source may equally well be "the plastic power of the human eye," the "best composer" that, combining with the laws of light, "integrates every mass of objects" (p. 12). The objectivity attributed to light's influence – "a sort of infinitude . . . like [that of] space and time" (p. 13) – is hardly reassuring to those who remember how quickly time and space vanish, both in Kant's Aesthetic and more proximately in the second half of "Discipline." The beauty of nature's forms, which seems at first autonomous, is finally rejected as "the least part." The more keenly these forms are pursued, the more they "become shows merely, and mock us with their unreality." The truth is in part moral, a warning against overanxiousness: " 't is only a mirage as you look from windows of diligence" (p. 14). But the "as" means "since" as well as "if." And the culprit is not merely the diligence with which we look, but the fact that we look at all.

The higher aspects of beauty are even more bound up with man's way of looking. Moral or spiritual beauty degenerates into a version of the pathetic fallacy ripe for parody. "In private places, among sordid objects, an act of truth or heroism seems at once to draw to itself the sky as its temple, the sun as its candle. . . . Only let his thoughts be of equal scope, and the frame will suit the picture" (pp. 15-16).[59] The single unembarrassing explication of this passage – that our mind makes nature *appear* to echo our moods, that the "drawing to" is really a "drawing of" – demands an idealist orientation. More simply, the very notion of a spiritual beauty is irrevocably joined to that of man's will. Though at first merely "found in combination" with the human will, high and divine beauty becomes finally this will's "dowry and estate. It

is his, if he will." What at the start of the chapter was "the" constitution of all things is revealed to be "his" constitution, the act of will by
which "he takes up the world into himself" (p. 15).

The ambiguity concerning the extent to which this taking up is the
actual cause of the world, this constitution its sole creation, is clarified
somewhat in the highest aspect – beauty as an object of the intellect.
That the relation of things to thought is higher than their relation to
virtue already implies the priority of the mental. In the mind, man
moves beyond the love of beauty as Taste to its actual creation as Art.
The power promised is rigidly circumscribed. Art as the expression or
result of nature has only one characteristic – its singleness and similarity,
that is, its unity. Just as commodity became the "endless circulations of
divine charity" (p. 11), the ultimate standard of beauty becomes the
"entire circuit of natural forms, – the totality of nature" (p. 17). All
artists work merely to concentrate the beauty of the whole "on one
point," to express "the same All" of which truth and goodness are but
different faces. As always, the ultimate source of power is uncertain.
Nature seems to maintain some independence, to make some autonomous "impression" on man. It "works through" his will as well as
"passes through" it. But however convincing Emerson's theory of
beauty, the simpler point is clear. Even if it does not annihilate reality,
as at times it seems to, the mind's activity of composing, drawing to,
and finally taking up the world points toward the mental self-sufficiency that provokes the skepticism of Chapter Six. And the transition
from will to virtue to unity that in "Discipline" gives rise to the noble
doubt is fully anticipated here in the progression from moral beauty as
will to intellectual beauty as unity.

In the problematic chapter on "Language," idealism not only informs
the structure of the argument but also accounts for some of its odd
conclusions. Its influence is partially hidden by the pseudosyllogism
that begins the chapter. The first statement – that words are the signs of
natural facts – is harmless but intellectually trivial, especially since
"sign" is so poorly defined. The first and second statements taken
together, however, do raise two interesting questions. The first concerns the necessarily pictorial character of language. The "radical correspondence between visible things and human thoughts" leads language
in its purest form to become more "picturesque" until "all spiritual
facts are represented by natural symbols" (p. 19). "Represent" and
"symbol" here are used no more carefully than was "sign" earlier. But
the general sense is that the words used to describe ("represent") spiritual facts are derived from or analogous to ("symbols" of) words used
to describe natural facts. This theory, though most immediately available to Emerson in Swedenborg and his American apologist Sampson

Reed, has a far more reputable heritage going back at least as far as the Battle of the Books and the Moderns' Adamic desire to make the word one with the thing.[60]

More important for our purposes, the argument is really just a variation on the Kantian theme, central to the sixth chapter, that consciousness presupposes the possibility (at least) of the experience of external objects. In its most general formulation, "thoughts without content are empty."[61] So for Emerson, "a man conversing in earnest, if he watch his intellectual processes, will find that always a material image, more or less luminous, arises in his mind, cotemporaneous with every thought, which furnishes the vestment of the thought" (p. 20). Emerson's insistence that "this imagery is spontaneous" may recall that "spontaneity" is Kant's term for the power of knowledge to produce objects through sensation.[62] So at the end of the chapter, his promised knowledge of "the primitive sense of the permanent objects of nature" looks forward to the crucial role permanence will play in stabilizing idealism, possibly alluding to Kant's similar emphasis in the Refutation. At the very least, he makes clear in his interpretation of a passage from Coleridge's Aids that the relationship between concepts and objects is causal, not contingent. Only "when interpreted and defined in an object" does unconscious truth become truly known and usable – "a part of the domain of knowledge, – a new weapon in the magazine of power" (p. 23).[63]

This Kantian argument about the relation between thoughts and things is, however, confused in this second section with another, far more dubious point about nature's role in interpreting man to man. Evidently Emerson equated the observation that some natural fact symbolizes every spiritual fact with the problematic one that "every natural fact is a symbol of some spiritual fact" (p. 18). The former is probably true. Our spiritual vocabulary is drawn chiefly from the natural world; it has no terminology of its own. But, as Kenneth Burke rightly reminds us by invoking Jeremy Bentham's "theory of fictions," the natural conclusion is that spirit is only a way of talking about reality and has no autonomous existence.[64] Yet so to conclude would jeopardize the priority of the mental, which is the first principle of transcendental idealism.

Instead Emerson proposes the extremely unobvious explanation of the radical correspondence between the world and the spirit: nature exists to supply the soul with a vocabulary to talk about itself. It is perhaps unwise to make too much of Emerson's overstatement here. Emerson himself trivializes the terminology nature provides as mere "pepper-corn informations" (p. 21). And the Swedenborgianism implicit in this chapter is, as we have seen, not really sustained later in the essay. As the sixth chapter reveals, nature and her vocabulary are already produced in part by the mind. The astonishing parallels between the two vocabularies, then, really prove little more than that man understands reality in terms of the concepts and categories with which he is equipped. Nevertheless it is important to recognize the extent to which the statements on language propel us toward the noble doubt: the awkwardness can be understood only by anticipating the skeptical idealism toward which the lower argument builds.

The chapter's third point is its most striking and perplexing.[65] The majesty of nature must have a higher purpose than to convey to man trivial particulars, "to expedite the affairs of our pot and kettle." The world must mean more than what we project on it as "emblems of our thought." Therefore "the [whole] world is emblematic. Parts of speech are metaphors because the whole of nature is a metaphor of the human mind" (p. 21). The second conclusion in no way follows from the first. That the world is a single symbol indicates nothing about what it symbolizes. If anything, it seems foolish to free natural particulars from the tyranny of our thoughts in order to reenslave them to the more universal subjectivism of "the human mind."

The urge toward unification – from emblems to emblem – should be familiar enough from the similar impulses in "Beauty" and "Discipline." But here the need to glorify the mind turns arbitrary, and Emerson capitulates to a two-world solution more fully than anywhere else in the essay.[66] Borrowing largely from Swedenborg and his followers, Emerson imagines a "visible world . . . the dial plate of the invisible," a "visible creation . . . the terminus or the circumference of the invisible world" (pp. 21, 22). Spirit becomes a distinct world of Ideas preexisting in the mind of God and necessarily manifesting themselves in material form. And for proof, Emerson merely responds that "it appears to men, or it does not appear" (p. 22); no materialistic skeptics need apply. Again, the long-range damage done by this overstated dualism is minimal. The axioms of physics have stopped translating ethics by the next chapter (pp. 21, 25), and correspondence is defined out of existence by the noble doubt. But the intensity of the momentary outburst marks the difficulty with which Emerson restrains his irrepressible idealism.

If the extravagance of "Language" represents the essay's most ebullient expression of nascent idealism, the end to "Discipline" – and to the whole lower argument – is its most melancholy one. By the time man has been taught all the lessons of will, morality, and finally unity, the lower argument is effectively complete, the world highly compressed into a ball of discipline waiting to be swallowed by the voracious doubt.[67] But the argument pauses and, as a kind of coda, Emerson doubles back to the question of human form – not now as a level of beauty but as an aspect of unity itself.

> Words and actions are not the attributes of mute and brute nature. They introduce us to the human form, of which all other organizations appear to be degradations. . . . We are associated in adolescent and adult life with some friends, who, like skies and waters, are coextensive with our idea; who, answering each to a certain affection of the soul, satisfy our desire on that side; whom we lack power to put at such focal distance from us, that we can mend or even analyze them. (P. 28)

The announced celebration of the power, the pure joy, of friendship is ridden with determinist language. Love turns compulsive, something we "cannot chuse" but do. The idealist point is obvious. People are "coextensive with our ideas," forms by which the eye is "always accompanied," because objects are necessarily bound up with the possibility of any experience. But such knowledge is threatening, and as objects of thought, persons seem thoughts merely.

Elsewhere Emerson makes the case more neutrally.

> Whatever does not concern us, is concealed from us. As soon as a person is no longer related to our present well-being, he is concealed, or *dies,* as we say. Really, all things and persons are related to us, but according to our nature, they act on us not at once, but in succession, and we are made aware of their presence one at a time. All persons, all things which we have known, are here present, and many more than we see; the world is full. . . . When he has exhausted for the time the nourishment to be drawn from any one person or thing, that object is withdrawn from his observation, and though still in his immediate neighborhood, he does not suspect its presence. Nothing is dead. (CW.III.142-43)

The passage combines Berkeley's claim that things cannot exist unperceived with Kant's that successions can be both real and apparent, irreversible and reversible.[68] Emerson concludes that although perception makes things seem to appear and disappear, live and die in succession, all really exist eternally.

In *Nature,* however, the emphasis is inverted. If the later treatment builds to the idea of eternal plenitude, here it ends with the perception of annihilation. With eternal presence subordinated to unconscious effect, the experience becomes simply one of absence and loss. "When [a friend] has, moreover, become an object of thought, and, whilst his character retains all its unconscious effect, is converted in the mind into solid and sweet wisdom, – it is a sign to us that his office is closing, and he is commonly withdrawn from our sight in a short time" (p. 29).

The passage may be an emotionally appropriate farewell to his brother Charles.[69] But intellectually this last disappearance – of other human beings – only broadcasts the difficulty the real world has in asserting its independence throughout the lower argument. In these four chapters, nature has been so exclusively directed away from objects and toward man that its ends seem mere means, a springboard to the only real world, that of spirit. Natural beauty, language, and finally people have been everywhere so evanescent that one scarcely need turn the page to read of the doubt spawned by sufficiency. And the question becomes not why Emerson imposed the noble doubt on the argument in Chapter Six, but rather how he was able to forestall it for so long.

IV

It is difficult, perhaps impossible, to determine the extent to which the failure of Chapters Two through Five is intentional. At times the argument seems naive, a perfectly conventional history of philosophy as Emerson learned it at Harvard. With Paley, Butler, and the argument from design as his guides, Emerson moves up the teleological ladder through the formal, spiritual, and intellectual aspects of the four ends of nature. The noble doubt is just the natural result of trying to take seriously a physicotheology that, like Unitarianism, customarily refused to face its own implications. And Kant is simply what you get when you push Paley to the limits: design means transcendental idealism if it means anything at all. At other times, however, Emerson seems in control of the ambiguities of the argument, or at least able to exploit them. In the most extreme version of this reading, the weaknesses of the lower argument are not honest confusion but rhetorical tricks to force his readers to see contradictions of which Emerson himself was fully aware from the start. By this account the lower argument becomes a fully strategic way of convincing one's mentors (or at least one's peers) of the radical implications of their own most cherished texts.[70]

Yet whether the lower argument is a lively discovery of contradiction or a rhetorical demonstration of it, the point about the centrality of idealism remains the same. However casually introduced, idealism, once present, tends to absorb all that came before it. It is not simply things that are swallowed – words, worlds, persons. Concepts too disappear. The very notions of experience, nature, and consciousness that first led to the noble doubt are thereafter derived from it, and epistemology becomes not the answer to the book's opening questions but their author. The priority of the mental, initially a psychological truism, ends a logical inevitability. And even the moral visions of unity and power to which the essay builds arise not out of the study of the mind's structures but within it.

The noble doubt of Chapter Six is, then, both a sophisticated Kantian formulation and an implicit part (even presupposition) of the lower argument. Centrality is not, however, a sufficient proof of appropriateness. Although the essay's idealism is neither silly nor imposed on the work at the last minute, it may be philosophically unsophisticated, that is, not well used in a single coherent argument. For, finally, the defense of the argument of *Nature* concerns less the presence of idealism than its meaningfulness. And the real question becomes whether idealism is for Emerson an epistemology or only a metaphysical predilection – not whether it is in the essay but whether it belongs there.

As always, the place to begin is with the noble doubt. Though by now the paragraph should seem fairly manageable, some striking peculiarities remain. Most troubling, perhaps, is that, however much the lower argument implies idealism, the noble doubt does not present itself as a logical outgrowth of that argument. Emerson has not, as we have seen, failed to piece together two separate essays of earlier drafts. He seems nevertheless intent on advertising some kind of discontinuity. The casual, parenthetic tone, of course, offers a sharp contrast to the rigid structure of the lower argument. But more important, universal skepticism is inimical to logic, and the noble doubt makes nonsense of the faith in argument implicit in the opening chapters. To some extent, Emerson is being intellectually honest: idealism has been so obviously presupposed throughout the earlier chapters that only the most disingenuous logician would pretend to induce it from such evidence. Emerson just admits that the hat was not much to look at after all, and lets the rabbit tumble out. Nevertheless the overstatement is surprising: presumably the rabbit need not eat the hat. Even the language is overprotective. The noble doubt "suggests itself" – perhaps an indication of the self-evidence of truth, but surely an insistence on the doubt's independence of the lower argument and, for that matter, of everything else.

This unwillingness to "prove" idealism – the insistence on its hypothetical character – might at first appear to make the doubt less absolute, a mere rhetorical strategy. Throughout the essay, Emerson's idealism seems to flirt with a pragmatic notion of usable truth (as does, at times, Kant's own account of the regulative principles).[71] In the lower argument, Emerson demonstrates nature's usefulness only by willfully ignoring the harsher aspects of her influence on man. So here, the final insistence that nature is useful and venerable "to me" suggests a pragmatic decision to take as true whatever works. And, indeed, the conclusion to the chapter seems explicitly to embrace just such a view. "The advantage of the ideal theory over the popular faith, is this, that it presents the world in precisely that view which is most desirable to the mind" (p. 36).

Yet one would want to think very carefully before conflating transcendental idealism and pragmatism, Kant and James. The personal emphasis that sounds willful may actually do no more than mark an epistemological place. Kant explained that the concepts of God, world, and immortality can be thought by analogy with experience (though these thoughts are not, of course, knowledge). "By means of this analogy, however, there remains a concept of the Supreme Being sufficiently determined *for us,* though we have left out everything that could determine it absolutely or *in itself;* for we determine it as regards the world and hence as regards ourselves, and more we do not require."[72] Like Kant's "for us," Emerson's "to me's" define only a perceptual framework, the limited realm of subjectivity that is the only kind of experience that man may be said truly to "know." The apparent power of the ME over the phenomenal world as NOT ME is thus held in check by the even greater reality of the truly not me, the thing-in-itself. And what might at first glance seem wildly assertive is really restrained, even apologetic.

But Emerson's idealism is unpragmatic in a more important sense. In James the criteria of "desirability" and "advantage" are roughly personal and can be applied to a number of specific problems like moral holidays and squirrels on trees. One does not try to measure a truth quotient apart from experience because its practical consequences in experience are, in fact, what is meant by its "truth." Truth cannot be identified before it happens. Emerson's intellectual context, however, is more traditionally metaphysical and assumes truth to exist before it is practiced. Truth is, in fact, that without which experience could not itself exist – less what we choose to believe than what permits the notions of choice and belief, even of personality. In James, because God allows for moral holidays, we trust in Him almost automatically. But one could imagine a world in which moral holidays (and therefore trust in God) were unnecessary.[73] Such alternative options and possible worlds do not exist for Emerson's doubt. It is not simply that in the absence of better evidence I might as well talk as if the world were ideal, were permanent. It is that a world independently real – like my experience a world, but nevertheless unexperienceable by definition – renders unintelligible any imaginable notion of experience. Equally meaningless is an experience that presupposes no stable collection of objects underwriting it. Unlike God and squirrels on trees, idealism and permanence are notions so fundamental that the failure to "choose" them results not in a different kind of experience but in no experience whatever.

The point is, quite simply, that whereas pragmatism studies truth in (or even as) experience, transcendental idealism asks what are the necessary preconditions for that experience. Kant asks not why do I feel as I actually do, but what are the minimal logical requirements for the kind of thing I would be willing to call experience, however loosely. His answer is, as we have seen, to argue that a whole set of notions come bundled together – consciousness, time, experience, self, and world. But, for the moment, we can focus on two of his arguments. The first – that of the Transcendental Deduction – is that for representations to be thought, they must be unified in one consciousness, called the "transcendental unity of apperception" or the "I think."[74] Consciousness requires conceptuability – the establishment of relations between intuitions – and self-consciousness in its most general sense defines the conditions under which (almost the place where) such relations occur. For an event to be an experience, it must include a sense of the experience as experienced – notions like "it seems" or "I feel" – and the transcendental unity of apperception identifies this need without defining too precisely what kind of thing is represented by the pronouns "it" or "I."[75]

This very unity of apperception further implies in the unstated dichotomy between seeming and being the possibility of external objects. The notion of something "seeming to be X" but perhaps not "being X" contains within it the definition of an external object X potentially (though unknowably) independent of all seemings. Thus – throughout the Analytic but especially in the Analogies and the Refutation – Kant makes specific points about substance, permanence, and causality to support a more general "objectivity thesis": the notion of experience presupposes the possibility of objects distinct from experience of them even as it also presupposes the possibility of a self-consciousness of experience as experienced.[76]

The necessity of Kant's thing-in-itself and self-in-itself clarifies the similar "desirability" of the noble doubt. Emerson's "advantageous" idealism is not pragmatic but inevitable, built like the more specific notion of permanence into the very structure of experience. But such transcendental determinism affects more than the initial paragraph of "Idealism." The lower argument's whole study of the "uses" of nature outlines less a convenient way of viewing objectivity than the only way it can be seen. And the moments of apparent intransigence actually mark not the truculence of will but the logical necessity of the dichotomies between object and thought, appearance and reality – man's need to see things grouped in certain ways if he is to see them at all.

Throughout the lower argument, apparent description is actually prescriptive, as Emerson analyzes less what is than what must be. Even so slight a statement as the conclusion to "Commodity" – that "a man is fed, not that he may be fed, but that he may work" (p. 12) – implies an epistemology as well as a praxis. Practically, man is to work at; philosophically, to work out. The dichotomy is not feed/be fed but only feed/work. Nature's epistemological "nourishment" – the possibility of objectivity that permits the possibility of experience – offers not direct support to the self but only a dynamic interplay. Similarly, the metaphors of picture and frame in "Beauty" and "Language" indicate not a shallow correspondence, a too easy suitability, but the self's need for objects. The "necessity in spirit to manifest itself in material forms" is "in" spirit exclusively – a mark only of what earlier in the chapter is glossed as the mind's inevitable image making (p. 22; cf. p. 20). Nature is perpetually "taken up into the self" not merely as a source of experienceables, but as a ground for consciousness as well.

This tyranny of consciousness is not a metaphysics of transcendence, but merely the logic (even logistics) of perception. And the apparently oracular summary – that "it appears to men, or it does not appear" – only neutrally records epistemological reciprocality. Earlier in the chapter, Emerson insists that "neither can man be understood without these objects, nor these objects without him" (p. 19). So now, the relation between man and matter appears "to men" because the relationship of the "I think" is necessary for consciousness to believe in itself, for men to be. The alternative that it may not appear merely marks the fact that, without men-ness, selfhood, and apperception, the complementary notions – of relation, of matter, even of seeming itself – have no place to exist. So, far from defining analogous epistemological worlds – one real, one derivative – Emerson's statements about language, then, may finally only examine the process by which we carelessly bundle notions together without regard for differences between definiendum and definiens.

The quirky, subservient character of nature in the lower argument, then, is not discovered empirically through observation but deduced logically from the necessary character of experience. The relentless unity of vision to which first each individual use and then the whole notion of usefulness builds is Emerson's dramatized version of Kant's initial precondition for experience – the transcendental unity of apperception. Even the unconvincing facility of the rhetoric derives from the requirements of Emerson's epistemology. The occasional resistance nature shows as she conforms, the implication that her holiday attire is for "not always" (p. 10), our very uneasiness with the psychological convenience of the whole lower argument: all illustrate the need for conflict embedded in the very notion of objectivity – that objects serve more to disagree with our perceptions than to agree with them. The notion of

seeming grounds consciousness in its own inaccuracy. Were my perceptions always identical to objective things, then self-consciousness could
not semantically exist – for "I think X" would mean simply "X." And
just as the lower argument's success proves transcendental apperception, so its failure proves Kantian objectivity.[77]

Whatever the apparent interests of the lower argument, then, it ultimately concerns not the pragmatically advantageous or even the objectively observable but the logically necessary. And only in the light of
such an emphasis can we fully understand the opening two chapters and
their questions about the relation between consciousness and the world.
Our examination of the later sections should now make plain the extent
to which here too the vocabulary is explicitly and precisely epistemological. The "criticism" of the opening sentences alludes not only to
"higher" biblical exegesis on historicist principles, but more generally
to Kant's whole philosophical emphasis. The initial impulse to discover
a theory of nature, in fact, seems – like the later paragraph on the noble
doubt – primarily an occasion to announce implicitly a philosophical
context by mentioning all the key Kantian terms in close succession.
Responding to attacks on "speculative" men, Emerson insists that "to a
sound judgment, the most abstract truth is the most practical," and the
test of its truth will be the way "it will explain all phenomena" (p. 8).
"Speculative," "judgment," "practical," and "phenomena" (at least)
are code terms, the peculiar vocabulary of the transcendental philosopher. Against this Kantian arsenal stands the repeated (ironic) use of
"impression" and "inquiry," which have been, since Hume, the most
common empiricist terms for sensation and the precritical philosophical
project.[78] Similarly, in the first chapter, the lover of nature is defined
not only by the Romantic, Neoplatonic preoccupation with the innocence of children but by the more explicitly Kantian dichotomy
between the inner and outward senses as well.[79] And the apparently
unmotivated use of the temporal terms "perpetual," "perennial," and
"always" anticipates the later argument for the necessity of permanence
as a defense against frivolity.

The abundance of specialized terminology does more, however, than
direct attention to current philosophical debates. It proposes two distinct frames of reference as a means of reconciling the apparent contradictions between empiricist and rationalist thought. Consider, for example, the final paragraph of the introduction. Earlier we argued that
the tyranny of the NOT ME over the mere "chippings" of the human will
seems to render meaningless the search for the "end" of nature. But, in
fact, the subtle use of prejudicial vocabulary suggests a way of resolving
the dilemma. Emerson admits that he conflates under the single term of
"nature" those essences untouched by man's will – the grand "impres-

sion" of the world on the mind – and the whole category of the NOT ME, both touched and untouched. But "in inquiries so general as our present one, the inaccuracy is not material; no confusion of thought will occur" (p. 8). Using specific empiricist terms – "inquiry," "impression," and "confusion" – Emerson makes a valid point about empirical realism. If we are talking from within about the particulars of perception, the givenness of sensation is superior to the effects of will, and no indistinctness or muddling of ideas ("confusion") will result.[80]

He says no more, however, and even warns us in the pun "not material" that what is irrelevant in one context need not be in another. The very subjectivity that is so unimportant when considering the mechanics of perception might be central to "super-material" questions about ontological status. His lists are equally equivocal. Among the unchanged essences he includes "space"; among the trivial chippings, "pictures." In "inquiries," such evaluations are fair. In "critiques," however, space is not the most absolute category, but a primary mark of subjectivity. Similarly, as Emerson makes clear later in "Beauty" and "Language," pictures represent not man's insignificant operations but the "use" of the natural world as a permanent "frame" or ground for subjectivity. This potential inversion of values is fully realized in the first chapter's "poetic" redefinition of nature as "the integrity of impression made by manifold natural objects" (p. 9). Here particular impressions are subordinated to the more transcendental concepts of "integrity" and "manifold," and the poet becomes the Kantian consciousness in his ability to "integrate all the parts."[81]

The first two chapters, then, are not quite the antinomies they seemed at first. Instead they work to intertwine empiricism and idealism – impression and integrity – much as Kant himself conceived empirical realism as a necessary corollary to transcendental idealism. A proper account of sensation and thought is the real motive behind the book's initial two questions about consanguinity and nature's end, and the paired Kantian concepts of apperception and objectivity are in effect the "answers." The ME of subjectivity, redefined as the apperceptive "I think," explains man's sense of unity with nature. Man will, of course, feel close to nature, for the notion of "I feel" must precede any recognizable sensation. Yet the NOT ME of objectivity ensures that the world's "impression" will remain "grand." For without the possibility of independent objects of perception, experience as "seeming" is an unintelligible concept.

It is in this philosophical context that we must consider the notorious image of the transparent eyeball. For the image, in its very exaggeration, characterizes well the purely formal quality of apperception. Nothing can be said of Kant's "I think." It is intellectually inaccessible (even incoherent), the mere possibility of self-consciousness without an empirical, objective self. So Emerson's eyeball, from which all personal selfhood ("mean egotism") is excluded, becomes simply the possibility of focusing, without even a particular retina on which to focus.[82] It represents the condition of eyeball-ness that is logically necessary for sight but is not itself an operating organ – a purely formal eye*ball*, just as Kant's apperception is a purely formal "I think." Moreover, the grotesqueness of this image makes impossible the kind of overinvestment in self by which Fichte and Hegel turned Kant's formal principle into an ontological one and his epistemology into an idealist metaphysic. In its very silliness, the eyeball avoids the subtle dangers of a concept like the Cartesian *cogito*, which in its restraint seems to prove more than it actually can. No one at least is tempted to ground a proof of personal existence on Emerson's eyeball, as many were tempted to do with Descartes's claim that "I think, therefore I am."[83]

But the eyeball is not merely comparable to Kant's apperception; it employs concepts themselves explicitly Kantian. "All mean egotism vanishes. I become a transparent eye-ball." In these short clauses, Emerson couples two of his most characteristic terms. "Vanishing" is that process by which apparent realities are discovered to be phenomenal. Here the empirical self – and later time, space, and disagreeable spiders – is declared only an inevitable function of perception, always present when perceiving but not necessarily relevant when studying how the mind perceives. Similarly, "transparency" is that condition phenomena enter when they are no longer essential to the epistemological frame of reference. It is not a question of disappearing, even less of annihilation. Instead things, while remaining in place, simply become invisible to reveal another layer of meaning, much as repeated sounds become inaudible when not the focus of attention. Thus, just as in Chapter Six objects will vanish or become "transparent" to reveal the causes and spirits behind nature, so does the self here to reveal the general conditions of unity and self-consciousness that ground it (pp. 30, 45).[84]

Emerson may be indebted to Kant for more than the concept. Kant and even Fichte use the same terms in similar circumstances. Summarizing in the Transcendental Aesthetic the first and most radical consequence of the Copernican revolution – the discovery that space and time are subjective and not absolute – Kant insists that without subjectivity "the whole constitution and all the relations of objects in space and time, nay space and time themselves, would vanish." Perceptions, whether clear or confused, are simply not the same as realities, and "even if that appearance could become completely transparent to us, such knowledge [of phenomena] would remain *toto coelo* different from knowledge of the object in itself."[85] "Vanishing" is a central term in

Kant, denoting not only the disappearance of the phenomenal in the noumenal but later that of the speculative in practical philosophy.[86] The point, here as in Emerson, is that each frame of reference has its own structuring principles, stable within that frame but inapplicable outside it. "Transparency," though not so frequent in Kant as "vanishing," is Fichte's characteristic term to mark that special kind of knowability wherein an unknowable object is absorbed into some larger known – usually subjectivity itself – and thereby known indirectly. Thus, in Fichte no less than in Emerson, the world is repeatedly "made transparent" in the presence of the higher reality of consciousness.[87]

If the I/eye of the first chapter is precisely transcendental, so is the notion of nature as NOT ME in the "Introduction." For the most part, such objectivity is subordinated to, even read through, consciousness: though apparently the opposite of the ME, it is actually contained within it as those aspects of the ME that do not seem wholly indigenous. But if not itself independent of the mental, the NOT ME does at least imply the possibility of such independence, and thus represent the autonomous thing-in-itself in the only form by which the self can know it. The point, like that of the apperception, is logical and not empirical. Earlier we associated with a Leibnizian concept of givenness the notion that the occult relation "takes me by surprise, and yet is not unknown" (p. 10). Now, however, the "surprise" seems more the result of a proto-Hegelian dialectic. Although the ME does not directly presuppose the notion of the thing-in-itself, the conception of the NOT ME does. Thus, in one sense, the ME is "taken" or captured by objectivity; in another, its power to "know" objects is what allows for the possibility of any NOT ME at all. Such dialectic inevitability accounts for the skewed time scheme whereby nature "already" answers unasked questions. Later Emerson will make the same point with a pun by claiming that the philosopher "postpones the apparent order and relations of things to the empire of thought" (p. 33). Conflating the two meanings of the verb "postpones," he suggests that consciousness "subordinates" objects to its own self-awareness by pretending that a logical antecedent can be "temporally put off" until later. In each case, however, the inadequacy of temporal language only emphasizes the degree to which the necessity transcends questions of priority. It is pointless to apply the subjective categories of time to those conditions that allow for subjectivity in the first place.

The real "end" of nature, then, is to fulfill Kant's objectivity requirement – to allow for the possibility of objects separate from the experience of them. Nature, which in the rough logic of the lower argument teaches the unity of consciousness, on a more fundamental level permits it. Such a nature is not that of traditional romanticism, affording (or at least recalling) to the poet a past splendor.[88] Nor is it that of the Puritan typologists, imaging and shadowing godhead. Least of all is it a Neo-platonic creation, the shabbiest, though most proximate, emanation of the divine. Nature in Emerson is not in any sense divine, and the road to divinity more likely moves away from her, putting her underfoot. Yet such lack of spirituality is not merely incapacitating. Underfoot, she supports as well as suffocates. Nature does not simply correspond to the mind but "corresponds to and authorizes" it (p. 9). Neither author nor creature, she is more exactly "authorizing," one of the conditions without which self-consciousness would be quite literally unthinkable. Instead of initiating transcendence, she does the opposite and firmly anchors consciousness to the realm of autonomous objects. But as there can be no self without world, no transcendence without objectivity transcended, she permits spirituality as (even because) she remains herself incontrovertibly substantial.

Emerson's solution to his initial questions about consanguinity and ends, then, is less to answer than to dissolve them in increasingly precise definitions of the meaning of experience itself. And in this light, the equivocation of the conclusion that power resides "in man or in a harmony of both" is not cowardly (as it seemed earlier) but necessary. The only sane explanation of how relationship is possible between world and mind is a dual one: in terms of consciousness, relationship is absolutely necessary; and, in terms of reality, absolutely nothing can be said absolutely. This epistemological strictness even defines the very notion of relationship – in the essay's most celebrated phrase, the "original relation to the universe."[89] The celebrity of the phrase makes us forget at times that we do not really know what it means. At the most basic level, an "original" relation, like the more famous "original genius" and "original man," is one without origin, arising wholly out of itself.[90] But in fact Emerson's phrase says more, for unlike the others it contains a submerged paradox. The strict definition of originality as *sui generis* explicitly denies the possibility of relationship; self-generation admits of no external influences. A relationship between two originals would be impossible, for each in its self-sufficiency would repel the other. Instead, originality-in-relation implies the far less evenhanded way in which an original relates "to" other things by allowing them to imitate it. Thus the implied equality between man and nature turns hierarchical, with man as the original and nature as the copy.

That the universe takes its cue from our originality already recalls the Copernican Kant, if not the solipsist Fichte. But, in fact, originality in Emerson may be even more fundamental, and more Kantian. For Kant, true originality measures logical nonderivativeness, not psychological integrity. I do not recognize "my" headache as my own by applying to it any criteria of mental identity, noting a characteristic feature or relating it to other mental states definitively mine. The headache must simply be mine to be experienced at all.[91] Kant indicates this ownership entailed in the "I think" by his most technical name for self-consciousness – the "original synthetic" unity of apperception or even "original" apperception.[92] So in Emerson, the most precise meaning of "original relation" may also be the most Kantian. It is not simply that we should see nature clearly, without interference from the past. Nor is it quite that in clear-sightedness we create nature. Instead the call for an original relation asks us to realize what is already, necessarily, the case: that anything we call experienced must be simultaneously both given and ours, that objectivity and originality – relationship itself – are the logical preconditions of our ability to perceive anything at all.[93]

V

The paired Kantian concepts of apperception and objectivity, then, show Emerson's argument in *Nature* to be surprisingly sophisticated and consistent. Whether he learned the point from Kant or Paley or from his own deductions, Emerson understands that the I/world coupling is primitive and irreducible. It makes no sense to question consanguinity – to search for its sources in "reality" – for the notion of relationship is built into the very concepts of "nature" and "mind" with which we start. In Kant's famous phrase, "thoughts without content are empty, intuitions without concepts are blind."[94] This claim that particular concepts are necessary for experience or thought – now called the "transcendental argument" – lies at the heart of Emerson's case in *Nature* for necessity as the way in which experience is "built."[95] And, in this sense, the (literary) structure of *Nature* and the (Kantian) structure of nature are finally the same. Not because, in some organic sense, the Romantic artist imitates natural germination in his literary constructs. But because the argument of the essay works to undermine its own questions about priorities – ends and means – by discovering in the supposed realities of nature and mind the two intellectual structures that Kant considered the inevitable preconditions for the very possibility of experience itself.

Emerson's idealism in the essay, then, is not merely personal – a metaphysical inclination or predisposition – but itself a controlled argument about the reason for all such predispositions. It would be foolish, however, to claim that these epistemological foundations can account for all the essay's assertions. However accurate his general understanding, Emerson is not always precise in his specific formulations. Although he can use it carefully, terminology as such never interests him. In "The

Transcendentalist," even as he explains correctly the theory of Kant's Copernican revolution, he wrongly calls these categories "intuitions of the mind."[96] Moreover, in *Nature*, he often allows his enthusiasm to lead him into overclaims about the power perception grants. The confusion of quantifiers seen in the Swedenborgian syllogism of "Language" is largely a product of such misplaced enthusiasm. As are the intimations of man's power in the passage near the end of "Idealism" on nature's "true position."[97]

Such overclaims need not disturb us too much. Nor should we judge Emerson too severely for his occasional tendency – like that of Fichte, Hegel, and Kant himself – to reify the Ideas. If there is a theoretical error, and one characteristically Emersonian, it originates less in his terminology or his misuse of the Ideas than in his peculiarly moral emphasis – his belief that "virtue subordinates [the world] to the mind" (p. 36). Here, of course, the real culprit is not German epistemology but the Unitarian establishment, whose ethical conservatism the essay means to overturn.[98] From the very first pages, Emerson tends to conclude from the logical unity of thought the moral unity of noumenal reality. In so doing, Emerson wrongly conflates the apperceptive unity of the Understanding with the urge to greater unity characteristic of the Reason.[99] The transparent eyeball adequately represents the former transcendental unity. But by claiming in his woods to return to "reason and faith," Emerson misleadingly suggests this unity to be the same as that impulse by which Reason glimpses the transcendent unities of God, freedom, and immortality (p. 10).

A similar blurring of epistemological and practical unity occurs in "Language," just before the more useful (and defensible) claim that men need objects, objects men.

> Man is conscious of a universal soul within or behind his individual life, wherein, as in a firmament, the natures of Justice, Truth, Love, Freedom, arise and shine. This universal soul, he calls Reason: it is not mine or thine or his, but we are its; we are its property and men. . . . That which, intellectually considered, we call Reason, considered in relation to nature, we call Spirit. (Pp. 18-19)

The vision of Reason as a universal soul – the realm of the truer worlds ("natures") of Freedom and Love – suggests one more reification of the Ideas. Emerson will himself try to retract this formulation in the noble doubt paragraph by ridiculing the notion of an Orion painted in "the firmament of the soul."

The general problem of practical morality remains, however, and in fact finds its fullest expression immediately after the retraction in the long middle section of "Idealism." Here Reason is shown to teach idealism as an "effect of culture." The overall argument is unobjection-able, and the logical necessity of idealism remains intact. Nature, poe-try, science, philosophy, religion, and ethics all indeed teach idealism – but as confirmation, not as discovery. Only after the noble doubt has occurred first in a purely theoretical context can idealism reveal itself through experience, which simply "conspires with" the revelation.

The section's imagery, however, gives back what its logic withholds. Not only is Understanding's use of sensation confused with Reason's abstractions concerning the Understanding. More simply, Reason's po-tentiality is depicted as an actual world. The Kantian notion of Reason's use of imagination is supplanted by the less defensible one of an "empire of thought." And the dynamic Ideas are conflated with their more static Platonic prototypes as "immortal necessary uncreated natures" (p. 34).

> We apprehend the absolute. As it were, for the first time, *we exist*. We become immortal, for we learn that time and space are relations of matter; that, with a perception of truth, or a virtuous will, they have no affinity. (P. 35)

Though impressive rhetoric, the passage is flawed epistemology. Rela-tionality cannot be so easily relegated to the realm of "matter." And the notion of a "perception of truth," like Kant's "intellectual intuition," is logically impossible in the positive sense that Emerson seems to imply. Thus, although Emerson does not confuse "transcendental" and "tran-scendent" on the level of the Understanding, he does in discussing practical Reason. And the problem is not that he reduces Kant's archi-tectonics to a bland contrast between reason and faith (as is so often claimed) but that he conflates them too completely and makes all Rea-son practical.

There is no easy way to explain away these problems. We will even-tually have to face directly the flaws in Emerson's moral vision. And to map out more carefully the character and range of his "apprehended absolute." For the moment, however, it is enough to realize that even these apparent errors are stated in terms of Emerson's epistemological interests. Whatever the psychological (even autobiographical) origins of his mistakes, they take in *Nature* a recognizable philosophical form – the same form in fact that they took in the history of German idealism. Emerson's reification is finally no different in kind from Fichte's Abso-lute Ego or Kant's two worlds. The crack in the essay is the crack in Kant (and perhaps in all modern epistemology): that between not mind and matter, "Nature" and "Spirit," but between pure and practical Reason – what Emerson quite exactly calls in the chapter's final para-graph "Reason, both speculative and practical" (p. 36).[100]

Whatever the essay's conclusion, then, its foundations are secure.

And if Emerson tries to take epistemology in directions it cannot comfortably go, it is at least still as epistemology that he tries to take it. The introduction and the first six chapters of the essay build upon a precise philosophical definition of the conditions necessary for the possibility of experience. In the paired introduction and first chapter, Emerson sketches the two essential requirements: the self-conscious apperception that unifies representations and the possibility of objectivity that stabilizes consciousness. In the lower argument, nature serves to justify, through the possibility of external objects, those distinctions between appearance and reality that make meaningful man's notion of consciousness. Although self-consciousness seems at times both temporally and logically prior, Emerson is careful to show that consciousness and things depend equally on each other for their existence. What occasionally seems argumentative intransigence is really an advanced, even modern understanding of truth: a true theory *is* "its own evidence" and does "explain all phenomena."[101] For, as Emerson carefully demonstrates, phenomena exist only inside a theoretical framework, never outside one. As independent standards are logically impossible, theories must be allowed to account for themselves, and the measure of truth becomes not external correspondence but internal coherence. Perhaps Emerson lacked the control to go no further. But the wonder is that he had the intelligence and discipline to go so far.

3

The practice of divinity

The transcendental idealism of *Nature* cannot be seen as Emerson's ultimate statement. Despite outcries against the essay's overelaborateness, however, the problem is not really formal. Although the book shifts through a bewildering number of narrative voices – from the cool philosophy of the ME/NOT ME dichotomy through the orphic rhapsody of the concluding prospects – each is in fact appropriate to its stage of the argument. Though Emerson never again adopts the rigid structure (or length) of this little book, the rhetorical strategies he experiments with here do reappear throughout the later essays.

Nor, despite charges of unbecoming terminology, is the problem in any simple sense intellectual. The philosophical (largely Kantian) vocabulary of the essay is carefully and wittily handled, as is the whole notion of a transcendental argument. If *Nature* remains somehow introductory to what we feel is Emerson's true career, it is not because he moved beyond argument and philosophy to other modes of discourse, but because the epistemological concerns so central to *Nature* could not account for everything the individual felt on the bare common. And if the ideas and idealism of *Nature* were not a sufficient answer to all the questions he asked, he did not give up his philosophical studies but pursued them further, seeking the solution in new ideas, in greater idealism.

I

In one sense, Emerson's epistemological examination in *Nature* ends with Chapter Six. In answer to his initial question about the end of nature – really about nature's relation to man – he offers the Kantian

solution of transcendental idealism and empirical realism, of apperception and objectivity. By his "theory of nature," man is necessarily
linked to the objective world, since the possibility of autonomous objects is what permits subjectivity in the first place. The whole question
of the relation is shown to be a false problem and Descartes's extension
and mind merely two sides of the same epistemological coin. But if
transcendental idealism provides a theory of consanguinity, it does not
adequately account for man's other feelings – of, say, immortality and
divinity. And so in his two final chapters – like the two introductions,
paired analyses from theoretical and personal points of view – Emerson
attempts to do justice to the "whole circumference" of man.

The personalized statement of "Prospects" causes fewer interpretive
problems, as the Orphic songs make good on the promise of the forest
visions in "Nature." So welcome, in fact, is the rhapsodic tone of these
final pages that some readers see the whole essay as a long preamble to
this moment, a philosophical dues-paying that permits the final, more
truly Emersonian mode of prophecy.[1] Indeed the Orphic Poet's two-
part myth does seem recognizable – thematically derived from familiar
Platonic and Gnostic creation myths and stylistically anticipating the
epigrammatic prose of Emerson's later essays.[2] Man, we are told, is a
"god in ruins." Echoing directly the language of the earlier eyeball
experience, the Orphic Poet recalls how man, "permeated and dissolved by spirit," once "filled nature with his overflowing currents."
Man has shrunk, so that the world he once filled is now too large, the
tight "fit" merely a loose "correspondence" (CW.I.42). But the resemblance still inspires man, and in the prophetic second half of the song,
the poet promises that once man conforms his life to the pure idea in his
mind, he will reenter his kingdom.

Yet one might wonder if "Prospects" does in fact endorse whole-
heartedly the prophecy it presents. The first half of the chapter, at least,
takes a very different tone. The point is perhaps visionary: knowledge
rests less in addition, subtraction, or other Lockean "comparisons" than
in "untaught sallies of the spirit" (p. 39). The vocabulary, however, is
self-consciously limited. The proclamation that "the highest reason is
always the truest" is not really transcendental, describing the more
rationalistic world of "inquiries," "laws," and "frames" (p. 39).[3] His
very interest in the "highest" reason makes clear his distance from Kant
and Coleridge: Kantian Reason is a faculty, not a quality, and admits of
no quantitative analysis, whether higher or lower. Similarly, the ironic
inversion whereby all "thought" of multitude or disparateness is lost in
a "sense" of unity implies that the emphasis is still largely empirical,
celebrating only a lower unity available to the senses (p. 40).

The same limitation informs the quotation from Herbert's "Man" that closes the first half of the chapter. The reappearance at greater length of the poem quoted briefly in "Commodity" reinforces the whole movement of the essay.[4] Just as the essay argues that the general subservience of nature means more than Paley and the Unitarians assume, so this reappearance implies that commodity – the lowest use of nature – really suggests the higher idealism underwriting that usefulness. Critics rightly note how Emerson's deletions shift the emphasis from Christianity to Neoplatonism by eliminating Herbert's prayer that God should someday inhabit the house He has so carefully built.

Less clear, however, is the irony of Herbert's own view of man, one heightened when Emerson repeats it two centuries later.

> "Man is all symmetry,
> Full of proportions, one limb to another,
> And to all the world besides.
> Each part may call the farthest, brother;
> For head with foot hath private amity,
> And both with moons and tides.
>
> "Nothing hath got so far
> But man hath caught and kept it as his prey;
> His eyes dismount the highest star;
> He is in little all the sphere.
> Herbs gladly cure our flesh, because that they
> Find their acquaintance there.
>
> "For us, the winds do blow,
> The earth doth rest, heaven move, and fountains flow;
> Nothing we see, but means our good,
> As our delight, or as our treasure;
> The whole is either our cupboard of food,
> Or cabinet of pleasure.
>
> "The stars have us to bed:
> Night draws the curtain; which the sun withdraws.
> Music and light attend our head.
> All things unto our flesh are kind,
> In their descent and being; to our mind,
> In their ascent and cause.
>
> "More servants wait on man
> Than he'll take notice of. In every path,
> He treads down that which doth befriend him
> When sickness makes him pale and wan.
> Oh mighty love! Man is one world, and hath
> Another to attend him." (CW.I.40-41)

The first stanza quoted is ambiguous. That each part of man may call the other "brother" is not perhaps negative, though in Herbert such fraternity is most commonly associated with the resurrection after death.[5]

The remaining stanzas, however, more clearly undercut the praise. Man's dominion seems overstated, especially since all the triumphs are phrased negatively. Man catches the world only as "prey," he "dismounts" the star, and his microcosmic role is notable primarily for its "little" scale. Even the homeopathic cure seems slyly critical: since like cures like, the "acquaintance" that herbs find in man is his poisonous nature. The claim that "the earth doth rest, heaven move" is probably ironic even in the seventeenth century; in the nineteenth, it is downright silly. And when, returning to the couplet quoted earlier, Emerson completes the stanza with the image of man treading down friendly herbs, we are meant to recall not only Herbert's previous reference to glad herbs but also Emerson's own ambiguous need in "Idealism" to put nature underfoot.

The tonal ambiguities of this first half of the chapter are not entirely overturned by the prophecies that follow. For as Barbara Packer rightly remarks, the Orphic songs themselves, though affirmative, are surprisingly muted.[6] The apocalyptic language does promise a return to divinity. But to forestall the concomitant annihilation, Emerson locates this promise in an ever-distant future. Man's sense of superiority arises from neither a Thoreauvian assurance of power (to be) regained nor even a Wordsworthian memory of power lost, but from the observation of power missing. Man knows he is a disinherited god less because he feels the divinity than because he sees the ruins. Infancy becomes not the truth he must be taught to disbelieve but the "perpetual Messiah" who "pleads" to an already fallen man.

The paradoxical result of this negative vision is that the passages on present loss seem more real – or at least more precise – than those on past glory or future gain. The myth of greatness is all too clearly spoken by the disembodied voice of an orphic poet.

> 'Man is the dwarf of himself. Once he was permeated and dissolved by spirit. He filled nature with his overflowing currents. Out from him sprang the sun and moon; from man, the sun; from woman, the moon. The laws of his mind, the periods of his actions externized themselves into day and night, into the year and the seasons.' (P. 42)

Whether the past tense refers to an aboriginal era or only more proximately to the bare common vision of the first chapter, that time is equally unrecapturable.

The voice of impotence seems more immediate, even human.

> 'Now is man the follower of the sun, and woman the follower of the moon. Yet sometimes he starts in his slumber, and wonders at himself

and his house, and muses strangely at the resemblance betwixt him and it. He perceives that if his law is still paramount, if still he have elemental power, "if his word is sterling yet in nature," it is not conscious power, it is not inferior but superior to his will. It is Instinct.' (P. 42)

The sense of loss is heightened by the brief reference to *Richard II*. Richard speaks the line after ceding his crown to Bolingbroke, when in fact his word is sterling no longer. His request, suggestively enough, is not for a return to dominion but only for a mirror in which to see his face bankrupt of majesty; and the speech that follows is full of puns on the Neoplatonic meanings of "shadow" – as "darkness," but also as "illusion" and a "sign of a more substantial substratum."[7] The reference thus reinforces our feeling that majesty in Emerson's prophecy is more compelling as absence than as presence.

It has become commonplace to view Emerson as a Puritan who no longer believes in original sin, a kind of universalized Edwards, extending to all what the Calvinist would claim only for the elect.[8] Yet Emerson's myth of the Fall is, in this one respect, more severe than that of his forefathers. The Puritans believe that man's salvation is evidenced in his renewed ability to fulfill the law: although disagreeing among themselves whether the agent of sanctification is man or only the Spirit within him, all still acknowledge the saint's power to do good.[9] Emerson, however, locates the sign of grace principally in man's inability to fill the mold he knows to be his own – a salvation without sanctification. Although divinity is in fact available not just to some but to all, Emerson emphasizes instead the difficulty all feel in sustaining spiritual exaltation. Reason does exhibit a "momentary grasp of the sceptre," but these "gleams of a better light" are only "occasional examples" in the midst of a more pervasive "darkness" (p. 43).[10] Even then, these efforts are entirely unconscious and unwilled, and what Emerson would have liked to call "intuition" is only mere "Instinct" (p. 42).

The Orphic Poet's second song is more obviously prophetic, anticipating a future triumph rather than recalling a past defeat. But even here the promise is circumspect, if not circumscribed. The passage encourages the reader in terms of the famous house image.

'Every spirit builds itself a house; and beyond its house, a world; and beyond its world, a heaven. . . . Build, therefore, your own world. As fast as you conform your life to the pure idea in your mind, that will unfold its great proportions. A correspondent revolution in things will attend the influx of the spirit. So fast will disagreeable appearances, swine, spiders, snakes, pests, mad-houses, prisons, enemies, vanish; they are temporary and shall be no more seen.' (Pp. 44-45)

Yet one might wonder if this imagery does not really devalue the previous song. There we were told that all nature was once our habitat, which we fitted and filled; the very discrepancy between this "house" and our modern, dwarvish bodies marked how much we had lost and could perhaps regain. But now the house is no longer available, and exhortations to build really ask to rebuild.[11]

Nor is the vocabulary encouraging. Earlier Emerson, in his own voice, spoke of aligning the axes of vision and of things. Now the same coincidence of life and thoughts is achieved through "conformity."[12] The word is characteristic of neither bards in general nor Emerson in particular, who has in fact on the previous page sneered at man's cowardly attempts to hide reality by "conforming" it to a spurious higher law. The "correspondence" of the revolution in things is equally unsettling. Correspondence has been throughout the essay a second-rate process, whether in the "soon-to-be-discarded" Swedenborgianism of "Language" or in the first Orphic song, where it measured man's fall from his primordial "fit." Even the "vanishing" of nature might give pause. Earlier "vanish" was used as a technical term to mark the disappearance of the phenomenal in the noumenal. What disappeared was less snakes and spiders than "all mean egotism," and the linguistic echo may suggest that the more radical annihilation accompanies this supposedly affirmative revolution as well.

The uncertain implications of vanishing signal only a greater ambiguity concerning Emerson's whole treatment of observation. Sight – the central metaphor of the paragraph, and indeed of the essay – is nevertheless curiously passive. The claim that "what we are, that only can we see" suggests not broadening horizons but tunnel vision, especially in light of Herbert's equally ironic evaluation of man's willfulness: "Nothing we see, but means our good" (pp. 45, 41). More distressing is the repeated claim that evil is merely disagreeable appearance and "shall be no more seen" (p. 45). Critics have rightly noted the allusion to "Lycidas," where "The Willows, and the Hazle Copses green,/Shall now no more be seen,/Fanning their joyous leaves to thy soft layes."[13] Yet it may make a difference whether it is the singer who disappears or the world. The situation in Milton is perfectly ordinary: the narrator will no longer see trees sway to the song because Lycidas sings no more in this world. Emerson's is far more troubling (and more Kantian), for it focuses entirely on sensation, remaining neutral on the nature of reality: whether or not trees sway, poets sing, and snakes and spiders contaminate the garden, they will be no more seen by the revolutionary eye. Similarly, the awaited apocalypse that ends the essay seems oddly static. The moment looked for "cometh not with observation" – almost, one is tempted to say, with not observation. And in a truly awkward grammatical inversion, man enters his kingdom "without more wonder" than a blind man who slowly regains his sight. Whatever one makes of this ungrateful blind man and his relation to the forest eyeball, it is clear that the exhilaration of the earlier transparency has, like mean egotism, vanished.

It would, of course, be foolish to deny entirely the prophetic overtones of "Prospects." Still it is important, here as everywhere in *Nature,* to be specific about what is and is not being asserted. Emerson himself warns us against overinvesting in prophecy. He characterizes the oracular final pages as merely "some traditions" about man and nature (p. 41). The songs present simply some of the things people say about the world; there are presumably other, less ebullient ways of talking. Even more, as he explains in the short interlude between the two songs, myths are intellectual crutches, which can take man only so far.

> The invariable mark of wisdom is to see the miraculous in the common. What is a day? What is a year? What is summer? What is woman? What is a child? What is sleep? To our blindness, these things seem unaffecting. We make fables to hide the baldness of the fact and conform it, as we say, to the higher law of the mind. But when the fact is seen under the light of an idea, the gaudy fable fades and shrivels. (P. 44)

In part Emerson is still struggling with his Swedenborgian inheritance, and the string of questions here derives from his opening list of unexplained phenomena. Earlier he had wanted to make all things meaningful. Setting up in the "Introduction" a problem answered in "Language," he complained, "Now many [phenomena] are thought not only unexplained but inexplicable; as language, sleep, madness, dreams, beasts, sex" (p. 8). But by the end of *Nature,* the Swedenborgian solution to supposed inexplicability seems as troublesome as the original question. We should not, as Swedenborg did, invent fabulous meanings to convince ourselves of the power of the initial perceptions; we should simply confront the fact not as sign or "gaudy fable" but as mere fact.[14]

Now admittedly Emerson's caution is not invigorating. The reticent (not to say niggardly) prophecy of "Prospects" is enough to send true mystics back to Blake and Thoreau.[15] Yet we should not miss the intellectual precision of the failed vision. Emerson's prospects, quite simply, treat a lower level of reality than we might have assumed. He is not at the end of *Nature* dissolving the phenomenal in the noumenal but only, as in the noble doubt paragraphs, showing the power of transcendental idealism over empirical realism. The topic of these projections is not nature or reality but "this tyrannizing unity in [man's] constitution" (p. 39), what we earlier associated with Kant's principle of formal unity, the transcen-

dental unity of apperception. And, finally, the various relations examined in the essay – the "original" one to the universe, the "occult" ones
between man and the vegetable, mind and matter, forms and the mind,
even the numerous "radical correspondences" – all reduce to the fundamental "relation between things and thoughts" (p. 40).[16]

> To the wise, therefore, a fact is true poetry, and the most beautiful of
> fables. These wonders are brought to our own door. You also are a
> man. Man and woman, and their social life, poverty, labor, sleep,
> fear, fortune, are known to you. Learn that none of these things is
> superficial, but that each phenomenon hath its root in the faculties and
> affections of the mind. Whilst the abstract question occupies your
> intellect, nature brings it in the concrete to be solved by your hands.
> (P. 44)

The Swedenborgian list appears one last time, only to be dismissed as
a false problem, something not at all inexplicable but in fact already
known. And the Orphic Poet's claim that the foundations of man are in
spirit is translated back into its more proper epistemological context:
the appearances of the world have their roots in the structures of the
mind.[17] We may not agree that Emerson has demonstrated his point.
The "therefore" seems a bit gratuitous: the gaudiness of fables does not
itself prove the beauty of facts, but only that, beautiful or not, facts are
the best we have. But his basic argument is clear. Abstractions and
intellect, concrete nature and constructive hands: things come bound
together, so that all experience describes the same situation – the insepa-
rability of transcendental idealism and empirical realism, what the Orphic Poet calls the perfection of phenomena, the world's existence "for
you" (p. 44).
    Yet if these poetic "Prospects" are more traditional and less radical
than they first appear, it is still hard not to feel that Emerson is flirting
with more dangerous formulations. The tyrannizing unity may be revealed finally to be only a formal principle of the mind's faculties and
affections. But this unity's access to divinity and archetypes seems peri-
lously close to a reification of the mental. And by the time Reason is
portrayed as a banished monarch warring to repossess his kingdom, it
is hard to tell the difference between Emerson's mind and Hegel's
world spirit on horseback. If Emerson ever faces directly the metaphysical implications of his epistemology, however, it is not in the
domesticated apocalypse of "Prospects" but in the more tangled theory
of "Spirit." For here alone in *Nature* does he move beyond the question
of perception to statements about an unperceivable noumenality, to find
not simply a "theory of nature" but a "true theory of nature and of
man" (pp. 8, 36).

This new focus is not itself antiepistemological. In the second half of the first *Critique,* Kant accounts for the mind's natural tendency to move beyond the bounds of experience in his notion of the regulative ideas of the Reason, which unlike the constitutive concepts of the Understanding imply nothing about real things. He argues that we can talk about the pure (i.e., nonexperiential) processes of thought without necessarily hypostatizing that conversation into a positive assertion about noumenal reality.[18] So, at the opening of "Spirit," Emerson's insistence that all true theories are "somewhat progressive" – that they allow an "infinite scope" to man's "activity" and everywhere "suggest the absolute" – in part reflects Kant's own emphasis on the unconditioned. Although the mutuality of objectivity and apperception is necessarily true of all experience, a complete analysis of "this brave lodging wherein man is harbored, and wherein all his faculties find appropriate and endless exercise" must also recognize man's need to think about things beyond his knowledge and faculties (p. 37). In Kantian epistemology no less than in Wordsworthian experience, intimations of immortality must be acknowledged.

Whereas Kant defines his absolute wholly in terms of the epistemological processes that generate it, however, Emerson insists on a qualitative difference between the two realms. Kant's Reason is propositional, operating much like a syllogism. Emerson's nature instead only "suggests" the absolute.[19] Recalling his previous characterization of the unspeakable but intelligible lessons of nature, he still admits that "he that thinks most, will say least." Yet metaphysical precision now seems inadequate, and the formerly admirable reserve of the thinker marks only the limits of analysis. "When we try to define and describe [God] himself, both language and thought desert us, and we are as helpless as fools and savages." Kant's momentous realization that knowledge is propositional is seen as irrelevant, for God's spiritual "essence refuses to be recorded in propositions." Epistemology must be replaced by theology, reason ousted by faith. In addition to the lessons of the lower argument, then, nature teaches the higher one of "worship," and its final use, the "noblest ministry of nature," is to stand as "the apparition of God" (p. 37). All experience turns "devout": causality becomes not categorical but "faithful," and even idealism itself speaks in biblical diction.

Rejecting idealism, which can explain only the "what" of matter, Emerson plunges into the "recesses of consciousness," regions indistinguishable from Christian (or even Neoplatonic) mysticism. One might wonder whether this vision of "the highest" is really a viable answer to questions about the "whence" and "whereto" of nature. No one surely would deny the truth of his answer. The "dread universal essence" – the "all in one . . . for which all things exist, and . . . by which they are" –

is by definition the origin and destination of matter, as it is of everything else (p. 38). Such an answer, however, does not so much solve
the problem as make it go away. The One can always swallow every
imaginable particular, including the "I think." But no argumentative
purpose is served by so radical an annihilation, which makes the noble
doubt seem tame by comparison. Emerson is not really renouncing the
philosophical precision of the first six chapters. To realize what is really
at stake, however, we must remember exactly what he has so far been
able to establish.

In the earlier chapters, especially "Idealism," Emerson demonstrates
the radical dependence of nature on man. Starting in the lower argument with the familiar eighteenth-century proofs of nature's adaptation
to man's needs, in the sixth chapter he derives from the timid physicotheology of a Paley the more extreme idealism of the noble doubt. At
the very least, of course, the subservience of nature assures the individual of a personal triumph: if he must, he can always put her underfoot.
But beyond this crass display of brute force – what he elsewhere calls
one more "weapon in the magazine of power" (p. 23) – the epistemological interrelations of objectivity and subjectivity may permit a more
subtle, balanced exchange between the two. The project then has been
to establish man's priority without simply enslaving the world.

So far Kant can take him. In "Spirit," however, Emerson tries to
give back to the world the equality that the first six chapters implicitly
denied. Here idealism cannot provide a proper balance.

> Idealism saith: matter is a phenomenon, not a substance. Idealism
> acquaints us with the total disparity between the evidence of our own
> being, and the evidence of the world's being. The one is perfect; the
> other, incapable of any assurance; the mind is a part of the nature of
> things; the world is a divine dream, from which we may presently
> awake to the glories and certainties of day. Idealism is a hypothesis to
> account for nature by other principles than those of carpentry and
> chemistry. Yet, if it only deny the existence of matter, it does not
> satisfy the demands of the spirit. (P. 37)

Idealism is, of course, preferable to the mechanical accounts of carpen-
try and chemistry, of Paley and Hartley. Yet it is not in itself sufficient.
In its simpler, Berkeleian form, it declares "nature" – now redefined as
mere "matter"[20] – to be phenomenal, not substantial. Such a bald dismissal of the world is obviously unsatisfactory, for it denies the very
feelings of fellowship in nature with which the essay began. "It baulks
the affections in denying substantive being to men and women. . . .
This theory makes nature foreign to me, and does not account for that
consanguinity which we acknowledge to it" (pp. 37-38). Berkeleian

idealism, by taking too seriously the old dualism of ME/NOT ME, gives power only at the expense of humanity.

Even the subtler transcendental idealism, however, is inadequately spiritual. "It leaves God out of me. It leaves me in the splendid labyrinth of my perceptions, to wander without end" (p. 37). Emerson's point is not mystical, but logical. It is not simply that idealism allows no active role to a real world, though Emerson does seem here to agree with those who find Kant's phenomenalism dangerously close to Berkeley's. Nor is it quite that the mind of the Kantian categories is, for all its precision, too complex and overdetermined, the architectonic too labyrinthine. Instead Emerson sees that the original apperception itself is threatened. Without some anchor outside the system, the very ME itself perpetually sacrifices its autonomy and is reduced to the merely adjectival role of identifying perceptions as "mine." Activating the pun implicit in his earlier formulation, Emerson worries that the mind may be too completely "a part of the nature of things."

Emerson's point finally is that it may not be possible to treat self-consciousness as purely formal: that if the ME is not some thing, then it may be nothing at all – that Kant's idealism is either a metaphysic or a mistake.[21] Although Kant himself was famously wary of statements about the noumenal reality supporting the "I think," of course, the possibility of an Absolute Ego behind empirical self-consciousness was exactly what most interested post-Kantian philosophers from Fichte through Hegel (at least). And in one sense the transition from "Idealism" to "Spirit" is simply the move from Kant to, say, Fichte.

What is interesting about Emerson's "Spirit," and particularly his notion of the God-in-me, however, is its relative conservatism compared to most post-Kantian absolutism. Access to divinity gives man no additional power. Nor could it. Transcendental idealism promises in its noble doubt that the mind will always be stronger than the world: no further help is needed by a mind already able to put nature underfoot. Instead, "spirit" acts to set an upper bound on human potential, and Emerson's "God," like Edwards's, serves as a constant reminder of human finitude. The God-in-me establishes not internal divinity but that greater part of God independent of man. Self-reliance may be God-reliance, as is so often said, but less because He is in me than because He is outside as well.

In part this external divinity affirms the reality of phenomena. The tree image measures the distance of this spirit from the powerful noble doubt of "Idealism." There "some god" merely painted a Berkeleian illusion in man's mind. Here "God" as the "Supreme Being" – the old-fashioned terminology is significant – proves the reality of other things, whether worlds or minds. The journal source for this image makes clear the multiplicity of minds: "the self of self creates the world through you, & organizations like you" (JMN.V.187).[22] More important in the essay, however, is that nature, though further removed from Being, is not inferior to man but more vital. The world is the "new branches and leaves [put forth] through the pores of the old" (p. 38). Though in some senses a "remoter and inferior incarnation of God," it exists independent of the human will. God as a triangulating principle measures man's distance from both Himself and His world. And His autonomy allows to nature surprising moments of truculence and unintelligibility: just as Berkeley's God permits objects to exist unperceived, Emerson's allows them by the end of the chapter to exist unaccommodating.

> We are as much strangers in nature, as we are aliens from God. We do not understand the notes of birds. The fox and the deer run away from us; the bear and tiger rend us. We do not know the uses of more than a few plants, as corn and the apple, the potato and the vine. (P. 39)

But more important than its returning to nature a degree of the independence missing in the earlier chapters of the essay, this notion of spirit grounds man's sense of self-consciousness. And the climactic question – "who can set bounds to the possibilities of man?" – may not be so rhetorical as it appears. No man, of course, can determine these bounds. But Spirit or God can, indeed must. In this sense, Emerson's positing of God operates much as does Kant's proof of the existence of objects in the Transcendental Deduction. One objection repeatedly made to Kant is that the positing of a limit necessarily presumes the existence of something beyond that limit. It was just this objection, in fact, that made Fichte and Hegel feel justified in their examination of noumenality. Kant, as we have seen, responded that the noumenal is accessible to man only negatively: it is that without which he could not have experiences. But it is otherwise totally unknowable. Emerson's God, like Kant's noumena, is proposed as a negative limit, grounding the reality of man's capacities in his inability to know perfection. As the difference between "seems" and "is" requires the existence of both the "I think" and objects, so it is the ME's failure to include all divinity that makes both ME and divinity possible. A God fully in the ME would either be indistinguishable or would disprove the existence of the ME itself. If I am only part or particle of the divine, both can exist; if I am identical to Him, one of us is a semantic redundancy.

"Spirit," then, does not quite offer the kind of "higher" idealism it appears to provide.[23] Instead it wishes only to protect what man has through the conservative concept of a God who represents what he lacks. The move is both striking and tantalizingly "transcendental": God is neither Puritan tyrant nor Unitarian gentleman but the epistemologically unknowable absolute that prevents the ME from becoming purely adjectival. In the imagery of the beginning of the chapter, spirit completes "the whole circumference" of man by serving itself as the permanent center for the circle, just as nature becomes the "fixed point whereby we may measure our departure" or degeneration (pp. 37, 39).

In light of this transcendental argument, whereby failure establishes reality, even the ambiguities of "Prospects" become somewhat more intelligible. As rewritten by the Orphic Poet, the question is less who can determine man's bounds than "who can set limits to the remedial force of spirit?" (p. 42). But the answer is the same. Spirit has no limits. But its remedial force makes spirit itself a kind of limit – a correction that rebukes even as it remedies. And the paradoxical tone of the essay's final prospects becomes perfectly appropriate. In a world where spirit is meaningfully in ME only to the extent that it remains apart from ME, the looked-for apocalypse will undoubtedly come without observation.

II

Although epistemologically sophisticated, even original, however, *Nature*'s notion of God as a negative limit in some senses begs the question. Philosophically it is an elegant concept: God serves as a kind of "self-in-itself" that underwrites the "I think" just as Kant's things-in-themselves underwrite the phenomenal world. Yet it does not really offer any direct explanation of the "tyrannizing unity" that Emerson feels so important. Nor does it resolve the tonal ambiguity of the ending, where an apparent call to action actually leaves nothing to do. When he tries to carry too far the notion of this negative God – as he does in his conflation of the unities of Understanding and Reason in "Nature" or in his "apprehension" of the absolute in "Idealism" – the carelessness of the formulations suggests that his heart, if not his mind, is elsewhere.

The problem marks *Nature*'s status as a preliminary statement.[24] From the beginning, Emerson implies that his true interest lies with "man's moral nature."[25] To such a study, the restrained affirmation of *Nature* is merely propaedeutic. In this first book, Emerson presents his unsystematic but informed account of current epistemological issues – in part to prove his philosophical credentials and in part to lay the groundwork for future explorations. But, like Kant, whose first critique defines (and denies) science to make room for the defense of truth in subsequent works, Emerson only hints at his true focus in *Nature*. For a full consideration of man's divinity, of the grounds for his feelings of transcendence, we must move to the Divinity School "Address."

The Divinity School "Address," however, poses its own problems. So clear are the psychological pressures shaping this notorious statement that it is difficult to separate the theoretical position presented from the emotional crisis that precipitated it. The story is a familiar one.[26] In 1837, Emerson was starting to curtail his activity at East Lexington, where, though never the official pastor, he had been preaching regularly since late 1835.[27] At the same time as he was making this shift from preacher to lecturer, he encountered in his own church at Concord the pedestrian sermons of the Rev. Barzillai Frost. Although only a year older than Frost, Emerson throughout his journals sneered at the "young preacher" and marked his discomfort with his own vocation by attacking Frost's inadequacy.[28] The year-long quarrel with Frost as alterego – climaxed in the famous description of the snowstorm and the spectral preacher – was incorporated into the Divinity School "Address" as a general attack on the uninspired preaching of the Unitarians.

But Frost was really only a convenient whipping boy.[29] More significant was the strife with his mentors, Henry Ware, Jr., and Andrews Norton. Ware had always been for Emerson something of an older brother, a model by which to measure his own failures. He was responsible in 1822 for the publication of Emerson's juvenile first essay. And it was Ware whom Emerson replaced in the pulpit of the Second Church in 1829. The competition was not purely psychological: on Ware's full retirement, Emerson was to receive half again as much salary. But the psychological pressures were real, since from the first Ware worked to restrain Emerson's heterodoxy. Emerson's earliest letters to Ware repeatedly thank him for "suggestions" about curbing his enthusiasms and supporting his positions with biblical texts. And Ware's own serious disease probably acted as a subtle rebuke to Emerson's more fanciful ailments. Whatever the nature of their early relationship, after the Divinity School "Address," Ware wrote Emerson two critical letters and published the first major refutation, his sermon on "The Personality of the Deity."[30]

The return to Divinity Hall, where Emerson had been a mediocre student, was bound to be psychologically charged for him. Emerson had always been sensitive about his academic record. In an earlier moment of bumptious self-confidence, he confided to his journal, "I was the true philosopher in college, & Mr Farrar & Mr Hedge & Dr Ware the false. Yet what seemed then to me less probable?" (JMN.IV.292).[31] And whether or not Ware played that day elder brother to Emerson's defiant prodigal, Andrews Norton willingly took on the role of unforgiving father. Unlike Ware, who was widely loved by his students, Norton, dubbed the "Unitarian Pope," was remote and dogmatic, with all too clear a capacity for Olympian rage.[32] It is as the spokesman not

for religious orthodoxy but for scholarly decorum that Norton announced the failure of the address. The question involved not Emerson's feeble heresies but how they came to be delivered "in the Chapel
of the Divinity College of Cambridge." The attack on religion and
historical Christianity was far less important than the "personal insult"
to "highly respectable officers of that Institution." And the true error
was committed by the "gentlemen" of the graduating class who had
invited Emerson in the first place and whose "exculpation or excuse"
Norton solemnly awaited.[33] Emerson recognized the intended slight,
and hurt and angry he wrote of the "old tyrant of the Cambridge
Parnassus," ironically reducing Norton's attack to a skillful piece of
prose whose style he praises without noting its content (JMN.VII.63).

But the psychological conflict may be even more literally oedipal.
For behind the substitute figures of Frost, Ware, and Norton lie the
blood relatives, Emerson's step-grandfather Ripley and his dead father
William. The references to Frost in the journals are often accompanied
by similar, more moderate attacks on Ripley, the senior pastor over
Frost.[34] And only two weeks before the address itself, Emerson's attacks turn both personal and bloodthirsty.

> Most of the Commonplaces spoken in churches every Sunday respect
> ing the Bible & the life of Christ, are grossly superstitious. Would not,
> for example, would not any person unacquainted with the Bible, al
> ways draw from the pulpit the impression that the New Testament
> unfolded a system? and in the second place that the history of the life
> & teachings of Jesus were greatly more copious than they are? Do let
> the new generation speak the truth, & let our grandfathers die.
> (JMN.VII.39)

As Joel Porte rightly sees, the substitution of "grandfathers" for the
more customary "fathers" is not innocent.[35] It is even possible to see
Emerson's preoccupation with antinomianism in oedipal terms; his
father's *Historical Sketch of the First Church in Boston* was largely a defense
of the establishment against the spiritist excesses of Mrs. Hutchinson.[36]

By the time of the address, all these various psychological pressures
seem to be jumbled together. And, indeed, the essay shows signs of this
psychic stress in its shifting tone. The ostentatiously un-Unitarian lushness of the opening, the stridency of the attack on miracles, and the
tasteless specificity of the paragraphs on Frost are the most obvious
signs of tension. But, finally, the real heart of Emerson's oedipal crisis
is his attack on historical Christianity itself, where the various psychological rivals are conjoined not in the minor threat of Frost but in the
major one of Jesus.[37] Although Christ enters the essay as one of the true

prophets, he soon comes to cut a very odd figure indeed. Emerson's powerful description of His influence is uncharacteristically impassioned and particularized. Christ becomes the means by which (perhaps even the agent whereby) man is "defrauded of his manly right" and virtue and truth are "foreclosed and monopolized."[38] At first, the pronouncement of disinheritance sounds merely descriptive and the pronouns generic – an anti-Orphic poem. "You shall not be a man even. You shall not own the world." But, by the end, the description turns specific and the pronouns personal. "You must subordinate your nature to Christ's nature; you must accept our interpretations" (CW.I.82). Not only does the "you" narrow to an autobiographical whine, but the "our" reveals the speakers to be not oracles but only the Cambridge faculty. The speech is less a prophecy of doom than a quotation from Emerson's most recent reviews.

The oedipal dimensions of the Divinity School "Address," then, are too striking to be ignored. At the same time, however, it must be admitted that though necessary to our understanding, they are not in themselves a sufficient account of Emerson's statement. For it is hard not to feel that the essential points in the oedipal debate – on miracles, the personality of the Deity, and the lack of inspired preaching – are really far from Emerson's main interests. His relation to the miracles controversy is perfectly representative here. The Unitarian establishment in general, and Andrews Norton in particular, held that the supernatural, absolute truth of Christ's teachings could not be established by unaided intellect. Miracles were therefore necessary to prove Christ's divine authority and, by extension, the divinity of His ethics.[39] The younger generation, largely Transcendentalists, attacked this position on two grounds. First, German higher criticism had shown the New Testament to be so corrupt a text as to disqualify its testimony concerning certain historical events, especially Jesus's miracles.[40] But more important, it became increasingly unclear how one could distinguish a divine event from a merely unusual one.

Emerson's Divinity School "Address" energized this controversy, a mild squabble since November of 1836. But during the ensuing two years of stormy exchanges, Emerson himself remained aloof, as much for intellectual as for temperamental reasons.[41] He had solved the problem, in his own mind, at least five years earlier. In 1831, Emerson delivered a sermon on "Miracles," itself based on "The Evidences of Revealed Religion" by William Ellery Channing, the leading Unitarian theologian and a particular favorite of Emerson's.[42] Although Emerson's early sermon is usually contrasted to the more radical Divinity School "Address," on the essential points the two are surprisingly similar. Channing, in the Dudleian lecture, articulated the most liberal Unitarian position when he spoke of an evidence "still more internal": "that conviction of the divine original of our religion. . . . a consciousness of the adaptation of Christianity to [men's] noblest faculties."[43]

When Emerson comes, ten years later, to echo Channing's formulation in his own sermon, however, he actually goes far beyond it.

> Internal evidence far outweighs all miracles to the soul. A reasoning Christian would think himself injured by the fortifying too scrupulously the outward evidence of Christianity. If the whole history of the New Testament had perished and only its teachings remained, the discourses of our Lord, the authority of holiness, and the heavenly standard of Jesus, the ardour and spirituality of Paul, the grave and self-examining advice of James would take the same rank with me that now they do. I should say, as I now say, that this certainly is the greatest height to which the religious principle of human nature has ever been carried and it has the total suffrage of my soul to its truth, whether the miracle was wrought, as is pretended, or not. If I did not acknowledge the doctrine as true, I should yield to the skeptic that this story of miracles, like other such stories, was false. But as the doctrine is true the miracle falls in with and confirms it. (YES, pp. 124-25)[44]

His point, he claims, is that miracles are only a "lower species of evidence," which not all will need or even want. But in fact he admits far more by concluding that miracles only "fall in with or confirm" a truth antecedently known as true. Acknowledging a page before that a miracle could not prove a negative truth, he concludes that "to make a miracle of any effect as evidence, it must accompany the revelation of a truth which, when made known, is agreeable to the laws of the mind" (p. 123).[45]

In 1831 Emerson may not have fully understood the implications of his position. But the recognition was not to take long. A little over a year later, on the eve of his resignation from the Second Church, he wrote in his journal:

> Every teacher when once he finds himself insisting with all his might upon a great truth turns up the ends of it at last with a cautious showing *how* it is agreeable to the life & teaching of Jesus – as if that was any recommendation. As if the blessedness of Jesus' life & teaching were not because they were agreeable to the truth. . . . It is a very operose way of making people good. You must be humble because Christ says, 'Be humble'. 'But why must I obey Christ?' 'Because God sent him.' But how do I know God sent him? 'Because your own heart teaches the same thing he taught.' Why then shall I not go to my own heart at first? (JMN.IV.45)[46]

The passage is crucial for a number of reasons. It makes clear that, at least this early, Emerson had connected the question of Jesus and His miracles with the problem of practical morality, of "making people good." Moreover, it explicitly announces that internal evidence makes the rest unnecessary, even "operose." Finally, it is the moment, four years before *Nature* and six before the Divinity School "Address," that Transcendentalism was truly born: a Unitarian like Channing might go to his heart, but only a Transcendentalist could go there "first."

The journal entries preceding the Divinity School "Address" evince the same sense of resolution. There is, surely, an uncertainty about how the world will receive his views. "What shall I answer to these friendly Youths who ask of me an account of Theism & think the views I have expressed of the impersonality of God desolating & ghastly?" (JMN.V.457). Yet this reluctance signals no great emotional intensity. Questions about miracles and preaching are ones he has resolved long ago, and his chief tone is intellectual weariness.

> The Divinity School youths wished to talk with me concerning theism. I went rather heavy-hearted for I always find that my views chill or shock people at the first opening. But the conversation went well & I came away cheered. (JMN.V.471)

He will, of course, be troubled by the personal animus of his audience's response. He gently reminds Ware of the implicit contradiction in taking so seriously the views of one already labeled a "chartered libertine." Yet whatever he feels to be the psychological pressures "in that place and presence," he is equally serious that his "conviction . . . is not very new."[47]

The historical record, then, asks us to separate the psychological pressures of the situation from its intellectual significance. But we need not go to outside sources at all. For the very form of the address, with its oddly disproportionate sections, suggests a tension between the controversial moments and Emerson's own interest in them. The stages of the argument are clear enough. After a brief theoretical introduction, Emerson announces that the greatest problem facing the church is its misrepresentation of the historical nature of Christianity and of the character of Jesus in particular.[48] The problem is most evident in two errors: one concerning the personality of Jesus, and the other the moral nature of man. This latter error of devaluing man's nature results in an excessively formal style of preaching. The solution to both problems – for they are inversions of each other – is to energize sermons through a direct personal attestation to the presence of spirit and divinity in the contemporary world.

What is interesting about this argument is that its overall structure and message are perfectly conventional.[49] The injunction to more lively preaching – if somewhat tactless in its anonymous reference to the poor

Reverend Frost–is surely the traditional, even expected topic for commencement addresses. Furthermore, the structure downplays the very points that would most infuriate. The problematic attack on the historical Jesus occupies only two pages of text and is far less important to Emerson's overall argument than his quintessentially Unitarian point about the moral nature of man.[50] And the notorious glance at the miracles controversy, though sufficient to revive the "storm in our washbowl," is itself a minor illustration of that first, less important error–a mere three-sentence throwaway.[51] Clearly, Emerson knew what he was doing in deemphasizing these points. But, just as clearly, current preoccupation with the psychological and historical context of the essay has obscured the work's own rhetorical emphases.

III

It will never be possible wholly to divorce the Divinity School "Address" from its historical and biographical context. Yet, for that very reason, history and biography may be the wrong places to start. We tend to think that anything in the address that Schleiermacher did not write, Freud did. But in fact there is much here that is neither hermeneutic nor oedipal. Some of the work comes directly out of the tradition of ethical philosophy. Even more of it seems simply odd, apparent nonsequiturs and perplexing juxtapositions. To understand the bulk of the essay as anything more than camouflage for a few guerrilla assaults in an oedipal war, then, we will have to double back to consider not merely the psychohistorical context of Emerson's arguments but their philosophical content as well.

The controversy about miracles in America really considered two questions. Most commentators addressed the first problem–of factuality and of the identifiability of a miracle. Here the issue was whether or not man possessed a natural standard that could rule on the supernatural status of an event. But there was also a related problem–of historicity and of evidence. Here the question was whether the canons of regularity by which we establish the truth of a past event do not inevitably exclude the miraculous–whether miracles do not imply the mutually exclusive propositions that any X must be a Y and that on one particular occasion X was not Y.[52] Although the two questions are closely related, their emphases do differ subtly: the first examines the range of man's nature; the second, the logic of observation, evidence, and natural law.

Although not entirely consistent on this point, Emerson was unusual among his contemporaries in addressing the second issue as often as the first.[53] The comparison with Channing's Dudleian lecture is, again, revealing. As we have seen, both men place their heaviest emphasis on the "internal" evidence of Christianity. But on other points they disagree. Hoping to explain how the notion of the miraculous does not contradict the notion of order it presupposes, Channing argues that Christianity is itself essentially miraculous. As a miraculous (i.e., nonrational) religion, Christianity cannot be discovered in "the ordinary exercise of [man's] powers, from the ordinary course of nature" (III, 107). Therefore God sends miraculous (i.e., intuitively striking) events to confirm His supernatural system. The argument is, of course, dangerously circular, as God offers unintelligible events to explain His own unintelligibility.

Emerson's solution is both more consistent and more radical. He claims that not merely Christianity but "all our life" is a miracle, and thus denies the conflict between the natural and supernatural orders by denying the notion of natural order altogether. "Our own being is a far more astounding and inexplicable fact, than, after life has once been exercised, could be the resurrection of a man from the tomb. . . . In other words I can believe a miracle, because I can raise my own arm" (YES, p. 122).[54] The solution solves the problem by doing away with the explanatory power of miracles and making all reality equally a question of faith.

More striking than Emerson's explicit revision of Channing, however, are his implicit excisions, those arguments he does not carry over. Perhaps caution, not acumen, persuaded him to forgo Channing's wrongheaded refutation of Hume, who in Channing's account said merely that miracles are by definition so unlikely that the "balance of proof" will always weigh against them (p. 115).[55] More surprisingly, Emerson eliminates Channing's argument from design, though that argument would seem especially congenial to Emerson. It summarizes what would become the lower argument of *Nature*, even to the point of concluding proleptically with Emerson that the true end – in Channing "purpose" – of nature is discipline – "the formation of Mind."[56]

Most perplexing, however, is his omission of Channing's best argument – on the nature of "conviction." Channing asserts that history records not the truth of facts but the state of other people's minds in regard to those facts, what he calls "conviction." We then are convinced of the events not directly, but by being convinced about the conviction.[57] Miracles reveal not the logical contradictions between unequivocal order and apparent departures but a conviction of departure that on certain historical occasions overruled the otherwise invulnerable conviction of order. The "internal" evidence on which he bases all other evidences is itself just one more, all-encompassing conviction –

that of "the divine original of our religion" (p. 135). This answer to
Hume may not be entirely convincing, for it seems to conflate the truly
believed with the true. But what is interesting for our purposes is how
Emerson avoids this, the one strong point in Channing's argument.

Although it is possible to overread Emerson's sermon – and especially
its omissions – his argument is suggestive both of his position on miracles and of the directions it will take. Channing's case builds to a
doubly psychological reading – of internal evidence and of convictions.
All of Emerson's changes emphasize instead the logical status of miraculous evidence. The only evidence that Emerson allows – internal
evidence – is different in kind from miracles (and from Channing's own
notion of internal evidence as conviction).

Emerson's focus is clearer perhaps in the journal passage partly examined earlier. The passage begins oddly as notes for a sermon on
"man's moral nature." But almost immediately the questions about
man are replaced (or subsumed) by ones about truth. "Has the doctrine
ever been fairly preached of man's moral nature? The whole world
holds on to formal Christianity, & nobody teaches the essential truth,
the heart of Christianity for fear of shocking &c." More important, this
moral truth is studied in purely formal terms, not for what it says but
for how it says it.

> Well this cripples [a minister's] teaching. It bereaves the truth he incul-
> cates of more than half its force by representing it as something second-
> ary that can't stand alone. The truth of truth consists in this, that it is
> selfevident[,] selfsubsistent. It is light. You don't get a candle to see
> the sun rise. Instead of making Christianity a vehicle of truth you
> make truth only a horse for Christianity. (JMN.IV.45)

Miraculous evidence fails in part because it implicitly depends upon
internal evidence and is therefore operose. But, more interestingly, it
fails (as by implication do all standards, internal or external) simply
because it misunderstands the nature of virtue. Virtue is not referential;
it neither needs nor even allows for proofs. Absolute truth is wholly
self-evidenced: it cannot be taught; like the *fiat lux*, it just is.[58]

Emerson's early confrontations with miracles, then, increasingly lead
him to see in the controversy not a truth about the nature of man but
one about the nature of virtue, finally perhaps even a truth about truth.
The same discovery underlies his larger argument about the personality
of the deity. The argument is a confusing one and too often reduced to
its oedipal implications. But there is a philosophical point here, as his
contemporaries well knew. Perhaps the easiest way to discover it is to
read backward from Ware's troubled but suggestive response in his
sermon on "The Personality of the Deity."

Although not entirely convincing, Ware's sermon is serious, and it is here (not in Andrews Norton's diatribes) that the intellectual heart of the Unitarian position lies.[59] Ware is clearly not concerned, as Norton is, with attacking the personal integrity of the Transcendentalists. "To the pure all things are pure; and some men will dwell forever in the midst of abstraction and falsehood without being injuriously affected" (p. 38). He even admits the validity of the Transcendentalists' general program to substitute higher laws for business ethics. Corruption arises less from "the ingenuity of an imaginative mind" than from "the hardening influences of a worldly career." For both Emerson and Ware the true villain is State Street, Jackson-*cum*-Babbitt (p. 39).

Despite their practical agreement, however, Ware thinks Emerson's ethics pernicious and works to refute him on his own theoretical terms. Interestingly enough, Ware immediately changes the focus from the exaggeration of the historical Jesus to the personality of the deity in general. On the simplest level this shift is unfair. The Unitarians are no clearer than Emerson about the divinity of Christ, and when Ware does approach this topic briefly in his sermon, he cannot really define what he thinks to be the special character of Christ's revelation.[60] Yet on another level the shift is justifiable. For Ware understands, as not all did, that the real thrust of Emerson's antipersonalism is to establish an antiauthoritarian definition of virtue and duty. And the single goal of Ware's sermon is to prove that a personal deity, and not merely a set of principles or code of laws, is necessary to "a true and happy virtue."[61]

Most of the sermon outlines the theoretical implications of an impersonal God, using traditional Unitarian arguments about design and the slander of the affections.[62] But two arguments relate directly to Emerson's presumed denial of virtue, defining the ethical tradition against which Emerson reacts. Ware claims that virtue entails the notion of responsibility and of someone to whom we are responsible. Responsibility to "the tribunal within the breast" is insufficient, for it is unattended by guilt and the "sentiment of approbation or disapprobation." Ware's argument, however, proves too much, insisting on God's personality by reducing Him to "the Living Lawgiver," a kind of moral policeman (pp. 34–36).

The other, more cogent argument claims that duty, in its notion of worship or reverence, presupposes an object of worship. Without such an object Ware is, like Emerson in his labyrinth, "left to myself, and to men as weak as myself." But, as Ware suspects, his argument, like Kant's objectivity thesis or Emerson's God-in-me, establishes nothing more than the reality of noumenal truth. To Ware's pleas for a more humane object of worship, an oracular voice chillingly responds, " 'The power that is over all sustains and guides; but, having no personality, it cannot appreciate affection, nor give it back in return; be satisfied to reverence and submit' " (p. 33).[63] In familiar Unitarian rhetoric, Ware refuses the response as a slander of the moral sensibility, the "affections." But his response is more emotional than logical, and his refusal to believe that "the altar at which he kneels is consecrated to a set of principles, and not to a 'living God' " indirectly concedes the logical superiority of Emerson's case (p. 34).

IV

Ware's sermon, then, shows the question of the personality of God to be chiefly a defense of a particular theory of virtue. A standard is necessary to uphold man's sense of duty and virtue. And for our own peace of mind, this standard must be a minimally human one. It is, one suspects, this double proof of virtue – of approbation and paternalism – that Emerson found truly operose. The real question is not how I recognize a miracle or whether the soul knows persons, but how I recognize virtue, know duty. And, in fact, it is in terms of such a theory of virtue that Emerson examines personality in the journals and lectures.[64]

In part, impersonality is a defense against the fear that the personalization of God is only inverted self-flattery, what Emerson calls in *Nature* "mean egotism." God's influence is "wholly impersonal; it passes through my whole being, and I cannot think without being affected by it, – but it refers me to all the world; and is as present to every other creature, as to me. It is the law of soul, and not of my soul. It melts all things into itself, for it is itself their ground of being" (EL.II.345).[65] The concept of personality seems to trivialize the divine. "I deny Personality to God because it is too little not too much. Life, personal life is faint & cold to the energy of God. For Reason & Love & Beauty, or, that which is all these, is the life of life, the reason of reason, the love of love" (JMN.V.467).[66]

But the psychological and theological implications interest Emerson less than the logical ones. All personality – whether of God or man – means particularity and is "dangerous," a division that signals the distance of the particular from the universal.

> I claim to be a part of the All. All exterior life declares interior life. I could not be but that absolute life circulated in me & I could not think this without being that absolute life. The constant warfare in each heart is betwixt Reason & Commodity. The victory is won as soon as any soul has learned always to take sides with Reason against himself; to transfer his *Me* from his person, his name, his interests, back upon Truth & Justice. (JMN.V.391)[67]

In the notion of God's paternal character, universal issues are falsely particularized or, as the lecture on "Holiness" says, "personated."

> Go at last into the cultivated class who ask, What is Beauty? How shall I be perfect? To what end exists the world? and you shall find in proportion to their cultivation a studious separation of personal history from their analysis of action and their study of things. Natural History is elegant, astronomy sublime for this reason – their impersonality. And yet when cultivated men speak of God they demand a biography of him as steadily as the kitchen and the barroom demand personalities of men. Absolute truth, absolute goodness must leave their infinity and take form for us. We want fingers and head and hair. (EL.II.354; cf. JMN.V.162)

The problem is purely rhetorical, one of an inelegant (and therefore false) bifurcation. Moral standards are referred to a personated adjudicator and ethics turns prudential: man does good because he hears that "God will give long life to the upright; God will punish the sinner in hell." It is simpler, Emerson insists, to admit the moral standard to be itself unified, and goodness its own reward – a doctrine Emerson usually calls "compensation."[68]

> As a spiritual truth needs no proof but is its own reason so the universe needs no outer cause but exists by its own perfection and the sum of it all is this, God is. Theism must be and the name of God must be because it is a necessity of the human mind to apprehend the relative as flowing from the absolute and we shall always give the absolute a name. (EL.II.354)[69]

The debate about the personality of the deity, then, like that about miracles, reduces to a struggle between two models of virtue – one dualist and prudential, the other monist and self-evidential. But although Emerson always saw the two controversies in terms of virtue, he did not usually approach the question of virtue in terms of them. And increasingly he came to define virtue less as a demonstrable doctrine than as a state of being, even an action.

In "Language" Emerson had concluded that "a fact is the end or last issue of spirit" (p. 22).[70] But he came to feel that this definition, though correct, was backward. It is this concern with facts, rather than with miracles or historical Christianity, that preoccupies him in the summer of 1838.[71] Although he never rejects facts outright, he increasingly sees them as means rather than ends. In a reworking of the indifference of the noble doubt, he asks, "who cares what the fact was, when we have thus made a constellation of it to hang in heaven an immortal sign" (JMN.VII.33). The process by which these facts are vitalized he most often calls "classification" and the moving force "thought" or "intellect."

> But Intellect & Intellection signify to the common ear something else, the consideration of abstract truth. It implies the power always to separate the fact from yourself, from all personality, & look at it as if it existed for itself alone. . . . The Intellect goes out of the Individual, & floats over its own being, & regards its own being always as a foreign fact, & not as I & mine. *I & mine* cannot see the Wonder of their existence. This the Intellect always ponders. . . . The subtle intellect detects the secret intrinsic likeness between remotest things, &, as a menstruum dissolves all things into a few principles. (JMN.V.446-47)

Here, as in his theological passages, Emerson examines the relation between personality and truth. But this vocabulary makes clear, as the other does not, that his examination is still epistemological and continues the questions of *Nature*. "Fact" is merely a new term for phenomenon or appearance, and the free-floating intellect that dissolves into principles is Emerson's new version of Kant's Understanding. It is on this distinction between fact and thought – as much as on any theological basis – that Emerson constructs the case against historical Christianity.

> I could not help thinking that there are two emphases that distinguish the two sorts of teachers[:] 1. *Human life.* 2. *Thought.* Those who remain fast in the first, respect facts supremely; & thought is but a tool for them. Those who dwell in the second, respect principles; – & facts & persons & themselves they regard only as slovenly unperfect manifestations of these; they care not for Christ, nor for Death, nor for resurrection, except as illustrations. (JMN.V.502)

The transformation of facts into thoughts is the subject of the two other major addresses of the period. "The American Scholar," delivered as the Phi Beta Kappa oration in late August 1837, is for the most part an aggressively untheoretical account of America's literary prospects, defining the scholar's relation to establishment tradition much as the Divinity School "Address" would discuss the preacher's similar problems. The crux of the essay, however, is Emerson's attempt, using the crucial fact/thought dichotomy, to outline a progressive theory of truth, to redefine the scholar's thinking as an action. In the first age, before the problem of belatedness, thought was inherently creative, and the scholar's primary activity was to transmute life into truth.[72] He received business, short-lived actions, dead fact and gave back poetry and immortal and quick thought (CW.I.55).

Yet subsequent scholars have found this process of vitalization troublesome. Transmutation involves particularization, and thoughts embodied for one generation appear to the next as dead facts. Although originally the soul was by definition "free, sovereign, active" (p. 56), now the previous unity of thought, truth, and action has disintegrated.

Thought, which early in the essay seemed identical to truth, is now preliminary to it, with action serving as catalyst. Although still necessary if thought is to "ripen into truth," action is itself only a "preamble of thought," "the transition through which it passes from the unconscious to the conscious" (p. 59). The intransitive definition of "action" as a state, a transition, represents grammatically the more general intellectual confusion.

Moreover, at the same time that thought, truth, and action come unraveled, facts take on an unwonted autonomy. The active fact is no longer identically a quickened thought but something intermediate – a "deed."

> The new deed is yet a part of life, – remains for a time immersed in our unconscious life. In some contemplative hour, it detaches itself from the life like a ripe fruit, to become a thought of the mind. Instantly, it is raised, transfigured; the corruptible has put on incorruption. . . . So is there no fact, no event, in our private history, which shall not, sooner or later, lose its adhesive inert form, and astonish us by soaring from our body into the empyrean. (P. 60)[73]

Presumably the "contemplative hour" signals that thought is still the efficient as well as the material cause of transfiguration. Nevertheless, the proliferation of terms and stages in the process is ominous, as is the "astonishment" with which the scholar confronts what was before his natural activity.

A similar confusion about the scholar's relation to action informs "Literary Ethics," delivered at Dartmouth College less than two weeks after the Divinity School "Address." Again the topic is the scholar and how his thoughts subdue a world of facts. In part the relation between the two seems more balanced. Explicitly refuting *Nature*'s banishment of snakes and spiders, Emerson announces, "No more will I dismiss, with haste, the visions which flash and sparkle across my sky; but observe them, approach them, domesticate them, brood on them, and thus draw out of the past, genuine life for the present hour" (CW.I.103). And combining the oration's embrace of the common with *Nature*'s visionary woods, Emerson celebrates in Miltonic tones the poetic possibilities of nature, where all is "new and undescribed . . . any and all, are alike unattempted" (p. 106).[74]

But in fact the apparent jubilation only masks the same struggle between thoughts and things that plagues "The American Scholar." If anything, the sense of belatedness so strong in the oration is even more striking here. Emerson claims – in a section on "Intellect as resource" – to see past successes as promises that he too can succeed.

> I console myself in the poverty of my present thoughts, in the paucity
> of great men, in the malignity and dulness of the nations, by falling
> back on these sublime recollections, and seeing what the prolific soul
> could beget on actual nature; – seeing that Plato was, and Shakspeare,
> and Milton, – three irrefragable facts. Then I dare; I also will essay to
> be. (Pp. 102-03)[75]

Yet the language betrays itself, especially the "factuality" of the previously great men.

Inverting the rhetoric of "The American Scholar," where facts soar up to become thoughts, Emerson argues at first that facts come from thoughts.

> [The scholar] is the world; and the epochs and heroes of chronology
> are pictorial images, in which his thoughts are told. There is no event
> but sprung somewhere from the soul of man; and therefore there is
> none but the soul of man can interpret. (P. 101)

But now he unfairly imports a third factor into the argument – that of simple being, action as existence. From the "fact" of Shakespeare I can conclude that once some soul thought. I might even interpret this conclusion as an injunction to attempt to think. But to derive my existence from that fact seems unwarranted – the *cogito* gone haywire.

The problem becomes clearer when Emerson turns from the resources of intellect to its task, its activities. Here he explicitly inverts the logic of the previous section. It is not that the world proceeds from soul "and therefore" I can interpret all events. Instead I am to interpret previously given facts "so as" to prove the power of my thought. Creative thinking is possible, but only by a denial of experience as ruthless as anything in *Nature*. The autonomy of an "alien" world, a world "not yet subdued by the thought," is so threatening that reality is reduced to the status of commodity, and life becomes simply raw material for the mind, "mere data and food for analysis" (pp. 106, 108).

Previous philosophical systems in particular – but all aspects of experience by extension – appear sufficiently phenomenal that the strong mind can immediately transcend them, putting all precursors underfoot.[76] "A profound thought, anywhere, classifies all things," and once man's knowledge is set afloat by thought, "then Plato, Bacon, Kant, and the Eclectic Cousin, condescend instantly to be men and mere facts" (p. 108). The condescension of these heroes gives the lie to the earlier heroes' ability to prove thought and being. And the transition from "irrefragable" to "mere" measures the unresolved tension in Emerson's relation to experience, the extent to which he has not yet found anything sufficiently spiritual for the scholar to do.

V

In the Divinity School "Address," these various models of man's moral nature – psychological, theological, epistemological – find their fullest, most coherent expression. Emerson succeeded here more fully in part because in virtue he found a subject that naturally included the problem of personality, such a troublesome undercurrent in the other works. Moreover, he discovered in the notion of duty a solution to the problem of action that had previously defeated him. But, most simply, the topic of virtue – unlike that of the scholar or literary ethics – grew logically out of his previous philosophical efforts. And in the Divinity School "Address" we find the natural extension of the epistemological theories Emerson began with in *Nature*.

The intellectual continuity is not felt immediately, for the opening of the Divinity School "Address" is calculated to disorient any audience, whatever its expectations.

> In this refulgent summer it has been a luxury to draw the breath of life. The grass grows, the buds burst, the meadow is spotted with fire and gold in the tint of flowers. The air is full of birds, and sweet with the breath of the pine, the balm-of-Gilead, and the new hay. Night brings no gloom to the heart with its welcome shade. Through the transparent darkness the stars pour their almost spiritual rays. Man under them seems a young child, and his huge globe a toy. The cool night bathes the world as with a river, and prepares his eyes again for the crimson dawn. The mystery of nature was never displayed more happily. The corn and the wine have been freely dealt to all creatures, and the never-broken silence with which the old bounty goes forward, has not yielded yet one word of explanation. One is constrained to respect the perfection of this world, in which our senses converse. How wide; how rich; what invitation from every property it gives to every faculty of man! In its fruitful soils; in its navigable sea; in its mountains of metal and stone; in its forests of all woods; in its animals; in its chemical ingredients; in the powers and path of light, heat, attraction, and life, it is well worth the pith and heart of great men to subdue and enjoy it. The planters, the mechanics, the inventors, the astronomers, the builders of cities, and the captains, history delights to honor. (CW.I.76)

The mischievousness of this opening has been fairly characterized as simultaneously voluptuary, shocking, and sacramental, and it is impossible to overemphasize the striking originality of the rhetoric and vocabulary of this most un-Unitarian of opening paragraphs.[77] At the same time, however, the argument should seem familiar, recapitulating as it does the first half of *Nature*. Perhaps the most obvious clue is the

stars, which pour their "almost spiritual" rays through a night predictably "transparent." The direct echo of the transparency highlights the
more subtle allusion in the "almost." We are expected to recall not only
the revered stars of the first chapter but the starry constellation Orion
vaporized by the noble doubt (pp. 8-9, 29). The stars are only "almost"
spiritual both because they are partly material and because they are
wholly phenomenal.

The second half of the paragraph, though apparently as celebratory as
the first, works increasingly to characterize the limitations of man's
field of perception. The "happiness" with which nature displays its
mystery marks only the accuracy of representation, not any special
adaptation to man. Nor is the sacramental communion particularly human. The corn and wine have been "freely dealt to all creatures." The
emphasis is less on the generosity of the gift than on its inscrutability:
the "old bounty" has never yielded one word of explanation.[78]

But the most obvious reminder of epistemological limitation comes in
the next two sentences. "One is constrained to respect the perfection of
this world, in which our senses converse. How wide; how rich; what
invitation from every property it gives to every faculty of man!" The
second sentence's intimations of wealth, breadth, and universality are
largely illusory, and the promise of the twin "every's" is sharply reined
in by the insistence that we are talking only about a secondary level of
reality, where psychological "faculties" perceive apparent "properties."[79]

The apparent paradox of a "constrained" respect for perfection is in
fact to be taken literally, as an allusion to the limits of transcendental
idealism.[80] The world is perfect, but merely as a conversation between
our senses and noumenality – a world shaped by our faculties, categories, and intuitions. Such idealism is, as before, less frivolous than fatal.
We do not merely respect the world but are "constrained" to do so.
Transcendental idealism entails empirical realism; thoughts require objects and concepts intuitions. This constraint, in turn, defines the ways
in which it is a "luxury" to draw the breath of life. Not only is the
summer so refulgent that one is drunk on its beauty, but, more narrowly, this breath – minimal objectivity – is what permits our sense of
self in the first place.[81]

The opening paragraph, then, recaptures in a few deft strokes
Nature's epistemological world of objectivity and apperception. The
second presents a revised version of the noble doubt. Invited to "subdue and enjoy" nature, the mind becomes so preoccupied with the
unity of the world that the reality of that world seems "mere illustration and fable" (p. 76). The logic is the same as in the earlier work. The
mind's argument for unity – here "lawfulness" – so sufficiently accounts
for the world that it is hard not to read this lawfulness as a product, or

at least a material cause, of mind. Unity is so exclusively for man that it seems of him.

Yet although the point is the same as in *Nature,* the tone is different. There Emerson moved very slowly to demonstrate the commonsense value of his radical reduction. Here he states the fact so baldly that he almost invites disbelief. A "curious" soul simply asks politely the Kantian questions of apperception and objectivity – what am I? and what is? – and the world vanishes. As Bishop rightly notes, the description of the world as mere illustration and fable seems ungallant, and the characterization of the imperfectly apprehended laws as the "entertainment" of the human spirit downright facetious.[82]

The next two paragraphs seem to reverse the restraint of the previous one as the mind (now assisted by the "heart") opens further to the "sentiment of virtue." The limitations of the previous paragraphs no longer apply. Man is not bemused by laws but liberated by them. They instruct him in what is above him, showing his being to be without bound. It is not so much that man knows more, but that the kind of propositional logic used earlier is now deemed worthless. The sentiment of virtue, unlike more objective intuitions, is less a sensation than "a reverence and delight in the presence of certain divine laws" (p. 77). In "The American Scholar," nature hastened "to render account of herself to the mind" (p. 54). The venerable law of the "Address" is more inscrutable: a mysterious imperative *"He ought,"* whose "sense" man "knows," "though his analysis fails entirely to render account of it." Clearly, these new laws transcend the apocalyptic discovery of the noble doubt. They "refuse to be adequately stated. They will not by us or for us be written out on paper, or spoken by the tongue." Although like the noble doubt "unspeakable," they are independent of our perception, and neither "by us" nor "for us," they "elude, evade our persevering thought" (p. 77).

Yet the difference between the second and third paragraphs should not be overstated. For if virtue does seem to transcend, even overturn, the idealism of *Nature,* it does so in an altogether familiar manner. Although Emerson avoids using the word at first, it eventually becomes clear that the sentiment of virtue is another term for the "moral sentiment." And in this form, the moral sense or sentiment has been implicit in Emerson's epistemology since his college days. Like most of his contemporaries, Emerson used the moral sense at first only to fill in some obvious gaps in current philosophical and theological discourse. At the simplest level, he wanted a way of talking about the sense of consanguinity and basic human adequacy felt in moments like the bare common experience. More technically, he wanted an ethical theory that could protect him from the ambivalence of Locke, the skepticism of Hume, and, most importantly, the savagery of Hobbes.[83]

By the time of *Nature,* however, "moral sense" seems to have a specific rhetorical function. Each of the four lower chapters discovers various levels of usefulness in the quality it studies. Thus, in "Beauty," objects delight in the simple act of perception, as signs of the higher beauty of virtue and as objects of the intellect. This general tripartite structure is most obvious in "Discipline," where the moral sentiment is contrasted to the purely objective "common sense" as the ethical character penetrating all nature.

> . . . every natural process is but a version of a moral sentence. . . . This moral sentiment which thus scents the air, and grows in the grain, and impregnates the waters of the world, is caught by man and sinks into his soul. The moral influence of nature upon every individual is that amount of truth which it illustrates to him. (P. 26)[84]

Yet although clearly important in *Nature,* moral truths are quite literally penultimate, always to be transcended by higher intellectual ones. Moral beauty gives way to intellectual beauty, much as in the Divinity School "Address" the beauty of summer and of laws gives way to the "more secret, sweet, and overpowering beauty" of virtue (p. 77). Moral lessons yield to the higher discipline of unity itself. But most important, the whole lower argument to which morality is bound in *Nature* is subsumed, virtually obliterated, by the introduction of idealism in the sixth chapter. The noble doubt merely makes the more gentle Platonism of the moral sense unnecessary, and ethics is reduced to the subservient role of helping idealism put nature underfoot.[85]

This subjugation is not permanent: although themselves purely epistemological, "Spirit" and the related notion of the God-in-me do foretell the eventual return of virtue. In *Nature,* Emerson is concerned only with epistemology, with "speculative Reason or philosophy." But he hints (in strikingly Kantian terminology) that there is also a "practical Reason or virtue."[86] In this epistemological context, virtue works only as a mediator, subordinating the world to the mind (p. 36). But the way in which spirit, though not itself a positive knowledge, "points to virtue" suggests that eventually Emerson will have something to say about virtue's independent activity (p. 38).

The Divinity School "Address" is that occasion when Emerson returns to these promises of "Spirit." Examining the same procedures from the point of view of virtue, he now looks not out from the mind on the world but in through the mind on absolute truth. The change in form is marked by the structural reorganization. In *Nature* moral sense suggested unity, which in turn suggested the noble doubt. In the "Address," although the lower argument still suggests the noble doubt, virtue appears not before idealism as the moral sense but after it as "duty." It is this new notion of duty or the "I ought" – embodied in a new third paragraph to replace the old chapter of "Spirit" – that is the essay's chief discovery and the heart of its theoretical introduction.

This shift in focus should not be read primarily as intellectual growth or a change of mind. Emerson has simply unpacked the "moral sense" to see behind the notion of a moral nature the notion of a nature of morality. The one is personal and psychological, the other universal and logical. Moral sense asks largely about man, morality about "ought" as a concept, even as a word. Yet the two notions are meant to be perfectly compatible, and the third paragraph, instead of going beyond the second, really only restates it in a different context.

The rhetoric, even the syntax, emphasizes the semantic equivalence of the two views. In Emerson's reformulation of the noble doubt, "But when the mind opens, and reveals the laws which traverse the universe, and makes things what they are, then shrinks the great world at once into a mere illustration and fable of this mind" (p. 76).[87] This syntactic formula of "But when A, then B" is one of Emerson's favorites, and might almost be called his preferred syntax of apocalypse. He first experiments with it at the end of *Nature*: "But when a faithful thinker, resolute to detach every object from personal relations, and see it in the light of thought, shall, at the same time, kindle science with the fire of the holiest affections, then will God go forth anew into the creation" (p. 44). This statement is more affirmative than most of the carefully circumscribed promises of "Prospects," and the first half of the sentence – with its talk of persons, objects, and thoughts – looks toward the formulations of 1838.

When he comes to rewrite this sentence for the Divinity School "Address," he simplifies the process by dividing it in two. In terms of epistemology, when man sees the laws, he recognizes the phenomenality of the world. But the same process has a moral dimension, and Emerson repeats the sentence in terms of duty.

> When in innocency, or when by intellectual perception, he attains to say, – 'I love the Right; Truth is beautiful within and without, forevermore. Virtue, I am thine: save me: use me: thee will I serve, day and night, in great, in small, that I may be not virtuous, but virtue;' – then is the end of the creation answered, and God is well pleased. (P. 77)

The two statements are not simply parallel: they are identical, as the identical syntax implies. The discovery of law that speculatively teaches the phenomenality of the world teaches practically the reverence of duty.[88]

Thus, although the third paragraph suggests a different focus from the second, perhaps even a different interest, it does not really depict a different model, a different world. And a theory of virtue that at first might seem to transcend the superficiality of the paragraph on idealism actually works to explain it. The identity of the two paragraphs and of the two apocalyptic formulae, however, really only points to the more radical identity within the statements themselves. For the two clauses of the statement are linked not causally but tautologically. Emerson claims not "if A, then (in response) B," but "when A, then (at the same time and by definition) B." A does not effect B but is identical to it.

If virtue is to be praiseworthy, it must be unconditioned and autonomous, carrying its own justification within itself. Its characteristics will exist instantaneously and eternally, not an "if/then" but a "when." The ought is not an "ought to do" any given thing: God is "well-pleased" with the intention, not its consequences or effects. Moreover, the ought is not even an ought "to please God." His "well-pleasedness" must itself be part of the ought – "oughting" must be what we mean by "pleasing God" – or His pleasure becomes only a "higher" consequence and duty a crass longing for His approbation, even admiration.

This issue of the autonomy of virtue is clarified in the second section of the introduction, a catalogue that enumerates "some of those classes of facts in which this element is conspicuous" (p. 77). The section is uneven, and the cogency of the explications varies directly with Emerson's ability to avoid the misleading vocabulary of temporality and sensation. In his first apocalyptic formulation he hedged about whether virtue was a state of "innocency" or an "intellectual perception." So, much of his subsequent enumeration wrestles with this Kantian problem of the "intellectual intuition."

Least successful perhaps is the explanation in terms of the unity of mind or will. The conflation of all values – love, justice, temperance – as parts of one mind seems simply reductive. The concept of one will is somewhat more complex. The argument here (as throughout the introduction) is structural: "will" identifies not a characteristic trait or effect but the way "things are made" (p. 78). Kant had noted that will is the only thing good without qualification. So Emerson concludes of his will that "good is positive." His subsequent conflation of that "good" with "benevolence" and rejection of evil as "merely privative," however, masks the purely formal character of good will. Any distinction between positive and negative – good will and evil – makes good will appear a thing that can be or not be, and thus flirts with the very subdivision of virtue he wishes to avoid.[89]

The discussion of energy is clearer on the autonomy of virtue. In a list ordered in terms of increasing epistemological importance, virtue is said to right wrongs, correct appearances, and bring facts into harmony with thoughts (p. 78). In both its forms – character and the affections – this energy is instantaneous and inherent. Like the "already" answered questions of *Nature,* character is "always" known. And the law's perfection necessarily expresses itself through the affections: "as we are, so we associate" (p. 78).

But (predictably) it is when discussing law itself that Emerson is most precise. The "perfection" of the laws of the soul – of which the moral sentiment is the "insight" – rests not in any particular characteristic but in their very self-contained nature. They are uncaused and "execute themselves" (p. 77). Not subject to the concepts of the understanding, neither are they to the intuitions of the sensibility, to "circumstance." They are quite literally "out of time, out of space." Their justice involves instant retribution, their enactment instant deification. The temporal emphasis is perhaps somewhat misleading. But here as elsewhere the language is prescriptive, not descriptive, with the instantaneousness of acts marking the tautological character of the statement. It is not a question of compensation – God's ultimately balancing every evil with a good. Rather, the just act is itself its own retribution: justice is identically what we mean by "being God," just as earlier the recognition of the Ought was tautologically the Christ and the "well-pleasedness" of God.

Both the merits and flaws of Emerson's exposition of his theory are epitomized in the final, most important class of virtue – the religious sentiment. The law of laws that awakens this sentiment is confusingly said to be "perceived." But this unfortunate choice of words is counterbalanced by the clarity with which Emerson depicts the nonreferential character of law. The sentiment is not really knowledge or perception but conviction, and the vocabulary moves beyond epistemology to a more Romantic "joy." "But the dawn of the sentiment of virtue on the heart, gives and is the assurance that Law is sovereign over all natures; and the worlds, time, space, eternity, do seem to break out into joy." In his infancy man "seeks to be great by following the great, and hopes to derive advantages *from another"* (p. 79). But when mature, he is able to turn and find all within guaranteed by "the deeps of Reason."

With the (long deferred) appearance of the Kantian "Reason," Emerson returns to one last formulation of his apocalyptic sentence. "When he says, 'I ought;' when love warms him; when he chooses, warned from on high, the good and great deed; then, deep melodies wander through his soul from Supreme Wisdom. Then he can worship, and be enlarged by his worship; for he can never go behind this sentiment" (p. 79). In this final variation, Emerson states precisely the element of formal necessity that earlier had been less evident. The soul's self-knowledge is not really perception – the sight of something else – but a simple declaration, the "I ought." Man can worship here because he must, because he has nowhere else to go. He cannot "go behind" his sentiment, presumably to the kind of "object" of worship that Ware longs for after hearing the "Address." For in practical terms the sentiment is the action, the declaration "I ought" the worship.[90]

The enumeration of the classes of morality, then, highlights the most striking characteristic of virtue's autonomy – its inherently active nature. Just as duty is identically worship, so the "I ought" is automatically an action. In this active practical dimension, it differs from its speculative counterpart, the "I think." The "I think" is purely formal, claiming that experiences must be owned without commenting in any way on the character of the owner. Grammatically it is transitive, always followed by a "that." The "I ought," however, is always intransitive: it neither requires a "because" nor permits one. Whereas experiences are innately personal, duties must be universal before they can be personalized. This autonomy makes saying "I ought" in and of itself a kind of promise, a declaration that something exists that should be done.[91] And after failing in "The American Scholar" and "Literary Ethics" to turn thought and scholarship into activities, here Emerson proves a theoretical position on virtue to be itself an activity – a duty-in-action.

The introductory section of the Divinity School "Address" works, then, to outline Emerson's theory of virtue. After summarizing the conclusions of *Nature,* he turns Reason from this speculative criticism of experience and epistemology to a practical analysis of virtue and duty. He examines various aspects of the moral imperative, in each case emphasizing its independence from external considerations of circumstances or effects. In a third section, he ends the introduction surprisingly, even grimly, with a myth of the fall.[92] At first the myth is stated only hypothetically: the moral sentiment as a principle of veneration is "sacred and permanent," surviving even in "man fallen into superstition, into sensuality" (p. 79). It is in the context of this vision of permanence that he first mentions Jesus, whose universal importance attests to the "subtle virtue of this infusion" (p. 80).

Yet the hypothetical fall is soon actualized by the introduction of the "one stern condition" – that the truth of virtue is an "intuition." In this generally Kantian context, the choice of terms is perhaps unfortunate; Emerson once again seems to imply the possibility of the very sort of intellectual intuitions Kant denies.[93] But his point is clear enough. The recognition must be direct, not received at second hand. Others cannot instruct me in this truth, but only "provoke" me to discover it myself. "What [another] announces, I must find true in me, or wholly reject; and on his word, or as his second, be he who he may, I can accept nothing" (p. 80).

The dependent clause with its lowercase pronouns, of course, implies how this doctrine will affect our sense of Christ and His teachings. But more important for the moment is Emerson's suggestion that the fall has already taken place. His verbs become increasingly immediate. He shifts from the eternal present tense of the previous paragraph to a predictive one. "Let this faith depart, and the very words it spake, and the things it made, become false and hurtful. Then falls the church, the state, art, letters, life." This imperative present then becomes the oracular voice of the Orphic Poet: "once man was all; now he is an appendage, a nuisance." And by the end of the paragraph, the present tense seems to describe an actual present, a consummated fall. Virtue is currently being denied to all but a few historical persons, and the "doctrine of inspiration is lost." Miracles, prophecy, poetry, the ideal life, the holy life – again the list increases in theoretical abstraction – become "ancient history merely" and therefore empty. "Life is comic or pitiful, as soon as the high ends of being fade out of sight, and man becomes near-sighted, and can only attend to what addresses the senses" (p. 80).[94]

The end of this paragraph – and of the whole theoretical introduction – does more, however, than announce the moral fallenness of the present generation. It doubles back to make our response to the voluptuousness of the introductory paragraph itself the proof of that fall. It is not simply that this luxurious opening does not belong in a commencement address or a Unitarian sermon. It does not belong in a theory of virtue either. This is the real reason it has been a "luxury" to draw the breath of life this summer: not because the air is so rich, or even because we need objects to exist as selves, but because we have become enslaved to the senses. Preoccupied with the smell of the meadow and the corn, we have ignored the higher "scent" of virtue.

The whole movement of the introductory section, then, serves to wean us from our love of that first sensuous paragraph. The world "in which our senses discourse" is, we are taught, comic or pitiful if we do not attend to more than what addresses the senses exclusively. The "delight" of history that ends the first paragraph is shown to be "history merely" in the last. And the luxurious breath drawn in the address's first sentence echoes throughout the introduction in the puns on the notion of "inspiration." Merely "to draw the breath" is too static, more pictorial than functional. For, finally, virtue is a "doctrine of inspiration." All things "conspire" with spirit, and truth measures the "aspiration" of society (pp. 79-80). True virtue does not absorb foreign influences: that is a doctrine not of inspiration but of "voices," the Holy Spirit turned spook (p. 80). Instead the emphasis is on the simple necessity of the act: virtue is life's breath – that without which nothing truly is.[95]

Thus the concept of the Ought carries with it its own kind of con-

straint. Man is at a lower level "constrained" to "respect the perfection" of the sensory world if he is to have any sense of self, an "I" that
thinks experiences. But more importantly, he is constrained to respect
"the perfection of the Law" (p. 78). The perfection, in ethics as in
epistemology, is not aesthetic but logical. Virtue, like experience, is
self-evidenced. Man, as Emerson says in his second apocalyptic sentence, is not virtuous, but virtue itself: his "I" is his "ought," just as in
Nature his "I" was his "think."[96] Duty, in this categorical sense, is not
the kind of thing that can be done for any particular reason – in obedience to eternal laws or because that is the way things have worked out
in the past. It simply must be done by definition; an unactivated duty,
like an unowned experience, is simply a logical contradiction.

VI

Emerson's introductory theory of virtue, then, has established
two basic points. First, virtue is autonomous – a law for its own sake. It
is intransitive and categorical, with a moral force deriving not from
external circumstances or consequences but from its own innate lawfulness. This necessity is logical, even semantic, and its universal applica-
bility is part of its form, something without which it would make no
sense. Finally, it is inherently active, and best expressed not as a nomi-
native "virtue" or "duty" but as the imperative "I ought."

The second point proceeds naturally from this initial premise of autonomy. Although virtue clearly has implications for the world of experience, it exists apart from experience, and man's knowledge of it is a
priori. There are really, then, two worlds in morality, as in epistemology there were the phenomenal and the noumenal. These worlds are
not hostile or in conflict: duty-as-action surely implies the necessity for
action in the world. At the same time, however, the two worlds are
philosophically distinct, and the logic and mechanics of one should not
be confused with the logic and mechanics of the other. Virtue quite
simply is one kind of thing and moral sense or conscience something
else.[97] And the rest of the essay attempts to sort out which world is
which and what response is appropriate to each.

Once Emerson's confusing positions on the autonomy of virtue and
the duality of the moral world are understood, the rest of the essay
offers few problems, but follows naturally as "abundant illustration" of
two current "errors" (pp. 80-81). Having predicted that man would fall
in two directions – into superstition and into sensuality – Emerson proceeds to outline the course of these two falls. The fall into superstition
is the less important error, because the more obvious. Here the church
substitutes some external standard for a self-validating virtue: rather

than realizing the "I ought" directly, the virtuous man is enjoined to imitate some outward sign of virtue, most temptingly the life of Christ with its double evidence of miracles. Perhaps the famous cry that "the soul knows no persons" is itself too personal a formulation: "the soul" seems a rather misleading term for duty-in-action. But the point is justifiable. Virtue needs no particularized standards, and the only things the moral can "know" are its own imperatives.

A better formulation comes in the short paragraph that follows, in which Emerson tries to relate the "I ought" to the language of "Spirit."

> That which shows God in me, fortifies me. That which shows God out of me, makes me a wart and a wen. There is no longer a necessary reason for my being. (Pp. 82-83)

The self-referring God-in-me makes my being necessary; the external God outside of me does not. Although the language and syntax clearly recall the earlier moment in *Nature,* however, the different emphasis reflects the difference between thought and virtue. In *Nature,* God was logically implied (in a purely negative way) as a ground for man's sense of self: since something thinks, therefore an "I" exists, with some sort of God behind that me. Duty, unlike thought, however, need not (indeed cannot) be owned; the God of the "Address" exists less in me than in the ought itself. "Obey thyself" really means that in doing duty I enter into the prior union of God and the ought; I make the ought "I ought," duty "my" duty, and thereby create a moral me, "give me to myself" (pp. 82-83). In both cases God must be in me, but in perception He need not be so completely there. In morality God is so identically duty that if He is outside me at all, the duty I thought done actually stays outside too.

The superstitiousness of historical Christianity, however, is finally only symptomatic. For superstition's substitution of a false moral standard for a true self-evidence is only a corollary of the more important error of sensualism.[98] The problem with false standards is not that they are false, but that they are not really standards. In the language of the two-world theory, sensualism takes the marks of a phenomenal, worldly piety to be moral noumenally. Such sensualism is the slander of "the Moral Nature." In Emerson's hands, however, this old Unitarian commonplace is transformed. No longer treating man's "internal evidence," as Channing and he had earlier, Emerson now sees the moral nature entirely in universal terms as "that Law of laws, whose revelations introduce greatness, – yea, God himself, into the open soul" (p. 84).

In restating his theory of the autonomy of virtue, Emerson is not simply returning to the theory of the introductory section. For in this central section – his explicit address to the graduating divinity students – his topic is not the noumenal but the phenomenal, not the soul but pastoral preaching. And what at times seems a traditional harangue on "The Dangers of an Unconverted Ministry" is actually a far more pragmatic account of the "condition" of divinity in the world, the "spiritual limitation of the office" (p. 84).[99]

The announced topic of preaching almost immediately gives way to the more universal one of soul.

> The soul is not preached. The Church seems to totter to its fall, almost all life extinct. On this occasion, any complaisance, would be criminal, which told you, whose hope and commission it is to preach the faith of Christ, that the faith of Christ is preached. (Pp. 84-85)

Clearly, the first sentence is a rallying cry, parallel to the earlier denial of the soul's knowledge of persons. Yet one might wonder whether the problem lies with the preachers or the soul itself. If, after all, the soul cannot be incarnated in people, neither can it be in words. If virtue is truly intransitive, then it cannot be externalized in sermons any more than in acts. The soul is not preached because logically it cannot be. And Emerson's case about preaching becomes less an injunction to preach the soul than to understand what preaching can and cannot do with respect to a soul that in its autonomy is basically inaccessible.

Although the argument is not trivial, this middle section of the essay clearly addresses a lower kind of activity than did the high-flying theoretical introduction. "Preaching is the expression of the moral sentiment in application to the duties of life" (p. 85). The language marks the shift in focus. "Duties" are not duty, nor is the "moral sentiment" identically the "I ought." And the word "application" puts us clearly back in the rationalist (not to say Ramist) world of the seventeenth-century theological textbook.[100] Man is indeed not made "sensible" that he is an infinite Soul, nor hears the "persuasion" that "imparadises" his heart. But as the vocabulary implies – especially the comic verb of transcendence – such spiritualization would be inappropriate in the world of sensation.

It is in light of this clear distinction between the noumenality of virtue and the sensualism of preaching that we must read the infamous attack on the Reverend Frost's formalism. There has always been an implicit contradiction in Emerson's position here. Having earlier attacked the personal doctrine of historical Christianity, he now seems to attack Frost for his impersonality. The "bad" preacher is not merely a dogmatist and formalist, but one who draws nothing from "real history," giving no indication of his family, country, culture, "or any other fact of his biography."

The capital secret of his profession, namely, to convert life into truth, he had not learned. Not one fact in all his experience, had he yet imported into his doctrine. . . . Not a line did he draw out of real history. The true preacher can always be known by this, that he deals out to the people his life, – life passed through the fire of thought. (p. 86)

The contradiction is only apparent. Experience, biography, and history dwell in the world of sensuality – of transcended luxury – and signal the extent to which preaching, unlike thinking or scholarship, is sensational. In exhorting the students to convert life into truth by passing it through the fire of thought, Emerson outlines not a noumenal activity – as he seemed to in "The American Scholar" and "Literary Ethics" – but only a phenomenal one. The joke about real snow and spectral preachers – like the one in *Nature* about flinging stones – only highlights the extent to which preaching, in its treatment of facts, thoughts, and history, is not morally transcendent. Although preachers may themselves operate on a higher plane of existence, their sermons belong to the phenomenal world of empirical realism. Such a clarification of levels does not denigrate the activity of preaching, for the personality that is impossible in the noumenal is necessary in the phenomenal. In the sensual world the preacher can imitate (at least negatively) the syntax of apocalypse: "Whenever the pulpit is usurped by a formalist, then is the worshipper defrauded and disconsolate" (p. 85).

Emerson's definition of formalism, however, does more than clarify the scholar's problematic relation to facts and thoughts. It redefines the proper, sensual role of Christ. Christ cannot attest noumenally to virtue: such a testimony would, however striking, still be secondhand and a posteriori. The historical Jesus and the formalist both "defraud" by pretending to impersonality, by denying their localization in time. Yet by implication, the very historicity that makes Christ too personal for noumenal virtue also makes Him the greatest of phenomenal preachers. Even His miracles, properly understood, have their function. It is not simply that they are "not one with the blowing clover and the falling rain," for epistemologically acts and clover are in fact "one," equally phenomenal (p. 81). It is only when asked to demonstrate an indemonstrable noumenality that they compromise the autonomy of virtue. Thus Jesus is virtually as great as the Unitarians claim; it is only a misunderstanding of the ontological status of preaching in general that causes the distortion. And the oedipal strife that infects the address ultimately is consistent with its intellectual point. Virtue does not depend upon an authoritarian external standard. Or, more simply, even the best preachers speak only for virtue, not as it.

There is, of course, an underlying irony (even tonal ambivalence) to Emerson's logic – one inevitable in a sermon on preaching by an ex-pastor about to stop preaching forever. Emerson's careful delineation of the spiritual limitations of preaching might suggest to his audience that they do not want to be preachers after all, that they want (in Emerson's academic pun) more than the "common degrees of merit" (p. 90). There is an implicit tension between his injunction to draw lines out of real history and his more orphic pronouncement later that "line is not in nature found." Nor would the insistence that the preacher delivers a historically localized message exactly console those brought up to be-lieve the true mark of divinity to be its eternal character, epitomized in Christ's historical dislocation.[101] And the awkward juxtapositions of the essay's conclusion, where the students are repeatedly admonished to act noumenally and to preach phenomenally, might finally seem counter-productive – even intentionally so.

But whatever the subtle undercurrents, Emerson's overt argument is clear and consistent. Virtue is autonomous and eternal, an intuition not to be learned secondhand. Preaching is a phenomenal, worldly activity, not teaching in any direct sense. Provocation, not instruction, is the only properly moral activity. But even this activity is not noumenal. Be yourself "a newborn bard of the Holy Ghost," but more to illustrate and acclimate your parishioners to a virtue with which they then must acquaint themselves "at first hand" (p. 90). Thus the ending, like "Pros-pects," takes away even as it gives. Since the remedy – both the efficient and the formal cause – is "first, soul, and second, soul, and evermore, soul," the current ecclesiastical structures, though not necessary, are surely adequate (p. 92).[102] Since the real activity is noumenal, the phe-nomenal locale is a matter of complete indifference. Moreover the Teacher awaited – who shall see the identity, the autonomy of the Laws – is really neither teacher nor person nor truly awaited. He is identically the list of his noumenal activities – especially his "Ought" – and happens not in time and for others but out of it and for himself. For the true advent is not of the Teacher, but of "the influx of the all-knowing Spirit, which annihilates before its broad noon the little shades and gradations of intelligence in the compositions we call wiser and wisest" (p. 91).

4

The revisions of self-reliance

Lively as readers find the intellectual muscularity of the early works, only with the two series of *Essays* is Emerson felt to discover his true voice.[1] Indeed, Emerson himself seems to agree, and even before publishing his first book on *Nature* looks forward to another, more important project.

> When will you mend Montaigne? When will you take the hint of nature? Where are your Essays? Can you not express your one conviction that moral laws hold? Have you not thoughts & illustrations that are your own; the parable of geometry & matter; the reason why the atmosphere is transparent; the power of Composition in nature & in man's thoughts; the Uses and uselessness of travelling; the law of Compensation; the transcendant excellence of truth in character, in rhetoric, in things; the sublimity of Self-reliance; and the rewards of perseverance in the best opinion? Have you not a testimony to give for Shakspear, for Milton? one sentence of real praise of Jesus, is worth a century of legendary Christianity. Can you not write as though you wrote to yourself & drop the token assured that a wise hand will pick it up? (JMN.V.40)

The paragraph is significant, and declares his intellectual intentions much as the earlier dedication to Dudleian eloquence defined his stylistic ones.[2] By 1840, of course, many of these projects are well underway: *Nature* and the addresses of 1837-38 have had much to say about the moral law, geometry and matter, the composition of thought, and atmospheric transparency. But other subjects – traveling, compensation, character, and self-reliance – still remain to be treated in this, Emerson's first full-length volume.

Modern preference for the essays, however, responds less to the topics than to the new mode of expression, the promise to "write as though you wrote to yourself & drop the token assured that a wise hand will pick it up." The earlier works seem at times too narrowly addressed to a specific audience and occasion, whether the imagined guardians of academic philosophy in *Nature* or the real-life oedipal figures of Norton and Ware in the Divinity School "Address." The essays are more experimental and personal. In the pun to which Joel Porte rightly calls attention, Emerson feels that he must "essay to be."[3] This intellectual freedom is matched by a new formal, rhetorical looseness. Unlike the earlier works, which are still closely tied to their origins in the sermons, the essays – it is argued – have no clear structure, no single argument.[4]

Again Emerson himself seems to support this interpretation. In revising the journals and lectures for publication, he protests that he is merely an anthologist, a compiler "arranging old papers," trying desperately to "spin some single cord out of my thousand and one strands of every color and texture that lie ravelled around me in old snarls."[5] His account of the last-minute tinkering is equally offhand.

> It is disgraceful when you thought you had done your chapters, to be obliged to waste days & weeks in parsing & spelling & punctuating, & repairing rotten metaphors, & bringing tropes safe into port, & inspecting suspicious places in your logic, and inventing transitions like solder to weld irreconcileable metals; and other such tinkering arts. (L.II.378)

We need not, in fact, take too seriously this comic self-deprecation. Actually Emerson made few changes in the galleys.[6] Moreover, whatever his mode of revision, the essays in their final, published form are more fully argued than is often thought.[7]

For, finally, the new tone and method represent less Emerson's changing his mind about his intellectual project than his sharpening his sense of its implications. The essays are not, of course, philosophical in quite the way the addresses were. Freed of the demands of a specific occasion – or even of a specific place in a lecture series – the pieces move casually over a whole range of topics, more anatomies or variations on a theme than systematic examinations of carefully delimited problems. But we must not confuse the method of the essays with their meaning, nor assume the heightened literariness to imply a decrease in philosophical interest. Emerson's "essaying to be" still allows him to say – even to assert and argue – and the aphorisms and organic structure have theoretic implications as well as stylistic ones. Unsystematic discourse is not unphilosophical, but instead a different kind of philosophy.[8] And the growing personal emphasis marks not only a new tone but a new topic, as behind the apparent autobiography lies a developing theory of personality and of the self.

I

Before examining the newness of the *Essays*, however, we must first recognize how much is old. The "I think" of perception and the "I ought" of duty have been sufficiently well established in *Nature* and the Divinity School "Address" that Emerson does not repeat here either demonstration. Yet their conclusions are taken for granted. The general concerns of the *Essays* are in fact extensions of those of the earlier works, and the topics, formulations, and rhetorical turns largely familiar. For – despite apparent claims to the contrary – continuity, even consistency, is Emerson's most striking intellectual trait.

Perhaps the most obvious continuity with his earlier idealism is Emerson's persisting attachment to the notion of one mind or, in its more mythic form, the One Man. Emerson had toyed with the concept of a universal mind as early as 1827, and it implicitly lies behind the Orphic myth in *Nature* of the God-in-ruins.[9] The fullest statement, however, is the myth of the One Man that opens "The American Scholar."

> It is one of those fables, which out of an unknown antiquity, convey an unlooked-for wisdom, that the gods, in the beginning, divided Man into men, that he might be more helpful to himself; just as the hand was divided into fingers, the better to answer its end.
>
> The old fable covers a doctrine ever new and sublime; that there is One Man, – present to all particular men only partially, or through one faculty; and that you must take the whole society to find the whole man. (CW.I.53)[10]

Here, in an uncharacteristically social version of the myth, Emerson argues first that the dispersed state of man requires cooperation among the disunited parts, and then that the scholar plays a special role as the mind of aboriginal Man – Man Thinking.

The essays, though less explicitly social, continue this general argument. Discussing early the desires of the dispersed "particular" man, "Compensation" builds to a vision of the unity of the "heart and soul of all men," of which even great men such as Jesus and Shakespeare are, like the farmers and scholars of the oration, merely "fragments" of an aboriginal "one" (CW.II.61, 72).[11] "Spiritual Laws" treats the same issue in the language not of the Phi Beta Kappa oration but of the companion Divinity School "Address." Rejecting "personal" ambition as mere "fanaticism," Emerson insists "that there is one mind in all the individuals, and no respect of persons therein" (p. 82).

The whole concept of an over-soul derives from such a notion of unity, depicted almost too graphically at the end of that essay as not a mind but a "heart of all": "not a valve, not a wall, not an intersection is there anywhere in nature, but one blood rolls uninterruptedly, an endless circulation through all men, as the water of the globe is all one sea, and, truly seen, its tide is one" (pp. 173-74).[12] But, of course, the most explicit statement of universality is the first – the opening paragraph of the first essay, "History": "There is one mind common to all individual men. Every man is an inlet to the same and to all of the same. . . . Who hath access to this universal mind, is a party to all that is or can be done, for this is the only and sovereign agent" (p. 3).

Yet it is not enough to identify the unity of mind as a leitmotif – even a first principle – of the essays, for Emerson uses this unity in many apparently different ways. He indicates the range of his interests in a journal passage outlining the "principles" for his upcoming lecture series on "The Philosophy of History," a series originally titled simply "One Mind."

> 1. There is a relation between man & nature so that whatever is in matter is in mind.
> 2. It is a necessity of the human nature that it should express itself outwardly & embody its thought. . . .
> 3. It is the constant endeavor of the mind to idealize the actual, to accommodate the shows of things to the desires of the mind. . . .
> 4. It is the constant tendency of the mind to Unify all it beholds, or to reduce the remotest facts to a single law. . . .
> 5. There is a corresponding Unity in nature which makes this just. . . .
> 6. There is a tendency in the mind to separate particulars & in magnifying them to lose sight of the connexion of the object with the Whole. . . .
> 7. Underneath all Appearances & causing all appearances are certain eternal Laws which we call the Nature of Things.
> 8. There is one Mind common to all individual men. (JMN.V.221-22)[13]

All Emerson's points can be related to the final principle that the universal mind is an absolute truth. And this principle not only becomes the center of the lecture series and the opening sentence of "History," but summarizes well the general approach to unity in the *Essays*. Yet in fact the corollary principles are more interesting, if only because more perplexing, and better represent the kinds of philosophical tensions that will characterize Emerson's subsequent works. The fifth principle, correspondence, is presumably a vestige of earlier interests and plays only a minor role in the essays.[14] More central are the remaining six, one pair of cosmic statements about relation and law, and two pairs on the processes of the mind – incarnation and idealization, unification and particularization. For in his manipulation of these six principles, which reappear individually or in groups throughout the essays, we can feel Emerson beginning to flex his intellectual muscles, see him trying to expand the original philosophical categories of the early works.

The first principle, of relation, is simply that notion of consanguinity with which Emerson (and we) began his epistemological explorations in *Nature*. In the lecture series Emerson insists that relationality accounts for *"how* man is strong." "His entire strength consists not in his properties but in his innumerable relations. There is nothing in the world that does not correspond to properties in him" (EL.II.155). The essay version of the same argument in "Spiritual Laws," though less direct, implies that the essence lies not in any specific personal traits but in a dynamic relation with the world. "My facts, my net of relations" are what determine my character. In this context, the unity of the world – what Emerson punningly calls "an identical nature" – merely explains how every man shares the potential for greatness: all are related to nature, and the conditions of that relationship are the same in each man (p. 95).

Yet Emerson is somewhat vague about the extent of this relation, the exact link between consanguinity and universal oneness.[15] The complexities are compounded in the second principle, of incarnation. Here questions of epistemology replace ones of ontology, and the propositional structure of relationality becomes its psychological necessity to human nature. The principle itself – man's need to embody thoughts in objects – is just a form of what we called in *Nature* the objectivity thesis. Yet with the logic of the noble doubt in our minds, we might wonder if man's psychological need for relationship does not create that relation, and if Emerson's first and second principles do not subtly undercut each other.

In the lecture series Emerson is clear on the extremity of the need. Man does not only define himself in part through relationships; without those relations he cannot exist.

> A man is a bundle of relations, a knot of roots, whose flower and fruitage is the world. All his faculties refer to natures out of him. All his faculties predict the world he is to inhabit as the fins of the fish foreshow that water exists and the wings of an eagle in the egg, presuppose a medium like air. Insulate a man and you annihilate him. He cannot unfold – he cannot live without a world. (EL.II.17)[16]

The essays are not, in general, so explicit on the necessity of world to thought, on the "predictions" of his faculties. Yet here too Emerson implies a necessary connection between things and thoughts in the concept of a "web of our unconsciousness," a fundamental store of relations from which man may select a fact, make it a subject of thought, and thereby objectify it into an "object impersonal and immortal" (p. 194; cf. p. 199). Even in "The Over-Soul" – at the same moment he insists that the soul "has no dates, nor rites, nor persons, nor specialities, nor men. The soul knows only the soul" – he admits, on the other side of the semicolon, the necessity of things to make thoughts visible: "the web of events is the flowing robe in which [the Soul] is clothed" (p. 163).[17]

A similar ambiguity about the causal relation between the universal mind and human nature infects the fourth principle, concerning the mind's need to unify all it beholds. Emerson has always had trouble describing the unifying tendency of mind. In *Nature,* the "tyrannizing unity" of consciousness pulled in two directions – acknowledging the transcendental unity of apperception, man's need to experience the world as stable, consciousness as one, and sensations as minimally his own; but more radically linking thoughts into the regulative principles of the transcendent Reason. Thus the logical unity of speculative thought was equated with the practical unity of noumenal morality. Similarly, in the essays, the principle of law functions at two levels – as the mind's tendency to unity and the universal orderliness that authorizes that tendency. At times law seems merely the mind's habit of classifying facts, the way in which "things are ever grouping themselves according to higher or more interior laws" (p. 107).[18] Too frequently, however, this tendency to order becomes itself a "fatal" ordering principle, the "Law" that makes the other "laws of cities and nations" (pp. 63, 59).[19]

These various tensions – between ontology and epistemology, psychological and semantic necessity, logical and moral imperatives – are most clear in the notion of compensation, which is central throughout the series, and especially in the third and fourth essays. Compensation claims simply that universal interrelation results in universal dualism. But everywhere Emerson hedges as to the status of the relation. At some level relationship is real, even material: all is related because (parodically) everything is made of "one hidden stuff," or (more seriously) because the relation of parts to the whole makes a "universal necessity by which the whole appears wherever a part appears" (pp. 59, 60).

But compensation as dualism and balance gives way to compensation as self-sufficiency, and the material necessity becomes a logical one. By this model God does not arrange a reaction for every action, but "every act rewards itself, or, in other words, integrates itself." Retribution is really twofold, and the circumstantial retribution seen by the senses is only the shadow of the self-fulfilling reality of causal retribution (p. 60).

Thus, in a move recalling the shift from the prudential morality of "Spirit" to the autonomy of the Divinity School "Address," Emerson rejects the otherworldly rewards promised in the doctrine of a Last Judgment (pp. 55-56).[20] Nemesis becomes less an avenging god of Give and Take than a self-affirming logic that "must also contain its own apology for being spoken" (pp. 63, 67, 88-89).[21] Yet here, as throughout the essays, logical necessity may be only psychological: what seems a statement about virtue is also a description of the self–the extent to which man cannot "be cheated by any one but himself" (p. 69).

The contradiction is only apparent. For as "Compensation" makes clear, both morality and psychology finally point beyond compensation entirely. And, borrowing his rhetoric from his beloved Dudleian lecture, Emerson ends his examination with a fact deeper than autonomy.

> There is a deeper fact in the soul than compensation, to wit, its own nature. The soul is not a compensation, but a life. The soul *is*. Under all this running sea of circumstance, whose waters ebb and flow with perfect balance, lies the aboriginal abyss of real Being. Essence, or God, is not a relation, or a part, but the whole. (P. 70)

Closing the self-evidential circle even tighter, he argues–as had the Platonists of the One (and God of Himself)–that all that can be predicated of unity is its being. Thus he moves beyond his four psychological principles about human nature to his seventh–that necessity is simply "the Nature of Things."

This principle is finally more radical than the other six. If the best example of self-evidence is the soul's being, then secondary instances, like self-fulfilling compensation, seem irrelevant. If necessity is cosmic, we cannot even talk about psychological necessity: the mind is forced to see things in a certain way not because of its own nature but because that is the way things really are. And it begins to seem as if the whole axiom of a Universal Mind and its psychological corollaries builds upon a series of puns in which the ineffable (in the earlier terminology "unspeakable") Nature of Things is conflated with the nature of reality (teasingly called the universal "mind") and the structure of the individual mind (teasingly called human "nature").[22]

II

The point, of course, is not to show Emerson's misuse of his philosophical categories, and certainly not to demonstrate intellectual discontinuity by an anthology of quotations that itself destroys any internal consistency the individual essays (not to mention the whole series) might have.[23] It is, however, important to see that in the essays, even more than in his early statements, Emerson works by paradox, ironic juxtaposition, and intellectual, even linguistic, conflation. Since his method is less to analyze systematically than to tease out apparent similarities and continuities from propositions, explication becomes increasingly difficult. It is clear that Emerson still examines the familiar concepts of apperception, objectivity, and autonomy. It is equally clear that his new more fluid tone and logic allow an energizing intellectual freedom in his treatment of these concepts. Yet the liberation at times seems extreme, and his capacity for paradox makes it hard to distinguish between interesting experiments and intellectual imprecision. To understand this new method fully, then, we must turn to the piece where he seems most completely in control of his ironies and juxtapositions – the much admired "Circles."[24]

The continuity between "Circles" and the other essays has not always been apparent, and "Circles" is often seen to mark a decisive shift in Emerson's career. As B. L. Packer rightly notes, it is the only essay in the series whose title is a process or pattern. Its topic is not a concept but a trope, a symbol that, in serving "to connect many illustrations of human power in every department," generates less a logical argument than a list (p. 179). Moreover, the tone is felt to be unusual – unsettled, restless, with a new sense of impermanence that brings out Emerson's more subversive impulses.[25] Yet such innovations in mode and tone should not obscure the importance of his meaning and rhetoric. Nor should the unsettled nature of the topic and the mutability of the image be read too quickly back into the form of the essay. "Circles" is indeed a great essay. And, as many have remarked, its imagistic invention and personal involvement are aspects of that triumph. But it is great for other reasons, too, reasons that perhaps better explain the general method of the essays and their overall place in Emerson's philosophical career. For this study of fragmentation is not itself fragmented, and when viewed as a whole the essay appears both more logical and less revolutionary than some of its parts might suggest.

The work has, after all, a perfectly clear structure and shape, and makes in its own desultory fashion a coherent argument. The basic premise, of which the essay's circles are the symbolic embodiment, is that there are no fixtures and that permanence is but a word of degrees. First, of course, there are no fixtures in nature. Emerson had insisted on such instability from his first works, at least so far as to establish mind's power over nature. Moreover, his next claim – that "the key to every man is his thought" (p. 180) – places this sense of fixturelessness within a specific intellectual tradition, Emerson's continuing interest in Presocratic relativism. That man (or, in Emerson's preferred formulation, "mind") is the measure of all things has been since the Sophists the traditional refutation of those realists, like the Pythagoreans, who believe that mathematical conceptions exist in a material universe.[26] Thus, in this first stage, he argues only the traditional position that "Line in nature is not found/Unit and Universe are round."[27]

Such relativism is "unsettling" only in a technical sense; a mere illustration of the mind's unifying tendency, it surely carries no psychological threat. The quick soul will resent all attempts by individual thoughts to solidify and hem in life. Every ultimate fact will be revealed as only the first of a new series; every universal principle as only one example of a bolder generalization.[28] But "the" thought that is each man's key, the idea after which all his facts are classified, remains itself inviolate, the constant center from which greater circles are generated. Fear not the new generalization, Emerson concludes.[29] The apparent attack on one cherished fact refines and raises another (pp. 181-82). And thus, at this elementary level, circles and compensation are the same theory, what at the start of the essay he called "the circular or compensatory character of every human action" (p. 179).

More emotionally unsettling than the lack of natural fixtures, however, is Emerson's subsequent claim that "there are no fixtures to men" (p. 182). Moods, relations, idealism, conversation, literature, religion, natural world, and virtue: all human traits illustrate man's essential instability. The list is admittedly an odd one. As everywhere in the *Essays*, the progression is not that of the overelaborate lower argument in *Nature*. It is unclear whether the examples are ordered in any incremental way, though the move toward "virtue" does seem both significant and characteristic. The treatment of the central topics of limitation and genius as subsets of the early category of "relations," however, is strained. And it is hard not to be surprised by the appearance of the natural world and its laws as a mark of man's lack of fixture, as if reality were a personality trait.[30]

Yet however idiosyncratic the list, Emerson has not at this point given up structure. It is important to remember that even the essay's most striking (not to say unsettling) statements are not individual observations but stages within an argument, illustrations of man's general fixturelessness. This is especially true of the most famous sentence in the essay: "I am God in nature; I am a weed by the wall" (p. 182). The formulation is so memorable that most readers hear in it a new sense of despondency, the recognition that man is really more weed than god.[31] Yet, in fact, his point is a familiar Emersonian (and Romantic) complaint about the inconstancy of temperament, and especially the infrequency of inspiration. The meaning and cadence, though not perhaps the intensity, recall *Nature*'s claim that the deifying relation between mind and matter "appears to men, or it does not appear" (CW.I.22).[32]

Similarly, we should beware overreading the apparent renunciation of idealism a page later. Here, of course, the statement is more extended.

> There are degrees in idealism. We learn first to play with it academically, as the magnet was once a toy. Then we see in the heyday of youth and poetry that it may be true, that it is true in gleams and fragments. Then, its countenance waxes stern and grand, and we see that it must be true. It now shows itself ethical and practical. We learn that God IS; that he is in me; and that all things are shadows of him. The idealism of Berkeley is only a crude statement of the idealism of Jesus, and that, again, is a crude statement of the fact that all nature is the rapid efflux of goodness executing and organizing itself. (Pp. 183-84)

The grim face here waxing stern and necessary seems far from the jubilation of *Nature*. Yet man's changing relation to idealism does not make the philosophy any less true, any more than the infrequency of inspiration made the moments of deification less divine. The little syllogism—that God exists, that He exists in ME, and that therefore all things are shadows of Him—explicitly reaffirms the argument of *Nature*, where the reality of spirit and the necessity of apperception established both the empirical reality and the transcendental ideality of objects.[33] And the move from Berkeley to Jesus to self-organizing goodness recapitulates implicitly the progress in the early works from epistemology to morality.[34] Indeed, idealism's presence on the list of fixturelessness reinforces rather than undercuts its centrality for Emerson. Only things presumed stable belong on a list exposing universal instability. Otherwise Emerson would seem to stack the deck.

But, in fact, transcendental idealism is even more central to the argument than this one paragraph would imply. At the end of his description of human instability, a skeptical voice interrupts him, arguing that he has arrived at "a fine pyrrhonism, at an equivalence and indifferency of all actions, and would fain teach us that, *if we are true*, forsooth, our crimes may be lively stones out of which we shall construct the temple of the true God" (p. 188). Emerson answers that he is indeed pleased that, by and large, things work out for the best. Yet not caring "to justify myself," he is less a prophet than a seeker.

> I am only an experimenter. Do not set the least value on what I do, or the least discredit on what I do not, as if I pretended to settle anything as true or false. I unsettle all things. No facts are to me sacred; none are profane; I simply experiment, an endless seeker, with no Past at my back. (P. 188)

This witty, allusive passage cannot be taken entirely seriously.[35] The skeptic's objection, which initially seems compelling, will not really bear examination. Emerson has nowhere claimed to transmute real crimes into real cornerstones, although he has said both that real crimes are self-punishing and that apparent crimes may appear holy in a higher realm. Nor is his own answer entirely straightforward. Even apart from his teasing allusions to Swedenborg, the claims to experiment and unsettle are disingenuous. As the previous pages have made clear, fixturelessness is not a function of man but a trait; the necessary movement is not generated by man, but by some unseen source defined mythically as a "flying Perfect" or, more tautologically, as the process of self-generation itself (pp. 179, 188). Nor is it entirely clear what the liberation from the "Past at my back" has to do with experimentation, which would surely require a minimal awareness of tradition, if only to distinguish the tried from the unattempted.

The rhetoric and language of this dialogue must be attended to carefully. Perhaps the images of lively stones and constructing temples refer back to previous passages where Emerson denied flinging stones and exhorted men to build their own houses.[36] More surely, the attack on equivalence and indifference recalls the role such concepts have played earlier in Emerson. In "Compensation," as we saw, it was the discovery of the "indifferency of circumstances" that uncovered the deeper fact of life.

> But the doctrine of compensation is not the doctrine of indifferency. The thoughtless say, on hearing these representations, – What boots it to do well? there is one event to good and evil; if I gain any good, I must pay for it; if I lose any good, I gain some other; all actions are indifferent.
>
> There is a deeper fact in the soul than compensation, to wit, its own nature. The soul is not a compensation, but a life. The soul *is*. (P. 70)

But behind both passages, and recalling them in tone, is the central Emersonian moment of the noble doubt as indifference: "What difference does it make, whether Orion is up there in heaven, or some god paints the image in the firmament of the soul? The relations of parts and the end of the whole remaining the same, what is the difference, whether land and sea interact, and worlds revolve and intermingle without number or end, . . . or, whether, without relations of time and space, the same appearances are inscribed in the constant faith of man?" (CW.I.29)[37]

The genealogy of the concept suggests two things. First, indifference in Emerson never represents stasis or paralysis, but only the logical impossibility of distinguishing between two things, the indifference of circumstances, surroundings, particulars. The inference in always positive and active. Whether Orion is real or phenomenal, I will reject the frivolous and treat it as real. Whether or not retribution is apparent to the thoughtless, virtue exists. Second, and more important, indifference is not only affirmative but the means by which the mind moves from one realm of reality to another. The very inability to determine logically the difference between things felt to be distinct is for Emerson proof that he is asking his question at the wrong level. One cannot distinguish between a sphere and a cylinder in a two-dimensional world. And so, indifference becomes a transcendental intimation of other worlds, other dimensions behind the perceptible.

Thus, as indifference moved Emerson in *Nature* from the lower argument of Paley to the higher one of Kant, and in "Compensation" from a prudential morals to an autonomous one, so in "Circles" the concept moves him from the fixtureless world of a generated man into the noumenal one of the generator itself. The shift is as explicit as it is subtle. Man appears fixtureless "if we appeal to consciousness," that is, in terms of transcendental idealism (p. 182). But in the realm of virtue, the noumenal is accessible. "When these waves of God flow into me," Emerson argues in a recollection of the eyeball passage, "lost time" is doubly lost. What appears squandered is compensated for by an infinite though instantaneous influx. And, more simply, the concept of time itself passes away with all other aspects of consciousness. Such omnipresence, beyond mere questions of "duration," "sees that the energy of the mind is commensurate with the work to be done, without time" – "commensurate" in the everyday sense of "sufficient" but also in the more exacting sense of "identical" (p. 188).[38]

Thus the noumenal response to the skeptical reader – delivered as much by a transparent eyeball as by any personal self – is highly deceptive. Out of time, the experimenter can honestly claim to have no personal past. But the discovery of the universality of progression is also a reification of the past, the recognition at every moment that what once was now has gone. And although the past is in one sense irrelevant, "no Past" as a null set – the everpresent awareness of absence – is the epistemological burden built into the very notion of succession. The progressive, circular man, without a past *at* his back, must always carry that awareness of loss, of "no Past," on it.[39]

The language – familiar from the noble doubt paragraphs and from their shared source in Kant – prepares the way for the next, even more recognizable move.[40] After the brief exchange with the skeptical reader, Emerson continues:

> Yet this incessant movement and progression, which all things partake, could never become sensible to us, but by contrast to some principle of fixture or stability in the soul. Whilst the eternal generation of circles proceeds, the eternal generator abides. (P. 188)

The casual "yet" should not obscure the importance of the intellectual shift. In part, of course, the claim seems simply common sense. A relatively stable backdrop is necessary to perceive change: if absolutely everything were in motion, there would be no standard by which to measure, no sense of something being one way and then being another. Yet Emerson is saying much more: in the phrase "by contrast to some principle of fixture," he clearly indicates his subject to be not "relative" but absolute stability, not any "perception" of things staying the same but the "principle" of permanence itself. He argues that without some prior concept of stability – the assumption that present reality is a modification of something that existed in an earlier form – change would be imperceptible.[41] The experience of progression entails the concept of continuity and behind it the principle of something mutable but stable, what he calls the "eternal generator."

Emerson's logic should by now be familiar as what we have called the transcendental argument – the claim that certain concepts are logically built into other concepts so that any subsequent attempt to separate them will be impossible. The very idea of transition presupposes the more fundamental one of stability, just as the image of an infinite series of concentric circles requires as its initial premise a stable (though not necessarily stationary) center. This argument that instability on the level of the "appeal to consciousness" must imply permanence at the higher level of soul is a traditional one – both in Emerson and in epistemology in general. In *Nature*, of course, the discovery of idealism immediately suggested the companion discovery of permanence. More strikingly, given the Kantian terminology throughout these final pages, in the Analogies of Experience permanence as "substance" is the necessary "principle" of all objects as they exist sensibly in time. Thus, paradoxically, the possibility of succession presupposes the existence of a more basic permanent substance.[42]

Whatever the philosophical precursors of Emerson's permanence, however, the real question is how to reconcile it to an initial premise that all is fixtureless and "permanence is but a word of degrees" (p. 179). Part of the answer, perhaps, lies in the falsely pejorative "but." When Emerson repeats the claim a page later, he drops the adverb and turns a valuative judgment into a semantic classification.[43] No one can deny that the word "permanence" does imply comparisons and standards, and none need conclude from that definition its unreality. Yet such verbal contortions suggest the need to reexamine the very concepts of circularity, unsettling, and succession. For the circle that started as an image of aimlessness seems increasingly to represent purposiveness, the assurance if not of a direction, at least of a generator. And what from the circumference may seem a model of endless succession is from the center an illustration of ubiquitous control.

"Circles" thus is more closely related to both the other essays and the earlier epistemology than was initially apparent. The essays have in one sense been full of intimations of circles. In "Spiritual Laws," to demonstrate that the soul's emphasis is always right, Emerson argues that the truth will always fulfill itself. His image for this impossibility of concealment is the circle, for from "an arc of the curve . . . a good mathematician will find out the whole figure" (p. 85).[44] More subtly, the notion of circularity is implicit linguistically in the prefices of "circumstance," "circumscribe," and of course "circumference." Emerson suggests that what seems to constrain may actually make meaningful, especially in his paradoxical use of "circumscribe," as both that which binds down and that which binds together, the limitation which enslaves and that which defines.[45] Concentric circles, rather than contradicting the optimism of the other essays, reinforce it, becoming themselves an image of the oneness present everywhere in the series. The final affirmation of the essay, which startles some readers, represents neither Emerson's characteristic digging in of his heels nor one more mood swing, but the inevitable working out of his first premises.[46] The initial hard line about where fixtures are not allows him to celebrate true centrality when it is located; it is the traditional denial of knowledge to make room for faith.

If "Circles" differs from the rest of the *Essays,* in fact, it is because it is intellectually more conservative, looking back more directly than the others to the original epistemological model of *Nature.* The general structural similarities – the tripartite division into world, consciousness, spirit; the dramatic shift in the transition from the second to the third stage; even the appearance of the concept of permanence as a presupposition of the final idealism – only point toward a deeper thematic continuity. "Circles" makes clear, as the other essays do not quite, that the necessity under consideration is logical and not empirical. However different the method, Emerson's topic is still the synthetic a priori – permanence and fixturelessness as categories of knowledge. "Circles" is finally not about how humans feel, or even how images work, but about what concepts are buried in other concepts. Its true intellectual allegiances lie not with the moodiness of "Experience," or even with the rhapsody of "The Over-Soul," but with the Kantianism of *Nature.* And we should not be surprised that the essay ends with a restatement in a muted form of the notorious apocalypse that annihilated snakes and prison houses. The context is admittedly a diminished one. By the same logic that turned the denial of history into an everpresent "no Past,"

Emerson warns that those who protest most loudly their escape from "black events" only keep the memory alive. "Vanishing" is too much to ask for. But the axis of vision still triumphs over appearances, if only as an apocalypse of fading and forgetting: "True conquest is the causing the calamity to fade and disappear as an early cloud of insignificant result in a history so large and advancing" (p. 190).

III

While tonally "Circles" may be something very new, then, it is intellectually something very old – an extended meditation on the logical place of permanence and substance in a world of flux. Critics are right to sense that something unusual is happening here. The strain, however, really surfaces only in the final paragraph, the moment after the apocalypse:

> The one thing which we seek with insatiable desire, is to forget ourselves, to be surprised out of our propriety, to lose our sempiternal memory, and to do something without knowing how or why; in short, to draw a new circle. (P. 190)

This definition of "seeking" is not what we might have expected.[47] Evidently one seeks not to approach a goal, or even to celebrate a process, but to simulate unconsciousness by pursuing something else. In the paradoxical phrase, man "loses" his memory not because it truly falls away. The past is, as we have seen, epistemologically inescapable. The very word insists on the impossibility of real loss; that which is "sempiternal" is not simply timeless, but cannot logically be created or destroyed.[48] Rather, man simply "misplaces" memory, drawing a circle in his wandering without himself having sufficient distance from the act to see either the figure transcribed or the center that generated it.

The brief portrait of the seeker is not finally central to the essay's overall depiction of generation and permanence. Yet this very extraneousness indicates Emerson's shifting interests. The tension in "Circles" between the dominant cosmological view and the more personal questions about what sempiternity "feels like" points toward a new topic in Emerson's epistemology, with the seeker a different kind of hero from the mythic Scholar or Thinker. Perception and duty are inherently impersonal concepts. Logical rather than psychological, the "I think" and the "I ought" are purely formal necessities yielding no positive knowledge about the status of the "I." Now Emerson, without denying this logical necessity, wishes to supplement his earlier studies by reconsidering the personality of that "I," more precisely called the "self."

Self is one of the most common terms in Emerson, both in the familiar hyphenates – self-respect, self-trust, self-knowledge, self-reliance – and in more troubled composites, like self-sustaining, self-possessed, self-authorized, self-subsistent, and self-existent.[49] In one sense, of course, Emerson had long ago resolved the issue, concluding from the start that in his pursuit of the absolute all mean egotism must vanish. An implicit hostility to "particular" persons is a ninth principle – the unstated, and for the most part unwelcome, corollary of the initial premise of universal oneness.[50] Yet without changing his opinion on their unintelligibility to the soul, Emerson increasingly comes to believe that there may be things to say about persons even after admitting that the soul knows them not.

Early in his examination of self, Emerson does not really distinguish between a personal and an absolute ego. Reference to the universal seems a way of validating the experience of the individual.

> I see no reason why I should bow my head to man or cringe in my demeanour. . . . When I consider my poverty & ignorance, & the positive superiority of talents, virtues, & manners, which I must acknowledge in many men, I am prone to merge my dignity in a most uncomfortable sense of unworthiness. But when I reflect that I am an immortal being, born to a destiny immeasurably high, deriving my moral & intellectual attributes directly from Almighty God, & that my existence & condition as his child, must be forever independent of the controul or will of my fellow children, – I am elevated in my own eyes to a higher ground in life & a better self esteem. (JMN.II.192)[51]

Minimally, such self-esteem permits mediocre singers moments of true majesty. Somewhat more boisterously, it allows Emerson himself to resist the antique charms of Europe: "Here's for the plain old Adam, the simple genuine Self against the whole world. Need is, that you assert yourself or you will find yourself overborne by the most paltry things" (JMN.IV.140, 141).[52] In neither case does the conflation of the personal and the universal seem especially dangerous.

Increasingly, however, these two selves seem discontinuous. In a justly famous passage from the journals, Emerson tries to define this problem of dualism.

> Who shall define to me an Individual? I behold with awe & delight many illustrations of the One Universal Mind. I see my being imbedded in it. As a plant in the earth so I grow in God. I am only a form of him. He is the soul of Me. I can even with a mountainous aspiring say, *I am God,* by transferring my *Me* out of the flimsy & unclean precincts of my body, my fortunes, my private will, & meekly retiring upon the holy austerities of the Just & the Loving – upon the secret fountains of Nature. (JMN.V.336)

The familiar rhetoric of transcendence, a more tangled version of
Nature's eyeball experience, gives way to an equally familiar complaint
against infrequency.

> Yet why not always so? How came the Individual thus armed &
> impassioned to parricide thus murderously inclined ever to traverse &
> kill the divine life? Ah wicked Manichee! Into that dim problem I
> cannot enter. A believer in Unity, a seer of Unity, I yet behold two.
> Whilst I feel myself in sympathy with Nature & rejoice with greatly
> beating heart in the course of Justice & Benevolence overpowering
> me, I yet find little access to this Me of Me. (P. 337)

Yet, surprisingly enough, the passage identifies the stumbling block as
not transcendence but personality: "Hard as it is to describe God, it is
harder to describe the Individual" (p. 337).

The inelegance of the pronouns indicates Emerson's growing uncertainty about the status of the ego. Earlier in *Nature* he spoke
merely of the ME and the NOT ME, vaguely implying that personal
feelings were ME, not nature. Here Emerson is much clearer on what
is purely personal – my body, my fortunes, my will. This clarity,
however, is achieved not by depersonalizing the ME but by subdivid-
ing it; the earlier dichotomy is now internalized wholly within the
ME to become a distinction between my ME and this ME of ME. Moreover the persistence of the adjectival "my" suggests that Emerson
may be trapped in an infinite regression: perhaps the ME of ME is still
too merely mine and needs further refinement to become the ME of
my ME of ME.

The final cry of the passage – "cannot I conceive the Universe without a contradiction" – wittily summarizes the multiple ironies Emerson
is beginning to uncover in his initial premise. First, of course, the
"uni-"verse, whose only condition is unity, seems nevertheless to split
apart. Furthermore, it is unclear whether the inevitable contradiction is
ontological or epistemological, a contradictory universe or a contradictory conception. But most important, the divisive element may be the
grammatical subject – the very notion of subjecthood. Emerson does
not fear personal incompetence, his intellectual inability to imagine how
a unified world might work. He sees instead that any "I" will force that
adjectival gap between experience and essence, implicitly labeling the
conceived universe "mine" and initiating the infinite regression.
Hume's skepticism about the objectivity of self may be faulty epistemology, but it does, as Emerson is beginning to sense, point to the
metaphysical bias of subject-predicate syntax. [53]

The problem of personality, then, is not merely that of inelegant
dualism, as Emerson tends to imply when treating the personality of

the deity.[54] For the bifurcation is as inevitable as it is inelegant. The only thing attributable to unity is, of course, unity itself. And thus what psychologically seems the infrequency of inspiration can be spoken of in logical terms as its exclusivity, the inherent struggle between subject and predicate in the phrase "I conceive."

> How many states of mind have I & those which are intense even in their mournful or practick influence, which refuse to be recorded. I can not more easily recall & describe the feeling I had yesterday of limited power, & the small worth to me of a day, than I could recall a fled dream. Only the impression is left; the self-evidence is flown. God has made nothing without a crack except Reason. (JMN.IV.362)

The very self-evidential character of truth that proves its validity also makes it useless as a personal point of reference, and man is forced by this universal "crack" to live most of his life at the lower level of the understanding and "impressions."[55]

It is in the context of this growing concern with the divided self that we must approach Emerson's most famous concept of self-reliance.[56] Emerson, of course, takes self-reliance in at least as many directions as he took unity. Fundamental to all is the need to resist outside influences. In the most famous early formulation, in "The American Scholar," self-trust, the scholar's first office, allows him subsequently to ignore convention and teach the oracles of Reason. Usually the threat is external, loosely called "society." "Let him not quit his belief that a popgun is a popgun, though the ancient and honorable of the earth affirm it to be the crack of doom" (CW.I.63). Consequently imitation becomes the most common failing. And true freedom is not the absence of all limitation but only of "any hindrance that does not arise out of his own constitution" (pp. 63-64).[57]

Yet, as the last phrase suggests, self-reliance teaches not only the rejection of external influences but the acceptance of internal ones. In part Emerson argues that the eternal in the soul will carry one over momentary lapses of judgment and commitment. Compensation works within the self as well as without, and the individual "has all the endowments necessary to balance each other in a perfect character; if only he will allow them all fair play" (JMN.III.198).[58] But at times he goes further to conclude from the eternal's support of the personal that the particular is merely the universal in disguise: "a soul in me infinitely beyond my art to puzzle out its principles."[59] Furthermore, occasionally the internal is simply praised for its own sake. In one of Emerson's most common arguments, man is exhorted to accept his own impressions in order to prevent having eventually to accept them as another's. The focus here is not on truth at all – the impressions are accepted in either case – but on mere pride, a defense against "mortification" (pp. 198-99).

Self-reliance, then, is a wide-ranging concept that Emerson uses in a variety of contexts for a variety of reasons. More interesting than these uses, in fact, are the reasons for his belief, the sources or grounds of self-reliance. In part, of course, the belief is empirical, even pragmatic, and warnings against the return of "rejected thoughts" merely offer encouragement to the timid. But whenever Emerson turns from the practice of self-reliance to its theoretical underpinnings in the notion of universal unity, the principle loses its ability to reassure.[60] Most often the unifying principle is religious, a spiritual union possessed only by the "meek."[61] In terms of the famous catch phrase, self-reliance is quite simply God-reliance.

Emerson explores these theological grounds most fully in an early sermon.[62] Proceeding from the text that "a good man shall be satisfied from himself," he sees self-distrust and a reliance on authority as the slander of God's gifts. "You are a judge of the truth or falsehood of any proposition the terms of which you understand." God "cannot make [man] perceive truth except by the use of his own faculties." In a striking anticipation of the Divinity School "Address" he explains,

> God does not use *personal authority*. It is the direct effect of all spiritual truth to abrogate & nullify personal authority, to make us love the *virtue,* & the person exactly by the measure of his virtues. God is no respecter of *persons*. Love is the reward of loveliness. . . . It is not his office, it is not his power, his renown, but his moral & intellectual being that are the objects of your regard. And these – how are these to be loved? *Only by means of yourself.* Yourself must be the mean through which only these exalted powers can satisfy your affections.

"A trust in yourself is the height not of pride but of piety, an unwillingness to learn of any but God himself." Therefore the doctrine may be safely preached "of a boundless reliance on himself[,] because that is a reliance on God."[63]

Obviously the specific model derives from Emerson's more general vision of unity, and especially from the related principles that every part is in the whole and that the whole is fully in every part. But as with Emerson's other statements about the self, the consequences of the doctrine are ambiguous. Throughout the sermon, the limits of self-reliance turn back on God to limit His exercise of power. Not only "cannot" He permit a knowledge beyond man's faculties. More simply, arguments for God's ignorance of individuals turn into ones for His unwillingness to use His personal authority. Thus the very self that God cannot respect becomes the sole "means" of perceiving His love.

The rhetoric is not, of course, really directed against God. But it does suggest how behind the theological controls on self-reliance lie more fundamental epistemological ones. Finally, the real cause of self-reliance is not spiritual omnipresence but ontological necessity, a limitation for God and man both. In the sermon, one senses the ominous overtones not only in God's entrapment but in the tautology that man may judge every proposition that he can understand. Emerson faces this problem of tautology directly in a journal passage three years later.

> Perhaps you cannot carry too far the doctrine of self respect. . . . For there is nothing casual or capricious in the impression [experiences] make (Provided always that I act naturally,) but they make this strong impression because I am fit for them & they are fit for me. (JMN.IV.317)

Emerson claims that this spiritual insight will not lead to antinomianism or even frivolity.

> Every man hath his own Conscience as well as his own Genius & if he is faithful to himself he will yield that Law implicit obedience. All these doctrines contained in the proposition Thou art sufficient unto thyself (Ne te quaesiveris extra) are perfectly harmless on the supposition that they are heard as well as spoken in faith. There is no danger in them to him who is really in earnest to know the truth but like every thing else may be a mere hypocrite's cloak to such as seek offence. (P. 318)[64]

The answer is an old one – that the limits are internalized as well as the power. But the solution is troublesome. First, the notion of fitting speaks more to the structure of the mind than to its content, proving not truths but processes. The casual tone suggests that perhaps the fittingness is not even epistemological but only linguistic, a definition of "self" as whatever the individual does.[65] More important, in assuring us of the harmlessness of the processes, Emerson has managed to internalize the dualism – to subdivide the self into cause and genius – without providing any guard against, or even test for, hypocrisy. Thus the overall effect of his argument is ironically to prove the inevitability of self-respect without demonstrating its desirability.

Increasingly the journals examine this self-validating character of self-reliance. "It occurred with sad force how much we are bound to be true to ourselves – (the old string) – because we are always judged by others as *ourselves* & not as those whose example we would plead" (JMN.IV.240). The objection here seems straightforward: we are judged by others' views of what we have previously been rather than by the example of what we would be. But, in fact, such stereotyping is even more inescapable, for exemplary action is as incomprehensible to the self as it is to others. "The truth is, you can't find any example that will suit you, nor could, if the whole family of Adam should pass in procession before you, for you are a new work of God" (p. 240). "Newness" implies insularity as well as independence, and a feeling of deracination overwhelms that of liberty.

Commenting on his temperamental differences from the fiery Fox and Penn, Emerson claims

> I see the World & its Maker from another side. It seems to me beauty. He seems to me Love.
>   Spiritual Religion has no other evidence than its own intrinsic probability. It is probable because the Mind is so constituted as that they appear likely so to be. (JMN.IV.364)

If, however, the mind's belief in spiritual truths measures not their self-evidence but its "constitution," then the consequences of self-reliance seem both morally empty and epistemologically fatal. The pragmatic tone of "you might as well trust your beliefs" turns hostile, and the return of rejected thoughts becomes less a minor irony than a grim description of the "nature of things," mortification as Nemesis. In this context, the original promise of freedom from all hindrances but those that arise out of man's constitution seems circumspect indeed.

The ironies (and tensions) in the concept of self-reliance are summarized in a late journal entry, written in October 1840 as the first series was in its final stage of revision.[66]

> And must I go & do somewhat if I would learn new secrets of Self-reliance? for my chapter is not finished. But selfreliance is precisely that secret, – to make your supposed deficiency redundancy. If I am true, the theory is, the very want of action, my very impotency shall become a greater excellency than all skill & toil.
>   And thus, o circular philosopher, you have arrived at a fine Pyrrhonism, at an equivalence & indifference of all actions & would fain teach us that *if we are true,* forsooth, our crimes may be lively stones out of which we shall construct the temple of the true God. (JMN.VII.521)

The passage is striking first for its cynical definition of self-reliance as a deficiency masquerading as a redundancy. The deficiency of the self, of course, results from its particularity. The source of its redundancy, however, is less clear: whether the soul's sufficiency is moral – a mark of God's participation – or logical – inherent in the very word "self" – all that is assured is excellency.[67] The teasing claim that inactivity is more excellent than activity – presumably because activity requires some sort of other, whether fellows, or tools, or only world – misses the point that whatever I do will be by definition part of my self.

More striking than this teasing deflation of the definition is the famous paragraph that follows it. The skeptic's anger actually seems more appropriate here than in "Circles": the argument has just claimed more than it should and concluded from indifference a kind of inverted superiority.[68] But, for our understanding of the essays, the specific contexts are finally less important than the general implications. That the objections raised (however fairly) against self-reliance should in the essays be made (however unfairly) against circularity suggests the complementarity of the two concepts. And we are forced to turn, if not quite away from the appealing "Circles," at least simultaneously toward the more problematic "Self-Reliance."

IV

"Self-Reliance" is, of course, Emerson's single most famous work, the concept and essay by which he is best known. Yet familiarity has in this case bred at least embarrassment, and critics have in general shied away from the piece.[69] The principle lies at the heart of most attacks on Emerson, especially those that find him antisocial.[70] Even admiring critics find it hard to be enthusiastic about the essay. His optimism here is at odds with what elsewhere seems the growing tragic sense. Nor, despite the famous sentences, does its style reflect the literary mode of the other essays. Its well-documented derivation from passages in the journals and lectures is all too frequently read as proof, if not of the work's naiveté, at least of its disunity. And ambiguous remarks about Emerson's "mosaic method" and the essay as an "anthology" of eight years' thought imply that the work makes no sustained argument.[71]

The objections, like similar ones we have seen, need not distress us too much. The empirical evidence is ambiguous; the essay is neither all that affirmative nor all that derivative.[72] Moreover the logic of these objections may not really hold. Personal optimism does not necessarily imply philosophical superficiality. Similarly, whatever the relation between ontology and phylogeny, the genealogy of the parts demonstrates nothing about their appropriateness to the whole.[73] The objections may, in fact, finally work more against themselves than against the essay. For if "Self-Reliance" is admittedly less personal, less imagistic, less organic than some of the other essays, perhaps this difference marks not the essay's failure but the general inapplicability of the categories. The real question, then, is not simply what makes "Circles" great but what elements of greatness the two essays share.

The answer leads away from the form of the essays and back to their theory. "Self-Reliance" is not a flowing piece but a tangle of jarring statements. This awkward mosaic, however, like the more carefully modulated circularity, has a rhetorical purpose. As the circles speed us gracefully on to the noumenal, so the jagged edges of "Self-Reliance" work constantly to undermine our fundamental assumptions about the self: as the one surprises us into a faith we scorned, so the other weans us of a confidence we cherished. In both, juxtaposition and logical shifts are the means by which Emerson makes his argument. The twice-told quality of this anthology of aphorisms is as necessary for its revolutionary conclusion as the intimate inevitability of the generating circle is for that essay's final celebration.

In one sense, in fact, the ironic, self-deflating structure of "Self-Reliance" is even more innovative than the organicism of "Circles." For the literal revisions of "Self-Reliance" made over the years in the journals (and recapitulated in the compilation of the essay) only anticipate the theoretical revisions of self-reliance the reader is asked to make in reading. Thus, in its very oracular tone, the essay actually demands a more personal involvement from the reader – every man his own editor. The goal of this impersonal essay is to work out the theory of personality only hinted at in the final paragraph of the more personable "Circles." And it is here, more than in the other famous work, that Emerson most explicitly moves beyond the theories of *Nature* and the Divinity School "Address" to the next stage of his philosophical program.

Emerson's revisionary motives are not immediately apparent. The opening paragraph at first sounds like nothing so much as a compendium of all his most familiar arguments. The call is once again to "originality," and the reader is given the standard lecture on his eternal parts. "To believe your own thought, to believe that what is true for you in your private heart, is true for all men, – that is genius. Speak your latent conviction and it shall be the universal sense; for the inmost in due time becomes the outmost, – and our first thought is rendered back to us by the trumpets of the Last Judgment." Predictably literature is dismissed as merely a stimulus to original thought. "Great works of art have no more affecting lesson for us than this. They teach us to abide by our spontaneous impression with good-humored inflexibility then most when the whole cry of voices is on the other side" (CW.II.27).

Yet for all its seeming familiarity, the paragraph consistently, even wryly, undermines Emerson's customary stance. Its tone qualifies more than reinforces the hortative rhetoric of "The American Scholar." The universality of man's convictions signals only some cyclic process during which the inmost by and by becomes outmost. That this universalizing apocalypse is here "the trumpets of the Last Judgment" might worry the suspicious. Does the advocated idealization only serve to hasten the final end?[74] The admission that Allston's verses instill a sentiment "of more value than any thought they may contain" seems oddly out of joint with the assertions of the divinity of man's idiosyncratic thought. Even the claims for genius seem ambiguous: what man speaks from his private heart is not Reason but only universal "sense," and the spontaneity he feels within is actually from without, not an intuition but an "impression."[75]

The clearest sign of the new perspective is the subtle transformation of the topos of the rejected thought. As elsewhere in Emerson, it is unclear for what reason we are to "abide" by our spontaneous impressions: is it that man should therefore accept his thoughts; or only that he might as well accept them; or even that he necessarily must accept them? But, more important, such abiding in spontaneity does not really solve the problem Emerson poses. In his timidity, man "dismisses without notice his thought, because it is his" (p. 27). Spontaneous acceptance, however, sidesteps the crucial issue of ownership by asking man to accept instantaneously an idea before asking whose it is. Only if man first recognizes his thought as his and then believes it to be true can he demonstrate the kind of genius Emerson advocates.

His revisionary ironies become clearer in the second paragraph, where Emerson explicitly rewrites previous formulations. Power becomes increasingly remote and man's role in the apocalypse – as the verbs attest – predominantly a passive one. The "corn" that in the Divinity School "Address" was "freely dealt to all" is now the "nourishing corn" that comes only "through his toil bestowed on that plot of ground which is given him to till." The roving eye of Nature itself is controlled: "the eye was placed where one ray should fall, that it might testify of that particular ray" (p. 28).

Most important, given the centrality of self-trust in "The American Scholar," the universal mind of that essay has disintegrated into a merely symmetrical monadology. Earlier unity was absolute, and the two concepts of identity and harmony were mutually exclusive. "But for the evidence thence afforded to the philosophical doctrine of the identity of all minds, we should suppose some pre-established harmony, some foresight of souls that were to be, and some preparation of stores for their future wants, like the fact observed in insects, who lay up food before death for the young grub they shall never see" (CW.I.58).[76] Now – with his growing sense of the individuality, even the insularity, of selves – Emerson accepts the discontinuity and grounds the truth of individual impressions precisely in such a "preëstablished harmony." "We but half express ourselves, and are ashamed of that divine idea which each of us represents. It may be safely trusted as proportionate and of good issues, so it be faithfully imparted, but God will not have his work made manifest by cowards" (p. 28). Man still "represents" the divine, but less in the sense of "standing for" than in the sense of "sending back." Man trusts himself not so much courageously or even jubilantly as "safely."

Emerson's distance from his own affirmation is most obvious in the climactic third paragraph.

> Trust thyself: every heart vibrates to that iron string. Accept the place the divine Providence has found for you; the society of your contemporaries, the connexion of events. Great men have always done so and confided themselves childlike to the genius of their age, betraying their perception that the absolutely trustworthy was seated at their heart, working through their hands, predominating in all their being. And we are now men, and must accept in the highest mind the same transcendent destiny; and not minors and invalids in a protected corner, not cowards fleeing before a revolution, but guides, redeemers, and benefactors, obeying the Almighty effort, and advancing on Chaos and the Dark. (P. 28)

Self-trust has, since the days of the oration, been the scholar's first duty, and it rhetorically serves that function here.[77] Yet Emerson's formulations are less compelling than those earlier in his career. Although individual geniuses "confide" their individuality to the "genius" of the age, the confidence only divides them from the trustworthiness within themselves. It becomes a mere "perception," the "betrayal" of which may be not a metaphoric "revealing" but a more literal "desertion." A similar remoteness infects the syntax of the paragraph's initial promise: "Trust thyself: every heart vibrates to that iron string." The imperative is not spoken directly in the essay by either Emerson or a more oracular voice. Instead it is a remembered slogan, implicitly in quotation marks – an echo of a former rhetoric, to which hearts sympathetically vibrate but which they no longer actually hear.[78] Moreover, when translated back into Emerson's proper voice in the next sentence, independence becomes acceptance – of circumstances, society, fate. Thus is apparent antinomianism reconciled to authority. Our originality merely imitates the originality of past masters. Individualism is advocated only because "great men have always done so." And the "guides, redeemers, and benefactors" of man are not those who speak the truth, or even see it, but those who "obey" (p. 28).

The same ambivalence informs the next section – on nonconformity. Initially the emphasis on time confuses. Infants are most self-reliant, boys still sufficiently so. Moreover, the attack on society as a joint-stock company in conspiracy against its members misleads by substituting a symptom for a cause.[79] But, as Emerson makes clear, the problem is finally not biological or social but epistemological. Man is "clapped into jail by his consciousness."

> As soon as he has once acted or spoken with eclat, he is a committed
> person, watched by the sympathy or the hatred of hundreds whose
> affections must now enter into his account. There is no Lethe for this.
> Ah, that he could pass again into his neutrality! (P. 29)

The first of many antiphilanthropic puns, "commitment" is an inevitable condition of personality, just as some imitation is the inescapable
result of using a common language. Although Emerson focuses on
those who "watch" to see man's next move, clearly the individual is
himself equally to blame. Without a minimal commitment–attachment
to remembered predicates–the acting subject would have no personal
identity but only a grammatical one.[80]

The allusion to Lethe at this point is suggestive. Usually amnesia
makes Emerson forget his greatest thoughts, threatening his general
trust by intimating an approaching apocalypse.[81] Here, however, the
problem is almost the opposite. History, in its most personal form as
the memory of individual experiences, automatically enslaves. What the
waters are to wash away is not divine inspirations but all particularity.
Man seeks not prophecy, or even youthful innocence, but simple obliv-
ion, "neutrality." In fact Emerson recognizes that, unlike the other, this
Lethe does not exist. But the longing for personal annihilation sharply
qualifies the apparent arrogance of nonconformity.

The section ends with a long (and notorious) summation.

> Whoso would be a man must be a nonconformist. . . . Nothing is at
> last sacred but the integrity of your own mind. Absolve you to your-
> self, and you shall have the suffrage of the world. (Pp. 29-30)[82]

Predictably the reason for the necessity of conformity is left unclear.
And, as always in Emerson, the most important word in the passage–
"integrity"–is also the vaguest. In part Emerson claims only the necessity of apperception and owned experiences. But both "sacred" and
"your own" point beyond epistemology to, on the one hand, a noumenal morality and, on the other, an individual dimension to thought.
These hints of a personal deification, however, are immediately withdrawn. Whatever the mechanism by which man absolves himself to
himself, the results are considerably less than in the journal original,
where self-absolution allowed him to "ray out light & heat,–absolute
good" (JMN.IV.275).[83] Now man wins only the suffrage of the world.
The language cuts two ways. First, of course, Emerson insists, as he
does throughout, that nonconformity properly understood is universal
obedience.[84] But more important, as the political "suffrage" wittily
suggests, man will be getting the votes of the very company he con-
temns, and a self-reliant nonconformity may not truly liberate but only
elect him chairman of the board.

As before, the concept is better defined in terms of why man does it than what it gets him. In the first of the essay's many responses to the charge of antinomianism, Emerson answers the "valued adviser" who worries that internal impulses may be demonic.[85]

> I remember an answer which when quite young I was prompted to make to a valued adviser who was wont to importune me with the dear old doctrines of the church. On my saying, What have I to do with the sacredness of tradition, if I live wholly from within? my friend suggested – "But these impulses may be from below, not from above." I replied, "They do not seem to me to be such; but if I am the Devil's child, I will live then from the Devil." No law can be sacred to me but that of my nature. (P. 30)

The most obvious answer to the friend's objections – that they do not seem so – is passed over very quickly. Evidently Emerson is willing to concede the subjectivity of moral judgments. Instead he takes a different tack: " 'if I am the Devil's child, I will live then from the Devil.' " The theological language is misleading, for the response is spurious demonology: all theologians would distinguish between demonic influences and demonic possession, between doing wrong and being Satan.[86] Despite his metaphor, Emerson is really substituting an epistemological determinism for a theological one and, rewriting the claim earlier in the paragraph, acknowledges that "no law *can* be sacred to me but that of my nature" (my emphasis).

But he goes even further, suggesting the problem to be as much linguistic as epistemological.

> Good and bad are but names very readily transferable to that or this; the only right is what is after my constitution, the only wrong what is against it. A man is to carry himself in the presence of all opposition as if every thing were titular and ephemeral but he. I am ashamed to think how easily we capitulate to badges and names, to large societies and dead institutions. Every decent and well-spoken individual affects and sways me more than is right. (P. 30)

The problem is not simply "my nature" and "my constitution," but more precisely that aspect of subjectivity by which it makes everything, including morality, "but names very readily transferable to that or this." The mind is nominalist only transcendentally, acting "as if" all were "titular" except its own operations. Yet its idealizing tendency is all too effective. We are too easily swayed by the speech of individuals and capitulate too quickly to mere badges and names.

To defend himself against this potential nominalism, which he associates particularly with speech, Emerson invokes the talismanic power of the written over the spoken. "I would write on the lintels of the door-post, *Whim*" (p. 30). The statement is not a declaration of overt antinomianism, parallel to the earlier claim to be a chartered libertine. The word "whim" does not accurately describe an absolute state: in the context of this relativist paragraph, such confidence would be absurdly misplaced.[87] Instead it is merely the engraving of an indeterminate sign, one itself chosen for its celebration of arbitrariness. Emerson writes the word not because whim is the thing sought, but because to claim to pursue anything more would be hubris. It is the act and not the sign's definition that is crucial; he in fact hopes that his interpretation is wrong, that it is more than whim after all.[88] But once the minimal affirmation – not of meaning but of meaningfulness – is made, he refuses to comment further. However inadequate, "whim" is a sufficient guard against nominalism and, for the rest, we cannot spend the day in what we would now call meta-explanation.

Yet such nominalism really only points to a more fundamental tension between the notions of conformity and personality. We usually define a person in terms of his peculiar traits, and especially particular intentions, of which whims are arguably the slightest – the smallest attributable expression of personal identity.[89] Such a definition is not pragmatic but necessary: it is only by the unusual characteristics that we can distinguish between otherwise identical substances. That person A, like everyone else, does X cannot help to identify which person A is. In terms of intentions, only the extraordinary – the perverse or the whimsical – is even visible: from the outside, it is impossible to tell whether someone does intentionally something that was bound to happen whether he intended it or not. By this light the conflict between personality and conformity is not moral but logical: an absolutely conforming person would be not unoriginal or self-distrustful but literally indistinguishable from the masses, scarcely a person at all. And thus, in some quite precise sense, he who would be visibly a man must indeed be a nonconformist.[90]

But nonconformity is itself not a very useful criterion for identifying character. The tension, as Emerson realizes, is not really between conformity and personality, but between personality and predictability. The nonconformist, to the degree that he is perfectly predictable, is as undistinguished (almost as indistinguishable) as the conformist. In its point-by-point inversion of society's categories, anticonformity actually valorizes them; solitude and society equally recognize the world's opinion. Thus conformity is doubly a game of blindman's buff. To those searching for some external "community of opinion," it is disastrously self-alienating. But it is equally so for those running away, and in rejecting wholesale the preacher's message, Emerson himself conforms. The preacher–who after all is no less "pledged to himself" than the nonconformist–fails by offering predictable moralisms. But Emerson is also guilty, for in his prediction of the preacher's message he actually preaches in anticipation the same sermon (p. 32).[91] True nonconformity is neither social nor antisocial. Better called "a-" or "un-conformity," it is simply a willed indifference to the category, a solitude in the middle of the crowd (p. 31).

Emerson's denials may, however, finally prove too much; by the end of the confrontation between the preacher and the skeptical Emerson, both conformity and nonconformity seem emptied of meaning, little more than theological puns. Emerson clarifies his position in his treatment of the related "other terror" of consistency. For his objection to consistency is, as that to conformity was not quite, purely a logical one. In one sense, of course, consistency is merely conformity internalized, and to attend to it too closely is to search for more personal communities of opinion. Tempted to "rely on [his] memory alone," man walks not simply with the past at his back but with his head constantly looking over his shoulder. Such excessive retrospection creates a phantom self, a hobgoblin. "With consistency a great soul has simply nothing to do. He may as well concern himself with his shadow on the wall" (p. 33). Not only is such self-scrutiny psychologically counterproductive and boring: it is in some absolute sense impossible, for the self that watches is included (or at least reflected) in the shadow it sees. The grammatical difference between the words is indicative: although one can intransitively "conform," one simply cannot "consist." Conformity may make the person invisible. But consistency does not make him even that; it poses an intellectually incoherent model of relation.

At the same time as the notion of consistency clarifies Emerson's theoretical objection, however, it also qualifies it. For, however confused a concept, consistency is necessary to self-identity in a way that conformity is not. It is true that checking up on one's own consistency is impossible, a kind of Humean shadow boxing. But without a minimal degree of consistency, that self cannot be identified (from within or without) as a single entity. The real problem with inconsistency is that it leads not to misunderstanding but to no understanding whatever. A wholly inconsistent self, as Emerson explains earlier, could not even be seen: "The eyes of others have no other data for computing our orbit than our past acts" (p. 33). Personal history provides the basic permanence against which variations can be measured. Without such an "orbit" we would not be distinguishable as the same person from moment to moment.[92]

Thus consistency, and to a lesser extent conformity and commitment, all pose the same kind of problem: though none will serve as a point of reference, being in some fundamental sense unexaminable, they are all nevertheless necessary – the logical conditions of constancy, permanence, and substantiality on which the self is grounded and without which it could not be. The great soul may have "nothing to do" with consistency; but if it is not itself minimally consistent, it cannot be the same "the." Like the lintel inscription, even the most mutable content must be contained within a relatively stable context, the most whimsical utterance within an utterable language.[93]

The contradictions inherent in the notions of commitment, conformity, and consistency are not resolved in this first section of the essay, which works only to undermine the reader's overconfidence in the power of self-reliance. A solution is, however, hinted at indirectly in Emerson's troublesome treatment of virtue. Virtue, of course, poses a problem for self-reliance, for the basically philanthropic orientation of the one seems at odds with the antisocial implications of the other. In response, Emerson tries to argue for the equivalence of the two by equating self-reliance's nonconformity with virtue's autonomy. At first, the conflict between virtue and conformity seems merely empirical, even historical. "In the popular estimate," it is generally admitted that virtues are nonconformities, "rather the exception than the rule" (p. 31). But this quantitative difference gives way to a qualitative one. Not only are virtues unnecessary, but they must advertise their unusualness if they are to be believed sincere. Just as your personality must be at least whimsical to be identifiable, so "your goodness must have some edge to it – else it is none," a mere word (p. 30).

Yet, in its autonomy, virtue is cut off from more than society and convention. It is also alienated from its source, the virtuous man. In part the problem is society's falsely prudential view of virtue. "There is the man *and* his virtues. . . . Their virtues are penances. I do not wish to expiate, but to live. My life is for itself and not for a spectacle" (p. 31). But the problem also involves virtue's essential autonomy. As in the Divinity School "Address," so here any duty that implies a "because" or even a "that" is insufficiently self-motivated. And thus, in light of Emerson's earlier moral theory, his outrageously misanthropic question – "are they *my* poor?" – makes a kind of grammatical sense (p. 30). Once again he objects that the possessive pronoun divides the subject from the very thing it was to possess. The notion of "my poor" creates a dualism of "mine" and "poor" when it means to assert simple unity and "spiritual affinity." And in the process the essential self-evidentiality of virtue is lost.

The situation is, however, more complex. For a prudential theory of virtue, though perhaps bad moral theory, seems good epistemology. If we regret what the division of man from his virtues does to ethics, we must admit that such attribution of traits to an individual is a necessary stage in individuation. In some sense we need the man *and* his virtues so that we can have the man *because* of his virtues. The claim, then, that "what I must do, is all that concerns me, not what the people think" cuts two ways (p. 31). What man does is, of course, more interesting than what people think of it. But, at the same time, what man does is what "concerns" or is appropriately attributed to him. Whatever the absolute ontology of the ought, man's assertion of it is the primary means by which he becomes visible to others.[94]

Emerson wishes to refuse even this minimal referentiality. But, in so doing, he moves the discussion abruptly away from virtue and toward life.

> I do not wish to expiate, but to live. My life is for itself and not for a spectacle. . . . I ask primary evidence that you are a man, and refuse this appeal from the man to his actions. I know that for myself it makes no difference whether I do or forbear those actions which are reckoned excellent. (P. 31)

Perhaps the shift is not so dramatic as it seems: the reflexive "for itself" and "for myself" may indicate that, as in *Nature*'s world of transcendental idealism, the indifference of action and virtue only measures the mind's inability to distinguish. Yet the shift still indicates the direction in which Emerson is headed. The notion of "my life for itself" suggests that it is not merely virtue that is autonomous but the self itself. Man's angle of vision offers no help in proving the existence of the self. To make life "for a spectacle" is to repeat Hume's proliferation of selves. In terms of existence – "for myself" – there is "no difference" between doing and forbearing action. What is needed instead is "primary evidence," which resides only in the simple existential predicate. "Few and mean as my gifts may be, I actually am, and do not need for my own assurance or the assurance of my fellows any secondary testimony" (p. 31).

Thus Emerson's apparent misanthropy may have an even deeper source than we suspected. The poor are not mine because an autonomous virtue cannot be subdivided into "my" and "poor." More simply, if *"my* poor" means anything, it does so because "my" had a meaning before "poor" was attributed to it. The problem of philanthropy and selfhood is what Emerson earlier called that of the operose proof. Virtue, neither good nor bad, simply cannot tell us anything about the self. If my poor are truly mine, the real source of selfhood must lie elsewhere. And if so, why then shall I not go to my own self at first?

V

The whole first section of the essay, then, works to undercut the reader's expectations and alert him to the new limits of the once boundless power of self-reliance. Increasingly self-reliance becomes something not to celebrate but to explore. The question is less what results from self-reliance than why it works at all, less how man should rely on the self than what it is on which the self itself relies. Action is viewed not in terms of morality but as a clue to the presence of something more fundamental; and to the traditional categories of thought and duty – the "I think" and the "I ought" – Emerson adds the more fundamental one of existence – the "I am." Despite its theological resonances, however, this assertion of self-existence is not one more insistence on potential divinity or a pipeline to the absolute. For, as the second and third sections of the essay indicate quite clearly, the self is not, like the other two, logically necessary, and its autonomy derives less from universality than from an almost recalcitrant particularity.

The change in tone is shockingly abrupt. After the "unrelieved *forte*" of the opening section with its two notorious paragraphs, Emerson gives it all away by admitting the affirmations to be empty, even tautological.[95] "I suppose no man can violate his nature" (p. 34). The casualness of the "I suppose" suggests a weariness with his previous mode of analysis: it has not been wrong, merely obvious and beside the point. Who are you, Emerson wonders, when you are allegedly out violating your nature?[96] The sentence does more than announce a tonal shift. It implies that the subsequent examination will be quite narrowly epistemological. After all, it is only in a precise philosophical context that self-violation is impossible. In everyday language, suicide is not a logical contradiction, and a man might easily be said to violate his nature by acting against his own best interests or even counter to custom. The very notion of tautology is a technical one; contradictions are never necessary, but only ironic, even whimsical.

The rest of the paragraph outlines the new philosophical topic – the sources of the stability of self. In *Nature* will was insignificant in "an impression so grand as that of the world on the human mind" (CW.I.8). Here it is subordinated to the greater law not of nature, but of man's being. "Character teaches above our wills" (p. 34).[97] What follows is a series of definitions of "character" – that is, self seen not absolutely but working in the world, what Emerson earlier called man's "orbit." Character is, he explains in a somewhat misleading simile, like an acrostic, not because it is constructed to read identically in all directions, but because it is by definition always itself. With distance the zigzag of variety disappears in the one tendency that unites all. This tendency does not imply a greater oneness behind itself, but only the way in which things "average" out.[98]

More suggestive than this visual metaphor is the concept of explanation itself. "Your genuine action will explain itself and will explain your other genuine actions. Your conformity explains nothing" (p. 34). In part Emerson is still answering the valued adviser, telling him that if an action is not self-validating, all subsequent explanations will be external and wasteful. Trading on his earlier notion of the invisibility of conformity, Emerson distinguishes between the genuine and the conforming act, unfairly collapsing empirical and intentional conformity—looking like and doing as. He thus denies the existence of a very important intermediate position, the genuine act that nevertheless "conforms" by choosing to do the accepted action.[99]

This conflation, however, does not really invalidate the overall argument. Emerson at this point is less concerned with self-explanation than with the more general notion of explanation itself. Earlier man was said to "represent" the divine idea, and later his failure to "correspond" to a tower-building force will lead to self-doubt. The problem, Emerson implies, is that man misunderstands his relationship to the world. He need not mirror it in any outmoded Swedenborgian sense of microcosm and macrocosm. It is sufficient that he "explain" it, that is, give it a context in which it can be described. In terms of the ubiquitous circle imagery, man is the center by which all is measured, though not necessarily the power from which it is generated.

> I will stand here for humanity, and though I would make it kind, I would make it true. . . . a true man belongs to no other time or place, but is the centre of things. Where he is, there is nature. He measures you, and all men, and all events. Ordinarily every body in society reminds us of somewhat else or of some other person. Character, reality, reminds you of nothing else; it takes place of the whole creation. The man must be so much that he must make all circumstances indifferent. (P. 35)[100]

Belonging to no other time or place, he is not entirely outside them, being really here and now. He does not remind, represent, correspond. And the indifference of circumstances marks not their unreality but their meaninglessness apart from the centering force of his being (Emerson emphasizes the verb, not the adverb). Explanation, like character, then, finally describes the self not as content but as context, virtually as process.[101] In his enigmatic phrase, "we pass for what we are" (p. 34).

The attempt to define character and explanation without turning them into absolutes climaxes in the long paragraph about the reason for

self-reliance. At first, this passage might seem to be exactly the opposite – one more reification of the self as a universal ground for reality.

> The magnetism which all original action exerts is explained when we
> inquire the reason of self-trust. Who is the Trustee? What is the ab-
> original Self on which a universal reliance may be grounded? What is
> the nature and power of that science-baffling star, without parallax,
> without calculable elements, which shoots a ray of beauty even into
> trivial and impure actions, if the least mark of independence appear?
> (P. 37)

These questions, however, are not really answered; in Emerson's precise formulation the explanation comes only "when" we ask.[102] The
language – of "inquiry" and "denotation" – immediately turns passive
and remote, and the only source Emerson acknowledges is not a reality
but a power or force, called variously "Spontaneity," "Instinct," or
"Intuition." For these capitalized abstracts Emerson is willing to claim
nothing but existence. They are "the last fact behind which analysis
cannot go," and the rest of the paragraph is filled with denials of
knowledge.

This being, so far as it is perceived as a "sense," exists on the same
level of reality as all other sensations – things, space, light, time, man.
And the argument returns quite explicitly to the empirically real, transcendentally ideal world of Nature.[103] The emphasis is perhaps shifted:
now the noumenality underwriting both apperception and objectivity
looms larger than their phenomenality.

> We lie in the lap of immense intelligence, which makes us receivers of
> its truth and organs of its activity. When we discern justice, when we
> discern truth, we do nothing of ourselves, but allow a passage to its
> beams. If we ask whence this comes, if we seek to pry into the soul
> that causes, all philosophy is at fault. Its presence or its absence is all
> we can affirm. (P. 37)[104]

But these transcendent noumena remain as inaccessible as ever. Emerson's revision of the transparent eyeball passage highlights the passivity,
the absence of mean egotism. And it explicitly banishes one of Nature's
overambitious questions – the "whence."

But, most important, the passage redefines the whole status of perception. Not only is sight demoted to discernment and the metaphoric
eyeball reduced to a mere "passage." Perception, as an earlier sentence
implies, is an aftereffect of a more fundamental state of pure existence.
"We first share the life by which things exist, and afterwards see them
as appearances in nature, and forget that we shared their cause" (p. 37).
The "I think," though still prior to experience, is itself superseded by
an indefinable sharing of life.

Thus a paragraph that seemed to begin in one more reification of the absolute moves finally in a different direction toward the depersonalization of perception – the separation of the "I think" and the "I am." And, in its last sentences, Emerson relinquishes his most beloved pun, and declares the I and the eye, the self and perception, to be not really the same.

> Thoughtless people contradict as readily the statement of perceptions as of opinions, or rather much more readily; for, they do not distinguish between perception and notion. They fancy that I choose to see this or that thing. But perception is not whimsical, but fatal. If I see a trait, my children will see it after me, and in course of time, all mankind, – although it may chance that no one has seen it before me. For my perception of it is as much a fact as the sun. (Pp. 37-38)

The passage, of course, plays with the dual meaning of perception. In part, a perception is only what Emerson earlier described as commitment – an *aperçu* that, once stated, becomes the inevitable formulation for subsequent generations. But "perception" is also meant quite literally as a sensation, and what once was mental and liberating becomes empirical and delimited, as much a fact as the sun.

This last line is crucial in understanding how the second section of the essay redefines the ambiguities of the first. The allusion is to Locke, who in trying to prove the reality of external objects claims as evidence the irresistibility of certain immediate sensations.

> *Sometimes I find, that I cannot avoid the having those* Ideas [of the existence of things] *produced in my Mind*. . . . If I turn my Eyes at noon towards the Sun, I cannot avoid the *Ideas*, which the Light, or Sun, then produces in me. . . . And therefore it must needs be some exteriour cause, and the brisk acting of some Objects without me, whose efficacy I cannot resist, that produces those *Ideas* in my Mind, whether I will, or no.[105]

In part, Emerson merely repeats Leibniz's proto-Kantian claim that consciousness is the only thing in the mind that is not first in the senses.[106] He warns Locke explicitly (and Hume implicitly) that their demonstrations do not disprove the "I think," which is as inevitably given as the sun. I can no more avoid perceiving in general than I can blank out any particular sense datum. Yet, unlike Leibniz, he emphasizes not the inevitability of perception but its fatality, its indifference to humanity. From the transcendental point of view, the "I think" is logically necessary, entirely impervious to personal wills or intentions. From the point of view of the empirical self, apperception is merely one more external "fact," an object like the sun. The very methods by which the mind gauges the truth of its ideas – called by Locke "corre-

spondence" and "conformity" – seem inherently at odds with a demonstration of a nonconforming self-reliance.[107]

Emerson's point in this paragraph is not to annihilate the self. Perception does not so much disprove the existence of the self as say nothing
one way or the other. It is either entirely formal or entirely empirical –
the empty "I think" or the merely factual "my thought" – and neither
extreme can provide knowledge about self-existence.[108] Instead Emerson wants only to separate two incompatible levels of discourse – to
suggest how perception is itself fundamental to the problem and not, as
in *Nature,* a road to salvation. A true proof of self will depend upon a
wholly different kind of experience, a new kind of language.

Emerson hints where such experiences might lie in his admission that
perception is not only fatal but "not whimsical." In the lecture on
"Ethics" he argued for the antipathy of self-reliance and whimsy.

> Self-Trust, that is, not a faith in a man's own whim or conceit as if he
> were quite severed from all other beings and acted on his own private
> account, but a perception that the mind common to the Universe is
> disclosed to the individual through his own nature. (EL.II.151)[109]

With the lintel inscription and now this rejection of an unwhimsical
perception, however, Emerson implies that perhaps self is not any kind
of absolute at all, but more like whimsy than like Universal Truth.[110]

There is, in fact, throughout this section a second tone, strikingly
different from the more dominant analytic one. The first mark of it
comes in the first paragraph, shortly after he admits the inviolability of
self.

> In this pleasing contrite wood-life which God allows me, let me re-
> cord day by day my honest thought without prospect or retrospect,
> and, I cannot doubt, it will be found symmetrical, though I mean it
> not, and see it not. My book should smell of pines and resound with
> the hum of insects. The swallow over my window should interweave
> that thread or straw he carries in his bill into my web also. (P. 34)

The content and even the rhetoric are unusual, both in the essay and
elsewhere in Emerson. The orphic prophecy and syntax of apocalypse
are here replaced by something much gentler – what can only be called a
supplication, even a prayer. The passage renounces willfulness in general and the intellectual aggressiveness of *Nature* in particular. Not only
is Emerson beyond "seeing," but he explicitly denies both retrospect
and prospect, almost literally the first and last words of the earlier
book.[111]

This initial hint is expanded upon in the paragraphs immediately
following the ostracism of fatal perception. The passage, one more

version of the apocalyptic return of power, differs from the others in its placidity, recapturing the previous paragraph's "sense of being which in calm hours rises, we know not how" (p. 37). Man, though fallen, is not the god in ruins Emerson once thought. Instead he is merely "timid and apologetic; . . . he dares not say 'I think,' 'I am,' but quotes some saint or sage" (p. 38). Man's failure to speak the two existential clauses is a predictable result of his fallenness. More extraordinary, and more indicative of the newfound restraint, is the absence of the "therefore," Emerson's unwillingness to permit man to combine those clauses and re-create the history of post-Cartesian philosophy.

The reason for this reticence is immediately explained in a recapitulation of the earlier naturalist passage.

> These roses under my window make no reference to former roses or to better ones; they are for what they are; they exist with God to-day. There is no time to them. There is simply the rose; it is perfect in every moment of its existence. . . . Its nature is satisfied, and it satisfies nature, in all moments alike. (Pp. 38-39)[112]

Referentialism is here explicitly declared the villain, as it had been implicitly in the attacks on commitment, conformity, and consistency. The marginally relational notions of spontaneity and immediacy give way to the "simple" unity of existence. In such a world, even logical links like the deleted "therefore" would be divisive: "the relations of the soul to the divine spirit are so pure that it is profane to seek to interpose helps." This soul, not the eye, is what effects the revolution. "Time and space are but physiological colors which the eye makes, but the soul is light." And the world once again vanishes, not through coincidence but through simplicity: "whenever a mind is simple, and receives a divine wisdom, old things pass away, – means, teachers, texts, temples fall; it lives now and absorbs past and future into the present hour" (p. 38).[113]

In this apocalyptic simplification, sight almost inevitably plays a negative role. Man's preoccupation with time, his postponements and remembrances, seems a function of his mode of perception, the way he laments the past "with reverted eye" or stands on tiptoe to "foresee" the future. Sight, after all, is inherently dualistic, and can only record other places, other times; it can never "see" the here and now. But the problem is less the process of perception than the false priority man tends to grant it. "If we live truly, we shall see truly" (p. 39). As earlier he shared the life before seeing the appearance, so here too things precede perception. And what man gets is not new but only newly discovered. The "new" perception will as much clear away rubbish as reveal different things. If a man lives fully, sight, simile, and even the grain refused him in the opening section will all duly return: "when a man lives with God, his voice shall be as sweet as the murmur of the brook and the rustle of the corn" (p. 39).

VI

The second section, then, works to clarify the ambiguity of the first by separating the two threads of perception and existence – to reaffirm the fatality of referentiality for the self while establishing personality apart from perception in purely existential terms. The third section moves beyond this theoretical clarification to suggest the consequences both for the superseded doctrine of self-reliance and for man's practical existence in the world. Once again we have moved beyond the purely speculative into the "unspeakable" realm of noumenality. "And now at last the highest truth on this subject remains unsaid; probably, cannot be said; for all that we say is the far off remembering of the intuition." All sensation is inadequate, especially sight. "You shall not discern the foot-prints of any other; you shall not see the face of man; you shall not hear any name" (p. 39). Beyond sensation, beyond persons, beyond even hope, fear, and joy, the soul "beholds" sensation and "perceives" self-existence: but the most it can conclude is a faceless, universal condition of "going well" (p. 40).

This emphasis on existence over essence subordinates thought and truth to the simple notion of process.

> Life only avails, not the having lived. Power ceases in the instant of repose; it resides in the moment of transition from a past to a new state, in the shooting of the gulf, in the darting to an aim. This one fact the world hates, that the soul *becomes*. (P. 40)

Such becoming involves more than Emerson's customary celebration of inspiration over tradition and authority.[114] It is a wholesale denial of referentiality of any kind. Transitory power is inherently unknowable, occupying no real place or time but only the invisible interstices. And life, like the roses, exists as not a continuum but an infinite extension of discrete though contiguous Nows. Self-reliance is redefined to be no longer a dualism: power as doing – not "confident but agent" – does not exist separately and therefore cannot be relied upon. "Why then do we prate of self-reliance? . . . To talk of reliance, is a poor external way of speaking. Speak rather of that which relies, because it works and is" (p. 40).

Speaking in the second section of character, Emerson defines the relation between action and existence by collapsing them, so that present firmness assures previous virtue and future triumph.

Act singly, and what you have already done singly, will justify you now. Greatness appeals to the future. If I can be firm enough to-day to do right and scorn eyes, I must have done so much right before, as to defend me now. Be it how it will, do right now. Always scorn appearances, and you always may. (P. 34)[115]

By the third section, Emerson has, without resolving the temporal tensions, at least purified his explanation. Reliance is now simply a function of working and existing, that which relies because it works and is. A temporal element is still implicit; the "because" marks some sort of priority. But Emerson refuses to make this relation precise. The priority may be not causal but phenomenal, and working and being merely the signs by which we tell that something previously did exist. The ability to rely implies only that the thing relied upon actually exists (or existed). By this account, Emerson preaches self-reliance not as an absolute way to the Good but more, in the manner of his Puritan ancestors, as a means of determining if God's gracious gift of salvation has indeed been given, a sign of not theological but existential election.[116] Perhaps the conjunction is not even empirical but merely linguistic, and "reliability" just the term used to describe working and being, as man is a bachelor "because" he is unmarried.

Emerson thus secures the reality of the self radically by cutting it off from all external standards. And self-reliance merely becomes the term to describe the existence, finally the self-existence, of the self. "Self-existence is the attribute of the Supreme Cause, and it constitutes the measure of good by the degree in which it enters into all lower forms. All things real are so by so much virtue as they contain" (p. 40). The definition is infuriatingly empty: things are real, in his pun on "virtue," only by the liveliness they contain.[117] What really emanates from divinity is less insight (of moral absolutes or even of self) than self-existence – "the" attribute, by implication the sole attribute, of the One. The "I think" has been entirely banished from this mutual exchange of working and being, wherein the "I ought" of duty proves the "I am" of existence. And even the priority of the "I ought" is only apparent: the visible sign of something that works "and" is only points back to pure self-existence itself. The absolute ground of such self-existence is indeterminable, for any such proof would necessarily refer to the very sort of external existence that self-existence denies by definition. Even divine self-existence is not a source of reality but only its "measure": I am not self-existent "in" the good but only "like" it. In the absence of any "other" standard, the "self-sufficing, and therefore self-relying soul" must be exactly that – sufficient (p. 41).

The process of "concentration" is then, as Emerson has always implied, also one of atomization, or at least of unknowable relationality. And the autonomy of the self–its logical independence of all standards–leads him to reconsider, in a considerably chastened tone, his misanthropy. "If we cannot at once rise to the sanctities of obedience and faith, let us at least resist our temptations; let us enter into the state of war, and wake Thor and Woden, courage and constancy, in our Saxon breasts" (p. 41). The self-righteousness is gone. He does not desert friends to pursue a higher genius. In fact, obedience and faith seem momentarily beyond him. Moreover, the very homogeneity that earlier seemed boring is now necessary; the Byronic refusals of external conformity and consistency are qualified by a new recognition of internal "constancy." The only question is how large an organism can productively sustain uniformity.

Even the famous renunciation of family relations is a qualified one.

> O father, O mother, O wife, O brother, O friend, I have lived with you after appearances hitherto. Henceforward I am the truth's. Be it known unto you that henceforward I obey no law less than the eternal law. I will have no covenants but proximities. I shall endeavor to nourish my parents, to support my family, to be the chaste husband of one wife, – but these relations I must fill after a new and unprecedented way. I appeal from your customs. I must be myself. (Pp. 41-42)

The passage is not a dramatic decision to be the truth's, but a sadder realization that man cannot live phenomenally "after appearances." The preference for proximities over covenants seems more fated than willful, a translation of Humean contiguity into the moral sphere. Recalling the early function of "essaying," the insistence that "I must be myself" states less who he must be than merely that he himself must be. Existence is not a group activity.

The most apparently antinomian of his claims is in fact the most hypothetical. "I will so trust that what is deep is holy, that I will do strongly before the sun and moon whatever inly rejoices me, and the heart appoints" (p. 42). It is hard not to read the second clause as independent: a declared intention to do strongly the inwardly rejoicing thing. Yet–as the parallel "thats" and the extra comma insist–the declaration is dependent, a wish that if I so trust I will have the courage to do strongly, just as I hope the deep will truly be the holy if it is trusted so to be. But the day is, once again, not to be spent in explanation.

The tone of this notorious renunciation, then, is more unsettled, less assertive than it appears–close in fact to the famous "Circles" paragraph whose project to "seek my own [truth]" it explicitly anticipates.[118] More important, it leads not to a celebration of liberty (as in fact it does in "Circles") but to the ominous return of consciousness.

> The populace think that your rejection of popular standards is a rejection of all standard, and mere antinomianism; and the bold sensualist will use the name of philosophy to gild his crimes. But the law of consciousness abides. (P. 42)

Emerson senses that this charge is more important than most leveled at him, and the "bold" sensualist who exploits self-reliance is more admirable than his other Emersonian avatars – the "thoughtless" in "Circles" or the "frivolous" in *Nature*. Self-reliance as self-existence is the rejection of all external standards, virtually all standards. What remains is the law of consciousness, apparently rejected near the end of the second section but – we now can see – only bracketed. Earlier this law was belittled as a jailor and a deterrent to self-reliance. Then, of course, it was called fatal. Now it is more clearly just something different. The notion of mean egotism has come apart – into "antinomianism," which can be mere or mean, and "egotism," which is logically necessary and morally neutral. Consciousness is no longer conflated with conscience. Having no practical, ethical dimension, it is the simple fact of perception, of the "I think" and of ownership.

Yet, though amoral, apperception still serves as a kind of upper bound. Having rejected indirect standards as threats to the self's autonomy, Emerson accepts this remaining direct one. And repeating his earlier phrase, he persists in his willingness "to absolve me to myself."

> You may fulfil your round of duties by clearing yourself in the *direct*, or, in the *reflex* way. Consider whether you have satisfied your relations to father, mother, cousin, neighbor, town, cat, and dog; whether any of these can upbraid you. But I may also neglect this reflex standard, and absolve me to myself. I have my own stern claims and perfect circle. It denies the name of duty to many offices that are called duties. But if I discharge its debts, it enables me to dispense with the popular code. If any one imagines that this law is lax, let him keep its commandment one day. (P. 42)

The mechanics of self-absolution are as unclear as ever, though the general idea seems to be that the existing self and the epistemological ME must accept each other's reality. But whatever the mechanics, the important change is obvious: self-absolution, though necessary, is an act without consequences. No "then" attends its fulfillment: man does not ray out absolute good, as in the journals, or even win the world's suffrage, as earlier in the essay. Consciousness is simply a law, a prerequisite for empiricism. In the world I simply am; therefore (or perhaps "because") I ought. But in another context, whose "I" may or may not be the same as the personal self of empirical realism, consciousness still abides, I also think.[119]

Thus, once again, Emerson builds his argument not to an absolute statement about the nature of reality but to a careful distinction between frames of reference. In this, the essay resembles most the Divinity School "Address." And, indeed, here too the essay reveals its general derivation from the sermon tradition by closing, after the three theoretical sections, with a final section of practical "applications."[120] Just as the "Address" ends with practical advice to ministers – parallel to but not causally related to the theory of duty propounded – so "Self-Reliance" ends with a cheerful list of what the individual can do – parallel to but not influencing the twin realities of consciousness and existence.

The categories – religion, traveling, imitation, art, society, and property – are familiar Emersonian concerns. Yet, as in the first section all was undercut, so here all seems anticlimactic. Will returns as a chief actor, although the central two sections have clearly subordinated that faculty to both character and perception. Society returns without its earlier conspiratorial strength as a mere corpuscular wave whose unity is phenomenal.[121] The very hortative rhetoric seems robbed of its energy. "Do that which is assigned you, and you cannot hope too much or dare too much." "Abide in the simple and noble regions of thy life, obey thy heart, and thou shalt reproduce the Foreworld again" (p. 47).

Moreover the early promises of "Prospects" are casually withdrawn. The ringing injunction to build one's own house and world becomes an overqualified assurance of the prudence of not imitating Gothic revivalism.

> If the American artist will study with hope and love the precise thing to be done by him, considering the climate, the soil, the length of the day, the wants of the people, the habit and form of the government, he will create a house in which all these will find themselves fitted, and taste and sentiment will be satisfied also. (P. 47)

And the famous vanishing of disagreeable appearances is wittily inverted to become the appearance of illusory hopes.

> A political victory, a rise of rents, the recovery of your sick, or the return of your absent friend, or some other favorable event, raises your spirits, and you think good days are preparing for you. Do not believe it. (Pp. 50-51)

With a paradoxical coupling of principles and yourself, the absolute and the particular, the essay abruptly ends.

Perhaps the key admission concerning "Self-Reliance" is simply that "my chapter is not finished." The separation of existence and consciousness – *esse et percipi* – is both logical and a possible answer to some of the philosophical limitations of the earlier formulations, especially the slighting of the empirical self. But the existential answer is decidedly preliminary. Emerson is not yet back to where he began in *Nature;* the what, whence, and whereto of the NOT ME remain unexplained. Self-reliance can teach man that if he is true, experience is irrelevant; or that since he experiences, he is true. It cannot, however, teach both at once. To learn of existence, Emerson brackets the question of the world. To proceed from this existential proof to "new secrets of self-reliance," however, he must remove the brackets.

5

The limits of experience

Less than two years after claiming his chapter on self-reliance to be unfinished, Emerson begins to record in his journals what will become "Experience." The essay is probably his greatest. It is surely the most universally admired, having no detractors, as do the earlier master-pieces – *Nature,* the Divinity School "Address," and "Self-Reliance." In it Emerson finds a solution to the problem of structure that has plagued him from the start and rejects the sermon form for a more supple "suite," the delicate dance of the seven lords. More important, he over-comes what recent readers have felt to be his oppressive assertiveness elsewhere. And by embedding the oracular and the epigrammatic in a more personal account, he discovers a new tone, more flowing and confessional, and thus more modern (not to say modernist).

The modernity of "Experience," however, tends to obscure other aspects of the work – both its relation to the *Essays: Second Series* as a whole and to Emerson's earlier statements. Critics are surely right to see this essay as the climactic statement of the middle period of uncer-tainty. And to see that, as in *Nature,* Emerson's personal situation strongly colors the intellectual intensity of the argument.[1] Yet whatever the initial impetus for writing, the form it takes is recognizably philo-sophical. Many of the questions seem familiar and offer recognizable (if not entirely predictable) reformulations of earlier problems. Moreover, the changes, though unexpected, seem internally consistent and of a piece. If psychologically Emerson shows an unsuspected willingness to treat the authentic facts of experience, philosophically he merely devel-ops the next stage of his epistemological argument. The ambivalences of "Experience" may seem far from the exhortations of "Self-Reliance." Yet the doctrine of world and other minds it proposes is the natural counterpart to, even the consequence of, the earlier theory of self. The work's newness measures less the extent to which he has moved outside of philosophy – beyond Kant to, say, Freud – than his move from one kind of epistemology to another – beyond Kant to, say, Wittgenstein. And the modernity of the essay rests as much in its philosophical argument as it does on top of it.[2]

I

The continuity is clearest perhaps if we consider the essay's position in the whole collection. The *Essays: Second Series* is generally felt to be less successful than the first.[3] Some falling off, of course, is inevitable in any such sequel. Having collected in the first series the best of twenty years of journal writing, in the second Emerson seems hard pressed to construct a companion volume from his considerably depleted sources.[4] Yet however it affects the style, the necessity of drawing on more recent material gives the second collection a kind of unity lacking in the first. These essays are not simply more immediate, but in some senses about their own immediacy. Many, of course, address contemporary issues, especially the various reform movements of the 1840s, and in this political focus anticipate the practical emphases of later volumes like *Representative Men, English Traits*, and *The Conduct of Life*. But more important, even those essays whose topics do not seem inherently contemporary are more concerned with the particular than the universal, even with articulating a theory of particularity.[5]

This shift in focus is perhaps most evident in the relatively minor "Politics," one of the oldest essays in the collection, drawn largely from a similarly titled lecture in the 1837-38 series on "The Philosophy of History."[6] In adapting the lecture to its final place in the *Essays*, Emerson deuniversalizes his earlier theory of politics. The lecture opens by praising the "idea of a State" for its depiction of the melting of many interests into one, and insists that the identity of mind is the presupposition that makes the notion of a single government possible (EL.II.69). Both this abstract opening and its reformulation in terms of individuals are eliminated in the essay. Emerson now argues instead that the state and its "particular" laws are not aboriginal but antecedent, lacking "roots" in eternal spirit and necessary only to the extent that they follow politely at a distance the history of culture (CW.III.117-18).[7]

The real mark of the series's emphasis on particularity, however, lies less in its explicit treatment of contemporary issues like politics and reform than in Emerson's more general attempts to understand the theory of sociability. Even in a short piece like "Gifts," seemingly coy advice on the proper selection of gifts actually disguises a serious question about the natural misanthropy of man: why man has so much trouble giving or getting anything. In part the problem lies in the falsely quantitative notion of giving: "there is no commensurability between a man and any gift," or, in the paradoxical opening statement, "the world owes more than the world can pay" (pp. 95, 93). Secularizing Anselm, Emerson argues that man cannot repay adequately repay an infinite debt of friendship and magnanimity.[8] But, more simply, the problem lies in the self-evidential character of personhood. There is a presumption in giving, an implication that the receiver is incomplete and that the giver himself has something to "bestow" (p. 94). Giving must not be willful or intentional but more nearly "indifferent." The gift must be not only quantitatively small but (so far as is possible) ontologically insignificant, so that its passing from one hand to the other will be merely like water moving at the same level.

The attempt in "Gifts" to clarify on a small scale the limits of selfhood suggests Emerson's growing concern with the relation between self and others throughout the series. Just as "Gifts" reworks the specific notion of misanthropy, the longer "Character" reformulates the whole concept of self-reliance. In "Self-Reliance," as we saw, "character" was Emerson's term for self working in the world. Here, as before, character is self-sufficing, even self-environing, "reminding" man of nothing but itself and offering new actions as the only possible "explanations" of inevitable misunderstandings (pp. 58, 63, 60). As the "moral order seen through the medium of an individual nature," character defines by enclosing (p. 56). Perception is again both fatal and penultimate. A man "animates all he can, and he sees only what he animates." And if not quite an eyeball, he is at least the "medium of the highest influence to all who are not on the same level," standing "to all beholders like a transparent object betwixt them and the sun" (p. 57).

Whereas "Self-Reliance" emphasized the self-evidencing exclusivity of self, however, "Character" focuses on its nonreferentiality. Character is not any sort of absolute. In the first series, both character and intellect were universals in their unintentional "teaching above will." Now character "repudiates intellect" even as it excites it, to occupy a middle ground between the purely whimsical and the absolutely true. No longer even "like" virtue, it is simply "nature in the highest form" (p. 61). The notion of "power" so confusing in "Self-Reliance" here tends to drop out of the earlier formulations about becoming, leaving "life" alone, which "goes headlong" (p. 65; cf. CW.II.40). As a result, character seems more fluid, even mercurial, and its very representative status seems undermined.

Nature never rhymes her children, nor makes two men alike. When we see a great man, we fancy a resemblance to some historical person, and predict the sequel of his character and fortune, a result which he is sure to disappoint. None will ever solve the problem of his character according to our prejudice, but only in his own high unprecedented way. Character wants room. (P. 63)[9]

A similar relativist bias is evident in his new essay on "Nature," both in its deuniversalization of the world and in its demythification of man.[10] In an apparently familiar opening, the harmony and perfection of the world celebrate a naturalism only slightly less luxurious than that of the Divinity School "Address."[11] Yet Emerson is now willing to admit the power of the phenomenal world. Formerly a pupil on whom nature attended a little too politely, man is now himself the inferior, a "parasite" living off her "roots," trying to "make friends with matter" and "nestle in nature" (p. 100).[12] The full implications of this shift become obvious only when Emerson turns from *natura naturata* or nature passive to *natura naturans* or efficient nature. To treat nature too completely as an end is a kind of dilettantism, to become a "fop of fields" (p. 103).[13] Nature as efficient cause concerns less the motive, direction, or end than the sheer vitality of the procedure. In a world of endless and even prodigal "motion," man's own position is one of comic "overfaith," itself only a specific form of "exaggeration" (pp. 107-09).[14] Although there is still law, identity, and unity, from his own ignorant station man experiences only a "something mocking, something that leads us on and on, but arrives nowhere."

> We live in a system of approximations. Every end is prospective of some other end, which is also temporary; a round and final success nowhere. . . . What is the end sought? Plainly to secure the ends of good sense and beauty, from the intrusion of deformity or vulgarity of any kind. But what an operose method! What a train of means to secure a little conversation! (P. 110)

And nature vanishes once again – not into a higher perceptual truth, but into the redundancy of her own referred existence.

> It is an odd jealousy: but the poet finds himself not near enough to his object. The pine-tree, the river, the bank of flowers before him, does not seem to be nature. Nature is still elsewhere. . . . It is the same among the men and women, as among the silent trees; always a referred existence, an absence, never a presence and satisfaction. (Pp. 111-12)

A similar admission of ignorance informs Emerson's treatment of fashion in "Manners." The very fact that he addresses the issue is suggestive; earlier, fashion would have been instantly dismissed as one of society's conspiracies.[15] Now he sees an implicit criticism of his earlier theories in the ease with which fashion successfully apes the individualism of self-reliance. He suggests, of course, various ways of distinguishing between the true and the false. But more interesting is his uncharacteristic (even Rabelaisian) willingness to accept the value of fashion without understanding it. "Let there be grotesque sculpture about the gates and offices of temples. Let the creed and command-ments even have the saucy homage of parody. The forms of politeness universally express benevolence in superlative degrees" (p. 85).

Like the "exaggeration" of the second "Nature," the "saucy homage of parody" marks a new kind of indifference. "What if the false gentle-man almost bows the true out of the world? . . . Real service will not lose its nobleness. All generosity is not merely French and sentimental" (p. 85). The distinction between levels does not, as in *Nature*, eliminate the dilemma. An Orion empirically real and transcendentally ideal is replaced by simple twoness – a service truly real yet largely unknow-able, or at least no longer merely useful and venerable to me. Within the world, cracks are never healed. All acceptance can effect is a salva-tion from the false problem of commensurability, and the new, limited apocalypse is one not of mind over matter but of matter purely. With-out glorifying the ideal by dismissing the disagreeable, it will at least allow a differentiation of experiences by elevating quality over quantity. "A man is but a little thing in the midst of the objects of nature, yet, by the moral quality radiating from his countenance, he may abolish all considerations of magnitude, and in his manners equal the majesty of the world" (p. 87).

But perhaps the clearest register of the new relativist focus of the series lies in the tensions of the volume's most troubled essay – "The Poet." At first "The Poet" might seem to contradict the overall direc-tion of the series. Its preoccupation with the single great man who speaks a universal truth seems far from the pluralism of the other es-says; and more than one critic has felt that, whatever the bibliographical evidence, it is this essay and not the second "Nature" that belongs more completely to the absolutist world of the first series.[16] "The Poet" seems to offer the fullest reconciliation of the conflict between thinking and acting, and – especially in the second section of the essay, on the poet's "means and materials" – comes as close as Emerson ever does to solving his vocational problem.[17] The poet is the namer and sayer, the sole "teller" in a world of knowers (p. 6). As in the first *Nature* (though not in the second), the world is fallen and language a "fossil poetry." "Language is made up of images, or tropes, which now, in their secon-dary use, have long ceased to remind us of their poetic origin. But the poet names the thing because he sees it, or comes one step nearer to it than any other" (p. 13). In his reattachment of words to things, he virtually makes the world anew, not only knowing the world but making his facts the "horses" of his thought.

> All the facts of the animal economy, – sex, nutriment, gestation, birth, growth – are symbols of the passage of the world into the soul of man, to suffer there a change, and reappear a new and higher fact. . . . The poet alone knows astronomy, chemistry, vegetation, and animation, for he does not stop at these facts, but employs them as signs. . . . for, in every word he speaks he rides on them as the horses of thought. (Pp. 12-13)

Yet it is hard, even without remembering Coleridge, to be entirely satisfied with Emerson's formulations.[18] The language theory of the middle section scarcely appears to be an advance on *Nature*'s fourth chapter, and the return of Swedenborg seems ominous.[19] The process of reattachment of things – of "even artificial things, and violations of nature, to nature, by a deeper insight" (p. 11) – is equally suspect, recalling in its "very easy" disposal of "disagreeable facts" the overstated facility with which in "Prospects" coincidence made disagreeable appearances vanish (p. 11; cf. CW.I.45).[20] Articulation seems, as did idealism at its worst, merely an enslavement: the way in which the world is "thus put under the mind for verb and noun" sadly echoes the hostility with which religion and ethics once "put nature under foot" (p. 12; cf. CW.I.35).

Moreover, it is unclear whether man is himself liberated in the process of articulation. Unenlightened man, Emerson explains, is merely one among many facts, all equally symbolic. "We are symbols, and inhabit symbols; workmen, work, and tools, words and things, birth and death, all are emblems." The poet is, of course, a genius able to break away from "being infatuated with the economical uses" and see that things are also thoughts. "The poet, by an ulterior intellectual perception, gives them a power which makes their old use forgotten, and puts eyes, and a tongue, into every dumb and inanimate object. He perceives the independence of the thought on the symbol, the stability of the thought, the accidency and fugacity of the symbol" (pp. 12, 244). Yet even here the freedom seems spurious, and "the independence of the thought on the symbol," in its awkward use of the preposition "on," appears implicitly to affirm the very dependence it explicitly denies.[21] His final triumph – as he "turns the world to glass, and shows us all things in their right series and procession" (p. 12) – not only reintroduces a suspect Swedenborgianism but may just return us to the blind transparency of *Nature*'s eyeball.[22]

Emerson's problems in defining the poet's role suggest his more general difficulty with the status of form throughout the essay.[23] In arguing for the "necessity of publication," Emerson in fact discovers the paradox of incarnation: for something to appear truly, it must become an appearance and thus appear merely.[24] A theory of beauty, to the extent that it offers thoughts on matter, seems oxymoronic, and even the famous claim that poetry is "not metres, but a metre-making argument" has trouble reconciling the general concern for inspiration and ecstasy with a more particular emphasis here on argument, logic, and structure. Increasingly one feels the distance between the poet-actor and his poetic action. Standing "among partial men for the complete man" (p. 4), the poet is less the sayer of beauty than himself the beautiful thing. The "indifference" of words and deeds, like that of stars and ideas, suggests the reality of activity – that "words are also actions, and actions are a kind of words" (p. 6) – but without proving that action to be significantly mine. And as earlier in Emerson man was divided from his virtue, so here he is from his power: "the man is only half himself, the other half is his expression" (p. 4). Finally, even the essay's most ringing claim, that poets are "liberating gods," leads primarily to the recognition of how greatly man needs such liberation and how deliverance is only from one dream to another, from the prison of one's thoughts to heaven itself a new prison (pp. 18-19).

As this distance between the action and the actor increases, the previously emblematic world gives way to one no less symbolic, but considerably less static. "For all symbols are fluxional; all language is vehicular and transitive, and is good, as ferries and horses are, for conveyance, not as farms and houses are, for homestead" (p. 20). A language previously oracular – all nouns and verbs – is now predicative, transitive, and the all too disciplinary houses and farms of Nature give way to more mutable horses and ferries. The poet who can see firmness is still looked for, but only "in vain," and his "possession" of the world entails the ironic sacrifice that the poet as sayer must finally "be content that others speak for thee" (pp. 21-24).

In such a world of "metamorphosis," insight is such a "very high sort of seeing" that it is scarcely seeing at all, but instead a "being where and what it sees."[25] Speaking is equally passive: "the condition of true naming, on the poet's part, is his resigning himself to the divine aura which breathes through forms, and accompanying that" (p. 15). His energy comes from "abandonment to the nature of things," and trusting to the instinct of the horses he rode earlier in the essay, man is simply caught up in the "life of the Universe" (pp. 15-16). And in one final revision of Nature, Emerson praises Swedenborg's ability to discover in the metamorphosis of things a perception of the different aspects objects can wear.

And instantly the mind inquires, whether these fishes under the bridge, yonder oxen in the pasture, those dogs in the yard, are immutably fishes, oxen, and dogs, or only so appear to me, and perchance to themselves appear upright men; and whether I appear as a man to all eyes. (P. 21)

No longer is perception a question of my mind versus reality or my apocalypse versus God's paintings. Now the issue is whether ontologically equivalent visions are in fact identical, whether my fish are your fish and whether I am me to you.

II

It is unnecessary for our purposes to sort out all the ambivalences of "The Poet," but simply to mark in the troubled essay the new interests of the second series as a whole.[26] Unlike the first collection, the second series addresses questions of variety and otherness – finally, of world – rather than those of unity and self, focusing on the integrity of the parts rather than their autonomy, their nonreferentiality rather than their self-existence. Questions of causality and absolute existence give way to those of interrelation and relative position. The concept of the over-soul pretty much drops out as a significant ground for or explanation of experience. Replacing it are various notions of particularity and pluralism, especially motion and metamorphosis. Perception, consciousness, and mind remain important topics, but only in relation to the more truly central ones of nature, experience, and other persons.

The second series, then, may best be seen as that moment, long forestalled, when Emerson tries to open the brackets he customarily placed around the NOT ME. And the triumph of the collection's only fully successful essay, "Experience," is identically the triumph of that reopening. Tonally the essay is unique in the series, standing among the generally upbeat essays – much as "Circles" did in the first series – as the one moment of quiet gloom. But it is also the fullest, most systematic exploration of the newfound worldliness. For in "Experience" Emerson asks what it feels like to live in the world, what are the epistemological consequences of existence, man's actually being an empirical self in the NOT ME of roses and woodlife.[27] As such the essay stands less as a tonal exception than as the philosophical summation of the series – more "Self-Reliance" than "Circles."[28]

"Experience" is perhaps Emerson's most self-allusive essay, and part of his method of portraying dislocation is to shore up the pieces with fragments from his earlier works.[29] Some of the most direct echoes, of course, are of other essays in the series and serve (at least in part) structurally to unify the collection. The ambiguous statement in "The Poet" that "dream delivers us to dream" is repeated verbatim to summarize the inevitability of illusion (pp. 19, 30). More generally, the rain falling copiously but inconsequentially at the end of "The Poet" returns to characterize those "dearest events" too easily repelled by the "Para coats" of self (pp. 24, 29).[30] The claim in "Experience" that extremes should yield to the golden mean – that "everything good is on the highway" – is explored at greater length in "Character" in the notion of the hero's constant motion, his being always "again on his road" (pp. 36, 60). And in the most striking echo of all, both essays insist (though with different pronouns) that man "animates all he can, and he sees only what he animates" (pp. 30, 57).[31]

The echoes within the series, however, only point to more general resonances with earlier works. Many have remarked the similarity between the stairs of the opening paragraph and the mysterious ladder in "Circles."[32] The notion that "ghostlike we glide" through the world registers the increasing importance of the verb in Emerson to mark restless natural motion (p. 27).[33] Moreover the concept of surface and the corollary injunction to skate well, though deriving in general from a famous passage in *The Prelude*, recall the more proximate source in the essay on "Prudence."[34] The related epidermal image of superficiality as only skin deep and "caducous" has an even older history, stretching back as far as the early lecture on "Prudence."[35]

It is, however, to "Self-Reliance" that "Experience" refers most directly and most often. The Lethe handed us at the beginning of the essay looks back to many similar potions in Emerson, most notably that in "Self-Reliance." In addition to the drink, the "sharp peaks and edges" with which Emerson hopes to prove the truth of reality (or at least the reality of grief) recall the "edge" that virtue must have if it is to be believed (p. 29; cf. CW.II.30). And the witty physician's attribution of creed to a man's liver echoes the less comic predictability of the much maligned conformist preacher (and perhaps their common source in Barzillai Frost).

Yet perhaps the most suggestive allusion to an earlier work is the least specific. For whether intentionally or not, Emerson has constructed his argument much as he did that of his first book, and the procession of the seven lords of life comments implicitly on the parallel development of the seven main chapters of *Nature*. There are some explicit verbal echoes, largely inversions. In both essays the kingdom comes without observation, though the second more clearly sees in this advent an implicit criticism of perception (p. 40; cf. CW.I.45). The commandments in *Nature* thundered at man by every chemical change, every leaf, every mute gospel of a farm are denied in "Experience."

"[Nature's] darlings, the great, the strong, the beautiful, are not children of our law, do not come out of the Sunday School, nor weigh their food, nor punctually keep the commandments" (p. 37; cf. CW.I.26). Similarly the "property" in the horizon possessed in *Nature* only by "he whose eye can integrate all the parts, that is, the poet" becomes the grimmer sense that, though people do not realize it, "it is the eye which makes the horizon" (p. 44; cf. CW.I.9).[36] And, of course, the transparent eyeball (never far away in Emerson) reappears in "Experience" in numerous guises – the beads, the glass prison, the correcting lenses.[37]

Such similarities should not really surprise us. Emerson's intellectual career is in general remarkably unified. Moreover since experience and nature are related at least in their shared preoccupation with the NOT ME, it would probably be unusual were there no overlap. It will not do, then, to argue too rigorously for the identity of the works. Nevertheless, the shapes of the two arguments are sufficiently similar that an analysis of the three main sections of "Experience" – its theoretical introduction, lower argument, and confrontation with idealism – in terms of the comparable three sections of *Nature* at least offers a convenient measure of how his philosophy has altered.

The first section, on the lord Illusion, roughly takes the place of the two introductory chapters in *Nature*, defining the general world in which the examination of particular aspects will occur. As critics have long remarked, the opening question – where do we find ourselves? – revises the equivalent moment in *Nature* when Emerson asked, to what end is nature?[38] The tone is subdued, less oracular, perhaps less arrogant, probably less hopeful. The grammatical shift is representative: finding replaces being, and the objectifying question about ends becomes a more straightforward question about us. The muted tone then infects the whole introductory paragraph, which, rather than setting forth some preliminary definitions about the ME and the NOT ME, merely presents a series of images of dislocation.

Yet although all realize that the opening takes a different tone, it is less often seen that it asks a different question. To wonder where we find ourselves is not to return, however chastened, to the what, whence, and whereto of *Nature*. Questions about the end or use of nature assume man's superiority. The world obviously does something for man, and the philosopher need decide only which among the many possibilities is the true *telos*. But "where are we?" is an altogether more primitive question: given our existence, what can we say about its conditions? The two questions are not mutually exclusive. Perhaps, in the end, superiority will reappear as one of the conditions of human existence. But at least at the start, examinations of our position require no comment one way or the other on any "theory" of nature. At the same time, however, this antitheoretical bias must not be read as anti-realist. Nature's movement here – the way in which things swim, glitter, and glide – far from demonstrating unreality, implicitly assumes that something exists. Nor is there any reason to conclude man's illusoriness from his uncertainty. The "I am" of "Self-Reliance" presumably still proves personal existence. Bracketing ontological problems, the project simply narrows its focus to describe what it feels like to exist – whether as man or as rose.

The first two sentences, then, must be taken perfectly straight, as serious question and adequate answer. "Where do we find ourselves? In a series, of which we do not know the extremes, and believe that it has none" (p. 27). The issue is not, as in the essays before "Self-Reliance," how can I find myself, what would constitute a sufficient proof of existence. Assuming the existence of both self and scale, Emerson instead questions the relation between the two, where the one is on the other. The commonsense reading, in fact, explicitly denies the possibility of more universal ones. Man cannot absolutely "find" his self in a Dantesque sense of coming to oneself, for this process creates a false dualism with no real place for the finder to stand. From within the system, however, he can talk a little about his condition – not "where exactly" or even "where the hell" am I, but only "where by the way and more or less." In this context, the answer is not sullen but precise. He is in the middle of a long series whose extremes literally cannot be known (and therefore not quite believed) because they involve the birth and death of the means of perception.[39]

The problem thus is one not of realism but of knowability. Man's gliding ghostlike through nature challenges neither his existence nor nature's. Instead it merely admits that our position, though real, cannot be reidentified, that we "should not know our place again." Or, in Emerson's explicit, though undervalued, formulation, "our life is not so much threatened as our perception" (p. 27). The tension between truth and knowability becomes increasingly clear in the mixed tone of the second paragraph, where images of actual success are coupled with those of apparent failure. The point is not, as it might be in a merely despairing context, that man is shafted, the plaything of the gods. In fact the paragraph is full of triumphs – accomplishments, wonders, wisdom, poetry, virtue, and even some heavenly days – and the gods' dice, if loaded, are clearly on the side of man and creation.[40] The possibility of such triumphs, however, does not lead, as it did in "Self-Reliance," to exhortations about self-trust. It is more simply descriptive. Whatever the theoretical implications of these triumphs, man experiences them as mere confusion, "a good deal of buzz, and somewhere a result slipped magically in." Even the "organic," which earlier had measured the integrity of the genius, is now organic merely, and marks purely personal "opinions," which "do not disturb the universal necessity" (p. 28).

The most obvious sign of the new focus, however, is the image of the self as a ship. In *Nature,* Emerson had explicitly denied such a reading: we "are not built like a ship to be tossed, but like a house to stand" (CW.I.30).[41] The change, however, measures less a new instability than a new relation between objects, not ships versus houses but my ship versus yours. "Every ship is a romantic object, except that we sail in. Embark, and the romance quits our vessel, and hangs on every other sail in the horizon" (p. 28). Illusion is itself illusory, and our life "looks" trivial only because we cannot really see it. The horizon that once had real "property" for the integrating eye of the poet now teaches only otherness, "perpetual retreating and reference" (p. 28). And in the querulous voice of the farmer, other grass is green but " 'my field . . . only holds the world together' " (p. 28).[42] Given Emerson's theory of perception, however, the farmer's complaint ironically moves in two directions at once. Beauty is not me, and envy universal. But without some self or "I think" to hold the world together – some purely formal "my field" of vision – there could, of course, be no perception of otherness at all.

The complex relation between this opening section and Emerson's earlier theories is implicit in the very titles he chooses. In *Nature,* the first chapter was also called "Nature"; there was apparently no discontinuity between the NOT ME and man's perception of (or "chippings" on) it. To rename the entire work "Experience" is to emphasize not the continuity but the homogeneity, not the fittedness but the indifference. "Experience" is, of course, Kant's term for sensation already passed through thought. By so naming his essay, Emerson makes explicit what is implicit throughout the second series: that bracketing questions of noumenality, even of existence – the transcendentality of epistemology – he now wishes to speak solely for our experience as empirically real.[43]

As with the retitling of the essay, renaming *Nature*'s first chapter as "Illusion" clarifies the philosophical focus without really altering the theoretical assumptions. By emphasizing the illusoriness of experience, Emerson in part acknowledges a greater range of sensations than in the earlier account of a somewhat too commodious world. More important, however, he internalizes that tension between being and seeming that by the end of *Nature* proved the world's objectivity. Here as there, illusion does not disprove noumenality but proves it. It is only the possibility that our perceptions might not be right that permits the existence of a separate standard of rightness. Without illusions or seemings, "I think X" would mean "X," and both the objectivity of the experience and my ownership of it as apperception would disappear.[44]

The introductory section, then, makes two related points. To the extent that we are in the world, nature as experience allows for no external standards: I and it are ontologically the same.[45] And to the extent that our intercourse with our own world is doubly reflexive, nature as illusion admits no certainty, except perhaps about its own procedural illusions. The very notion of occasionally being right means that we must generally seem wrong. Thus the bitter sentence at the beginning of the second paragraph holds a kind of truth. Generally, of course, it is one of life's little ironies that we understand least when we try most to do so. But in the more precise Kantian distinction between the phenomena we "know" and the noumena we can only "think," if any of us did "know" our actions and directions, it would be "when we think [that] we [should] best know" (p. 27).

It is in this context that we must read the section's most notorious passage – on the pain of the death of his son Waldo. Structurally if not thematically equivalent to the bare common experience, the paragraph stands as that introductory moment that the rest of the essay teaches us to understand and accept. Yet critics have perhaps more trouble here than with the eyeball. And although all recognize the power of the prose, they find it difficult not to condescend to the content – to ask not what is he saying, but how could he say that.

A few dismiss the paragraph outright as a mark of Emerson's deficient humanity, his constitutional coldness. More important, those who defend it do so in terms of its psychological validity – showing, on the one hand, that the death did affect him deeply and, on the other, that grief is a hard emotion to feel.[46] Such an answer, however, accepts too fully the opposition's assumptions. By couching the argument in the psychological vocabulary of what Emerson had come to feel was true, this defense unwittingly readmits the conclusion it meant to banish – that it is unfortunate that Emerson did not come to feel a little more.[47] Yet the passage can also be viewed as a theoretical statement about the nature of the world he has constructed, and by this light it is logic and not Waldo that teaches him the nature of grief.

Although the autobiographical elements confuse the situation somewhat, the point Emerson makes is one about disaster, specifically emotional disaster, as an apparently unusual experience.

> What opium is instilled into all disaster! It shows formidable as we approach it, but there is at last no rough rasping friction, but the most slippery surfaces: we fall soft on a thought: . . . People grieve and bemoan themselves, but it is not half so bad with them as they say. There are moods in which we court suffering, in the hope that here, at

least, we shall find reality, sharp peaks and edges of truth. But it turns out to be scene-painting and counterfeit. The only thing grief has taught me, is to know how shallow it is. That, like all the rest, plays about the surface, and never introduces me into the reality, for contact with which, we would even pay the costly price of sons and lovers. Was it Boscovich who found out that bodies never come in contact? Well, souls never touch their objects. An innavigable sea washes with silent waves between us and the things we aim at and converse with. (P. 29)

The basic assumption – leading back through empiricism's distinction between impressions and ideas all the way to Descartes's notion of the clear and distinct – is that clarity is a mark of indubitability.[48] Moreover, as with a nonconformist virtue, the negative and unusual – the rough, rasping, and sharp – will be the most easily discerned. Logically, therefore, the truly disastrous should in its negative clarity be undeniably real and free from illusion. Yet the search for the sufficiently calamitous is in vain. Looking for a sharp sensation or impression, "we fall soft on a thought" and the gap between ideas and real things remains unbridgeable.

Emerson in this passage focuses on what we now call the mind-body problem. Furthermore he locates the heart of the matter in what has come to be seen as the central topic of suffering and grief or, more generally, pain.

Grief too will make us idealists. In the death of my son, now more than two years ago, I seem to have lost a beautiful estate, – no more. I cannot get it nearer to me. If tomorrow I should be informed of the bankruptcy of my principal debtors, the loss of my property would be a great inconvenience to me, perhaps, for many years; but it would leave me as it found me, – neither better nor worse. So is it with this calamity: it does not touch me: something which I fancied was a part of me, which could not be torn away without tearing me, nor enlarged without enriching me, falls off from me, and leaves no scar. It was caducous. I grieve that grief can teach me nothing, nor carry me one step into real nature. The Indian who was laid under a curse, that the wind should not blow on him, nor water flow to him, nor fire burn him, is a type of us all. The dearest events are summer-rain, and we the Para coats that shed every drop. Nothing is left us now but death. We look to that with a grim satisfaction, saying, there at least is reality that will not dodge us. (P. 29)

Whatever its status as emotion, grief is a peculiar sort of sensation in that it is not deniable in the way that most sensations are. Although we can recognize a difference between being in the presence of heat and feeling hot, there is no equivalent distinction between true and false griefs (though there is one, of course, between real and counterfeit). To feel pain is to be in pain. Suffering is not the sort of thing one can be wrong about, and the statement "I thought I hurt but now I see that I was mistaken" is not intelligible.[49]

Yet – and this is for Emerson the important point – this incorrigibility does not in fact really help man. "Grief too will make us idealists." The "too" returns us to *Nature*'s list of idealizing influences.[50] But now the proof has turned fatal. Like nature, poetry, philosophy, science, religion and ethics, grief "too" teaches man the phenomenality of sensation, but the shift from public influences to an intensely private one marks the disheartening internalization of the ME/NOT ME dichotomy. With the earlier categories, it was their uncertainty that proved idealism: since I can invert the world by standing on my head, I must myself be more stable than nature. Now, however, doubt is unnecessary. That single thing that is inherently undeniable (even more so than doubt itself) nevertheless still proves dualism.

The inherent stability of grief as phenomenon has no noumenal consequences: "That, like all the rest, plays about the surface, and never introduces me into the reality. . . . I cannot get it nearer to me" (p. 29). If at times it looks as if we might mirror the ideal in the material, we can surely not reverse the process and elevate matter to the noumenal. Perhaps "we may have the sphere for our cricket-ball, but not a berry for our philosophy" (p. 29). Moreover, the undeniability of grief doesn't say anything practical about the real world either: as grief cannot introduce Emerson to his ME, neither can it get him any closer to "real nature." The problem, as in any vaguely Cartesian context, is one of misplaced concreteness.[51] As in "Manners," so here what is needed is a liberation from the false standard of quantity. Earlier, man's dissatisfaction with the quantitative proof – how few men are great, how much time is wasted – obscured the results slipped magically in. So now in his unsympathetically archaic formulation, "people grieve and bemoan themselves, but it is not half so bad with them as they say." It is not "half so bad" not because they do not care enough, but because they cannot.

Yet this rejection of quantification is in fact more radical than it seems. Emerson understands that pain is less a matter of decibels than of logic. But such a recognition implicitly admits that pain is not really an experience, or, more precisely, that what makes pain true is only contingently related to what makes it painful. Something that cannot be denied does not exist in the real world in any interesting way; to exist undeniably as a matter of logic is in some sense not to exist as an experience at all. Thus Emerson is more correct than his critics on the epistemic status of grief and answers proleptically the charges against his insufficient sensitivity. His detractors click their tongues and say that it is a pity Emerson could not feel more deeply. But Emerson sees that grief is not really a question of degree – that it derives its truth not from its intensity but from its inherent undeniability. Pain is real so self-evidentially that quantitative considerations are irrelevant. And Emerson's complaint that he cannot feel grief sufficiently to make himself feel real is simply his recognition that there is no end to grief – no conditions either psychological or logical under which one could honestly say, "Yes, now I have grieved enough." The question is not how Emerson could have said this of his son's death but how anyone could say anything else. And the burden of proof lies not with those who doubt the sufficiency of grief but with those who trust in it.

Emerson, then, in this first section of the essay examines illusion not merely as an empirical reality but as a necessary condition of experience, of being wholly within a system. Theoretically illusion is simply the possibility of wrongness that allows for the possibility of rightness, the intimation of standards however indeterminate. Yet the interdependence of illusion and reality does not really work both ways. And if the possibility of illusion allows for the possibility of reality, its experience does not prove realism. The Lethe is in this sense mixed too strong. Certainty only tells man what is necessary, not what is sufficient, and all the incorrigibility of grief proves is the insufficiency of perfect clarity – his inability for direct strokes or for relations not casual or oblique. Emerson ends teasingly with the notion that in death we have "a reality that will not dodge us." But the promise is a hollow irony, for as the opening sentences made clear, it is the very absence of end points that introduced relativity into the human condition. And birth and death are ways not to define the system but only to leave it.

III

Illusion, then, is an introductory section, serving to characterize all experience in a general, negative, though not despairing way. The next four sections – Temperament, Succession, Surface, and Surprise – treat specific aspects of this general illusoriness, commenting especially on how illusion is experienced in the world and how an understanding of the mechanics of illusion can help explain its necessity. With their emphasis on human experience, these four sections stand as something of a "lower argument." By describing where we find ourselves, they hope, like the introduction, to distinguish between a necessary indeterminacy and a debilitating incoherence.

The first section, Temperament, offers the most personal (and familiar) explanation of illusion. Illusion is neither good nor bad but the mere fact of perception, the inescapability of thought. "Life is a train of moods like a string of beads, and, as we pass through them, they prove to be many-colored lenses which paint the world their own hue, and each shows only what lies in its focus. . . . Temperament is the iron wire on which the beads are strung" (p. 30). Temperament is simultaneously the history of moods and the unifying principle of that history, the train and wire both.[52] The vibrating iron string that in "Self-Reliance" sang of self-trust is now itself the self on which the beadlike particulars of personality are strung.[53]

Inverting *Nature*'s initial question of to what end nature, Emerson asks the use of temperament.

> Of what use is fortune or talent to a cold and defective nature? Who cares what sensibility or discrimination a man has at some time shown, if he falls asleep in his chair? . . . Of what use is genius, if the organ is too convex or too concave, and cannot find a focal distance within the actual horizon of human life? . . . (P. 30)

The very formulation, an adaptation of the rhetoric of indifference, seems defeatist and leads to the ironic claim of the witty physician – a near relative of the conformist preacher – that there is a direct correlation between digestive disorders and religious creeds. Yet the cynicism should not be overstated, for temperament does have a use, albeit a diminished one. "We animate what we can, and we see only what we animate. . . . It depends on the mood of the man, whether he shall see the sunset or the fine poem. There are always sunsets, and there is always genius; but only a few hours so serene that we can relish nature or criticism" (p. 30).[54] The point is the purely Kantian one of the Copernican revolution: temperament measures the structuring power of the mind, the adaptation of world to thought. And its own irregularity – what Emerson calls its "more or less" – actually implies the stability of the things-in-themselves, the eternality of sunsets and genius.

The first explanation of the illusoriness, then, rehearses the familiar idealist point about the consequences of unknowability. Yet Emerson immediately suggests the insufficiency of this explanation by claiming that temperament not only explains illusion but itself "enters fully into the system of illusions" (p. 31). The problem, implicit in self-knowledge, becomes explicit in our understanding of other persons. For "there is an optical illusion about every person we meet" (p. 31). Using the traditional argument from analogy, Emerson claims that we see in others the signs of life and therefore impute to them the kinds of feelings or "impulses" that we as selves feel.[55] Yet what "in the moment . . . seems impulse" over a longer period of time reveals itself as "a certain uniform tune which the revolving barrel of the music-box must play" (p. 31).[56]

From the platform of ordinary life or of physics, the irresistible conclusion is "the contracting influences of so-called science." All physicians, witty or not, become phrenologists and implicit materialists in their assumption that temperament proves determinism. "The physicians say, they are not materialists; but they are: – Spirit is matter reduced to an extreme thinness: O *so* thin! – But the definition of *spiritual* should be, *that which is its own evidence*" (p. 31). The only solution is to insist on the importance of inscrutability and the liberating whispers of intellect. Thus, though adequate as a veto or limitation-power, a restraint on the preoccupation with illusoriness, temperament cannot itself disprove the possibility of the unusual, "original equity" (p. 32). The argument – with its emphasis on the self-evidence of truth and on temperament as a negative limit – seems Emerson's usual one. Yet the vehemence and dogmatism of his tone are surprising. More, however, is at stake here than the liberation of other minds. For in perceiving the imprisonment of others in their temperaments, Emerson fears he may also prove indirectly his own enslavement. As part of a system of illusions, temperament not only limits others but "shuts us in a prison of glass which we cannot see" (p. 31). The transparent eyeball thus becomes not the perfectly clear lens of *Nature* or even the many-colored ones earlier in Temperament. It is now quite literally an invisible prison.

The next section, Succession, offers a partial solution to the instability of temperament by emphasizing the ironically stabilizing implications of movement.

> The secret of the illusoriness is in the necessity of a succession of moods or objects. Gladly we would anchor, but the anchorage is quicksand. This onward trick of nature is too strong for us: *Pero si muove.* When, at night, I look at the moon and stars, I seem stationary, and they to hurry. (P. 32)

Movement is, of course, one of the central concerns of the second series, especially evident in the inchoate motion of the second "Nature." But the concept of "succession" as movement in time harnesses this surging power to an orderly sense of progression (if not quite of progress).[57]

The issue is not the location or even the reality of the succession, but its necessity. And the particulars of succession – whether internal moods or external objects – are less important than the mere possibility of change. Anchorage is quicksand, for in stasis man discovers his imprisonment in temperament, without even the compensation of knowing precisely where his jail is. The experience of succession, although solving the problems of neither temperament nor illusion, mitigates both by establishing the existence of an objectivity unknown yet necessary. As Kant showed in the second Analogy of Experience, the possibility of experience presupposes an objective ordering, the reality not of the *"subjective succession* of apprehension" but of the *"objective succession* of appearances."[58] Although Kant's exposition here is notoriously problematic, the point is at its lowest level justifiable. The experience of an event in time involves the sense of that event's date or order in a sequence. Dates and orders, however, are not themselves part of the experience, but largely discovered after the fact. As a logical construct, then, such datedness, although not defining the relation to an objective order, at least assumes its possibility. Thus the experience of any succession or change, whether in moods or objects, requires the prior notion of an objective, necessary order – in Kant's formulation, that "everything that happens . . . presupposes something upon which it follows according to a rule."[59]

Yet despite claims for the possibility of "symmetry" and of man's part in "the gaining party," Emerson does not find this answer sufficient.[60] The child is simply not reassured, as he might have been in an earlier work, that his inconstant interests measure his universality, his being "born to a whole" (p. 33). In part this hostility to the particular threatens the status of other "persons," who become – as they did at the end of "Discipline" – merely "representatives of certain ideas, which they never pass or exceed. They stand on the brink of the ocean of thought and power, but they never take the single step that would bring them there" (p. 33). But the insufficiency of others infects the empirical self as well. The earlier explanation of perception as truly active and animating is now rewritten to seem, like all human activity, merely partial and necessitated. "We do what we must, and call it by the best names we can, and would fain have the praise of having intended the result which ensues" (pp. 33-34).

The symmetry and stability of succession thus deny personal achievement, what Emerson calls "expansion" or "elasticity." Yet the next lord suggests that this apparent desperation only marks the limits of the ways man can know things. The lord's name, Surface, and the physical images of superficial travel – skating, being "on the highway" or in the "mid-world" – seem to imply that the shallowness is qualitative. Yet, in fact, superficiality is offered only as a corrective to what in the previous lords seemed excessive depth – the tendency to send down roots into quicksand. "But what help from these fineries or pedantries? What help from thought? Life is not dialectics. We, I think, in these times, have had lessons enough of the futility of criticism. . . . Intellectual tasting of life will not supersede muscular activity" (p. 34).

The denial is partly directed against the absolutism of the previous lords, especially Temperament. The power and form that in Succession seemed separate are now equally mixed in life; it is in fact the super-abundance of each man's peculiarity that constitutes the needed propor-tion or symmetry (pp. 35, 38; cf. p. 34). Boscovich's theory, which earlier seemed to prove atomism, now teaches the simpler lesson of antiessentialism – not no contact between souls and objects, but no inside to the world (p. 37; cf. p. 29). And most strikingly, the denial of "dyspepsia" and praise of the "temperate" zone teasingly qualify what had earlier seemed the total enslavement to temper (p. 36).

Like the previous lords, then, Surface works in part to redefine the tyrannical implications of those who have come before him. But the real revisionary force of the section is directed less against the early pages of this essay than against the early absolutes of Emerson's whole career. And the true target of the section is not so much Succession or Temperament but *Nature*. It is in this section, as we have seen, that Emerson makes his most explicit revision of *Nature*, denying nature's gospel lessons and her thundering of the commandments. Moreover, his new willingness to settle for the "potluck of the day" probably glances back to the moment in "Language" when nature's message explicitly transcended "the affairs of our pot and kettle" (p. 36; cf. CW.I.21).

But the most extended revision is also the most puzzling. In *Nature* the mark of man's potential divinity was the contrast between himself and his house, the world. "We are as much strangers in nature, as we are aliens from God. We do not understand the notes of birds. The fox and the deer run away from us; the bear and tiger rend us" (p. 39). This difference was then read by the Orphic Poet to prove that "the founda-tions of man are not in matter, but in spirit" (p. 42). The logic and even the vocabulary are repeated in Surface, immediately before the return of Boscovich.

> We fancy that we are strangers, and not so intimately domesticated in the planet as the wild man, and the wild beast and bird. But the exclusion reaches them also; reaches the climbing, flying, gliding, feathered and four-footed man. Fox and woodchuck, hawk and snipe, and bittern, when nearly seen, have no more root in the deep world than man, and are just such superficial tenants of the globe. (P. 37)

The point is now different, as the neutral use of the loaded word "gliding" implies. The mild paradox that the "wild" are more truly "domesticated" because less strangers in the world gives way to the more sweeping charge that all are equally excluded.[61]

The denial of "deep worlds" and "insides" is not, however, merely the denial of spirit, though it does suggest one way of avoiding the pseudospirit of the materialist physicians. It is, as Emerson implies in one final allusion to *Nature*, a rudimentary theory of indifference.

> Objections and criticism we have had our fill of. There are objections to every course of life and action, and the practical wisdom infers an indifferency, from the omnipresence of objection. The whole frame of things preaches indifferency. Do not craze yourself with thinking, but go about your business anywhere. Life is not intellectual or critical, but sturdy. Its chief good is for well-mixed people who can enjoy what they find, without question. (Pp. 34-35)

In *Nature*, of course, the rhetoric of indifference taught the inevitability of transcendental idealism: in my inability to discover a standard against which to check sensations, I must admit the phenomenality of knowledge. And at the beginning of Temperament, a similar rhetoric of "uselessness" taught the neutralization of genius through personal excess. Here, however, indifferency is not a trope but a category, part of the "whole frame of things," nature's sole sermon.

The point is not anti-Kantian. Criticism is rejected throughout this section as futile. But futility does not necessarily prove inaccuracy: questions for which answers cannot be discovered are not questions for which no answers exist.[62] Instead, "practical" wisdom's inference of indifference, like practical reason's of the imperative, is merely the suspicion that the world is not limited to what can be known with certainty. Or at least the injunction not to "craze" oneself by seeking to know the unknowable, but instead to settle for what can be done "without question" – one's "business." As Emerson explains in one last restatement of man's power of control, "so many things are unsettled which it is of the first importance to settle, – and, pending their settlement, we will do as we do" (p. 37). No longer animating, yet neither entirely will-less, man should simply go on as he will without seeking to know further.

This argument for indifference is most strikingly summarized in the case for other people. "Let us treat the men and women well: treat them as if they were real: perhaps they are." Prescinding from questions of noumenality, even admitting tacitly that so far as they can be "known" people are phenomenal, Emerson nevertheless chooses to "treat" them as if they were real. "Men live in their fancy, like drunkards whose hands are too soft and tremulous for successful labor. It is a tempest of fancies, and the only ballast I know, is a respect to the present hour" (p. 35).[63] Transcendental idealism ensures that experience will always be illusion, a tempest of fancies. Yet the answer is not merely succession as empirical realism but the further ballast of the indifference of surface–a respect to the present hour. Logically we can presuppose stability; psychologically we can respect the present.

> We should not postpone and refer and wish, but do broad justice where we are, by whomsoever we deal with, accepting our actual companions and circumstances, however humble or odious, as the mystic officials to whom the universe has delegated its whole pleasure for us. (P. 35)

The argument is familiar and the allusion to "Self-Reliance" clear. In the earlier essay, man established the existence of self "without prospect or retrospect." Here he believes in others by not postponing or referring or wishing. There, few and mean though my gifts might have been, I actually was. So in a similar "broad" justice, however humble and odious are the companions and circumstances that the universe delegates–however mean their gifts–they too are "actual," they too actually are (cf. CW.II.31). In part their existence is necessary as the relatively stable backdrop against which change can become apparent. "They give a reality to the circumjacent picture, which such a vanishing meteorous appearance can ill spare." But more simply, they are merely that other part of reality that Emerson had bracketed in his attempt to define precisely the autonomy of self. And as in "Self-Reliance" he had banished father, mother, wife, brother, and friend, so here–the brackets removed–he readmits them to experience (or at least those of them who are still alive). "In the morning I awake, and find the old world, wife, babes, and mother, Concord and Boston, the dear old spiritual world, and even the dear old devil not far off" (p. 36).[64] Within a circumscribed system of "beautiful limits"–the "kingdom of known cause and effect"–then, all is defined because surface and indifference deny in principle the relevance of the undefinable. Thus the problem of illusion drops out, and temperament's enslavement becomes nothing more than a pun, the derivation of man's peculiar nature from nature's own "irresistible nature" (pp. 39, 38).[65]

Yet the ease of the solution suggests its insufficiency, even inaccuracy, and the next lord, Surprise, stands to remind man of the extent to which "fate" will not allow such circumscription. "Power keeps quite another road than the turnpikes of choice and will, namely, the subterranean and invisible tunnels and channels of life. . . . Life is a series of surprises, and would not be worth taking or keeping, if it were not" (p. 39).[66] The formulations are not new and, in fact, repeat exactly points made in earlier sections. The definition of power recalls the extent to which, throughout the essay, life has been a mixture of power and form, though Surface tended to emphasize the latter (pp. 35, 38). And however much indifference seemed a kind of willfulness, it is not in any significant sense a choice. Moreover the stability of succession depends only on its serial quality, not on the individual character of the moments. What seemed earlier the superfluity of parts, man's mere "tricksiness," made life "not worth the taking" (p. 34). Now Emerson insists that life would be equally "not worth the taking or keeping" without the capacity for the extraordinary that transforms succession into a series of surprises. And the whispering that freed man from the prison of temperament now returns as the "angel-whispering" that, on a larger scale, "discomfits the conclusions of nations and of years" (pp. 32, 39).

Yet the force of such unpredictability is not, as might first appear, antinomianism or liberation of any kind. The cause of inevitable surprise is not irrationality but ultimate rationality – here called God. Its function is not so much to mystify experience as to relocate the power away from man. As in "Self-Reliance" and Surface, so here man lives without prospect or retrospect. Such spontaneity, however, is not chosen but imposed.

> God delights to isolate us every day, and hide from us the past and the future. We would look about us, but with grand politeness he draws down before us an impenetrable screen of purest sky, and another behind us of purest sky. 'You will not remember,' he seems to say, 'and you will not expect.' (P. 39)

The impossibility that earlier seemed liberating is now more logical, even mechanical and biological. "The art of life has a pudency, and will not be exposed. Every man is an impossibility until he is born; every thing impossible until we see a success." Life has an "art," is created or made; and the apparent limitlessness of potentiality really only measures man's inability to create, his lack of a certain kind of imagination. "The ardors of piety agree at last with the coldest skepticism, – that nothing is of us or our works, – that all is of God. Nature will not spare us the smallest leaf of laurel. All writing comes by the grace of God, and all doing and having" (p. 40).

Although the vocabulary is theological, the point is epistemological, even linguistic. The failure of man's will measures the greater intransigence of life itself. Frivolous idealism would make the world whatever man says it is, and surface seems to condone this trivialization of the external. Surprise, however, asserts the essential unmalleability of experience. In one sense the world is given, not created; and however great may be his power to shape it by choosing which questions to ask, man still cannot blink the whole thing away.[67] The power of surface is that of description and "conversation"; the corrective of surprise, that of life itself.

At times Emerson connects this inaccessibility merely with our perspective. Seeing only a small segment of history, man cannot comment on the direction of the whole. "The persons who compose our company, converse, and come and go, and design and execute many things, and somewhat comes of it all, but all unlooked-for result." But at his best he realizes that the problem cannot be corrected by a broadening of his view, that in one sense holism is a logical as well as an empirical impossibility. "I can see nothing at last, in success or failure, than more or less of vital force supplied from the Eternal. The results of life are uncalculated and uncalculable" (p. 40). The inability to see anything but vital force from the Eternal is, of course, empirical, a denial of the visibility of any "will of man." But it is also analytic, a definition of the Eternal as identically that supply of vital force. And in repeating his claim that "the individual is always mistaken," Emerson moves from the insufficiency of individual persons to the insufficiency of individuality as such, the "irreducibleness of the elements of human life to calculation" (p. 40).[68]

This last move, though in some ways just one more example of the liberator turned enslaver, is actually different in kind and effectively signals the end of the lower argument. In his survey of the lords Temperament, Succession, Surface, and Surprise, Emerson has offered four partial explanations for the illusoriness of experience. Now with the sixth lord, Reality, he declares the problem a false one. The ancients' reification of irreducibleness into a false deity, Chance, implicitly suggests not only the dangers of calling surprise a lord but also the problem of choosing illusion as a starting point. For surprise and illusion, in their essential dualism, their very irreducibleness, suggest equally the need for a shift in perspective. "The miracle of life which will not be expounded, but will remain a miracle, introduces a new element" (p. 40). The notion of the "unexpoundable" recalls *Nature*'s use of the "unspeakable" to mark the existence of other realms of discourse. And it suggests the same inversion of subject and object by which the noble doubt introduced Kant's Copernican revolution into the world.

The method of Reality is to claim that what in the lower argument seemed a defect in our ability to experience is actually a defining characteristic of experience as such. The amnesia that earlier marked a flaw in our perception is now essential to experience, the fact that "life has no memory" (p. 40). Similarly, before, without defining absolutely the tendency or direction of progress, succession at least stabilized it in the notion of a time sequence. Now, however, man's ignorance of tendency does not mark the partiality of his perspective on his own succession but proves reality's essential nonsuccessiveness. "That which proceeds in succession might be remembered, but that which is coexistent, or ejaculated from a deeper cause, as yet far from being conscious, knows not its own tendency" (pp. 40-41). The relative instability of experience is less explained away than it is used to relocate stability elsewhere. "Life is hereby melted into an expectation or a religion" (p. 41). And "our life seems not present, so much as prospective" (p. 42).

The fullest proof of this greater reality just beyond experience, however, lies not with the lords themselves but with a "critical" meta-experience, "the mode of our illumination." Man does not proceed toward a goal (or at least steadily toward one), as he does when searching for water to end his thirst. He is simply "apprised" of his closeness to an area of unspecified excellence. Thought or study gives no continuity to his progress, but only reveals in momentary glimpses the nature of his goal. This discontinuity prevents any sense that man creates the experience, for each individual insight points away from itself. "But every insight from this realm of thought is felt as initial, and promises a sequel. I do not make it; I arrive there, and behold what was there already" (p. 41).

Yet the very discontinuity suggests the possibility of continuity.

> If I have described life as a flux of moods, I must now add, that there is that in us which changes not, and which ranks all sensations and states of mind. The consciousness in each man is a sliding scale, which identifies him now with the First Cause, and now with the flesh of his body; life above life, in infinite degrees. (P. 42)

Returning to the opening image of the series and degrees, in all its Swedenborgian quirkiness, Emerson now sees consciousness not quite as that which unifies the series, but as the scale against which unification becomes possible.

As always, the principle of unity itself, though undeniable, remains unapproachable – or, in Emerson's customary trope, unnameable. "The baffled intellect must still kneel before this cause, which refuses to be named, – ineffable cause" (p. 42). Yet though the intellect remains humbled in its bafflement, it is ironically that very bafflement that assures it of the potential for clarity elsewhere. The tendency of experience, whose independence throughout the lower argument measured man's distance from reality, now establishes that reality in the mere possibility of having rules at all. "It is for us to believe in the rule, not in the exception. . . . It is not what we believe concerning the immortality of the soul, or the like, but *the universal impulse to believe*, that is the material circumstance, and is the principal fact in the history of the globe." And experience, though still uncontrollable, nevertheless becomes coherent and even satisfying. "I am explained without explaining, I am felt without acting, and where I am not. Therefore all just persons are satisfied with their own praise. They refuse to explain themselves, and are content that new actions should do them that office" (pp. 42-43).

IV

A kind of pattern, then, may be discovered in the lower argument of "Experience." Each lord in turn is offered both as an explanation of the general problem of the illusoriness of nature and as a possible means of curbing the excesses of the previous lord. All are thus presented as initially liberating forces that turn enslaving when left unchecked. And the measure of each lord's power – positive or negative – is how it alters man's view of other people. Not only Illusion, with its famous denial of Waldo, but each section builds to and is tested by its effect on the self's relation to others – whether as optical illusions, unexpansive partialists, hypothetical people, or mistaken individuals. And, as in *Nature* the whole lower argument finally collapsed into the noble doubt of "Idealism," so here the lower procession of the lords of Temperament, Succession, Surface, and Surprise halts with the introduction of the more absolute condition of reality.

Thus "Experience" can – at least in these early lords – be read as Emerson's inversion of his initial philosophical project. In *Nature,* Emerson found that if he started with the objective world and asked its purpose, he could deduce through the noble doubt the constitutive dimension of mind. In "Experience," he shows that if he starts at the other end with experience as something constructed (even misconstrued) by mind, he can still work his way back to the notion of objectivity as Reality. Yet however adequately this pattern describes the shape of the essay, it does not really account for the work's peculiarly unsettling quality. The failure of the section on Reality itself marks the peculiarity: though the rhetorical climax of the first half of the argument, Reality is far less compelling than Surface or even Surprise. But a more striking example is the role of memory both here and in the earlier passages on Lethe.

Here the question is not what memory is but why Emerson spends so much time on it. The answer, as we might expect from our analysis of "Self-Reliance," lies in the concept of personal identity. In that earlier essay, Emerson cuts his notion of self off from time: without prospect or retrospect, I actually am. Yet this solution solves the problem of existence without addressing the related notion of identity: existence alone cannot establish the unity of selves – whether for Emerson or the roses. Something might exist in many bodies, many consciousnesses – or even in none. What is needed, according to most of Emerson's contemporaries (and some recent philosophers), is a common store of remembered knowledge. In Locke's crucial formulation,

> Since consciousness always accompanies thinking, and 'tis that, that
> makes every one to be, what he calls *self;* and thereby distinguishes
> himself from all other thinking things, in this alone consists *personal
> Identity,* i.e. the sameness of a rational Being. . . . Consciousness, as
> far as ever it can be extended, should it be to Ages past, unites Exis-
> tences, and Actions, very remote in time, into the same Person, as
> well as it does the Existence and Actions of the immediately preceding
> moment: So that whatever has the consciousness of present and past
> Actions, is the same Person to whom they both belong.[69]

Thus consciousness, particularly in its ability through memory to connect discontinuous temporal events, establishes identity.

Yet Locke's position, though true, is not a sufficient account of personal identity. As many of his contemporaries understood, memory
presupposes the concept of personhood. The claim that "John was the
one who understood X if and only if he could remember it" is wrong
for all meanings of "could" except the one that presupposes his identity
as witness – that no one else "could" because he actually did.[70] Thomas
Reid's formulation of this objection is particularly suggestive here.
"There can be no memory of what is past without the conviction that
we existed at the time remembered. . . . The moment a man loses this
conviction, as if he had drunk water of Lethe, past things are done
away; and, in his own belief, he then begins to exist."[71] Similarly Reid's
definition of personality resonates strongly with Emerson's ironic characterization of Waldo as a mere piece of real estate.

> When a man loses his estate, his health, his strength, he is still the
> same person, and has lost nothing of his personality. If he has a leg or
> an arm cut off, he is the same person he was before. The amputated
> member is no part of his person, otherwise it would have a right to a
> part of his estate, and be liable for a part of his engagements. . . . A
> person is something indivisible, and is what Leibnitz called a *monad.*[72]

Emerson's denials of memory throughout the lower argument, then,
in part attest to its insufficiency as a proof of personhood. Yet if memory is not a sufficient proof of personality, it is still a necessary one, for
one condition of personal identity is reidentifiability – our ability, in
Emerson's terms, to know our place again. To be a person, one must
be able not merely to recall the store of one's past experiences but to
reidentify the experiencer as the same self – to know not simply that
John once was X but that the John who was X at T is the same John
who is now Y at T'.[73] In terms of the essay's initial question, how can I
distinguish between a single self at many places – where*s* do I find my
self? – and a simple multitude of persons – where do I find my selves? In
this context, the denial of reidentifiability of place is the denial of exter-

nal criteria. Although other people may identify me in terms of my sustained behavioral patterns, I cannot bring this objective criterion close enough to my own subjectivity to convince me of self-unity. This body seems the same body, this place the same place. But this sameness does not make them any more convincingly mine or establish my integrity through my apparent ownership of these experiences.

Moreover, the denial of memory rejects a still more internal criterion. The claim that life has no memory, like the claim that the world has no inside, implies that within the system of experience there is nothing that could test the memory of recollections. I think I remember experience X, or feel the same sensation S as I did at time T. But in the absence of objective standards for X, S, and T, I cannot be certain that my memory of their definitions is accurate. In Wittgenstein's famous analogy, to use one memory as the subjective justification of another is like using a mental image of a timetable to check the train's departure time or, worse, to buy duplicate copies of a single newspaper in order to demonstrate the truth of the news.[74] In such a context, it is not surprising that Emerson glances back nostalgically toward his earlier Swedenborgianism. For the mystic's belief in the absolute nature of language and his attendant ability to construct dictionaries of spiritual signification would provide the very kind of objective standard needed to establish personal stability in the midst of relativist experience.

In part, then, what Emerson explores in the lower argument is the lack of objective criteria for the ascription of place, memory, and, by extension, of self-identity itself. In this context, the opening question provokes Hume's response that we find ourselves nowhere, that every attempt to find self as an object reveals some particular perception or another, but never a self without a perception or anything but a perception.[75] Other people, the standard against which the lords are measured throughout the lower argument, only aggravate the problem. Though they seem to demonstrate the reality of other selves, even the unity of these selves, they do not solve our personal problem. For, as Emerson later admits, "we believe in ourselves, as we do not believe in others" (p. 45). It is not merely that we believe in self so much more; the very ways in which we establish this belief are different.

This last recognition—that self-belief is a special kind of experience—however, suggests the solution in its very statement of the problem. If self cannot be studied as object, perhaps it can as subject. And the whole issue of the absence of objective criteria redefines itself to study the special conditions of subjectivity—especially the criterionless self-ascription of identity. The multiple perspective is implicit even in the opening. Hume's inability to answer positively the opening question in one sense calls a halt to the Cartesian project by showing that there is no "place" for mental events, no "where" to grief. Yet both Kant and Wittgenstein reopen the question, though not within Cartesian coordinates.[76] For Kant, man finds his self not in any real place but in the formal unity of consciousness – the transcendental unity of apperception. Wittgenstein, attending more specifically to the meanings of the terms, argues that "I," when used as a subject, does not really denote a possessor any more than "here" does a place or "now" a time.[77] The implication is, then, that the proper answer to Emerson's opening question of where is "In the 'I think' " or even simply "Here." To demand a more complete definition of place or self is simply to misunderstand the function of the two concepts.[78]

This shift in focus, then, solves some of the problems the essay poses by showing them to be misstated. In general, the whole problem of a plurality of selves passes away. To the extent that the I – whether in Kant's version or Wittgenstein's – is purely formal, there is no question of disunity. Either unity is inherently part of the definition from the start, or it drops out as an empirical consideration irrelevant to any such formal definition. It is, in fact, the conflation of these two conditions – the unity of experience and the experience of unity – that for Kant constitutes metaphysical "illusion" in the Dialectic.[79] In Emerson's version, illusion is perceived as such only when experience is asked to comment too explicitly on the self. Even as it demonstrates the greater unity of Reality as objectivity, the lower argument characterizes the experience of the empirical self as necessarily one of moments: not merely that we see only "what" we animate, but that we see only "when" as well. The "exclusion" that the living feel from the absolute – from deep roots and insides – results in the total fragmentation of personal experience. Each moment is independent, neighborless; and the Romantic problem of infrequency gives way to the more metaphysical one of discontinuity – what has been more recently called the "solipsism of the moment."[80]

This fragmentation represents for Emerson less a dilemma than an antinomy, resulting from the delusive search for objective criteria. As he says at the beginning of the essay, the problem of experience is not really a question of objectivity but of subjectivity, not of life but of perception. And the false dilemmas of solipsism and the failure of objectivity – the questions about multiple selves – should turn man back to the deeper question of subjectivity – of what it means to be really "in me." The issue here is the cluster of notions concerning the apparently criterionless self-ascription of identity – what is now called privacy. Ever since Descartes isolated the mind as a distinct entity, philosophers have noted that our knowledge of consciousness is learned in a different way from our knowledge of the world. The mind's ideas seem inherently first-person and private, especially some of its sensations and propositional attitudes.[81] Some thoughts are "incommunicable" and can be known by their thinker but not conceivably by anyone else. To some, the thinker has "private access" and can detect their existence in at least one way that others cannot. Finally, some ideas are "incorrigible" in that his claims for their existence cannot be overridden.[82] It was this privileged status of thought, and especially the last notion of incorrigibility, that led Descartes to discover in the mind the kind of clarity and indubitability needed to overturn his methodological doubt.

Even as it dismisses certain questions as pseudoproblems, however, the emphasis on the privacy of mental events makes other problems seem central. The test case for studying all three types of privacy – trivially in Descartes, Locke, and Kant, and centrally in much recent philosophy – became sensations, especially, as we have seen, those of pain.[83] First, in the uniqueness of our "mode of observation" – our certainty about the "special felt qualities" of pain – privacy tends to posit the existence of separate mental entities somehow unlike physical ones. This proliferation of concepts of interiority – mind, inner space, mental events, private experiences – then generates a whole complex of skeptical paradoxes about the relation between these interior entities and external ones, whether bodies or words (of which the most famous is currently the possibility of a private language).[84] Furthermore the reification of "our" mind raises the question of the existence of "other minds." Given that we know our own minds in a way both private and inaccessible, do we really have any adequate criteria for the belief in other "minds" behind the appearances we see? Or any reason for assuming that behavioral patterns roughly comparable to what we know to be our own in certain situations are actually the mark of similar, though inaccessible, mental events in other minds?

It is with such questions of internality, more than the nature of experience as such, that Emerson is most concerned in this essay. Experience as the problem of existence within a system focuses increasingly on the question of the experience of experience – the special problem of what it "feels like" to have a mind. The reification of mind has always been a problem for Emerson. His customary solution is to distinguish between realms of discourse – in the second series, "platforms of reality" – asserting that the mind's operations are transcendentally knowable, though its transcendent reality is unspeakable. In "Experience," however, which takes place entirely within the sphere of the knowable, such a solution seems less conclusive, though Emerson does in fact invoke it briefly in Reality. Instead Emerson's project is to determine not the logical conditions of knowledge but its felt experience, and his proof of the mind's existence emphasizes not its transcendent necessity but its epistemic incorrigibility.

The answer comes early in the essay, near the end of Temperament, during the attack on the "mental proclivity" of the physicians. In one sense the passage is odd, and expends far too much energy (even spleen) exposing the crypto-materialism of the phrenologists. Yet Emerson is after bigger game than Spurzheim. The attack on those who would deduce the "law of [man's] being" from his beard or his bumps is by extension, of course, a denial of all external criteria and finally of all criteria. But the real problem is less the way they conceive the mental than their need to conceive it at all – less a proclivity concerning the mental than a proclivity toward it. Mental entities are, by this light, as materialist as vibratiuncles (and, indeed, philosophy of mind has always had to fight its own behaviorist tendency).[85]

In substituting the notion of the self-evidentiality of spirit, Emerson acknowledges the privacy of the mind but implicitly denies the possibility of substantiation, even within its own realm. Self-evidence is a special kind of privacy: in claiming that P, though not necessary, is asserted truly if asserted at all, self-evidence argues for the truth of an assertion without admitting its necessity or even its existence.[86] The claim that mind is free from the universal exclusion of reality – that "it is impossible that the creative power should exclude itself" (p. 32) – claims not its closeness to the noumenal but only its epistemic independence, even isolation. And the real thrust of the assertion that souls never touch their objects is not the trivial (and probably wrong) conclusion that objects are unreal, but the more perplexing one that souls are – or at least that they are sufficiently distinct from reality that the sensory metaphor of touching is inapplicable.

Emerson's preoccupation in the essay with skepticism about other minds is even clearer than his worries about the reification of the mental. Each of the sections in the lower argument builds, as we have seen, to the question of other persons as a test of the lord's power. But, as before, the real question is what Emerson means to do with this problem – not how we might know about other minds, but why Emerson asks the question when he does. The great problem of experience has been implicit in the definition of experience itself: how can one know from within a closed system; what could possibly serve as a standard or criterion? Our knowledge of other minds, then, stands as a representative example of this problem in its double circumscription. Not only are we within the system we wish to examine, but the quality of mentality we wish to discover is not – or at least is discovered in our own minds in a nonsystematic way.

In Temperament, Emerson focuses attention on the failure of analogy, our discovery that the impulsiveness we impute to others in the moment turns out in the lifetime to be a barrel-organ tune. His point,

however, is not to deny other minds but simply to discredit the argument from analogy traditionally used to prove them.[87] Not only does
the argument fail to establish the reality of other minds, but in the
process it tends to make our mind seem just as rule bound and calls into
question our own impulsiveness. Thus the praise of "other" temperaments begins to look to an embattled Emerson like an implicit refutation of subjectivity and privileged access; and unless further defended,
private truth may become not self-evidential but personal and even
moody. Yet as Emerson insists, "temperament is a power which no
man willingly hears any one praise but himself" (p. 31). In part Emerson only notes a curious anomaly about our use of the word: "my"
temperament means only my quirkiness; "yours," however, implies
your obstinacy. Yet he suggests a more significant difference (perhaps
itself the source of the linguistic one). Temperament as moodiness in
part identifies those episodic thoughts and images that are inaccessible
because their public expression is a perfectly voluntary matter, those
minimal intentions he would elsewhere call "whims." Thus to hear
someone else praise their impulses is to doubt one's own; to do so
"willingly" is to deny the possibility of lintel willfulness that inaccessibility is meant to prove.[88]

Analogy, then, challenges privacy and the notion of will it supports. In
the remaining sections, Emerson tries to imagine how one might believe
in other minds without analogically doubting one's own. In Succession
the child's dissatisfaction with his mother's explanation that change implies universality marks a more general discomfort with a treatment of
people as particulars. If people are merely "representatives" of certain
ideas, they are sure to seem partial and unexpansive (p. 33). "I cannot
recall any form of man who is not superfluous sometimes" (p. 34). The
problem is less with the individual than with our way of perceiving
him – the representative theory of knowledge and especially memory.
As Reid responded to Hume, the very notion of recollection, and especially recalling a "form" of a man, by placing an idea between the past
impression and the memory experience, ensures the impossibility of
learning "by experience" of the connection.[89] Memory too leads back to
privacy, and the "special talent" by which man remembers must be
treated not as "representative" but as self-validating.

The solution to the problem of other minds – in the two sections
Surface and Surprise – is not realistic but hypothetical, even pragmatic.
To treat minds as like anything else is to deny the essential privacy by
which we define our own minds and therefore to undermine the definition from the first. The first-person experience is so built into our
understanding of "mind" that the phrase "other minds" is an oxymoron.[90] The failure is not of reality but only of expression – language,

categories, dialectics. And the obvious solution is to treat people "as if" they have all those things associated with "my mind" without asking what it would mean for them to have such things. The individual will always be mistaken conceptually. The things that he feels about his private situation will always be wrong – applicable to neither himself nor others – because he thinks he has ideas and knowledge when he only has incorrigibility and privileged access – intuitions without concepts. But as in Illusion's magic result, the discontinuity between activity and result does not interfere with the functioning of either. The parallel worlds of actions and ends continue unaffected. "The persons who compose our company, converse, and come and go, and design and execute many things, and somewhat comes of it all . . . . [The individual] designed many things, and drew in other persons as co-adjutors, quarrelled with some or all, blundered much, and something is done" (p. 40).

Thus Emerson's skepticism about other minds reduces to skepticism about minds altogether. And the solution of hypothetical indifference toward the existence of other people suggests an equal indifference about the meaning of personality itself – a refusal to explain the ineffable irreducibility of the elements of human life. Throughout the lower argument, the question has been not so much, as it first appeared in Illusion, why does knowledge never work to evaluate experience. Instead it is, how can I use the tension between the logical impossibility of such knowledge and my apparent experience of it to understand further the logical peculiarities of being an I within a larger system? Or, in terms of the opening question, less where do we find ourselves than why do we find ourselves as such: what is it about the nature of our existence that makes us experience things in the way we do?

It is in this light that we can most fully understand the point of Emerson's difficulties with Waldo's death. Despite apparent claims, he is not out to prove reality by locating the authentically sharp peaks and rough edges. Such attempts to locate things become increasingly suspect throughout the essay, as "where" comes to look like simply the wrong question. Since the whole lower argument works to show that reality proves itself – or at least that reality and illusion are two sides of the same coin – the special revelation of grief seems unnecessary. Nor is the passage about the nature of grief itself. Grief teaches nothing but its own superficiality, and the grief about Waldo gives way to a meta-grief about the shallowness of grief.

Instead the passage examines the experience of grief. In one sense, to have a grief, or more generally a pain, is not a possessing or even a content of any kind, but a behavioral act. "I have a pain" is not a description but an expression, an extended groan.[91] Thus those who object to the insufficient humanity of the passage are actually complaining that Emerson does not groan loud enough. The point is fair: Waldo's death as such is not a significant aspect of the passage. Yet the deficiency lies not in Emerson's emotion but in logic and language, and an increase in decibels still could not establish the reality Emerson supposedly seeks. Pain as a privileged sensation is incorrigible, without need of demonstration. Moreover, as an essentially private one, it is not really part of the meta-discussion we apparently have about it, and drops out, like Wittgenstein's celebrated beetle or his wheel that turns no part of the mechanism.[92]

Yet a reading of the paragraph as expressive behavior, though fair, is not sufficient. For if the passage makes no point about Waldo or even about pain, it nevertheless is significantly about "my pain" and what it means to "have" a pain (whatever kind of thing that pain may be). In "Self-Reliance," Emerson asked, "Are they my poor?" and decided that they were not, that the conditions of selfhood were established independently of any relation to others. The same autonomy of self remains obviously, even trivially, true of pain. There is no interesting way of establishing my identity through my pains. They do not introduce me into reality or real nature, though such a failure does not of itself suggest the phenomenality of me, reality, or nature.

But pain is even more deeply private. In "Self-Reliance" my whims were incommunicable and inexplicable as a matter of choice: the day could in fact be spent in explanation, but Emerson chose not so to waste his time. My pain, however, is incommunicable in a more fundamental sense. There is no common vocabulary by which the self-validating nature of private pain can be correlated with the sharable behavioral patterns of public expression.[93] We have quite simply no real notion of what it is to "have" a pain and therefore mean very little by our use of the possessive "my": "I cannot get it nearer to me."[94] Though a pain may be undeniable, I do not "know" or even "believe" I have a pain. I do not wonder whose pain this is and then identify it by comparing it with characteristics quintessentially mine.[95] The very undeniability of the sensation makes talk of knowledge and possession nonsensical.

This last lesson of skepticism turns on itself. Incorrigibility as a mark of the mental is also the implicit denial of mentality as a category. Grieving teaches only the inapplicability of the category of grief as knowledge: I grieve that grief can teach me nothing. But this ultimate failure of discipline, although not quite a lesson, is not without its implications.[96] And the inaccessibility of the ME of privacy becomes itself the occasion for grief: the grief that grief, in its incorrigibility, is neither knowable nor haveable – not merely psychologically difficult, but epistemologically incoherent.

V

In part, all Emerson has done in the lower argument is to rediscover the purely formal nature of the "I think." The unity of consciousness is a logically necessary condition for any experience, but such necessity imparts no knowledge about a thing called "consciousness." In this sense, the denial of Waldo is not only structurally parallel to the eyeball passage; it carries the same message about transparency as unknowability. Were the essay to end here, it would represent merely a more sophisticated version of *Nature*. But, in fact, the lower argument moves not only to the conclusion of Reality, but beyond it to the epistemological despair of Subjectiveness. It is this last transition that shows the real meaning of Emerson's interest in experience and the true thrust of his apparent modernism. For in this final attempt at honesty, Emerson confronts the consequences of the discontinuity in experience – what it means to "experience" a logically unexperienceable, transcendent privacy.[97]

The shift from Reality to Subjectiveness is structurally equivalent to that in *Nature* from "Idealism" to "Spirit." There Emerson used the notion of a God outside of man as a negative limit on what might otherwise have seemed the unlimited power of the noble doubt. Here, however, the subordination of experience to reality needs no external limit, but is itself a kind of limitation. Reality in fact ends with an insistence on the inevitability of limits, how skepticism too is part of the self-explanatory dimension of reality and must be assimilated to it. "For, skepticisms are not gratuitous or lawless, but are limitations of the affirmative statement, and the new philosophy must take them in, and make affirmations outside of them, just as much as it must include the oldest beliefs" (p. 43). Yet the anticipation of new affirmations leads instead to a focusing in on a single skepticism – our discovery of self-consciousness.

> It is very unhappy, but too late to be helped, the discovery we have made, that we exist. That discovery is called the Fall of Man. Ever afterwards, we suspect our instruments. We have learned that we do not see directly, but mediately, and that we have no means of correcting these colored and distorting lenses which we are, or of computing the amount of their errors. Perhaps these subject-lenses have a creative power; perhaps there are no objects. Once we lived in what we saw; now, the rapaciousness of this new power, which threatens to absorb all things, engages us. Nature, art, persons, letters, religions, – objects, successively tumble in, and God is but one of its ideas. (Pp. 43-44)

The abrupt change in tone suggests that, though structurally equivalent to "Spirit," Subjectiveness recalls as well "Idealism" and the noble doubt. Not that the two skepticisms are the same. The noble doubt concluded from the commodiousness of the world the primacy of the mind: nature serves, therefore I think. The fall of man is an entirely subjective, even second-level skepticism, discovering in our existence as consciousness the suspect nature of all experience: I think as the "I think," therefore nothing is directly. The very formality of the first two sentences – with the clinical (almost Austinian) "unhappy" – suggests that the problem is purely technical, though no less disastrous for that.[98] Notions of our seeing give way to our sight of sight, and all particulars – nature, art, persons, letters, religions – are subsumed under and dissolved by the very idea that there are ideas.[99] The list is one more version of Swedenborg's list of unexplained wonders – language, beasts, sex – first seen in *Nature*.[100] But now the problem has been normalized: the question is not why oddities exist but how any object can, and God himself – once the boundary and guarantor of reality – tumbles in as just one more idea, one more thought on which to fall soft.[101]

The inaccuracy of perception, then, really points only toward the more fundamental issue of its mechanics – the difference between "living in what we saw" and merely "being engaged by" the power itself. Emerson has, after all, recognized the subjectivity of sight from the beginning, and there is no real reason why an idealism that left him indifferent in *Nature* should now paralyze him. But the true problem of Subjectiveness is not, as it might first appear, that of the other lords – the inability to discover from within the system some external objective criterion or standard. For, as the image of the horizon suggests, the mind is not so much trapped in the system as wholly outside it. Earlier, the question was, how can I know the real status of the constellation Orion? Now, revising formulations earlier in the essay and in his career in general, Emerson claims, "People forget that it is the eye which makes the horizon, and the rounding mind's eye which makes this or that man a type or representative of humanity with the name of hero or saint" (p. 44). No longer does he wonder if stars in the heavens are really out there, but asks only whether the pattern called Orion is man's creation or reality's. On this point, subjectiveness scores an easy victory.

Yet the triumph has disastrous implications. Earlier in the essay Emerson insisted that true genius was useless if its organ could not find a focal length adjusted to "the actual horizon of human life" (p. 30). The point, like that of *Nature*'s transparent retina, was that the image must be adapted to the eye, the experience to the system within which it occurs. Now when he turns to the eye itself, however, he sees that the idea of an "actual" horizon is misleading. Sight quite simply is the system, not within it, and questions about the representative status of its functions are incoherent. The horizon is not a sensation but a process, a side effect of perception itself. As such, there is outside sight no horizonal entity, no real thing represented well or badly.[102] This particular variety of optical illusion (or better, optical construction) combines with the earlier hypothetical emphasis to vaporize more than we might have hoped.

> Jesus the "providential man," is a good man on whom many people are agreed that these optical laws shall take effect. By love on one part, and by forbearance to press objection on the other part, it is for a time settled, that we will look at him in the centre of the horizon, and ascribe to him the properties that will attach to any man so seen. But the longest love or aversion has a speedy term. (P. 44)

Treating Jesus "as if" divine is not merely a prescinding from questions about categories for which we have no objective standards. It ascribes to him a neutrality that, like the horizon, is entirely phenomenal.

The reconceptualization of the horizon is not simply one more attack on tradition – whether as historical Christianity or as world. And subjectiveness is not merely higher idealism. For the real question is whether the subject-object dualism can hold at any level. The whole notion of self-consciousness – of turning one's glance inward or using one's inner eye – is in some strict sense incoherent. In an inversion of Hume, one could argue that the self's invisibility is not discouraging but the strongest possible proof of its absolute existence – its unpredicability. That omnipresence is a kind of exclusion is implied in Kant's apperception. And stated overtly in Wittgenstein's early insistence that "the subject does not belong to the world; rather, it is a limit of the world."[103] It is the fatality of this exclusion that Emerson tries to capture in his distinction between living in our perceptions and being engaged by them.

> The great and crescive self, rooted in absolute nature, supplants all relative existence, and ruins the kingdom of mortal friendship and love. Marriage (in what is called the spiritual world) is impossible, because of the inequality between every subject and every object. (P. 44)

Self is outside the system: it is this independence that accounts for both its power and its unintelligibility.

The tone here should not be misread.[104] The self is great and absolute. But what it supplants, though merely "relative," will nevertheless be missed. "Ruins," always an important word in Emerson, is here the key. In Nature, man's status as a god in ruins, though depressing, also marked – in a customary Kantian inversion – his potential for recovering his kingdom. Subjectiveness as an anti-orphic poem carries with it no equivalent promise. If "ruins" as a noun implies the possibility of rebuilding, "ruins" as a verb does not–and may even imply its impossibility.

Nor should we miss the ironic dismissal of the Swedenborgianism flirted with earlier in the essay. Marriage in the spirit world is, of course, one of Swedenborg's most famous topics.[105] The parenthetic qualification of "what is called" suggests Emerson's disbelief, his realization that spirit as mentality and world as externality are uncomfortably yoked in the oxymoron. But, more important, Emerson admits, as he does not elsewhere, that the real problem with Swedenborg is not his static symbolism but his faulty philosophy. Swedenborg is acknowledged to be a code name for sloppy epistemology, a kind of burlap Kant, and his system fails not through unimaginativeness (or silliness) but through "impossibility": "the inequality of every subject and object."[106]

Emerson ends this long introductory paragraph with a summary. At times the problem seems, as with Swedenborg, the quantitative one of "inequality": love can never make consciousness and ascription "equal in force." Yet the more important issue is qualitative. The "same gulf" exists between all mes and thees, and considerations of the varying width of that gulf are secondary. The failure does not lie, as in *Nature*, in the incoherence of ascription and representation, but in the distance between this mode and the entirely different one of consciousness. In the terminology of the section's opening, to the extent that spirit is by definition unmediated and experience by definition mediated, there cannot logically be any such thing as an experience of spirit. The relation between subjects and objects is similar to that between originals and pictures; we simply do not ask the same questions of the one as we do of the other. The "proper" or particular deity that "sleeps or wakes" in every subject may perhaps make it superior to every object. But the admission of the irrelevance of activity–its sleeping or waking–qualifies the personality of the power, nullifying all the earlier dream imagery and especially Surface's injunction to favor one's "private dream."[107]

The very inevitability of relationship prevents a more intimate union: the universe remains a perpetual bride whose marriage is never consummated. "Though not in energy, yet by presence, this magazine of substance cannot be otherwise than felt" (p. 44). In part, of course, this undeniable presence is stabilizing, the legacy of the lower argument's realism. Yet this "magazine of substance" has quite explicitly lost its "energy" since its introduction in *Nature* as "the magazine of power" (cf. CW.I.23). The inevitability of feeling really marks the impossibility of thought; and substance's inability to be "otherwise than felt," its inaccessibility to Reason and consciousness, its unknowability.

The summary ends with the triumphant claim that "all private sympathy is partial" (p. 44). Yet this apparently familiar embrace of the universal is in fact more ominous than earlier claims. "Privacy" in this essay is not trivially idiosyncratic, meanly egoistic. It is instead, like the "private dream," that element of personal experience that, in its privilege and incorrigibility, is absolutely unassailable. To say, then, that this logically necessary truth is nevertheless merely partial is not to hold out the hope of a greater universality, but to deny such a possibility altogether. The very autonomy of privacy forbids the feeling "with" that sympathy implies.

The affirmation that follows – the central paragraph for both this lord and the whole essay – is striking in its indirection. In attempting to define the conditions and consequences of privacy, Emerson is forced to emphasize (in predominantly negative constructions) simply what experience is not. Although life can be imaged or depicted, it cannot be divided or doubled. As soul, it is not twin born and admits of no co-life. And in the paragraph's most ringing sentence – and its most explicit definition of the notion of privacy – we believe in ourselves as we do not believe in others. Not only do we think of ourselves in a qualitatively different way. This difference effectively prohibits belief in others at all; the very necessity of the one makes the other a kind of logical impossibility. Though time and appearance are necessary in life's self-revelation – the realm of empirical realism – they are "fatally" subordinated to the greater power of unity. Moreover it is not even clear that we truly believe in ourselves. Selfhood is an undeniable condition, a logical presupposition of experience. But like the mystic's One, of which nothing can be said, the absolute privacy of consciousness does not allow any predicates – even of the belief in its existence.

The outrageous example of these discontinuities – between subject and object, but also between subject and subject – is man's relation to his crimes, even to his murders. As always, Emerson's point is not moral but logical. Consciousness as unity has no inherent conditions, but judges law and fact alike, as if there were no difference between the event and its rule. In part this conflation measures mind's indifference to quantity; in absolute terms, no one possesses and all steal.[108] But, more simply, consciousness is self-contained and inimical to the particularizing tendency of essentialist language. "The intellect names [sin] shade, absence of light, and no essence. The conscience must feel it as essence, essential evil. This it is not: it has an objective existence, but no subjective" (p. 45). Quite simply, that which *is* essence does not name itself; or, in the earlier language of privacy, the expression of pain obviates the need (or even the ability) to know it. Just as they were not my poor, and it not my pain, so ultimately it is not my murder. And, finally, what has no subjective existence is less charity or pain or sin than subjectivity itself.

It is possible to argue that Emerson is here conflating different unities—much as he did in the reification of unity as an over-soul.[109] But whereas earlier such conflations turned the subject into an absolute, now they empty it of all content. "Thus inevitably does the universe wear our color, and every object fall successively into the subject itself. The subject exists, the subject enlarges; all things sooner or later fall into place" (pp. 45-46). The falling into the subject, like the earlier fall into self, does not consolidate but annihilates. The subject exists and enlarges, but it is not something that can itself be the literal subject of predicates. For it is not really a thing at all: spirit—as self or subjectiveness, self-evidence or privacy—is not part of man's experience but is instead its limit. Everything else falls into "place," the Cartesian outside of "extension." And, ironically, the grammatical "I," which must be attached to statements for them to become experiences, is by definition self-validating and private, something that cannot function as the subject of a sentence.[110]

In one last reformulation of his vaguely Cartesian dictum, Emerson claims, "As I am, so I see; use what language we will, we can never say anything but what we are" (p. 46). The possibility of unity still precedes that of experience. But as the shift from singular to plural suggests, the two are not more intimately connected. Man cannot say anything but what he is: there is no escape from subjectiveness as temperament. The "what" never becomes a "where": man cannot pinpoint his relative existence within the system. Neither does it become a "that": man cannot conclude from the formal necessity of subjectivity anything substantial.[111] In this light, the old argument from indifference takes on a new dimension. Like the original pair of Orion and its starry image, so here Kepler and the sphere, Columbus and America, a reader and his book, puss and her tail all are equivalent. But the identity no longer marks their usefulness "to me" or even my inability to distinguish. Now all are reduced to their categorical function as a subject and an object; and once the galvanic circuit is completed, "magnitude"—one might almost say particularity or substance—adds nothing more.

In one sense, this conclusion is only the inevitable collapse of subjectiveness into temperament. Much as in "Prospects" nature seemed to collapse into its lowest end of commodity, so now Emerson admits "our constitutional necessity of seeing things under private aspects, or saturated with our humors" (p. 46). The point, however, is less the truth of temperament than the logical gap between a formal unity and its existential consequences—between spirit and experience. To examine our experiences is to assume a unitary consciousness underwriting that experience; and the same philosophical move that proves we necessarily exist forces us to look behind that existence, even behind that experiencing "we," to the self-validating "I" of subjectiveness. Man is encouraged not to speak of temperament and its deterministic implications, for nothing practical will come of it. Yet it is this "private aspect" of the mental that is in fact its theoretical justification: "And yet is the God the native of these bleak rocks." This God is not the tumbled-in deity of the section's opening, but–as the superfluous article suggests–the more general possibility of godliness. If man would look for "the" God, any absolute, it is only in the logical necessity of subjectivity–the incorrigibility of privacy–that he can find it. The crimes that in "Circles" appeared to be lively stones for building a new temple now turn out to be merely bleak rocks. But nevertheless it is on such bareness–a purely formal, logical condition–that an absolute will depend.[112]

This discontinuity between Reason and experience is complete. The former is an absolutist "poverty," "cold, and so far mournful" (p. 46). But it is at least not conditional or consequential, the "slave of tears, contritions, and perturbations."

> It does not attempt another's work, nor adopt another's facts. It is a main lesson of wisdom to know your own from another's. I have learned that I cannot dispose of other people's facts; but I possess such a key to my own, as persuades me, against all their denials, that they also have a key to theirs. (P. 46)

Emerson does not really claim to know wisdom as such, to know wise things. Still he is aware of knowledge as possessible and able to distinguish wisdom as "my own." Thus, even though unable to know where he is, he does not wonder if wherever he is is his place or another's.

This minimal knowledge of wisdom as unintelligible but owned then permits the return of analogy in an equally diminished form. Emerson is unable to dispose of "other people's facts," because he is effectively unable to "dispose" of his own, the disagreeable appearances once so easily vanquished. Nevertheless the knowledge, not of the meaning of his own key, but merely of his possession of it, is sufficient to persuade him that others have comparable keys. The reduced argument does not make the traditional mistake of equating private evidence with public behavior: insofar as others address the issue, they in fact deny their keys. Nor does the analogy imply a moral reciprocity–whether Christic or Kantian. Charity would not only foolishly conclude from the existence of the two keys their identity; it would more falsely conclude from my ability to believe in and use my key my knowledge of it.

There is, then, another ruin that, though less inevitable than that of subjectiveness, is finally more dangerous. In absolute terms, the noumenal ruins relative existence: there is no continuity between the evidence for self-belief and the assumption that experience is grounded. But at the more empirical level of the speakable, in our "talking America," we can be equally "ruined" by listening too closely to our good nature and to all sides. The threat lies not simply in the frivolity of others. *Nature* dismissed such frivolity as harmless; and Surface showed it to be in some circumstances even desirable. Instead others are "importunate" in their frivolity and tend to distract us. The solution is "preoccupied attention."

Such attention is not an otherworldly preoccupation or stoic denial of harsh realities. It is quite literally preoccupied – a sense of self that admits the logical priority of the private, what here he calls the "conviction of the irreconcilableness of the two spheres" and elsewhere "the incommunicable objects of nature and the metaphysical isolation of man" (pp. 47, 80). Divinity is a "surcharge," added on without relation to the rest. Man can presumably effect much without specific reference to it. But if he wishes to follow the logic of his assumptions – to court epistemic honesty – it is to the "divine answer" of "disparity" that he is inevitably led (p. 47). The twoness that Emerson has felt from the beginning now reveals itself as a kind of Cartesian schizophrenia: not merely a dualism that he happens to meet whenever he tries to think unity, but a tension between experience and its presuppositions that logically requires a simultaneous unity and duality.

VI

"Experience" offers no real "Prospects" – not simply because self-evidence is timeless, without prospect or retrospect, but because the bleak autonomy of the noumenal self effectively calls a halt to any epistemological enterprise. Since *Nature*, Emerson has pursued the Kantian project of deducing from the logic of experience some knowledge about its conditions. Man cannot escape thought to know the absolute reality of things. Yet by examining the "transcendental" conditions for the possibility of knowledge, he can determine the canon of a priori principles concerning the correct employment of certain faculties of knowledge.[113] Thus, although not piercing through the veil of ideas to reality, he can discover a kind of absolute in the necessary conditions of what we call experience.

In *Nature*, his most explicitly Kantian essay, Emerson examined the necessary connection between transcendental idealism and empirical realism – the extent to which the very possibility of experience is predicated on the unity of apperception or the "I think" and on the existence of an objective realm apart from that apperceptive unity. In the Divinity School "Address," he examined the logical conditions of virtue in terms of the self-enacting autonomy of the moral imperative, "I ought." Finally, in "Self-Reliance," he explored the nature of the empirical self and particularly the self-evidence of personal identity – the nonreferentiality of the existential claim "I am."

"Experience," however, undermines the validity of this whole project by admitting that the "I's" of these three statements are not identical, and that behind the empirical self lies a formal or transcendental self, both outside experience and prior to it. Experience means three things in the essay. Most simply, it is the condition of being within a system, the inherently unfinished, serial quality of what Emerson calls "life." More specifically, it is the recognition implicit in the rule of the various lords that experience is a construct, not simply given but controlled by various laws both internal and external to man. But most distressingly in the final lord, it is also the discovery that one aspect of experience – its mentality – seems different in kind from the others. Mental events in their self-validation, like Kant's apperception in its formalism, are essentially unknowable. And what really disappears is not Waldo, grief, or God, but the mind itself – the regulative potential of Reason that in Kant seemed to establish the reality of all that man most wants to know about truth and morality.

"Experience," then, is that moment when Emerson finds that his pursuit of autonomy has ended on the bleak rocks of tautology. In *Nature*, he found in experience the possibility of objectivity that delimited the self. Now, looking at the same mutuality from the opposite direction, he sees the self as the limit of experience. Yet, as a limit, it is essentially outside the system – necessary, but not necessary as such. Emerson abandons the attempt to imagine with Kant that certain logical conditions can be thought even though they cannot be known. And in so doing he rejects the mind as the "place" of such knowings and thinkings. To the extent that formal unity is necessary, it is purely formal; the rest is just personal – necessarily experienced but not necessary. Thus, if in most senses Swedenborg is for Emerson a lesser Kant, in this one tendency to substantialize thought processes (though in this tendency alone) Kant is only a greater Swedenborg – one more physician with a quirky myth of the spiritual.

Nothing is really destroyed in this abandoning of epistemology – neither the stability of nature nor of self. Tautology is not solipsism, and all that is given up is the pride of knowledge – the understanding of relationship.[114] The lords' order, though coherent in this highly structured account, is not, Emerson recognizes, absolute but only "as I find them in my way" (p. 47). More generally, in a recapitulation of the paragraph on Waldo, all experience is contingent.

> Life wears to me a visionary face. Hardest, roughest action is vision-ary also. It is but a choice between soft and turbulent dreams. People disparage knowing and the intellectual life, and urge doing. I am very content with knowing, if only I could know. That is an august enter-tainment, and would suffice me a great while. To know a little, would be worth the expense of this world. (P. 48)

People understand knowing no better than their grief, and action, like disaster, falls "soft." The costly price of sons and lovers becomes the sacrifice of the world's wealth. And the grief for grief is reformulated as the (grammatically awkward) counterfactual of my content with knowl-edge if I could know.

Knowledge thus remains only as the recognition of its impossibility. "I know that the world I converse with in the city and in the farms, is not the world I *think*" (p. 48).[115] Epistemology posits two worlds, both stable and real in their way. Thought is always possible, as is experience or conversation. But the interconnection between the two, which lies at the heart of all epistemological questions, though it may occur, is logi-cally unknowable. "All I know is reception; I am and I have: but I do not get, and when I have fancied I had gotten anything, I found I did not" (p. 48).[116] Discrepancy, like the "disparity" in Flaxman's portrait of Apollo, becomes the condition of human experience, the thought of self as other than experience. "I observe that difference, and shall ob-serve it. One day I shall know the value and law of this discrepance" (p. 48).[117] And though the stability of the world is unchallenged, the clarity and knowledge that ground epistemology are rejected as delusions. "I have not found that much was gained by manipular attempts to realize the world of thought" (p. 48). In one last, phlegmatic echo of *Nature*'s prospects, he admits:

> I observe, that, in the history of mankind, there is never a solitary example of success, – taking their own tests of success. I say this po-lemically, or in reply to the inquiry, why not realize your world? But far be from me the despair which prejudges the law by a paltry em-piricism, – since there never was a right endeavor, but it succeeded. (P. 48)

Distancing himself from his own early exhortation to build your own world, he now rejects man's identifications of failures (or by implica-tion successes) as a paltry empiricism, even while hypothetically admit-ting the necessary connection between right action and success.[118]

Turning ironically skeptical, Emerson inverts Hume's famous will-ingness to live in the world of backgammon and beef by announcing his own intention to reascend to his study. "We dress our garden, eat our dinners, discuss the household with our wives, and these things make no impression, are forgotten next week; but in the solitude to which every man is always returning, he has a sanity and revelations, which in his passage into new worlds he will carry with him" (p. 49).[119] And the essay concludes with the relegation of Kant to the world of the purely fictional. "The true romance which the world exists to realize, will be the transformation of genius into practical power" (p. 49). Transcendental idealism still requires empirical realism. But their "existence to realize" each other is relocated in some distant infinitive. And though power is still imaginable, perhaps even realizable, this romance of transformation is less declared a truth than practical truth a romance.

6

After epistemology

"Emerson came late into his force" begins Whicher's dramatic little book. It is just as true – and even sadder – that he left it early. Not only did he suffer from decreasing productivity and finally aphasia.[1] With the defeat of epistemology, he seemed to have lost the intellectual tension generated by his long confrontation with philosophical idealism. There were many works after "Experience" – some new and some new compilations.[2] His lecturing continued, bringing him more fame and revenue than it had in the Transcendentalist decades of the 1830s and 1840s. But the energy of youth disappeared with the defeat of his youthful philosophy. And the late essays, though beautifully crafted, move toward a universalism that is disappointing after the muscularity of the earlier works.

It is tempting to see the shift in the essays after "Experience" as largely stylistic. Surely there is for Emerson, as for James, a late style, though not necessarily a major phase. The early works tend toward a somewhat overelaborate logical structure and terse, even elliptical pronouncements. The later works invert these priorities. The essays become increasingly free-flowing and less sermonic. Although the sentence structure remains simple, the aphorisms are fewer and less memorable. Instead the rhetorical force lies in the paratactic catalogues, which are more fully Whitmanian than anything else in Emerson.

The stylistic change, however, is of a piece with the intellectual one. It is hard not to hear in the vocabulary anticipations of modernism – existentialism, absurdism, even deconstruction. But, as always in Emerson, these means of expression arise from the message. The excellence of the prose suggests that the unargumentativeness of the works does not mark waning imaginative powers. Although the energy and rigor of the great essays are not sustained, Emerson is not merely regressing to the tentativeness of his earliest positions. Instead the failure of epistemology has taught him the falseness of a certain kind of clarity. And acquiescence becomes itself a kind of philosophical position, an unwillingness to pretend to a knowledge fundamentally inaccessible, an admission that energy and rigor themselves may not be all they are cracked up to be.

I

The attempted readjustment begins almost immediately after the defeat of epistemology in "Experience," in the neglected "Nominalist and Realist." Though saddled with a ponderously abstract title, this essay is actually a practical, even slangy, account of considerable charm, and stands as the comic masterpiece of the second series much as "Experience" does the tragic.[3] Addressing the same formlessness and relativity that makes experience illusory, it finds the tension not soporific but exhilarating. And instead of a paralyzing disparity, it discovers in man, as in nature, an invigorating duality.

At first the essay seems one last lecture on the transient and the permanent, as Emerson rehearses long discarded arguments on the superiority of the universal to the relative and representative. "In the famous dispute with the Nominalists, the Realists had a good deal of reason. General ideas are essences." Despite a "proclivity to details," man is in fact "saturated with the laws of the world" (CW.III.136). So unified is the world that "it will appear as if one man had made it all." Recalling the "giant" who in "Self-Reliance" "goes with me wherever I go," Emerson now insists that "wherever you go, a wit like your own has been before you, and has realized its thought" (pp. 136-37; cf. CW.II.46). If anything, this giant is more genial than the other. In "Self-Reliance" such anticipations proved the self to be sad and unrelenting; here, however, they are more neutral, and look back even further to the "helpful" instinctual giant of the innocent days of "The American Scholar" (CW.I.61). Equally familiar (and innocent) is the unity of literature, "the appearance, that one person wrote all the books" (p. 137). Like the giant, Emerson's famous claims that "I read for the lustres" and that his interest lies not with the author but with the "author's author" echo the oration's untroubled position on literature.[4]

Yet this almost anachronistic praise of essences may not be so placid as it seems. The very ubiquity of phenomenal terms – especially the various forms of "appear" – asks us to question the reality of our conclusions, and the Realists' "good deal of reason" reduces to a pun (p. 136). Moreover, however familiar the argument, the ironic tone seems to undercut what it would establish. It is a dreary proof of the wit of the One Man, if all he can make is markets, customhouses, and business offices. Similarly the complaint in "Experience" against the uselessness of genius is trivialized into the account of the gluttonous angel. "I verily believe if an angel should come to chaunt the chorus of the moral law, he would eat too much gingerbread, or take liberties with private letters, or do some precious atrocity" (pp. 134, 262).[5]

Affirmations of the universal, even when convincing, seem oddly to undercut earlier formulations. The elevation of magnetism over the poor empirical pretensions of the individual filings less defends general power than burlesques earlier claims of its existence in the genius.

> Yet we unjustly select a particle, and say, 'O steel-filing number one! what heart-drawings I feel to thee! what prodigious virtues are these of thine! how constitutional to thee, and incommunicable!' Whilst we speak, the loadstone is withdrawn; down falls our filing in a heap with the rest, and we continue our mummery to the wretched shaving. (P. 135)[6]

Similarly Emerson's restatement of his aesthetic theory from "The Poet" turns back on itself. "Lively boys write to their ear and eye, and the cool reader finds nothing but sweet jingles in it. When they grow older, they respect the argument" (p. 138).[7] Earlier, the jingles of the music box were the real failures of a nonargumentative poet. Now that the error is in the reader's cool eye, however, all judgments—whether of jingles or arguments—seem compromised.

Most indicative of this ironic restraint is his image of the invisible arc. In "Spiritual Laws," Emerson used the image to represent man's ability to know (and compulsion to publish) the whole truth: the good mathematician can deduce the whole figure from a single arc (CW.II.85). Later, in "Intellect," he admitted this model of completion to be too simplistic: the curve turn outs to be a parabola, whose arcs will never meet (CW.II.201). Now, however, he goes one step further to find the systematic pursuit of character not merely impossible but based on a false notion of consistency. "We have such exorbitant eyes, that on seeing the smallest arc, we complete the curve, and when the curtain is lifted from the diagram which it seemed to veil, we are vexed to find that no more was drawn, than just that fragment of an arc which we first beheld" (p. 133).[8]

Perhaps the most obvious sign of this irony is the first section's conclusion that exceptions also prove the rule. Emerson, of course, regularly uses such inverted logic: skepticism, for example, through limitation proves Reality in "Experience." But the rhetoric here is self-consciously careless. Recalling *Nature*'s list of the momentary triumphs of Reason – Mesmerism, Swedenborgianism, Fourierism, et al. – Emerson concludes that "these abnormal insights of the adepts, ought to be normal, and things of course" (p. 138). As a proof of integrity and normalcy, the argument fails by assuming the very thing it sets out to prove. Moreover the inference is shocking in its Leibnizian complacency: since "on every side we are very near to the best," it "seems not worth while to execute with too much pains some one intellectual, or aesthetical, or civil feat." And the section ends blithely but ominously with a pseudo-Shakespearean couplet: "whilst we are waiting, we beguile the time with jokes, with sleep, with eating, and with crimes" (p. 138). The final element in this version of *Nature*'s list of the unexplained – and especially its willful refusal to rhyme – suggests the section's apparent universalism to be no more creditable than the essay's pompous title.[9]

The whole first section, then, works ironically to undercut the very premises of the essentialism it "appears" to praise. The second section makes this ambivalence explicit. Beginning with a jaunty summary of his anti-personalism, Emerson claims:

> I wish to speak with all respect of persons, but sometimes I must pinch myself to keep awake, and preserve the due decorum. They melt so fast into each other, that they are like grass and trees, and it needs an effort to treat them as individuals. (Pp. 138-39)

Yet the apparent confidence backfires, and Emerson immediately denies what he has just affirmed.

> But this is flat rebellion. Nature will not be Buddhist: she resents generalizing, and insults the philosopher in every moment with a million of fresh particulars. It is all idle talking: as much as a man is a whole, so is he also a part; and it were partial not to see it. . . . You have not got rid of parts by denying them, but are the more partial. You are one thing, but nature is *one thing and the other thing,* in the same moment. She will not remain orbed in a thought, but rushes into persons; and when each person, inflamed to a fury of personality, would conquer all things to his poor crotchet, she raises up against him another person, and by many persons incarnates again a sort of whole. She will have all. Nick Bottom cannot play all the parts, work it how he may: there will be somebody else, and the world will be round. (P. 139)[10]

Emerson's redefinition of nature here as "one thing and the other thing" represents an important advance on (or at least a clarification of) his previous theories. Privacy made self into something so autonomous that any analysis of the logic of knowledge was futile. Now, however, Emerson notes a similar anomaly about nature. Nature is naturally, even linguistically, unified – one of those words like "life" or "mind" that cannot profitably be divided. At the same time it "is" one, it means "the other." Privileged access is really exclusion, and things do not so much tumble into thought as rush out of them to be incarnated as people.[11] Yet the incarnation of one assumes the incarnation of many. If there will be someone else, then there will be "a sort of whole" and the world will be round.

Ironically recasting earlier formulations, this middle section of the essay then goes on to suggest how experience might look to nature. "For nature, who abhors mannerism, has set her heart on breaking up all styles and tricks" (p. 140). Disdainful of human pretensions to "honesty," nature has "set her heart" on attacking all the "tricks" that in "Experience" allowed man to live in the world. To counter the trick of personality, man's tyrannical tendency, Emerson embraces mere multifarity. "Since we are all so stupid, what benefit that there should be two stupidities! . . . If John was perfect, why are you and I alive? As long as any man exists, there is some need of him. . . . Every man is wanted, and no man is wanted much." And in his most explicit denial of the earlier absolutism of *Nature* or the Divinity School "Address," Emerson admits that "we came this time for condiments, not for corn" (p. 141).[12]

Nature's project is not to balance man's essentialism and realism off against her own pluralism and nominalism. Instead she works, like Emerson's argument itself, merely to problematize reality, "to embroil the confusion, and make it impossible to arrive at any general statement" (p. 141). Her method derives not from science but from games. No longer concerned whether the divine dice are honest, Emerson now claims that we are the dice. "For though gamesters say, that the cards beat all the players, though they were never so skilful, yet in the contest we are now considering, the players are also the game, and share the power of the cards." The game's only characteristic is continuity as alternation: " 'Your turn now, my turn next,' is the rule of the game."[13] And the focus is not completion but motion. "The universality being hindered in its primary form, comes in the secondary form of *all sides*: the points come in succession to the meridian, and by the speed of rotation, a new whole is formed" (p. 142). Succession may, as in "Experience," still establish substance, but it is rotation or mere change that accounts for the whole.

This emphasis, although not antiessentialist, tends to direct attention away from absolute questions. "If we cannot make voluntary and conscious steps in the admirable science of universals, let us see the parts wisely, and infer the genius of nature from the best particulars with a becoming charity" (p. 143). "Becoming," which was in "Self-Reliance" almost a thing in itself, is now merely adjectival, a movement toward the charitable communication that earlier seemed impossible. And the essay ends with a recapitulation and softening of the subjectivist dilemma of "Experience." "The end and the means, the gamester and the game, – life is made up of the intermixture and reaction of these two amicable powers, whose marriage appears beforehand monstrous, as each denies and tends to abolish the other. We must reconcile the contradictions as we can" (p. 143).

The marriage between subject and object, though theoretically incoherent, even monstrous, can nevertheless be embraced hypothetically. Antinomies need not prove metaphysical illusion, but can instead simply be accepted as one of the limitations of language. "No sentence will hold the whole truth, and the only way in which we can be just, is by giving ourselves the lie. . . . All the universe over, there is but one thing, this old Two-Face, creator-creature, mind-matter, right-wrong, of which any proposition may be affirmed or denied" (pp. 143-44). And in a self-deflation as pointedly anti-Emersonian as anything in Thoreau, he admits the triviality of his distinction between universal and particular. "We fancy men are individuals; so are pumpkins; but every pumpkin in the field, goes through every point of pumpkin history" (p. 144).[14]

The old problems do not disappear. Man still longs for "security against moods" and bemoans the difference between his ease in "saying all that lies in the mind" and the "incapacity of the parties to know each other" (pp. 144-45). And as in "Experience," privacy as a way of belief is still the inevitable villain. "Is it that every man believes every other to be an incurable partialist, and himself an universalist?" But the shift in terms marks a shift in expectations: privacy and knowledge are quite simply one kind of vocabulary, universalist and partialist another. The solution is not to solve the metaphysical dilemma – to seek further among the bleak rocks – but to give up the hope of that kind of answer altogether. By accepting such limitations, in fact, Emerson need not even force out one last hymn to patience or prospects. And this generally upbeat essay, unlike the more tortured ones, ends quite simply with the melancholy conditional that to know of others' existence would be satisfying, though it is probably impossible.

> Could they [two visiting philosophers] but once understand, that I loved to know that they existed, and heartily wished them Godspeed, yet, out of my poverty of life and thought, had no word or welcome for them when they came to see me, and could well consent to their living in Oregon, for any claim I felt on them, it would be a great satisfaction. (P. 145)[15]

II

Emerson's experiment with looser, less epistemological categories in "Nominalist and Realist" continues in his next major publication – *Representative Men*.[16] The shift is not simply from philosophy to biography: his questions are still vaguely philosophical, though not quite metaphysical and surely not epistemological. Biography has, of course, always interested Emerson: one of the earliest lecture series treats the topic, and in the first series of essays he largely equates it with history in general.[17] Yet in this later work, his focus is more theoretical. He wants to understand not the tests but the uses of great men – not who the great are but what are the conditions and limitations of their greatness.[18] And, in some sense, the whole series is less a collection of biographies than an exploration of the meaning of "representativeness."

The collection starts traditionally enough – both for Emerson and for heroic theories in general. The great man, by personally demonstrating the existence of spirit, makes the world both meaningful and real. "Nature seems to exist for the excellent. The world is upheld by the veracity of good men: they make the earth wholesome. . . . Life is sweet and tolerable only in our belief in such society; and, actually or ideally, we manage to live with superiors" (W.IV.3). The possibility of such virtue, like that of stability in *Nature*, is a "necessary and structural action of the human mind" (p. 4). And from the subordination of the "great material elements" to "his thought," man concludes the existence of "one essence" (p. 5).

Yet this examination of the meaning of greatness is preliminary to Emerson's real interest: "the kinds of service we derive from others" (p. 5). Other men are merely the lenses through which we learn self-respect. The great may seem angelic: the unique members of their "class" as angels are of their species (p. 19). But, in fact, these representatives are themselves "determined" by their constituency (p. 11). The very possibility of greatness that they illustrate undoes the "excess of influence" of their own "peculiar" greatness (p. 27), and after teaching his lesson of self-respect, each great individual is supplanted in nature's inevitable "rotation" (pp. 23, 19).[19] Greatness transcends any particular great thing: "great men exist that there may be greater men" (p. 35). And *Nature*'s rhetoric of disappearance reappears, in this unepistemological context, to deny not the disagreeable but the particularized in any form. "If the disparities of talent and position vanish when the individuals are seen in the duration which is necessary to complete the career of each, even more swiftly the seeming injustice disappears when we ascend to the central identity of all the individuals, and know that they are made of the substance which ordaineth and doeth" (p. 33).

This theory of the uses of great men recapitulates many traditional Emersonian concerns – about explanation, relation, giving, and reminding.[20] Yet it does so largely without reference to the questions of perception and knowledge earlier so central. This dereification of representation is taken to its fullest extreme in the most interesting essay in the series – "Montaigne; or, the Skeptic." In many ways the work is an anomaly. Unlike the accounts of Plato, Shakespeare, Napoleon, and Goethe, it treats a figure only marginally great and a topic not clearly inevitable – skepticism.[21] Moreover it is even less biographical than the others: Montaigne quickly becomes merely a synonym for skepticism, and after a delayed entrance passes out of the essay a little past the halfway mark.[22] But most important, skepticism is, even more than the "philosophy" of Plato, an epistemological concept, and its unphilosophical presentation here measures Emerson's increasing disaffection from his earlier project.

The essay begins with familiar claims for dualism. Emerson avoids his customary pairing of sensation and thought, here defining thought as the mediator between sensation and its true opposite, morals. In general, however, the pairings are predictable – Infinite/Finite, Absolute/Relative, Real/Apparent – and are merely the means to characterize "predispositions" in man to either a "perception of difference" or a "perception of identity." Each perception, though neutral in itself, betrays a tendency to exaggeration or "arrogance." Those predisposed to identity disdain matter or "realizations." And in an implicit denial of the ennobling beggar's dream of "Self-Reliance" – and behind it the intimations of divinity in Nature – Emerson rejects those who speak and act "as if" their ideals were already "substantiated" (W.IV.150-51).[23] Equally misleading is the implicit materialism of those pursuing difference, for it leads to "indifferentism" and "disgust," finally to mere cynicism (pp. 153-54).

Unlike earlier dualisms, whose tensions are necessary and unresolvable, however, the conflict between the abstractionist and the materialist requires a solution – the synthesis of the skeptic. Rejecting both the idealist's certainty about abstract ideas and the materialist's rootedness in matter, the skeptic simply refuses to comment. "But I see plainly, he says, that I cannot see. I know that human strength is not in extremes, but in avoiding extremes. I, at least, will shun the weakness of philosophizing beyond my depth." Recalling the rhetoric of indifference, he argues, "What is the use of pretending to powers we have not? What is the use of pretending to assurances we have not, respecting the other life? Why exaggerate the power of virtue? Why be an angel before your time? These strings, wound up too high, will snap" (p. 156).

His position is actually less that of epistemological indifference than of pragmatism. The objectionable doctrines are not logically impossible but merely dangerous. Metaphysical precision or tautness is so little an illusion that, if pursued, it will snap the strings of life. In response, like the seeker of "Circles," he recommends not the absolute but the "approximate solution." "I neither affirm nor deny. I stand here to try the case. I am here to consider, σκοπεῖν, to consider how it is" (p. 156). Recognizing that "there is much to say on all sides," the skeptic takes the ground "of consideration, of self-containing; not at all of unbelief; not at all of universal denying, nor of universal doubting, – doubting even that he doubts; least of all of scoffing and profligate jeering at all that is stable and good" (pp. 157, 159). And, explicitly inverting *Nature*'s earlier assertion that man is built like a house to stand, not a ship to be tossed, he concludes,

> We want a ship in these billows we inhabit. An angular, dogmatic house would be rent to chips and splinters in this storm of many elements. No, it must be tight, and fit to the form of man, to live at all; as a shell must dictate the architecture of a house founded on the sea. (P. 160; cf. CW.I.30)

Clearly the skeptic continues from "Experience" Emerson's program of honesty. And his refusal to lie about the hostility of experience is admirable. Yet his refreshing honesty should not obscure the limitations of his position. For it is unclear whether he has resolved the problems of idealism and materialism or only internalized them. His claim that materialists mistake for adamant the chaotic movement of nature less denies materialism than replaces it with a higher atomism. Similarly his concern with "the prudent" reinforces our suspicions that he may only be a materialist in disguise (pp. 155, 159). Moreover his objection that the studious abstractionists are their own victims, pale and underfed, cannot be taken seriously. His own faith in the plainly seen and the certainly known suggests the degree to which, for all his sneers against Cartesian doubting of doubt, he has failed to free himself from the myth of indubitability (pp. 155, 156, 167). At the very least, Montaigne's appreciation of pain "because it makes him feel himself and realize things" seems naive after "Experience" (p. 169).

The inconsistencies in the skeptic's program only suggest the more general ambiguity in Emerson's tone toward it.

> Let us have a robust, manly life; let us know what we know, for certain; what we have, let it be solid and seasonable and our own. A world in the hand is worth two in the bush. Let us have to do with real men and women, and not with skipping ghosts. (P. 159)

Although the sentiment is admirable, it is hard not to distrust the expression. The desire to "have" a robust, manly life seems egoistic:

unless life is inherently manly, it is unlikely that man's "manipular" attempts will add anything. Nor is the subordination of manliness to certainty reassuring: stability and even possession seem more the moving forces than does honesty. Emerson's revision of the pragmatic cliché hardly speaks well for the skeptic's deference to nature, and the "skipping" ghosts trivialize the gliding ones of "Experience." As Montaigne himself later makes clear, the project seems less to confront reality than to keep your nose clean. " 'If there be anything farcical in such a life, the blame is not mine: let it lie at fate's and nature's door' " (p. 167).

Perhaps the clearest indication of Emerson's reservations, however, is his subtle use of George Herbert in this section. In characterizing the skeptic's superiority to the abstractionist scholar – his failure to "be betrayed to a book and wrapped in a gown" – Emerson quotes from Herbert's "Affliction (I)."[24] The allusion, of course, qualifies the skeptic's triumph. The betrayer in Herbert's poem is God, and the afflicted the naive Christian who only imperfectly understands the meaning of his commitment. The final inversion, wherein the speaker realizes that there is no escape from God – that failure to love Him would be the punishment as well as the cure – suggests that Emerson's skeptic may similarly misconceive man's relation to truth.[25]

Emerson's point, like Herbert's, is not to reassert authority – whether of God or ideas – but to redefine the notion of relationship. And having demonstrated the skeptic's corrective to the excesses of the materialist and the idealist, he abruptly shifts gears about halfway through the essay.

> Shall we say that Montaigne has spoken wisely, and given the right and permanent expression of the human mind, on the conduct of life? We are natural believers. (P. 170)

The drama of the rhetoric is obvious: the essay's shortest paragraph introduces the essay's shortest sentence. And although the "no" is not explicit, it is clear that natural belief denies the possibility of skepticism, and only slightly less clear that the "we" for whom it is denied is not men of Emerson's temperament but mankind in general. Rejecting the skeptic's moderation, his fear that strings may snap if wound too tight, Emerson explains that threads are presuppositions, the possibility of lawfulness that cannot be denied. "We are persuaded that a thread runs through all things: all worlds are strung on it, as beads; and men, and events, and life, come to us only because of that thread: they pass and repass only that we may know the direction and continuity of that line."[26] To imagine the string as breakable quite literally "dispirits us," for it is such linearity that permits the possibility of relation and coherence, of spirituality in general. Skepticism as the pursuit of the clearly seen and known dissolves in the more general question of belief. "Seen or unseen, we believe the tie exists" (p. 170).

The rejection of a certain kind of skepticism is not, however, a rejection of skepticism as such, and the remainder of the essay works to clarify how the indeterminacy of knowledge does not necessarily imply the impossibility of belief. Although unbelief is immediately dismissed as sour and dumpish, a more general skepticism as "equilibration" is acceptable, even necessary (p. 171). Very quickly, however, Emerson takes this Montaignesque unwillingness to comment one way or the other in a direction far from Montaigne's own. For the first form of this skepticism is a disinterest in particulars except in their more universal tendency and spirit (p. 172). Somewhat more traditional perhaps (though still characteristically Emersonian as well) is the skeptic's hostility to action over thought: although politically progressive and something of a reformer, he is nevertheless a "bad citizen" in his antipathy to all organization or association, whatever its political bias.

The clearest mark of the new meaning of skepticism, however, is the "honest" doubts it raises. The materialist's skepticism about spirit is irrelevant, merely the "quadruped opinion." More significant is the levity of intellect, which repeatedly overthrows tradition. Yet since what is overthrown is merely superficial – baby-houses and crockery-shops – knowledge does not challenge true earnestness and ultimately "the intellect and moral sentiment are unanimous" (p. 175). Somewhat more threatening is the question of temperament, which seems to deny the possibility of belief to the extent that "the [alternation of] beliefs and unbeliefs appear[s] to be structural" (p. 175). Yet, finally, this very structural dimension of moods denies the mere temperamentality of indigestion or "stomach evidence." For "rotation," although it guarantees no single opinion, still implies a more general principle that may be believed in and trusted to – the "record of longer periods" (p. 176). The greatest challenge to affirmation lies in the "doctrine of the Illusionists," which denies free agency by emphasizing the disproportion between Reality or Law – which is eternal but only occasionally visible – and human performance – which, though always practicable, seems to have no direct bearing on reality.[27]

The real significance of the doubts, however, lies less in their honesty than in their unimportance to Emerson. Man's inability to name or know virtue is not to keep him from virtue. The man of earnest and burly habit who wants more than traditional instruction has "a right to insist on being convinced in his own way" (p. 180). Skepticism as disbelief, equilibration, or postponement of judgment is redefined as a deeper need for and right to conviction, and the doubts become simply hobgoblins, redirecting attention from their tepid paradoxes to a more fundamental belief.[28] Even skeptics "must needs have a reflex or parasite faith; not a sight of realities, but an instinctive reliance on the seers and believers of realities. The manners and thoughts of believers astonish them and convince them that these have seen something which is hid from themselves" (p. 181). Emerson argues in an inverted analogy that though they differ in their knowledge, both believer and unbeliever "love" beliefs. Whether accepting or denying the specific affirmations of the soul, both implicitly admit that there is something there worth discussing.

Just as the sensualist necessarily believes, so the believer necessarily doubts, and is "driven to express his faith by a series of skepticisms" (p. 181). The specific beliefs of charity, doctrine, tradition, and the masses all fall in customary Emersonian fashion before the greater belief in the moral design of the universe. The very possibility of lying, of "make believe," suggests a more essential belief not so manufactured (p. 182). Superficial skepticism becomes impossible in the revelation of order, and as in "Nominalist and Realist" man was saturated with law, so here "the world is saturated with deity and with law" (p. 183; cf. CW.III.136). Compensation as each desire's prediction of its own satisfaction is rejected. But the more basic "expansive nature of truth," in its inability to be surrounded, permits man a vision of "the permanent," if not an access to it. "Man helps himself by larger generalizations. The lesson of life is practically to generalize" (p. 185).

It is hard not to be angry with the "larger generalizations" of the essay's final paragraphs—to feel that the honesty of the early pages was merely a stratagem.[29] Yet our anger should not obscure Emerson's point about skepticism and the naturalness of belief. The epistemological project from Descartes on has been basically negative, pitting belief against knowledge—attempting, in Kant's phrase, to make room for faith by denying knowledge. But, as Emerson's gradual redefinitions of skepticism are meant to show, disbelief—even when it is not simply greater, unconventional belief—still necessarily admits the existence of the affirmations believed in and denies only their importance. It is not without irony, then, that Emerson includes in his portrait gallery a paradoxically "representative" skeptic, one who representatively denies the significance of representation. Belief is not what is left over when the bounds of knowledge are accurately mapped out. Not the residue from a Kantian separation of thought and knowledge, it is instead present at a different level from the beginning. And its "naturalness"— the impossibility of being skeptical about belief, whatever one's doubts about knowledge—suggests less an obstinate reaffirmation of constitutional hopefulness than a different, nonepistemological kind of necessity, that of unknowable faith.[30]

III

Since *Nature*, questions of belief and faith have always implied the possibility of "practical power," in both the Kantian sense of a behavioral determinant and the more general sense of an action in the world. In the last major series of essays, this practical emphasis comes to the fore in the organizing concept of a "conduct of life." Avoiding the Kantian distinction between a reason purely speculative and a motive purely practical, however, Emerson defines practice more simply as how one gets on in the world. The series opens paradoxically, even ominously, with the idea of fate, that very limiting force that would seem to inhibit individual "conduct." Yet the essay, for all its depressing "honesty," does not restrict action or the belief that attends it. Knowledge of a Kantian apodeixis is rejected. But the more general project of limitation pursued in "Experience" is still valued, though removed from the specifically epistemological context of the earlier work. And what starts as an account of the negative aspects of circumstance defines itself to become a philosophical definition of the implications of limitation–a preliminary study not of how I might conduct myself, but of what my apparent ability for any conduct means.

The essay, though long, has a fairly simple structure. After a brief preface summarizing the argument, Emerson–to counteract America's "bad name for superficialness" (and his own)–honestly states the facts in an extended, almost gleeful, catalogue of nature's negative aspects. Although most of these "odious facts" have been implicit in earlier accounts of nature's lack of sentimentality, the energy (and length) of the presentation is new, and this section, by far the most famous, tends to overshadow the rest.[31] The world, by this reckoning, is full not only of "rude" shocks and ruins but of the more general tyrannies of organization and structure–race, temperament, sex, climate, talent–that permeate all aspects of politics, science, and even statistics.

A brief second section, however, qualifies this lively negation by redefining fate as limitation, thus permitting the gradual rebuilding of confidence in the final sections of the essay. Reviving the dualist emphasis of the preface, the third section argues that power is the natural counterpart of fate and antagonizes it even though itself limited by it. More specifically, intellect annuls fate in three ways. Trivially, it can use fate to teach man a fatal courage. But more importantly, the revelations of both thought and the moral sentiment locate within fate a kind of freedom. The fourth and final section, in characteristic Emersonian fashion, resolves this dualism into a higher unity. Not only can odious facts be understood and exploited, but the whole tendency of fate is toward melioration. Nature's economy of means suggests the universal fitness of things, which in turn suggests the ultimacy of unity.

As in "Montaigne," the ease with which Emerson reconciles the odious to the beautiful is highly suspicious. And as always when Emerson talks of unity, his arguments collapse different kinds of similarities. Moreover he confuses questions of time and perspective with those of melioration. Not all these problems, of course, can be explained away. Some of the apparent contradictions, however, can be resolved (or at least softened) by understanding exactly where the main focus lies in the essay. For, as in "Montaigne," Emerson is here less concerned with knowledge than with belief, and after epistemology the kinds of questions, even the ways of talking, are subtly different.

Part of the difficulty resides in the meaning of the central concept, and by one reading the essay exists merely to refine its own notion of fate.[32] Yet in fact – when we eliminate those definitions that describe less its nature than its uses – fate fairly consistently means limitation in its broadest sense of existence within a system, called most often "condition."[33] Alluding to the Hindoos' poetic belief in fate as "deeds committed in a prior state of existence," Emerson equates this definition with Schelling's claim that man feels "that he has been what he is from all eternity, and by no means became such in time" (W.V.12-13). Eliminating the emphasis on time, Emerson explains in a third redefinition (his own) that "in the history of the individual is always an account of his condition, and he knows himself to be a party to his present estate" (p. 13). "Condition" at this level of generality means simply "what there is" and, as the "always" implies, the only true time is an empty Now. As he explains a few pages later, reality is itself conditional, and what we have is a "conditional population; not the best, but the best that could live now" (p. 16). Conditionality is marginally necessary, describing the state under which things can happen. Revising his earlier sense in "Prospects" of the constructive power of visual coincidence, Emerson now sees that whatever the origin of the system, it becomes a limit once built. "Every spirit makes its house; but afterwards the house confines the spirit" (p. 9).

Similar to Kant's structuring principles of the mind or his conditions necessary for the possibility of knowledge, this conditional necessity is in fact freer than Kant's logical inevitability.[34] As Emerson explains later in the essay, the house is less a limit than a measure of man's growth (p. 30). The change in vocabulary – from category to condition – is etymologically suggestive. Unlike the perceptual language of epistemology, "condition" derives from the vocabulary of speech.[35] As Emerson implies, existence is not like a science or a mind (let alone a science of the mind), but more like a language, whose "what is" marks what can be said in that system. In the gnomic statement of the preface, "if there be irresistible dictation, the dictation understands itself" (p. 4). The rules of the language are not arbitrary: like condition, language is delimited. But what can be said within that language is fairly free: the irresistibility of the dictation does not prevent conversation and even understanding. So condition is simultaneously limited and free. As that which is, it cannot not be; but within that irresistible existence, there still remains the possibility of multiple "dictions," different descriptions.[36]

Yet "condition" is only one of the essay's poles. "Fate" is the first work in a series on the conduct of life, and opens by explicitly announcing this interest. Recalling the odd coincidence that during the same season a number of men (including himself) delivered lecture series on the Times, Emerson admits:

> To me, however, the question of the times resolved itself into a practical question of the conduct of life. How shall I live? We are incompetent to solve the times. . . . We can only obey our own polarity. 'T is fine for us to speculate and elect our course, if we must accept an irresistible dictation. (P. 3)

In part this opening merely rejects the earlier epistemological pursuit of knowledge. Rather than the earlier questions about the end of nature or even about where we are – of speculations and solutions – Emerson now wants to know only how he "shall" live.

The absence of the conditional "should" may be significant. The question is directed less toward ethical choice than biographical prophecy, and the paragraph ends with a determinist emphasis on absolutes and irresistibility. Later this notion of conduct is explicitly connected with nature. "The Circumstance is Nature. Nature is what you may do. There is much you may not. We have two things, – the circumstance, and the life. Once we thought positive power was all. Now we learn that negative power, or circumstance, is half" (pp. 14-15). Evidently nature is the language of conduct much as fate is the language of condition.

Yet the interrelation is not so simple. In the division of power into virtue and life, circumstance is said to be both negative and natural. But according to the earlier sentence, nature is not what you cannot do but what you can. Equally confused is the relation between condition and conduct. To the extent that fate equals condition and nature conduct, conduct seems to be the possibility of relative freedom within the greater system of fate. But, as Emerson says, "the right use of Fate is to bring up our conduct to the loftiness of nature" (p. 24). By this definition, nature seems to stand for the condition of the world, with fate a kind of cosmic model for conduct.

These tensions – between conduct and condition, action and description, doing and saying – seem to imply something far more sophisticated about the nature of systems. The problem is clearest when Emerson considers how "criticism," the self-conscious attempt to understand the system, alters the system. In one account, "Fate then is a name for facts not yet passed under the fire of thought; for causes which are unpenetrated" (p. 31). This highly Kantian definition depicts fate as reality, not merely Kant's logically necessary objectivity but the real ding-an-sich behind intuitions.[37] More suggestive, though still cryptic, is his claim that "To hazard the contradiction, – freedom is necessary. If you please to plant yourself on the side of Fate, and say, Fate is all; then we say, a part of Fate is the freedom of man." The irony that fate is everything, including its negation, is too easy; but at least the formulation makes clear, as the other did not, that if the system is all, then there is nothing beyond it.

Emerson clarifies this emphasis in the sentences immediately following: "Forever wells up the impulse of choosing and acting in the soul. Intellect annuls fate. So far as a man thinks, he is free" (p. 23). Choice in this context is not moral but linguistic, the mere selection among possibilities that creates meaning within the limits of rules. Intellect "annuls" fate in the Hegelian sense of the term, putting it aside by rising above it but also putting it aside to protect and preserve it. And – again the term is Hegelian – the unity that results does not abolish distinctions but preserves them through "reconciliation." "If Fate is ore and quarry, if evil is good in the making, if limitation is power that shall be, if calamities, oppositions, and weights are wings and means, – we are reconciled" (p. 35).[38]

The positive point that determination implies meaning as well as limitation is one that Emerson has understood at least since "Self-Reliance." The system within which we exist is necessitated by definition: it cannot be what it is not, and no man can violate his own nature. The negative point, however, is both new and striking. If nature is what you can do, what is the status of the negative half – what you cannot? To the extent that what cannot be done is truly determined, it cannot be done by anyone within the system. But such necessity is not itself within the system, nor is the impossible act. It makes more sense, then, to speak of it as incoherent than as impossible: if nature is what is, then what is not natural simply is not relevant because we have no terms with which to talk about it.[39] To the extent, however, that an impossible thing does exist at least potentially within the system, it must be potentially practicable – either by you or by an imaginable someone else. And to say of this sort of impossibility that it cannot be done is only to say that as yet it has not been. Labeling such an event necessitated is, as Emerson knows, paltry empiricism. Even if the impossible task is impossible only to me, I am not thereby determined. If it is necessarily impossible, I would not be me if I did it; and if it is only unlikely, I must patiently await the end of time before commenting on the absolute nonrelation of me and it.

A similar paradox attends the sayable. Man's "condition" is the range of possible descriptions that can be applied to the system of nature as what man can do. Condition is marginally freer than conduct, for it involves the choice among a number of descriptions, each necessarily within the system but none necessarily described. Everything is a doing; a not doing is simply incoherent. But not everything is a saying: within the system one can say any number of things, or even not say anything. It is this freedom presumably that accounts for the essay's rhetorical looseness, its tendency especially in the first section to become a catalogue of all kinds of negativity. The possibility of choice as a preference among sayings, however, does not extend to the literally unsayable. To the extent that saying is a specific form of doing, the freedom lies less in what you say than in that you say. To say the unsayable, like doing the undoable, is not freedom but incoherence.

Although Emerson's terminology may seem cumbersome and abstract, it does in its very imprecision correct some of the false implications of epistemological rhetoric. There is no distinction between knowing and thinking or even, as in "Experience," between thinking and conversing. There is only conversation, man's condition; and his criticism of that condition is itself more condition, a self-reflexivity that merely produces "meanness" if pursued too relentlessly (p. 23). The metaphor of sight, always too palpable, is implicitly overturned in the essay. The quirky "eye-ball" of *Nature* is replaced, in the image of the drowning man, by the "eye-beam" that keeps him afloat (p. 19). The substitution permits the notion of intellect as something that supports, even buoys up, without having to be too precise about the beam's relation to (or swallowing of) the object it sees.[40] Moreover the transparency explicitly associated earlier with perception now characterizes men in general (p. 43).

In a striking summation Emerson admits, "As once he found himself among toys, so now he plays a part in colossal systems, and his growth is declared in his ambition, his companions and his performance. He looks like a piece of luck, but is a piece of causation" (p. 42). Implicitly rejecting idealism, the "toy" of "Circles," he now finds the proper metaphor to be systematization.[41] And the distinction between what he looks like and what he is reduces to a more general one between his reality as performance and his appearance as feeling, even description.

The point, finally, is that systems, if misunderstood, encourage an illusory self-alienation. In examining the naturalness of belief in *Representative Men*, Emerson discovered the paradox of skepticism: by admitting that there is a disagreement, the skeptic tends implicitly to acknowledge the existence of the entity he means to doubt. In "Fate," a related paradox informs the whole notion of a system. "When there is something to be done, the world knows how to get it done" (p. 39). The world's knowledge is necessary not ontologically but logically. It is not inevitable in the state of things but is identically that state: if nature is what can be done, there can be nothing to be done that is not nature.

Like the skeptic worrying the relation between thought and world, however, man tends to misinterpret the implications of negativity and to create the false problem of Fate by imagining necessity as something apart from his life.

> The secret of the world is the tie between person and event. Person makes event, and event person. . . . The same fitness must be presumed between a man and the time and event, as between the sexes, or between a race of animals and the food it eats, or the inferior race it uses. He thinks his fate alien, because the copula is hidden. But the soul contains the event that shall befall it; for the event is only the actualization of its thoughts, and what we pray to ourselves for is always granted. The event is the print of your form. It fits you like your skin. What each does is proper to him. Events are the children of his body and mind. (Pp. 39-40)

The proliferation of terms is confusing, but the outlines of the argument are clear. It is only man's limited perspective that gives the "illusion" of alienation, of outsides. In fact, all is interrelated and conductional – a "web of relations."[42] Each man does the "proper" thing not because he does it rightly but because he does it as his own. To imagine that I do something not my own is merely a logical confusion, like thinking I can have someone else's headache or another person's pain.[43]

Finally, then, the conduct of life is quite literally what I "shall" do – what will be as what is. Nature is what can be done, as is fate. Evidence is conditional and therefore necessary, an inevitable doing that permits a kind of freedom in what we say about it. This is the sole vocabulary of existence: all else is unintelligible. "One key, one solution to the mysteries of human condition, one solution to the old knots of fate, freedom, and foreknowledge, exists; the propounding, namely, of the double consciousness" (p. 47). The formulations here, as everywhere in the essay, are erratic. To the extent that the "double consciousness" is one more description, a "propounding" roughly equivalent in epistemic status to a Platonic "myth," the imprecision need not bother us.[44] Yet to the degree that Emerson seems to posit two real horses, two real worlds, he is mistaken. Leaving the daemon to side with the deity is not a shift of place but only of perspective: within the system, man is always simultaneously with both and never sufficiently removed completely to understand either.

The more accurate formulation is the one that closes the work. "Let us build altars to the Blessed Unity which holds nature and souls in perfect solution, and compels every atom to serve an universal end." The restraint implicit in the injunction to build not houses but altars is appealing; the falling back on the universal, less so. But this "blessed unity" is not, as at least one critic fears, just an "anthropomorphized figment."[45] Emerson says that this preference for the unified over the particularized really marks "the necessity of beauty under which the universe lies; that all is and must be pictorial; that the rainbow and the curve of the horizon and the arch of the blue vault are only results from the organism of the eye" (p. 48). The passage is difficult but suggestive. Particulars like rainbows, skies, and horizons cannot be praised too enthusiastically, for they are, after all, only a function of our mode of perception. Yet rather than concluding that the mind is prior, Emerson states instead that all is pictorial – in the sense both that pictures are interrelated wholes and that they must be described to be activated.[46] The first point – about the pictorialness of relationship – suggests that meaning is internal. There is no image reflecting some separate meaning, nor even an external key to link together the picture's parts; there is only the one picture. Moreover, since meaning lies wholly within the system, to be realized it must be picked out or described: it is this sense of interpretation as selection – and not as true creation – that accounts for the eye's power over bows and skies.

To build altars, then, to the "Beautiful Necessity" of blessed unity is really to recognize that in the necessity of beauty lies both the fated stability of the system and the relative freedom of man's descriptive ability. Anything less than stability would seem not freedom but chaos. "If we thought men were free in the sense that in a single exception one fantastical will could prevail over the law of things, it were all one as if a child's hand could pull down the sun" (pp. 48-49). Exceptions do not challenge the whole but show man's ability to shape it through conceptualization. But, as Emerson has long insisted, local redescription requires that the whole remain fundamentally the same, or the change would not be discernible. It is perhaps too exclusively with this beauty of necessity that the essay ends. But in the notion of the pictorial dimension of nature – the necessity of beauty as well as the beauty of necessity – Emerson outlines a proto-pragmatic theory of truth that permits both general stability and local freedom, without flirting with the reifying tendency of his earlier epistemological formulations.

It is unnecessary (probably even counterproductive) to decide whether or not this final stage really represents an intellectual falling off – the acquiescence of an ebbing vitality. Emerson had always pursued a number of topics, and even in terms of his philosophical interests, epistemology was only one of his many concerns. Yet though not necessarily an end, the shift does mark a change in focus. In the late essays in general and "Fate" in particular, Emerson seems to confess his disinterest in the epistemological project so prominent up through "Experience." The pictorial quality of the beautiful necessity may point toward William James – or even beyond him to Wittgenstein. Wherever it points, however, clearly epistemology and the rigorous argumentative mode that accompanied it have shown themselves inadequate and been discarded. For the final result of the long hard look at philosophical idealism that occupied the center of Emerson's literary career was to teach him to look somewhere else.

Notes

1. EMERSON AS PHILOSOPHER

1 Comparing the aesthetic assumptions of English and American literature has been common since at least Irving and Cooper and lies at the heart of classic statements by D. H. Lawrence, Richard Chase, and especially Harry Levin. For recent explicit discussions, see Edwin M. Eigner, *The Metaphysical Novel in England and America: Dickens, Bulwer, Melville, and Hawthorne* (Berkeley: University of California Press, 1978); and Jonathan Arac, *Commissioned Spirits: The Shaping of Social Motion in Dickens, Carlyle, Melville, and Hawthorne* (New Brunswick, N.J.: Rutgers University Press, 1979). It has been argued that such transcontinental readings invalidate attempts to define nineteenth-century America in terms of its Puritan origins. There seems, however, no reason why both influences might not be worth studying, though, in general, academic specialization tends to lead individual scholars to pursue either one influence or the other.

2 The term originates with Stephen Whicher. See his article "Emerson's Tragic Sense," reprinted in Milton R. Konvitz and Stephen E. Whicher, eds., *Emerson: A Collection of Critical Essays* (Englewood Cliffs, N.J.: Prentice-Hall, Inc., 1962), pp. 39-45; and his book *Freedom and Fate: An Inner Life of Ralph Waldo Emerson* (Philadelphia: University of Pennsylvania Press, 1953), pp. 109-11.

3 See, for example, Quentin Skinner's discussion of the various mythologies of textual autonomy in "Meaning and Understanding in the History of Ideas," *History and Theory* 8 (1969), 6-39. See also John Dunn, "The Identity of the History of Ideas," *Philosophy* 43 (1968), 85-104; and J. G. A. Pocock, *Politics, Languages, and Time: Essays on Political Thought and History* (New York: Atheneum, 1971), pp. 3-41. Although these articles usefully identify certain errors common to intellectual historians, they seem committed to a problematic notion of intention wherein "what the author meant" is treated as totally independent of "what the historian makes the author mean." Since there is no such thing as presuppositionless history, however, it is hard to see how one could tell an imposed coherence from a discovered one, except in terms of a subtly prescriptive (and probably circular) notion of the historically "likely."

4 Critics have wisely cautioned against equating Emerson and the Transcendentalist "children" he describes in the essay. Yet this distance seems more to characterize his emotional commitment to the movement than his sense of its intellectual sources. See, for example, Joel Porte, *Emerson and Thoreau: Transcendentalists in Conflict* (Middletown, Conn.: Wesleyan University Press, 1966), p. 6; and Lawrence Buell, *Literary Transcendentalism: Style and Vision in the American Renaissance* (Ithaca, N.Y.: Cornell University Press, 1973), p. 52.

5 The key statements here are by Porte, *Emerson and Thoreau*, pp. 45-92; and especially René Wellek, "Emerson and German Philosophy" (1943), reprinted in *Confrontations: Studies in the Intellectual and Literary Relations between Germany, England, and the United States during the Nineteenth Century* (Princeton, N.J.: Princeton University Press, 1965), pp. 187-212. For an opposing view, see Henry A. Pochmann, *German Culture in America: Philosophical and Literary Influences, 1600-1900* (Madison: University of Wisconsin Press, 1957), pp. 153-207. For more general source studies, see J. Russell Roberts, "Emerson's Debt to the Seventeenth Century," *American Literature* 21 (1949), 298-310; Cameron Thompson, "John Locke and New England Transcendentalism," *New England Quarterly* 35 (1962), 435-57; Merrell R. Davis, "Emerson's 'Reason' and the Scottish Philosophers," *New England Quarterly* 17 (1944), 209-28. On Platonism in Emerson, see John S. Harrison, *The Teachers of Emerson* (New York: Sturgis and Walton, 1910); Stuart Gerry Brown, "Emerson's Platonism," *New England Quarterly* 18 (1945), 325-45; George Mills Harper, "Thomas Taylor in America," in *Thomas Taylor the Platonist, Selected Writings*, ed. Harper and Kathleen Raine (Princeton, N.J.: Princeton University Press, 1969), pp. 49-57; and Gay Wilson Allen, *Waldo Emerson: A Biography* (New York: Viking Press, 1981), pp. 269-74 et passim. On Swedenborg, the most complete source is Clarence Paul Hotson, "Emerson and Swedenborg," Diss. Harvard 1929. See also Hotson's articles, "Sampson Reed, Teacher of Emerson," *New England Quarterly* 2 (1929), 249-77; "Emerson and the Doctrine of Correspondence," *New-Church Review* 36 (1929), 47-59, 173-86, 304-16, 435-48; "Emerson and the Swedenborgians," *New-Church Review* 38 (1931), 46-78; and Sherman Paul, *Emerson's Angle of Vision: Man and Nature in American Experience* (Cambridge, Mass.: Harvard University Press, 1952), pp. 60-70. On Kant and Schelling (through Coleridge), see Joseph Warren Beach, *The Concept of Nature in Nineteenth-Century English Poetry* (New York: The Macmillan Co., 1936), pp. 318-45. On Schelling, see Henry David Gray, *Emerson: a Statement of New England Transcendentalism as Expressed in the Philosophy of Its Chief Exponent* (Stanford, Calif.: Stanford University Press, 1917). On Cousin, see Georges J. Joyaux, "Victor Cousin and American Transcendentalism," *French Review* 29 (1955), 117-30; and Emerson R. Marks, "Victor Cousin and Emerson," in Myron Simon and Thornton H. Parsons, eds., *Transcendentalism and Its Legacy* (Ann Arbor: University of Michigan Press, 1966), pp. 63-86. On Coleridge, see Frank T.

Thompson, "Emerson's Indebtedness to Coleridge," *Studies in Philology* 23 (1926), 55-76; and Kenneth Walter Cameron, *Emerson the Essayist,* 2 vols., (Raleigh, N.C.: Thistle Press, 1945). On Carlyle, see Frank T. Thompson, "Emerson and Carlyle," *Studies in Philology* 24 (1927), 438-53. A useful overview of these various influences is in Whicher, *Freedom and Fate*, pp. 175-81 et passim.

6 For Emerson's own (somewhat contradictory) comments on his knowledge of German, see L.I.154-55, 254, 377; V.42; VI.188, 190, 204; CEC, p. 269; JMN.IV.293, V.319. See also Pochmann, *German Culture in America*, p. 597, n. 163. The first English translation of Kant was not published until 1838, although numerous summaries were available, some with extensive quotations from the original.

7 See especially Wellek, "Emerson and German Philosophy," pp. 188-95. The best overviews are Cameron, *Emerson the Essayist*, Paul, *Emerson's Angle of Vision*, pp. 13-70, and, more generally, Buell, *Literary Transcendentalism*, pp. 1-54.

8 Wellek, "Emerson and German Philosophy," p. 193. Most critics repeat some version of this objection. For Kant's distinction, see Immanuel Kant, *Critique of Pure Reason,* trans. Norman Kemp Smith (New York: St. Martin's Press, 1965), pp. A295-96=B351-53. [Page references to the first *Critique* traditionally cite the page numbers of the first edition (A), the second edition (B), or both.]

9 CW.I.33. See Wellek, "Emerson and German Philosophy," pp. 188-89. For the Kantian original, see Kant, *Pure Reason*, p. A307=B364. Coleridge does not explicitly attribute the formulation to Plato, but only identifies it as Plato's "grand problem"; see *The Collected Works of Samuel Taylor Coleridge,* Vol. IV: *The Friend*, sec. II, essay V ("Essays on the Principles of Method"); ed. Barbara E. Rooke (Princeton, N.J.: Princeton University Press, 1969), I, 461. For an interesting distinction between Emerson as a seer and Bronson Alcott as a mystic, see Octavius Brooks Frothingham, *Transcendentalism in New England* (Gloucester, Mass.: Peter Smith, 1965), pp. 224-42, 249-54. Frothingham's general account of Transcendentalism remains one of the best.

10 See Wellek, "Emerson and German Philosophy," pp. 193-95, and especially Porte, *Emerson and Thoreau*, pp. 53-61.

11 For this interpretation of Kant and Emerson's misuse of him, see Wellek, "Emerson and German Philosophy," pp. 211-12. Similar conclusions are reached in Wellek's "The Minor Transcendentalists and German Philosophy" (1942), reprinted in *Confrontations*, pp. 153-86; see especially pp. 178-79.

12 For Emerson's sense of the unpopularity of German philosophy in America, see L.III.346. More generally, see the attacks by Andrews Norton and Francis Bowen on Transcendentalism as "German barbarisms," and the responses by George Ripley and especially Orestes Brownson. Many relevant passages are reprinted in Perry Miller, ed., *The Transcendentalists: an Anthology* (Cambridge, Mass.: Harvard University Press, 1950), pp. 173-246. Miller, however, probably overemphasizes the political dimension of Transcendentalism.

13 It is at least reassuring that the modern editors of Coleridge fail to note the error; see *The Friend*, II.v ("Method"); I, 461-62. Perhaps the real point is less Coleridge's and Emerson's ignorance of Kant than their sense, shared with many Romantics, that Plato is himself best interpreted as a forerunner of German idealism.

14 For a representative reevaluation of Cousin, see Etienne Gilson, Thomas Langan, and Armand A. Maurer, *Recent Philosophy: Hegel to the Present* (New York: Random House, 1966), pp. 232-37. For more general accounts of how historians of philosophy have underrated the French influence, see Hans Aarsleff, *From Locke to Saussure: Essays on the Study of Language and Intellectual History* (Minneapolis: University of Minnesota Press, 1982); and Norman Fiering's two volumes, *Moral Philosophy at Seventeenth-Century Harvard: A Discipline in Transition* and *Jonathan Edwards's Moral Thought and Its British Context* (both Chapel Hill: The University of North Carolina Press for the Institute of Early American History and Culture, 1981). At the very least, it is clear that the traditional distinction between French rationalism and English empiricism creates a false dichotomy and obscures the extent to which, for example, Hume was far more aware of Descartes and Malebranche than of Berkeley.

15 On Kant's knowledge of Hume, see T. E. Wilkerson, *Kant's Critique of Pure Reason: A Commentary for Students* (Oxford: Clarendon Press, 1976), pp. 4-6; and especially Norman Kemp Smith, *A Commentary to Kant's 'Critique of Pure Reason,'* 2nd ed. (London: Macmillan Press, Ltd., 1923), pp. xxv-xxxiii. For a more thematic treatment of the relation between the two, see Jonathan Bennett, *Kant's Analytic* (New York: Cambridge University Press, 1966), pp. 153-63. Kant claims that Hume awoke him from his dogmatic slumber in the introduction to the *Prolegomena to Any Future Metaphysics,* ed. Lewis White Beck (New York: Bobbs-Merrill Co., Inc., 1950), pp. 257-62. (Page references to the *Prolegomena* traditionally cite the page number in the fourth volume of the Academy edition.)

16 For claims that the only proper way to be a Kantian is to accept Kant's whole system, see Wellek, "Minor Transcendentalists and German Philosophy," pp. 163-66; H. J. Paton, *Kant's Metaphysic of Experience: A Commentary on the First Half of the Kritik der reinen Vernunft* (New York: Humanities Press, Inc., 1976), I, 16; and Gian N. G. Orsini, *Coleridge and German Idealism: A Study in the History of Philosophy, with Unpublished Materials from Coleridge's Manuscripts* (Carbondale: Southern Illinois University Press, 1969), p. 142. Orsini's work offers a fine summary of Kant's idealism; see pp. 57-148. Pochmann usefully collects Emerson's statements against systematic philosophy; see *German Culture in America,* p. 586, n. 1. It is probably for his systematic approach as much as his philosophical acumen that Brownson seems to Wellek more informed than Emerson; it is at least clear that both make about the same number of technical errors.

17 See P. F. Strawson, *The Bounds of Sense: An Essay on Kant's Critique of Pure Reason* (London: Methuen and Co., Ltd., 1966), p. 18; Jonathan Bennett, *Kant's Dialectic* (New York: Cambridge University Press, 1974), p. 267; and Smith, *A Commentary,* pp. 73-76. This terminological distinction becomes increasingly problematic as Kant moves from the Analytic to the Dialectic. For examples of possible misuse, see Kant, *Pure Reason,* pp. B44, A297=B354, and A308-09=B365-66. For a defense of the distinction, see Paton, *Kant's Metaphysic,* II, 430.

18 Although it is customary to speak loosely of the two "halves" of the *Critique* as the Analytic (including the Aesthetic) and the Dialectic, this quantitative distinction does not correspond to Kant's announced structure. The book in fact divides into the Elements (about four-fifths of the work) and the Method. The Elements is divided into the 30-page Aesthetic and the 500-page Logic. Only within the Logic itself are the two divisions – the Analytic and the Dialectic – roughly comparable in length. Behind such observations often lies the implication that Kant's faulty notion of an architectonic committed him to an inappropriate structure. Such an objection is fundamental to Francis Bowen's account, *Modern Philosophy from Descartes to Schopenhauer and Hartmann,* 6th ed. (New York: Charles Scribner's Sons, 1891), pp. 202-03, 229-30. For modern interpretations, see Smith, *A Commentary,* pp. 77-78, 579-81; and in reply, Paton, *Kant's Metaphysic,* I, 235-37.

19 See Bennett, *Dialectic,* p. viii. Paton, who examines only the first half, suggests that "the rest of the argument should offer no insuperable difficulty" (*Kant's Metaphysic,* I, 18). Few modern commentators agree, and the work of Strawson and Bennett in particular exposes the problematic nature of the Dialectic's concept of Reason. Wellek has himself admitted, with respect to his work on Kant and Coleridge, that his emphasis on Kant's anticipation of Hegelian dialectics was overstated; see *The Attack on Literature and Other Essays* (Chapel Hill: University of North Carolina Press, 1982), p. 147.

20 Kant makes his condescending references, *Pure Reason,* pp. B274-75, B71; see also *Prolegomena,* pp. 290-94. Strawson countercharges that Kant's transcendental idealism is closer to Berkeley's psychological idealism than Kant admits; see *The Bounds of Sense,* pp. 21-22, 35, 133-50.

21 See JMN.VII.283. It is useful to remember that, in summarizing Kant's philosophy, Bowen similarly elevates the Analytic, and that Brownson (like Paton in our century) treats only the first half of the *Critique.* See Bowen, *Modern Philosophy,* p. 219; and *The Works of Orestes A. Brownson* (Detroit: Thorndike Nourse, 1882), I, 186-213. (All subsequent references to Brownson will cite this first volume of the *Works.*)

22 Wellek, "Emerson and German Philosophy," p. 193. Again, most subsequent scholars repeat this charge. Porte offers a spirited attack; see *Emerson and Thoreau,* pp. 83-87. It is useful, however, to recall that most critics themselves have trouble with the distinction. See for example, Mme. de Staël, *De L'Allemagne* (Paris: Librairie Hachette, 1959), IV, 120-24 (and Porte, *Emerson and Thoreau,* p. 88); Coleridge, *The Friend,* II.ix, xi ("Method"); I, 491, 520; Brownson, *The Works,* I, pp. 186-87; and various statements by Ripley, Hedge, and Brownson in Miller's *Transcendentalists,* pp. 65, 69, 87, 244. Even in our century, both Porte (*Emerson and Thoreau,* p. 88) and the Harvard editors (CW.I.xxii) tend to treat "intuition" as intuitive, even innate. For Kant, however, "intuition" is a term of art more closely related to "sensation" than to current meanings of "intuition"; see, for example, Kant, *Pure Reason,* pp.

A19-22=B33-36; A248-54=B308-11. Equally troublesome is Emerson's general misuse of the distinction between Reason and Understanding, an error he probably learned from Coleridge. See, for example, the passages collected from the journals by Cameron, *Emerson the Essayist*, I, 191-94; and especially the famous letter to his brother, L.I.412-13. For the Coleridgean sources, see *Aids to Reflection*, "Aphorisms on that which is indeed Spiritual Religion," no. VIII; ed. James Marsh (Burlington, Vt.: Chauncey Goodrich, 1829), pp. 142-45; see also *Biographia Literaria*, x; *Collected Works*, VII, ed. James Engell and W. Jackson Bate (Princeton, N.J.: Princeton University Press, 1983), I, 173-75, 203; and *Friend*, "The Landing-Place," v; I, 154-61.

23 For representative uses of the distinction in the published works, see CW.I.23-24, 43, 81, 184. It is one of the chief contentions of this book that unpublished material, however indicative of the development of Emerson's thought, must not be cited against him as evidence of his philosophical immaturity.

24 J. G. Fichte, *The Science of Knowledge*, ed. and trans. Peter Heath and John Lachs (New York: Cambridge University Press, 1982), I, 101-05; cf. I, 305, 320. For the characteristically Fichtean notion of "striving" that results from the Ego's posits, see I, 261-62. [Page references to Fichte traditionally cite the edition of his son, I. H. Fichte (1834-46).] For a useful summary, see Frederick Copleston, S.J., *A History of Philosophy* (Garden City, N.Y.: Doubleday & Co., Inc., 1962-77), VII, i, 64-68.

25 See Kant, *Pure Reason*, pp. A642-704=B670-732; and the *Critique of Practical Reason*, trans. Lewis White Beck (Indianapolis: Bobbs-Merrill Co., Inc., 1956), pp. 4-5, 134-36. (Page references to the second *Critique* traditionally cite the page number in the fifth volume of the Academy edition.) For neutral discussions of the problem of regulative ideas, see Copleston, *A History*, VI, ii, 94-97, 125-37; and Beck, *A Commentary on Kant's Critique of Practical Reason* (Chicago: University of Chicago Press, 1960), pp. 48, 251-65. For more critical approaches, see Strawson, *Bounds of Sense*, pp. 33-38; and Bennett, *Dialectic*, pp. 137-42, 270-80.

26 See, for example, Fichte, *Science of Knowledge*, I, 468-91; and Hegel, *Logic*, being Part One of the *Encyclopaedia of the Philosophical Sciences*, trans. William Wallace (New York: Oxford University Press, 1975), §§ 40-60; pp. 65-94; and Arthur Schopenhauer, *The World as Will and Representation*, trans. E. F. J. Payne (New York: Dover Publications, 1969), I, xv, 415-534 (preface to the first edition and appendix to the first volume).

27 Thus the anger of Porte's account, which drew much criticism and for which he subsequently apologized, is in this one sense simple honesty – an admission of the condescension implicit in all such claims.

28 On the limitations of the concept of influence, see Quentin Skinner, "The Limits of Historical Explanations," *Philosophy* 41 (1966), 199-215. On the dangers of overemphasizing "continuities," see John Passmore, "The Idea of a History of Philosophy," *History and Theory*, Beiheft 5: *The Historiography of the History of Philosophy* (1965), 1-32.

29 Skinner, "Meaning," p. 29. For Skinner's tempering of this statement, see his "Motives, Intentions and the Interpretation of Texts," *New Literary History*

3 (1972), 405. For my own reservations about the myth of "endowed coherence," see note 3.

30 The two arguments are not entirely compatible. Critics of Emerson's maturity employ the notion of influence only to exploit its negative implications, damning him by association with his more disreputable mystical sources. Moreover they push the influence argument forward, as the others do not, to show that Emerson's own influence has been pernicious. The failures of his disciples – both in his age and in ours – are read back into his own philosophy as the realizations of its dangerous potential. This argument, however, implicitly grants to Emerson's ideas the kind of authenticity that the other denies them. Although Wellek would see Emerson's idealism as enervated, Winters admits it to be very powerful indeed. And the irony of their position is that repeatedly this second group of critics finds itself attacking the strength of formulations whose content is meek and genteel, Emerson's ability, as it were, to awaken people into somnambulism. The key statements here are George Santayana, "Emerson," in *Interpretations of Poetry and Religion* (1900), reprinted in Richard Colton Lyon, ed., *Santayana on America: Essays, Notes, and Letters on American Life, Literature, and Philosophy* (New York: Harcourt, Brace & World, Inc., 1968), pp. 258-67; Henry Bamford Parkes, *The Pragmatic Test: Essays on the History of Ideas* (San Francisco: The Colt Press, 1941), pp. 32-62; Yvor Winters, *In Defense of Reason* (Denver: Alan Swallow, 1947), pp. 262-82, 577-90; and Quentin Anderson, *The Imperial Self: An Essay in American Literary and Cultural History* (New York: Random House, 1971), pp. 3-58, 216-44. It is interesting that Santayana, who had no love for idealist metaphysics, feels Emerson's epistemology to be the equal of his German masters' and intuitively superior to Hegel's (p. 261).

31 Henry James, Jr., *Partial Portraits* (New York: The Macmillan Company, 1899), p. 31. Earlier, less public forms of the charge were made by Herman Melville and Henry James, Sr. It has subsequently been repeated by, among others, T. S. Eliot, W. B. Yeats, D. H. Lawrence, Santayana, Winters, Parkes, and Anderson. See also recent popular statements by A. Bartlett Giamatti and John Updike. For F. O. Matthiessen's reservations in his otherwise positive account, see *American Renaissance: Art and Expression in the Age of Emerson and Whitman* (New York: Oxford University Press, 1941), pp. 4-5, 73-75, 180-84.

32 The first response is Newton Arvin, "The House of Pain," reprinted in Konvitz and Whicher, *Emerson*, pp. 46-59; the second is Whicher's own in *Freedom and Fate*, p. 109. See also Frederic Ives Carpenter, *Emerson Handbook* (New York: Hendricks House, Inc., 1953), pp. 143-52; and Chester Eugene Jorgenson, "Emerson's Paradise Under the Shadow of Swords," *Philological Quarterly* 11 (1932), 274-92.

33 See, for example, Santayana, *Santayana on America*, p. 266; Winters, *In Defense of Reason*, pp. 267-69; and especially Parkes, *The Pragmatic Test*, pp. 34-35, 47-58. Perry Miller gives the fullest expression in his "From Edwards to Emerson," reprinted in *Errand into the Wilderness* (Cambridge, Mass.: Harvard University Press, 1956), pp. 184-203. Yet one might want to suspect this formulation, especially given Miller's barely suppressed hostility to Emerson

throughout his career. By historicizing the optimism argument as "Edwardse-anism without original sin," Miller establishes the Americanness of Emerso-nianism without affording it any of the intellectual muscularity he finds so congenial in the Puritans. His Emerson thus becomes indistinguishable from Winters's, one of "shallow optimism and insufferable smugness," and in his anthology he blithely tells the story of Transcendentalism without him.

34 The exception here is, of course, Henry James himself, who in defining Emerson's blindness to evil does so by contrasting him to the more purely Puritanical Hawthorne.

35 *The Pragmatic Test,* p. 4. Parkes discusses the Puritans' failure, pp. 21-32.

36 *In Defense of Reason,* p. 269.

37 *American Renaissance,* p. 4.

38 Thus recent critics can acknowledge the truth of Whicher's account without changing the overall shape of their criticism. Anderson's response is the most revealing. Admitting the naiveté of previous attacks on Emerson's optimism, he nevertheless insists on Emerson's unwillingness to accept the value of social experience. By this account, there was no place in his theory for evil, and the problem of optimism, though banished from the biography, returns to damn his metaphysics (*The Imperial Self,* pp. 51-58).

39 Harold Bloom himself acknowledges the debt in *The Ringers in the Tower: Studies in Romantic Tradition* (Chicago: University of Chicago Press, 1971), pp. 218-19. For Bloom's various statements on Emerson, see *Ringers,* pp. 217-26, 291-304; *A Map of Misreading* (New York: Oxford University Press, 1975), pp. 160-76; *Kabbalah and Criticism* (New York: Continuum, 1975), pp. 95-126; *Figures of Capable Imagination* (New York: Seabury Press, 1976), pp. 46-75; *Poetry and Repression: Revisionism from Blake to Stevens* (New Haven, Conn.: Yale University Press, 1976), pp. 235-66; *Wallace Stevens: The Poems of Our Climate* (Ithaca, N.Y.: Cornell University Press, 1977), pp. 1-11; and *Agon: Towards a Theory of Revisionism* (New York: Oxford University Press, 1982), pp. 145-78. Bloom confronts Winters directly on the topic of Emerson in *Figures,* pp. 51-53.

40 See, for example, Charles Feidelson, Jr., *Symbolism and American Literature* (Chicago: University of Chicago Press, 1953), pp. 119-61; and Sacvan Berco-vitch's two books, *The Puritan Origins of the American Self* (New Haven, Conn.: Yale University Press, 1975), pp. 157-86, and *The American Jeremiad* (Madison: University of Wisconsin Press, 1978), pp. 182-85, 199-203.

41 *Santayana on America,* p. 259.

42 This concept is, of course, central to the work of Jacques Derrida. See, for example, *Of Grammatology,* trans. Gayatri Chakravorty Spivak (Baltimore: Johns Hopkins University Press, 1976), pp. 10-26. For analyses, see Spivak's introduction, pp. xxi-liv; and Jonathan Culler, *On Deconstruction: Theory and Criticism after Structuralism* (Ithaca, N.Y.: Cornell University Press, 1982), pp. 89-110. For explicit attempts to reconcile Emerson to deconstruction, see Joseph Kronick, "Emerson and the Question of Reading/Writing," *Genre* 14 (1981), 363-81; and Donald Pease, "Emerson, *Nature,* and the Sovereignty of Influence," *Boundary 2* 8, iii (1980), 43-74. Bishop's sense of Emerson's tonal puns, Packer's of his "contempt for intelligibility," and perhaps even Poirier's of American language as "elsewhere" all flirt with generally deconstructive readings. See Jonathan Bishop, *Emerson on the Soul* (Cambridge, Mass.: Harvard University Press, 1964), p. 139; B. L. Packer, *Emerson's Fall: A New Interpretation of the Major Essays* (New York: Continuum, 1982), p. 18; and Richard Poirier, *A World Elsewhere: The Place of Style in American Literature* (New York: Oxford University Press, 1966), especially pp. 56-70. My own sense of Emerson's intentional (though not necessarily conscious) ironies is more conservative, meaning to show Emerson's deconstruction of others' positions without giving him over totally to linguistic indeterminacy.

43 For William James's own attempts to answer questions about the relation between pragmatic truth and experience, see *Pragmatism: A New Name for Some Old Ways of Thinking [and] The Meaning of Truth: A Sequel to* Pragmatism (Cambridge, Mass.: Harvard University Press, 1978), pp. 104-08, 320-25.

44 For an argument concerning the positivist bias of history, see the exchange between Gordon S. Wood and Jackson Lears in *The New York Review of Books* (Dec. 16, 1982), pp. 58-59. For more extended accounts of the literariness of history, see Louis O. Mink, "History and Fiction as Modes of Comprehension," *New Literary History* 1 (1970), 541-58; W. B. Gallie, *Philosophy and the Historical Understanding* (New York: Schocken Books, 1968); and Hayden White, *Metahistory: The Historical Imagination in Nineteenth-Century Europe* (Baltimore: Johns Hopkins University Press, 1973), pp. 1-42.

45 The divorce of an idea from its effects has not always seemed easy. Critics have finally declared illegitimate the conflation of Nietzsche, Wagner, and Hitler that so jeopardized that philosopher's reputation. And they are only now beginning to learn to separate Heidegger's philosophy from his politics – to assume that questions about his reification of *Da-sein* are different from (though related to) questions about his Nazism.

46 For this famous passage in Hume, see *A Treatise of Human Nature,* I.iv.7; ed. L. A. Selby-Bigge (Oxford: Clarendon Press, 1973), pp. 269-74. Subsequent references to the *Treatise* will cite this edition by book, part, chapter, and page. For a useful review of the theory about the "compatibility" of the apparently contradictory notions of freedom, autonomy, and determinism, see Lawrence H. Davis, *Theory of Action* (Englewood Cliffs, N.J.: Prentice-Hall, Inc., 1979), pp. 107-41. For Hume's own most extended treatment of the issue, see *An Enquiry Concerning Human Understanding,* VIII.i.62-81; eds. L. A. Selby-Bigge and P. H. Nidditch (Oxford: Clarendon Press, 1975), pp. 80-103.

47 For possible models of literary history, see the essays by Geoffrey Hartman and Paul de Man in Morton W. Bloomfield, ed., *In Search of Literary Theory* (Ithaca, N.Y.: Cornell University Press, 1972), pp. 195-267; the exchange between Wayne C. Booth and M. H. Abrams in Booth's *Critical Understanding: The Powers and Limits of Pluralism* (Chicago: University of Chicago Press, 1979), pp. 138-94; and more generally the work of Hans Robert Jauss, especially *Toward an Aesthetic of Reception,* trans. Timothy Bahti (Minneapolis: University of Minnesota Press, 1982), pp. 3-45. For this problem as it infects Americanist scholarship, see Michael J. Colacurcio, "Does American Literature Have a History?" *Early American Literature* 13 (1978), 110-32.

48 My notion of truth as separable from experience does not imply an ideal truth separate from it. For a related view of truth as distinct from time, see Gordon Graham, "Can There Be History of Philosophy?" *History and Theory* 21 (1982), 37-52. For a more general account of the continuity between meaning and theory, see Walter Benn Michaels and Stephen Knapp, "Against Theory," *Critical Inquiry* 8 (1982), 723-42.

49 For this reason, the Kant of my account is closer to the stripped-down versions of modern neo-Kantians like Strawson and Bennett than the more historically accurate ones of Wellek and Paton. In the early stages of grappling with a philosophy, explication seems more important than interpretation. And in the cases of *very* hard philosophers like Kant and Wittgenstein, that preliminary period seems to last forever. But the distinction is only apparent. For the real problem – as Bloom implies with his sense of strong and weak readings – is that all explication is interpretation, although with very conservative presuppositions.

50 The claim is made by John Dewey, Emerson's most sympathetic philosopher-reader. See Konvitz and Whicher, *Emerson*, p. 24.

51 Here I merely paraphrase Paton's analysis of Kant; *Kant's Metaphysic*, I, 40.

52 On the relation between Emerson and Nietzsche, see Hermann Hummel, "Emerson and Nietzsche," *New England Quarterly* 19 (1946), 63-84; Rudolf Schottlaender, "Two Dionysians: Emerson and Nietzsche," *South Atlantic Quarterly* 39 (1940), 330-43; Grace R. Foster, "The Natural History of the Will," *American Scholar* 15 (1946), 277-87; and S. L. Gilman, "Nietzsches Emerson-Lektüre: Eine unbekannte Quelle," *Nietzsche Studien* 9 (1980), 406-31. A more general sense of the continuity lies behind much of Bloom's work; see especially *Kabbalah*, pp. 113-21.

53 Santayana exploits this crack most fully in asserting that Emerson's kind of poetic prose is inimical to fact; see *Santayana on America*, pp. 262-63. See also Brian M. Barbour, "Emerson's 'Poetic' Prose," *Modern Language Quarterly* 35 (1974), 157-72. Winters offers the more traditional explanation that Emerson possessed "the gift of style without the gift of thought"; see *In Defense of Reason*, p. 600. Dewey denies both by insisting that the distinction between philosophy and literature is a false one; see Konvitz and Whicher, *Emerson*, pp. 25-26. In terms of current Emersonian scholarship, the dilemma is perhaps best represented in the two Emersons of Joel Porte. Not only does Porte offer two accounts – a negative evaluation of Emerson's philosophical sources and a positive one of his style. His apology, in his second account, for his initial hostility takes two forms – an admirable willingness to be "more sensitive to the nuances of Emerson's thought" and a questionable belief that Emerson is to be read only by the "sufficiently Transcendental." Although there is a real tonal difference between Porte's two books, however, they are not intellectually incompatible, but only two ways of drawing the same conclusions. Perhaps the best explanation of Emerson's prose is simply the most generous: not that Kant was the better epistemologist, but that Emerson was the better stylist. For Porte's "renunciation," see *Representative Man: Ralph Waldo Emerson in His Time* (New York: Oxford University Press, 1979), pp. xxi-xxiii.

54 In addition to the statements by Bloom and Poirier, see also Roy Harvey Pearce, *The Continuity of American Poetry* (Princeton, N.J.: Princeton University Press, 1961), pp. 41-42, 153-64.

55 See William H. Gass, *Fiction and the Figures of Life* (New York: Random House, 1972), especially pp. 3-26; and Richard Rorty, *Consequences of Pragmatism (Essays: 1972-1980)* (Minneapolis: University of Minnesota Press, 1982), pp. 90-109. Rorty treats Emerson in this context (pp. 64-68) and has extended his general comparison of literature and philosophy in "Deconstruction and Circumvention," *Critical Inquiry* 11 (1984), 1-23.

2. THE STRUCTURE OF NATURE

1 See Henry David Gray, *Emerson: A Statement of New England Transcendentalism as Expressed in the Philosophy of Its Chief Exponent* (Stanford, Calif.: Stanford University Press, 1917), p. 15; and Odell Shepard, *Pedlar's Progress: The Life of Bronson Alcott* (Boston: Little, Brown, & Co., 1937), p. 159.

2 I paraphrase Stephen E. Whicher in his edition *Selections from Ralph Waldo Emerson: An Organic Anthology* (Boston: Houghton Mifflin Company, 1957), p. 13; hereafter, *Selections*. Those writers who agree, with Jonathan Bishop, that *Nature* is "our primal book" still tend to treat the work only in parts, with particular attention to the first and last chapters; see Jonathan Bishop, *Emerson on the Soul* (Cambridge, Mass.: Harvard University Press, 1964), p. 9. And even those who, like B. L. Packer, give it extended treatment often see the book as a problem to be explained. The most interesting exception is Warner Berthoff, who, in his facsimile edition of the first edition of *Nature*, finds the awkwardness simply that of a novice author that in no way reflects on his intellectual project [San Francisco: Chandler Publishing Company, 1968), p. xi].

3 The Unitarian is Francis Bowen, the Transcendentalist Orestes Brownson. Both responses are reprinted, along with other useful source material, in Merton M. Sealts, Jr., and Alfred R. Ferguson, eds., *Emerson's* Nature: *Origin, Growth, Meaning,* 2nd ed., enlarged (Carbondale: Southern Illinois University Press, 1979); see especially pp. 76, 81.

4 That Emerson thought of his project as preliminary is clear from his famous statement about the "entering wedge" (CEC, p. 149). All the relevant passages on the writing of *Nature* are reprinted in Sealts and Ferguson, *Emerson's* Nature, pp. 38-46; they are usefully summarized in CW.I.3-6.

5 The most interesting reading of the passage is Berthoff, *Nature,* pp. xlvi-lvi. Berthoff's sense of Emerson's philosophical adequacy is close to my own, and in some senses my reading of *Nature* only expands upon claims implicit in his introduction.

6 For the traditional view, see Octavius Brooks Frothingham, *Transcendentalism in New England* (Gloucester, Mass.: Peter Smith, 1965), pp. 107-28; and Perry Miller, ed., *The Transcendentalists: an Anthology* (Cambridge, Mass.: Harvard University Press, 1950), pp. 45-48 et passim. For modern reevaluations which stress the continuities between Unitarianism and Transcendentalism, see Lawrence Buell, *Literary Transcendentalism: Style and Vision in the American Renaissance* (Ithaca, N.Y.: Cornell University Press, 1973), pp. 4-54; William R.

Hutchison, *The Transcendentalist Ministers: Church Reform in the New England Renaissance* (New Haven, Conn.: Yale University Press, 1959), pp. 1-51; Conrad Wright, *The Liberal Christians: Essays on American Unitarian History* (Boston: Beacon Press, 1970), especially pp. 34-40; and for a special focus on Emerson's Unitarianism, David Robinson, *Apostle of Culture: Emerson as Preacher and Lecturer* (Philadelphia: University of Pennsylvania Press, 1982).

7 On the Romantic concept of "joy," see M. H. Abrams, *Natural Supernaturalism: Tradition and Revolution in Romantic Literature* (New York: W. W. Norton & Co., Inc., 1971), pp. 123, 276-77, 431-37 et passim.

8 Emerson's revision of the line to the famous "glad to brink of fear," though in most respects an improvement, does lessen the quantitative dimension of gladness implicit in the original "how glad." Cf. CW.I.10, 288. For praise of the revision, see Bishop's famous reading in *Emerson on the Soul*, pp. 11, 14.

9 These objections are made respectively by Bishop, *Emerson on the Soul*, pp. 14-15, and Barbara Packer, "Uriel's Cloud: Emerson's Rhetoric," *Georgia Review* 31 (1977), 326-28. Packer treats the same topic, with less emphasis on *Nature*, in her book, *Emerson's Fall: A New Interpretation of the Major Essays* (New York: Continuum, 1982), p. 5. Expanding on Matthiessen, Packer rightly notices that Bowen, one of the first to object to the image, associates it with passages we now admire. Her conclusion – that Bowen objects to the rhetorical perversity that she praises – is less certain. It is unclear whether Bowen attacks merely Emerson's indecorousness or his use of striking diction to disguise the radical nature of his intellectual argument. See Packer, "Uriel," p. 328; Matthiessen, *American Renaissance: Art and Expression in the Age of Emerson and Whitman* (New York: Oxford University Press, 1941), pp. 38-39n; and Bowen in Sealts and Ferguson, *Emerson's Nature*, pp. 81-82. For other readings of the passage, see James M. Cox, "R. W. Emerson: The Circles of the Eye," in David Levin, ed., *Emerson: Prophecy, Metamorphosis, and Influence* (New York: Columbia University Press, 1975), pp. 57-67; and especially Berthoff, *Nature*, pp. lxi-lxix. The most radical reading of the linguistic tensions in the passage is in Richard Poirier, *A World Elsewhere: The Place of Style in American Literature* (New York: Oxford University Press, 1966), pp. 56-70. For more general treatment of eye imagery in Emerson, see Kenneth Burke, "I, Eye, Ay – Emerson's Early Essay 'Nature': Thoughts on the Machinery of Transcendence," in Myron Simon and Thornton H. Parsons, eds., *Transcendentalism and Its Legacy* (Ann Arbor: University of Michigan Press, 1966), pp. 13-14; and Sherman Paul, *Emerson's Angle of Vision: Man and Nature in American Experience* (Cambridge, Mass.: Harvard University Press, 1952), pp. 71-102 et passim.

10 Emerson emphasizes this selflessness in his revision of the journal original, from "I become happy in my universal relations" to "I am nothing"; cf. JMN.V.18 and CW.I.10. For a reading that emphasizes the selflessness to answer Bishop, see Robinson, *Apostle of Culture*, pp. 88-89.

11 As many critics have noted, the very fact that the awkward image of the eyeball is added to the journal passage suggests that awkwardness to be intentional; see JMN.V.18, Berthoff, *Nature*, p. xxxvi, and Packer, "Uriel," pp. 327-28.

12 On the general structure of the essay, see Robinson, *Apostle of Culture*, pp. 87-96; Richard Lee Francis, "The Architectonics of Emerson's *Nature*," *American Quarterly* 19 (1967), 39-52; Barry Wood, "The Growth of the Soul: Coleridge's Dialectical Method and the Strategy of Emerson's *Nature*" (1976), revised and reprinted in Sealts and Ferguson, *Emerson's* Nature, pp. 194-208; and Richard Tuerk, "Emerson's *Nature*–Miniature Universe," *American Transcendental Quarterly* 1 (1969), 110-13. For a more theoretical approach, see Julie Ellison, *Emerson's Romantic Style* (Princeton, N.J.: Princeton University Press, 1984), pp. 85-96.

13 On the relation between Egyptology and writing implied in Emerson's use of the word "hieroglyph," see John T. Irwin, *American Hieroglyphics: The Symbol of the Egyptian Hieroglyphics in the American Renaissance* (New Haven, Conn.: Yale University Press, 1980), especially pp. 11-14. For a more historical account, see Irwin's article, "The Symbol of the Hieroglyphics in the American Renaissance," *American Quarterly* 26 (1974), 103-26, which lies behind the book's first chapter.

14 For Fichte's famous distinction between the ME and the NOT ME, see J. G. Fichte, *The Science of Knowledge,* ed. and trans. Peter Heath and John Lachs (New York: Cambridge University Press, 1982), I, 93-105. Emerson's most probable sources are Victor Cousin, *Introduction to the History of Philosophy* (Boston: Hilliard, Gray, Little, and Wilkins, 1832), pp. 149-53, 159-62; and Thomas Carlyle, "Novalis," *The Works of Thomas Carlyle in Thirty Volumes,* centenary edition (New York: Charles Scribner's Sons, 1896-99), XXVII, 22-27. For Emerson's well-established knowledge of these secondary sources, see Frank T. Thompson, "Emerson and Carlyle," *Studies in Philology* 24 (1927), 438-48; and René Wellek, "Emerson and German Philosophy" (1943), reprinted in *Confrontations: Studies in the Intellectual and Literary Relations between Germany, England, and the United States during the Nineteenth Century* (Princeton, N.J.: Princeton University Press, 1965), pp. 188n, 196-98 and n.

15 For a similar application of "Ramsey's Maxim" to Kant, see Lewis White Beck, *Essays on Kant and Hume* (New Haven, Conn.: Yale University Press, 1978), pp. 11-19.

16 JMN.V.336-37. For further discussion, see pp. 115–17.

17 Emerson's "occult" may refer to Berkeley's preferred term to attack the notion of material substance in Locke and of scientific entity in Newton. See *De Motu,* §§ 4-6 and, more generally, *The Principles of Human Knowledge* (PHK), I, §§ 16-17, 68-81, and *The First Dialogue between Hylas and Philonous*; in *Berkeley's Philosophical Writings,* ed. David M. Armstrong (London: Macmillan Co., Ltd., 1965), pp. 251-52, 67, 89-94, 161-64. For the source of the problem, see John Locke, *An Essay Concerning Human Understanding,* II.xxiii; ed. Alexander Campbell Fraser (1894; reprinted New York: Dover Books, 1959), I, 390-423. For a more general use of the term, see Thomas Reid, *Essays on the Intellectual Powers of Man,* I.iii; (Cambridge, Mass.: MIT Press, 1969), p. 42.

18 For the source, see G. W. Leibniz, *New Essays on Human Understanding,* II.i; trans. and ed. Peter Remnant and Jonathan Bennett (Cambridge: Cambridge University Press, 1981), p. 111. (References to Leibniz traditionally cite pages in the Academy edition of the *Nouveaux essais*.) For Emerson's knowledge of the passage, see, for example, JMN.I.202 and CW.I.206-07.

19 For a reading that sees in this tension a Hegelian synthesis, see Wood, in Sealts and Ferguson, *Emerson's* Nature, p. 202.

20 For this fourfold division, see Whicher, *Selections*, p. 487. The division, though useful, is of course arbitrary, especially in its attempt to distinguish between classical Platonism and a more general mysticism, a distinction that Neoplatonism explicitly denied.

21 See Melville's famous letter to Hawthorne on his affinities with Goethe in *The Letters of Herman Melville*, ed. Merrell R. Davis and William H. Gilman (New Haven, Conn.: Yale University Press, 1960), pp. 130-31. On Emerson's own mysticism, see Frederic Ives Carpenter, *Emerson and Asia* (Cambridge, Mass.: Harvard University Press, 1930).

22 For a more neutral use of the term, see Carlyle, *Sartor Resartus,* II.ix; and *Past and Present,* I.iii, III.xv; *The Works,* I, 148; X, 16, 229.

23 For Berkeley's view, see the "Second Dialogue"; Armstrong, pp. 174-78. For recent controversy on this point, see the articles by J. D. Mabbott, Jonathan Bennett, and E. J. Furlong in C. B. Martin and D. M. Armstrong, eds., *Locke and Berkeley: A Collection of Critical Essays* (Garden City, N.Y.: Doubleday & Company, Inc., 1968), pp. 364-408; and Bennett's extension of his position in his *Locke, Berkeley, Hume: Central Themes* (Oxford: Clarendon Press, 1971), pp. 165-88. For Emerson's more traditional view, see his undergraduate essay "The Present State of Ethical Philosophy," in Edward Everett Hale, *Ralph Waldo Emerson* (Boston: Brown and Co., 1899), p. 122.

24 The real lines of philosophical inheritance are far more complex. Thomas McFarland, for example, suggests that the notion of faith passing to Coleridge indirectly from Fichte and directly from Jacobi itself derives from Humean sources. So even before Emerson borrows the idea from Coleridge, it has already traveled from England to Germany and back again. See McFarland, *Originality and Imagination* (Baltimore: Johns Hopkins University Press, 1985), pp. 52-53.

25 For the Newtonian sources of the concept, see, for example, *Sir Isaac Newton's Mathematical Principles of Natural Philosophy and His System of the World*, ed. Florian Cajori (Berkeley: University of California Press, 1934), I, 6-8. Absolute space is, of course, one of the occult entities that Berkeley attacks; see *PHK*, I, §§ 110-17; Armstrong, pp. 106-10. For a useful summary of the issue, see Alexandre Koyré, *From the Closed World to the Infinite Universe* (Baltimore: Johns Hopkins University Press, 1957), especially pp. 160-66, 221-28.

26 For a general treatment of Emersonian correspondence, see Paul, *Emerson's Angle of Vision,* pp. 60-70. For a useful summary of Swedenborg's use of the doctrine, see Inge Jonsson, *Emanuel Swedenborg* (New York: Twayne Publishers, 1971), pp. 104-08.

27 The insufficiency of a correspondence theory of truth – and related theories of representation – is the theme of much recent philosophy, especially that of Richard Rorty. See A. N. Prior, "Correspondence Theory of Truth," *The Encyclopedia of Philosophy*, ed. Paul Edwards (New York: Macmillan Co. and The Free Press, 1967), II, 223-32. For useful introductions to current formulations of the problem, see Mark de Bretton Platts, *Ways of Meaning: An Introduction to a Philosophy of Language* (London: Routledge & Kegan Paul, 1979), pp. 9-67; George D. Romanos, *Quine and Analytic Philosophy: The Language of Language* (Cambridge, Mass.: MIT Press, 1983), pp. 107-52; and Richard Rorty's various statements, including *Philosophy and the Mirror of Nature* (Princeton, N.J.: Princeton University Press, 1979), pp. 179-82, 299-305, 333-42; and *Consequences of Pragmatism (Essays: 1972-1980)* (Minneapolis: University of Minnesota Press, 1982), pp. xv-xix, 12-18. For the theory (and the term) in Kant and Fichte, see *Pure Reason,* pp. A104, A373-76; and *The Vocation of Man,* II, 244-47; ed. Roderick M. Chisholm (Indianapolis: Bobbs-Merrill Company, Inc., 1956), pp. 80-82.

28 This is presumably the real thrust of the *cogito*: whatever the status of the ego, doubt is the kind of thing that cannot be disproved.

29 For Berkeley, sensation proved the existence of God; see the "Second and Third Dialogues"; Armstrong, pp. 174-76, 193. For Fichte, it discovered in Kant's unity of apperception the very sort of "intellectual intuition" that Kant denied; see *Science of Knowledge,* I, 463-91. The validity of both responses is still debated. On the difference between the varieties of idealism, see P. F. Strawson's distinction between descriptive and revisionary metaphysics in *Individuals: An Essay in Descriptive Metaphysics* (Garden City, N.Y.: Doubleday & Company, 1963), pp. xiii-vi.

30 Kant saw his idealism as half of a necessary dualism: the true transcendental idealist was also an empirical realist. For an explanation of this concept in terms of time, see *Pure Reason,* p. A35=B52. In fact, according to Kant, it was Berkeley's transcendental realism – his belief in space and time as absolutes – that led him to empirical idealism in the first place; see pp. B274-75 and A369-80.

31 "I might be content that this material world beyond me should vanish into a mere picture, or be dissolved into a shadow; I am not dependent on it." *Vocation of Man,* II, 241; Chisholm, p. 76. Although the work was not published in English until 1848, general assessments of Fichtean idealism were readily available. In addition to Cousin and Carlyle, see, for example, Francis Bowen, *Modern Philosophy from Descartes to Schopenhauer and Hartmann,* 6th ed. (New York: Charles Scribner's Sons, 1891), pp. 310-26. *Note:* In treating the availability of certain concepts in nineteenth-century America, I mention three sorts of materials: eighteenth- and nineteenth-century texts (like those of Reid and Cousin) that Emerson was familiar with; eighteenth- and nineteenth-century texts (like those of Berkeley) that he probably knew, at least indirectly; and nineteenth-century texts (like those of Bowen and Brownson) that he could not have known but which nevertheless indicate the degree of sophistication that an interested person could attain in the mid-nineteenth century. This highly schematic survey is not offered as a historical proof of Emerson's knowledge, but only as an answer to the more general objection that the kind of understanding I attribute to Emerson is in principle unavailable to any American Transcendentalist. Let me again insist, however, that my own argument is both much simpler and less historical: if one wants to read Emerson in a vaguely Kantian context, the texts permit and even assist such a reading.

32 "What therefore becomes of the sun, moon, and stars? What must we think of houses, rivers, mountains, trees, stones; nay, even of our own bodies? Are all these but so many chimeras and illusions on the fancy? Whatever we see, feel, hear, or any wise conceive or understand, remains as secure as ever, and is as real as ever," *PHK*, I, § 34; Armstrong, p. 74.

33 *PHK*, I, § 38; Armstrong, pp. 75-76. Berkeley's notion of God's condescension anticipates Edwards's notion of God's importance in underwriting personal identity; see *Original Sin*, IV.iii, in *The Works of Jonathan Edwards*, III, ed. Clyde A. Holbrook (New Haven, Conn.: Yale University Press, 1970), pp. 398-405.

34 Kant, *Pure Reason*, p. A39=B56. This last phrase I take to make exactly the same point as Emerson's claim for the indifference between a real Orion and an apocalypse of the mind. Francis Bowen discusses this issue in *Modern Philosophy*, pp. 181-83. Brownson gives an unsympathetic but fundamentally accurate summary of this point in *The Works of Orestes A. Brownson* (Detroit: Thorndike Nourse, 1882), I, 186-88.

35 Although Kant was circumspect on the subject, his hostility to Berkeleian idealism is apparent in his condescension to "the good Berkeley" and in his rejection of dogmatic idealism as a "scandal"; see *Pure Reason*, pp. B69-71 and Bxxxix-xli n. See also *Prolegomena*, Remarks II and III, and Appendix, pp. 288-94, 374-75. For more general analyses of the relation between the two, see Colin M. Turbayne, "Kant's Refutation of Dogmatic Idealism," *Philosophical Quarterly* 5 (1955), 225-44; Margaret D. Wilson, "Kant and 'The *Dogmatic* Idealism of Berkeley,' " *Journal of the History of Philosophy* 9 (1971), 459-75; George Miller, "Kant and Berkeley: The Alternative Theories," *Kant-Studien* 64 (1973), 315-35; Henry E. Allison, "Kant's Critique of Berkeley," *Journal of the History of Philosophy* 11 (1973), 43-63; Richard E. Aquila, "Kant's Phenomenalism," *Idealistic Studies* 5 (1975), 108-26; M. R. Ayers, "Berkeley's Immaterialism and Kant's Transcendental Idealism," *Idealism Past and Present*, Royal Institute of Philosophy Lecture Series: 13 (New York: Cambridge University Press, 1982), pp. 51-69; and Professor Wilson's recent "The 'Phenomenalisms' of Berkeley and Kant," in Allen W. Wood, ed., *Self and Nature in Kant's Philosophy* (Ithaca, N.Y.: Cornell University Press, 1984), pp. 157-73. (I am grateful to Professor Wilson for allowing me to see an earlier version of this piece in typescript.)

36 It is unclear how seriously Emerson intends the notion of a "procession" toward nature's end. It is, however, suggestive that Kant uses the notion of a succession in a similar (and similarly confusing) way in the Second Analogy; see *Pure Reason*, pp. A189-211=B232-56. For analyses of Kant's theory and the ship metaphor he uses to demonstrate his point, see P. F. Strawson, *The Bounds of Sense: An Essay on Kant's* Critique of Pure Reason (London: Methuen and Co., Ltd., 1966), pp. 133-39; and Jonathan Bennett, *Kant's Analytic* (New York: Cambridge University Press, 1966), pp. 219-29. Kant's emphasis on succession was well known and discussed in accounts by Bowen, *Modern Philosophy*, pp. 177, 180, 216-18, and Brownson, *The Works*, I, 196, 199. The concept is treated indirectly in Coleridge's notion of the link chain. See *Biographia*, xii; I, 266-67; see also xv; II, 23-25. Carlyle makes a related point about perseverance in *Sartor*, III.v; *The Works*, I, 189.

37 Although Emerson is saying a number of things at once, he never really claims that the independence of objects presupposes the existence of "*some other Mind*," as does Berkeley. Kant and Emerson do not have God as a given; Berkeley does. Or, more precisely, Kant and Emerson want most to establish the existence of objects; Berkeley, of God. For Berkeley, see the "Second Dialogue"; Armstrong, pp. 174-75. Kant's own consideration of God's existence (*Pure Reason*, pp. A567-642=B595-670) takes place within a different intellectual context, largely concerned with the illusions of an overweening metaphysics.

38 *Pure Reason*, pp. B274-79; see also p. A177=B219. Bowen treats the "Refutation" with extensive quotation in *Modern Philosophy*, pp. 215-17. Brownson alludes to it unsympathetically in *The Works*, I, 207.

39 For critiques of Kant's attack on Berkeley, see Strawson, *Bounds of Sense*, pp. 149-50; T. E. Wilkerson, *Kant's Critique of Pure Reason: A Commentary for Students* (Oxford: Clarendon Press, 1976), pp. 81-82; and Bennett, *Analytic*, pp. 184-87, 215.

40 Praise of Kant's position on permanence or stability – both in the Refutation and the First Analogy (*Pure Reason*, pp. A182-89=B224-32) – has become common since Strawson; see *Bounds of Sense*, especially pp. 125-32.

41 See also YES, p. 188. The vagueness of the sermon passage, with its theistic definition of stability as steadfastness, highlights the greater precision afforded Emerson by the epistemological focus of *Nature*.

42 For the most famous examples of these images in Kant, see for the house, *Pure Reason*, pp. A2=B3, B162; and for a house compared with a ship, pp. A190-92=B235-38. The house image itself is, of course, fairly common in both secular and quasi-religious contexts. For the latter, see Carlyle, *Sartor*, III.vii; *The Works*, I, 199.

43 Emerson seems here to conflate two distinctions common to English philosophers. The first is that between sensation and reflection; see Locke, *Essay*, II.i.1-4; I, 121-24. The other is Reid's distinction between the "intellectual" powers of the mind, such as knowledge and understanding, and the "active" powers, such as will. See, for example, *Intellectual Powers*, I.vii; pp. 65-66. Emerson's juxtaposition of Locke and Kant seems unwise, though perhaps the allusion to Reid, implicit critic of the idealism of both, suggests Emerson to be more farsighted than he appears.

44 For a similar observation, see Berthoff, *Nature*, p. lii. For the metaphysics of constellation imagery, see McFarland, *Originality*, pp. 38-43. For Kant's famous image of the "starry heavens," see *Practical Reason*, pp. 161-62; also Lewis White Beck, *A Commentary on Kant's Critique of Practical Reason* (Chicago: University of Chicago Press, 1960), pp. 281-82 and n. Bowen quotes the passage in Hamilton's translation, *Modern Philosophy*, pp. 249-50.

45 See *Science of Knowledge*, First Introduction; I, 429-35. Coleridge takes a roughly comparable position in the *Biographia*, xii; I, 254-58.

46 *Pure Reason*, p. A699=B727. Although all Emerson's sources recognize the purely logical emphasis of Kant's distinctions, none comments specifically on his notion of indifference. For a far more emotional use of the term, see Teufelsdrockh's "centre of indifference" in *Sartor*, II.viii; *The Works*, I, 146. For the concept without the term, see Kames's claim that "whether our perception of the reality of external objects correspond to the truth of things, or whether it be a mere illusion, is a question, which, from the nature of the thing, cannot admit of a strict demonstration"; quoted in David Fate Norton, *David Hume: Common-Sense Moralist, Sceptical Metaphysician* (Princeton, N.J.: Princeton University Press, 1982), p. 185. Norton's book contains very useful overviews of the commonsense philosophers.

47 For general analyses of the distinction between regulative and constitutive, see Norman Kemp Smith, *A Commentary to Kant's 'Critique of Pure Reason,'* 2nd ed. (London: Macmillan Press, Ltd., 1923), pp. 543-58; and T. D. Weldon, *Kant's* Critique of Pure Reason, 2nd ed. (Oxford: Clarendon Press, 1958), pp. 232-45; for a highly critical account, see Jonathan Bennett, *Kant's Dialectic* (New York: Cambridge University Press, 1974), pp. 137-42, 270-80. For Kant's account, see *Pure Reason*, pp. A642-704=B670-732; for a representative overclaim, see p. A497=B525. Brownson raises this objection in *The Works*, I, 176. See also Bowen, *Modern Philosophy*, pp. 224-26.

48 The example is Bennett's, *Dialectic*, pp. 277-78.

49 Again, the conclusion follows from the logical nature of doubt. Just as one cannot exactly disprove a doubt, so one cannot "believe" but only "have" or "entertain" it.

50 The point is clearer in the inelegant journal source. To challenge the "absolute being" of corn or pasture is not to challenge "their phenomenal being," which "I no more dispute that I do my own. I do not dispute but point out the just way of viewing them" (JMN.V.124). This notorious claim has been ridiculed, especially by Christopher Cranch, whose portrait of Emerson as a complacent pumpkin seems nastier than his eyeball drawing. Paul reprints both drawings. See also Thoreau's revision of the idea in *Walden*; in *The Writings of Henry D. Thoreau*, ed. J. Lyndon Shanley (Princeton, N.J.: Princeton University Press, 1971), p. 111.

51 It is possible that "object" and especially "ground" are meant to recall the Kantian context. For the way in which Kant avoids the issue of causality by substituting the apparently neutral "ground" for "cause," see Rorty, *Mirror*, p. 151n. Fichte, of course, makes the same objection in more general terms.

52 The Berkeleian sources of this image are clearer in a later passage in "Spirit" that revises it. There it is argued that God "does not build up nature around us, but puts it forth through us" (CW.I.38). As the journal source makes clear, this built-up world is one "God paints . . . around your soul" (JMN.V.187). Emerson's posttheological notion of God merits more examination than it has yet received in the criticism; for a very brief treatment, see pp. 69–71, 183.

53 The pictorial dimension of truth is a motif in recent philosophy. See especially Ludwig Wittgenstein, *Tractatus Logico-Philosophicus* (London: Routledge & Kegan Paul, 1961), 2.1-3.01. (References to the *Tractatus* traditionally cite proposition numbers.)

54 For a review of the traditional scholarship, see Merton M. Sealts, Jr., "The Composition of *Nature*," in Sealts and Ferguson, *Emerson's* Nature, pp. 175-93.

Sealts revises this view to argue that "Idealism" and "Spirit" are not last-minute additions. Packer reinforces this view in *Emerson's Fall*, pp. 236-37. The passages on which I focus most fully are not in the journals but written for the essay itself. These late additions need not, however, be seen as mere structural stratagems; that Emerson paused in the final stages to work out more fully the implications of his idealism, in fact, might argue for its centrality.

55 JMN.IV.237, L.II.26.

56 The passage, of course, quotes one of Satan's more famous lines; see *Paradise Lost*, I.254. For Fuller's similar use of the same phrase, see *The Letters of Margaret Fuller*, ed. Robert N. Hudspeth (Ithaca, N.Y.: Cornell University Press, 1983), I, 209. It is also possible that the notion of place is present etymologically in "epistemology" from the start; although the immediate root of the word is ἐπιστήμη or "knowledge," behind both lies the standard verb of position, ἵστημι or "I stand."

57 For the notion of a "lower" argument, see Whicher, *Selections*, p. 474.

58 See Whicher, *Selections*, p. 13; and Maurice Gonnaud, *Individu et Société dans l'oeuvre de Ralph Waldo Emerson* (Paris: Didier, 1964), p. 172.

59 That the attack is not far off can be seen in the overly "sympathetic" sun of the eighteenth chapter of *The Scarlet Letter*; see my "Hester's Labyrinth: Transcendental Rhetoric in Puritan Boston," in *New Essays on The Scarlet Letter*, ed. Michael J. Colacurcio (Cambridge: Cambridge University Press, 1985), pp. 57-100. More important than the parody, however, is the extent to which the Emersonian passage belongs to a tradition of spiritist language, in its image of the sun as the candle of a higher beauty. One of the stories lying behind my study of idealism in the American Renaissance tells of how spiritist language used by the Puritans is revived by the Transcendentalists. The most notorious example of this inheritance is Emerson's recapitulation in the journals of the arguments of the Antinomian controversy almost two hundred years before: he repeats verbatim the spiritists' assertion that "you don't get a candle to see the sun rise" (JMN.IV.45). Although the image is common in the seventeenth century, and especially associated with Benjamin Whichcote, the more suggestive source here is John Cotton, with Jonathan Edwards as a probable intermediary. See, for Cotton, *The Antinomian Controversy, 1636-1638: A Documentary History*, ed. David D. Hall (Middletown, Conn.: Wesleyan University Press, 1968), pp. 67, 105.

60 Although the immediate source here is surely Swedenborg's American apostle, Sampson Reed, Emerson would probably have also known the seventeenth-century origins of the tradition in Sprat, Wilkins, and their opponent Swift. For a good overview, see Richard Foster Jones, *Ancients and Moderns: a Study of the Rise of the Scientific Movement in Seventeenth-Century England* (Gloucester, Mass.: Peter Smith, 1961); and his essays collected in *The Seventeenth Century: Studies in the History of English Thought and Literature from Bacon to Pope* (Stanford, Calif.: Stanford University Press, 1951), pp. 10-160. For a recent reappraisal, see Hans Aarsleff, *From Locke to Saussure: Essays on the Study of Language and Intellectual History* (Minneapolis: University of Minnesota Press, 1982), pp. 225-77. For the importance of this tradition to the Romantics, see M.

H. Abrams, *The Mirror and the Lamp: Romantic Theory and the Critical Tradition* (New York: W. W. Norton & Co., Inc., 1958), pp. 265-71, 285-89, 303-12. For a general review of language theory in mid-century America, see Philip F. Gura, *The Wisdom of Words: Language, Theology, and Literature in the New England Renaissance* (Middletown, Conn.: Wesleyan University Press, 1981), especially pp. 15-31.

61 *Pure Reason*, p. A51=B75. The passage is paraphrased in *The Collected Works of Dugald Stewart, ESQ., F.R.S.S.*, ed. Sir William Hamilton (Edinburgh: Thomas Constable & Co., 1854), I, 593, n. xx. See also Bowen, *Modern Philosophy*, p. 167; and Brownson, *The Works*, I, 190.

62 See, for example, *Pure Reason*, pp. A50-52=B74-76. It was Kant's use of this term in reference to the initial awareness of self-consciousness that led some followers to argue that ego was not a formal unity but an intellectual intuition. See p. B132; and in response Fichte, *Science of Knowledge*, I, 476, 141, 231-34; and Coleridge, *Biographia*, xii; I, 243, 289n. See also Coleridge, *The Philosophical Lectures*, ed. Kathleen Coburn (London: Pilot Press Limited, 1949), p. 388. These lectures were not published in Emerson's lifetime, though they were summarized in newspaper accounts.

63 The point in Coleridge is a much more straightforward one about man's inability to predict the ultimate usefulness of ideas; Coleridge's context is almost exclusively religious. See *Aids*, "Aphorisms on that which is indeed Spiritual Religion," no. IX; pp. 150-51.

64 See Burke in Simon and Parsons, *Transcendentalism*, p. 18.

65 It is presumably against such moments of Swedenborgian rhetoric that Whicher directs his charge of "borrowed terminology," *Selections*, p. 13; see also *Freedom and Fate: An Inner Life of Ralph Waldo Emerson* (Philadelphia: University of Pennsylvania Press, 1953), p. 53. For a more general analysis of the chapter, see Gura, *The Wisdom of Words*, pp. 92-98.

66 On Kant and the problem of the two-world solution, see Beck, *Commentary*, pp. 281-83; and H. J. Paton, *The Categorical Imperative: A Study in Kant's Moral Philosophy* (Philadelphia: University of Pennsylvania Press, 1971), pp. 223-41. Bowen discussses the issue in *Modern Philosophy*, pp. 252-54. Coleridge seems to duplicate Kant's error in *Biographia*, xii; I, 242. In this context, Kant's sense of "the starry heavens above me and the moral law within" may be problematic.

67 Much later, in 1840, Emerson would record in the journals a dream in which the world appears to him as an apple that an angel bids him eat; see JMN.VII.525. Bishop discusses the representativeness of this dream and its relation to the essays in *Emerson on the Soul*, pp. 41-42.

68 The center of Kant's discussion of succession is the Second Analogy, *Pure Reason*, pp. A189-211=B232-56. For discussions, see Strawson, *Bounds of Sense*, pp. 133-46; Wilkerson, *Kant's Critique*, pp. 76-81; Bennett, *Analytic*, pp. 219-29; and W. H. Walsh, *Kant's Criticism of Metaphysics* (Chicago: University of Chicago Press, 1976), pp. 135-42. Stanley Cavell emphasizes the importance of succession in later Emersonian texts in "Thinking of Emerson," *New Literary History* 11 (1979), 169.

69 The claim is Whicher's; see *Selections*, p. 474. For more general treatments of the death, see Ralph L. Rusk, *The Life of Ralph Waldo Emerson* (New York: Columbia University Press, 1957), pp. 230-32; Gay Wilson Allen, *Waldo Emerson: A Biography* (New York: Viking Press, 1981), pp. 263-69; and for a psychoanalytic approach, Bishop, *Emerson on the Soul*, pp. 175-76. For a general analysis of this characteristically Transcendentalist response, see Perry Miller's comments on the "syndrome of sensibility" in his edition of *Consciousness in Concord: The Text of Thoreau's Hitherto "Lost Journal" (1840-1841)* (Boston: Houghton Mifflin Company, 1958), pp. 102-03.

70 It is in fact possible to imagine at least four reasons for Emerson's setting up the argument as he has: a biographical one, where Emerson himself hears of Kant after studying Paley and Berkeley and duplicates this progression in his essay; a rhetorical one, where he realizes that though he reads Kant, his audience reads the other two; a historico-philosophical one, where he announces that Kant is the man who legitimizes Paley and Berkeley; and an empirico-philosophical one, where he realizes that what the bare common teaches him is the transition from Paley to Kant. Whatever his reasons, it is important to see that the rhetoric is not simply deconstructive; it conflates historical moments but does not necessarily undermine them. Kant himself respects the physico-theological argument more than we do today: see *Pure Reason*, pp. A620-30=B648-58; and for commentary, Kemp Smith, *A Commentary*, pp. 538-40, and Weldon, *Kant's Critique*, pp. 231-32.

71 The similarity between Kant and James focuses on their apparently similar use of "as if" rhetoric; see, for example, *Pure Reason*, pp. A670-75=B698-703. On the difference between the two, see Beck, *A Commentary*, p. 254; and A. C. Ewing, *A Short Commentary on Kant's* Critique of Pure Reason (Chicago: University of Chicago Press, 1938), p. 246. Barry Stroud usefully compares "conventionalist," "transcendental," and "pragmatist" arguments in his "Transcendental Arguments," *Journal of Philosophy* 65 (1968), 243-44. A distinction between the two is, of course, central to Rorty's reappraisal of pragmatism; see, for example, *Consequences*, pp. 160-75.

72 *Prolegomena*, §58; pp. 357-58; see also *Pure Reason*, p. A702=B730. For a discussion of this rhetoric in Kant, see Ewing, *Short Commentary*, p. 247; and more generally Bowen, *Modern Philosophy*, pp. 313, 320. For a similar use of the rhetoric in Coleridge, see *Biographia*, xii; I, 285.

73 See William James, *Pragmatism: A New Name for Some Old Ways of Thinking [and] The Meaning of Truth: A Sequel to* Pragmatism (Cambridge, Mass.: Harvard University Press, 1978), p. 41. In fact, it is a modified rejection of both holidays and God that James chooses for himself (p. 43).

74 Kant, *Pure Reason*, pp. B131-36; cf. pp. A117-18 and n. Most contemporary commentaries discuss these famous passages, frequently in detail. See, for example, Bowen, *Modern Philosophy*, pp. 193-95, 198-200; Brownson, *The Works*, I, 205-06; and especially Coleridge, *Biographia*, ix, xii; I, 145 and n, 153, 241, 279-80, 289. On this last, an especially likely source for Emerson, see the notes to the Princeton edition and Thomas McFarland, *Coleridge and the Pantheist Tradition* (Oxford: Clarendon Press, 1969), pp. 239-40.

75 It is Strawson who revives modern interest in the transcendental unity of apperception in terms of the "necessary unity of consciousness"; see *Bounds of Sense*, pp. 89-117. See also Bennett, *Analytic*, pp. 100-17; and Richard Rorty, "Strawson's Objectivity Argument," *Review of Metaphysics* 24 (1970), 230-34. For a response, see Stroud, "Transcendental Arguments," and Ralph C. S. Walker, *Kant* (London: Routledge & Kegan Paul, 1978), pp. 74-86. For Kant's insistence that this transcendental "I think" is not the empirical, individual "I," see, for example, *Pure Reason*, p. A350.

76 The emphasis on Kant's "objectivity thesis" is also Strawson's; see, for example, *Bounds of Sense*, pp. 97-112 et passim. The argument is related to Strawson's own position in *Individuals*, pp. 81-113. See also Rorty, "Objectivity," pp. 212-23; and in response, Walker, *Kant*, pp. 116-20. The objectivity thesis is summarized (though not with post-Strawsonian sophistication) in Coleridge, *Biographia*, xii; I, 255-60. See also Bowen, *Modern Philosophy*, pp. 186-88, 217.

77 The emphasis on the difference between "being" and "seeming," and the resulting definition of a physical object as the possibility of seeming to be X without actually being so, is Rorty's; see "Objectivity," pp. 212-13 and n et passim. In some senses, this aspect of the objectivity thesis treats epistemologically what Derrida approaches linguistically as *différance*.

78 For "inquiry," see the titles to Hume's works, among others; for "impression," see the opening section to Hume's *A Treatise of Human Nature*, ed. L. A. Selby-Bigge (Oxford: Clarendon Press, 1973), pp. 1-4 et passim. Much has been written about the strange list of "unexplained phenomena" that follows this passage. Its origins seem vaguely Swedenborgian; the apparent anomaly of "madness" on a list otherwise largely concerned with phenomena may be explained in part by the fact that madness was a late addition; cf. CW.I.286. See more generally Packer, *Emerson's Fall*, pp. 22-23.

79 For the Romantic origins of the passage, see Abrams, *Natural Supernaturalism*, pp. 412-13. Yet in fact the inner/outer dichotomy seems at least as interesting as the child/adult one. It is in terms of the distinction between inner and outer space that Bennett redefines Strawson's objectivity thesis; see *Analytic*, pp. 15-60. For the use of the distinction before Kant, see Rorty's review of the progression from Descartes's invention of "inner space" to Kant's innering of "outer space" in the Copernican revolution, in *Mirror*, pp. 131-55. For an older but equally critical view, see Etienne Gilson, *The Unity of Philosophical Experience* (New York: Charles Scribner's Sons, 1937), pp. 125-239. The two points of view are remarkably similar, as Rorty himself admits in *Mirror*, pp. 50-51n.

80 For the empiricist definition of "confusion," see Locke, *Essay*, II.xi.3; I, 204. For Kant's response to this reading, see *Pure Reason*, pp. A43-44=B60-61.

81 The inclusion of "Locke" among the owners of fields is probably not innocent. He is not so included in the journal passage from which the sentence derives, though in fact there one of the farmers is an equally suspicious "Mr. Bacon" (JMN.V.113). This revision suggests that here, as elsewhere, Emerson is both covert and careful in his philosophical allusions.

82 It is interesting, though scarcely conclusive, to recall that Wittgenstein uses just such an image of an eye to define his modern notion of solipsism; see *Tractatus*, 5.633-6331.

83 Anti-reification is certainly the focus of Kant's most extended critique of the Cartesian *cogito*; see *Pure Reason*, pp. B422-23n. For a more general treatment of the relation between the two, see (in addition to the Rorty and Gilson analyses cited above), Kemp Smith, *A Commentary*, pp. xxxix-xlv; and Weldon, *Kant's Critique*, pp. 10-17.

84 For a review of passages on transparency in the essay, see Burke in Simon and Parsons, *Transcendentalism*, pp. 13-14; and Packer, *Emerson's Fall*, pp. 75-76. Packer offers an exciting analysis of the relation of these passages to the history of optics, pp. 73-81; and at greater length in her article, "The Instructed Eye: Emerson's Cosmogony in 'Prospects,' " in Sealts and Ferguson, *Emerson's Nature*, pp. 209-21. For a more experimental, sexual reading, see Eric Cheyfitz, *The Trans-Parent: Sexual Politics in the Language of Emerson* (Baltimore: Johns Hopkins University Press, 1981), pp. 3-4, 51-68.

85 Kant, *Pure Reason*, pp. A42=B59, A44=B61.

86 For uses of the term *verschwinden* in the first *Critique*, see pp. B5, A38=B54, A42=B59, B208, A168=B210, A174=B216, A183=B226, A185=B228, A203= B248, A297=B353, A297=B354, B424, B428, A413=B440, A422=B449, A451=B479, A473=B501, A613=B641, A617=B645, A847=B875. Kemp Smith does not, of course, always translate the word the same way. For similar references in Fichte, see *Vocation*, II, 241, 244, 256, 260; Chisholm, pp. 76, 79, 91, 95. For a similarly heightened use of the term in Coleridge, see *Biographia*, xii; I, 239.

87 For uses of the terms *"durchschauen"* and *"durchsichtige"* in Fichte, see *Vocation*, II, 229, 258, 268; Chisholm, pp. 64, 65, 93, 104. For a similar use in Coleridge, see *The Friend*, II.xi ("Method"); I, 513, 522. See also Packer, *Emerson's Fall*, p. 77. Bowen uses the concept of transparency, though not the word, to describe Kant's notion of time (*Modern Philosophy*, p. 178). For the religious and stylistic implications of Emerson's use of the term, see Robinson, *Apostle of Culture*, pp. 66, 87-89; and for its sexual implications, see Cheyfitz, *The Trans-Parent*, especially pp. 53-62.

88 By such a reading, Emerson is distinguishable not only from Coleridge but also from Wordsworth, with whom he is frequently compared. For more traditional views of the English Romantic connection, with particular emphasis on Emerson's Wordsworthian "freshness of sensation," see Joseph Warren Beach, *The Concept of Nature in Nineteenth-Century English Poetry* (New York: The Macmillan Co., 1936), pp. 368-69; Abrams, *Natural Supernaturalism*, pp. 412-13; and Joel Porte, *Representative Man: Ralph Waldo Emerson in His Time* (New York: Oxford University Press, 1979), pp. 71-73.

89 Related points could be made about the similar phrases "occult relation" and "radical correspondence" (CW.I.10, 19).

90 The classic treatments of "original genius" are Edward Young, *Conjectures on Original Composition*; William Duff, *Essay on Original Genius;* and to a lesser extent Edmund Burke, *Enquiry into . . . the Sublime*. For analyses, see Abrams, *The Mirror and the Lamp*, p. 12 and n; Samuel H. Monk, *The Sublime: A Study of*

Critical Theories in XVIIIth-Century England (Ann Arbor: University of Michigan Press, 1960), pp. 101-33; and James Engell, *The Creative Imagination: Enlightenment to Romanticism* (Cambridge, Mass.: Harvard University Press, 1981), pp. 84-86. For an attempt to relate this concept to modern psychological theory, see Thomas Weiskel, *The Romantic Sublime: Studies in the Structure and Psychology of Transcendence* (Baltimore: Johns Hopkins University Press, 1976), pp. 98-99. For representative uses of the concept of the "original man," see Carlyle, *On Heroes, Hero-worship and the Heroic in History* (1841), ii; *The Works*, V, 45-46.

91 Bennett, *Analytic*, pp. 109-11.

92 Kant, *Pure Reason*, p. B132; see also pp. B72, B140, A617=B645, A770=B798. Wilson discusses this concept in the context of Berkeley in Wood, *Self and Nature in Kant's Philosophy*, p. 171n. See also Kames's suggestive phrase in the *Essays* that one of the internal senses is an "original perception or consciousness of himself" (quoted in D. F. Norton, *Hume*, p. 185); and Thomas Reid's characterization of sensation as an "original principle of belief" in *An Inquiry into the Human Mind*, ed. Timothy Duggan (Chicago: University of Chicago Press, 1970), pp. 24-26. Coleridge uses the term in a vaguely Kantian context in, *Biographia*, ix; I, 153; see also xii; I, 262. See also Bowen, *Modern Philosophy*, p. 194. For a more general treatment of the "paradox" of Romantic originality, see McFarland, *Originality*, pp. 1-30. Emerson himself uses Reid's phrase in his Bowdoin prize essay (in Hale, *Ralph Waldo Emerson*, p. 116).

93 In this special sense of ownership, Emerson has re-created (and resolved) the traditional Puritan conflict between sainthood and antinomianism. And to this extent he does not deserve the attacks of his Unitarian teachers, for his egotism really does escape "meanness."

94 *Pure Reason*, p. A51=B75.

95 The focus on transcendental arguments is, again, a legacy from Strawson. See, for example, *Individuals*, p. 30. The value of such arguments has been widely criticized. See, for example, Walker, *Kant*, pp. 14-27; and Barry Stroud, "Transcendental Arguments," pp. 241-56. For a useful review of the current state of the debate, see Richard Rorty, "Transcendental Arguments, Self-Reference, and Pragmatism," *Transcendental Arguments and Science*, ed. P. Bieri, R.-P. Horstmann, and L. Kruger (Dordrecht: D. Reidel Publishing Co., 1979), pp. 77-103. The controversy turns, in part, on whether transcendental arguments prove the necessity of certain concepts for thought (Stroud) or whether they simply identify a logical strategy (Rorty). I use the term, even more loosely than Rorty, merely to name the argument that claims certain concepts to be contained within (rather than developed from) other concepts. I hope so loose a definition, although it will please few, will anger none.

96 CW.I.207. For similar errors in other authors, see Chapter 1, note 22. Part of the problem may be Emerson's desire to activate the pun of "internal teaching" implicit in "intuition," though such a desire would not of course excuse his misleading diction.

97 For discussion of the problem of "intellectual intuition," see pp. 212–13.

98 German epistemology, of course, is not uninterested in moral philosophy, and it is as a moralist that Fichte most impressed Americans. See, for example, Bowen, *Modern Philosophy*, pp. 324-26.

99 For Kant's explicit warning against conflating the two unities, see *Pure Reason*, pp. A306-07=B363-64.

100 The distinction between the two terms is, of course, available almost everywhere to Emerson. The argument that Kant did not successfully negotiate the transition from the first to the second *Critique* is less common but still made; see, for example, Bowen, *Modern Philosophy*, pp. 238-44.

101 By this account, Emerson is at least minimally Kantian in his espousal of a coherence theory of truth. Kant's theory of truth has become important in recent discussions of hermeneutics. For a more traditional account of Dilthey's post-Kantianism, see Richard E. Palmer, *Hermeneutics: Interpretation Theory in Schleiermacher, Dilthey, Heidegger, and Gadamer* (Evanston, Ill.: Northwestern University Press, 1969), pp. 100-02; and Josef Bleicher, *Contemporary Hermeneutics: Hermeneutics as Method, Philosophy and Critique* (London: Routledge & Kegan Paul, Ltd., 1980), pp. 19-24. For a suggestive comparison of Hirsch's theory of meaning and Kant's regulative ideas, see David Couzens Hoy, *The Critical Circle: Literature, History, and Philosophical Hermeneutics* (Berkeley: University of California Press, 1978), pp. 33, 109.

3. THE PRACTICE OF DIVINITY

1 The project of distinguishing the authentically Emersonian in Emerson is articulated most clearly in Jonathan Bishop, *Emerson on the Soul* (Cambridge, Mass.: Harvard University Press, 1964), p. 15. The claim that prophecy is the essence of *Nature* is present in most of Harold Bloom's statements; see especially *Poetry and Repression: Revisionism from Blake to Stevens* (New Haven, Conn.: Yale University Press, 1976), p. 247; and *Agon: Towards a Theory of Revisionism* (New York: Oxford University Press, 1982), pp. 156-59, 164-66. That *Nature* builds to its true voice of prophecy is one of B. L. Packer's solutions to what she sees as the "problem" of the book; see *Emerson's Fall: A New Interpretation of the Major Essays* (New York: Continuum, 1982), pp. 63-84.

2 For an analysis of the Platonic element in the passage, see Gay Wilson Allen, *Waldo Emerson: A Biography* (New York: Viking Press, 1981), pp. 271-74. For the Gnostic sources, see Bloom, *Agon*, pp. 169-78. For a more general survey of the creation myths in question, see Hans Jonas, *The Gnostic Religion: The Message of the Alien God and the Beginnings of Christianity*, 2nd ed. (Boston: Beacon Press, 1963), pp. 209-36. It is interesting to remember that by the time Emerson inherited this tradition, it had been assimilated to other traditions as well. Thus, for example, the dichotomy between man as giant and man as dwarf had by this time been taken over by the scientific movement (in the debate between the ancients and the moderns), and it would be difficult to decide which tradition was Emerson's more immediate source.

3 The sources for "inquiries" and "laws" are, of course, obvious. For the special relevance of "frames" to this tradition, see Newton's famous claim to "frame no hypotheses" in *Sir Isaac Newton's Mathematical Principles of Natural Philosophy and His System of the World*, "General Scholium"; ed. Florian Cajori

(Berkeley: University of California Press, 1934), II, 546-47. On this passage, and especially its possible mistranslation, see Alexandre Koyré, *From the Closed World to the Infinite Universe* (Baltimore: Johns Hopkins University Press, 1957), pp. 223-34. For other uses of the term, see Berkeley, *The Principles of Human Knowledge* (PHK), I, § 23; in *Berkeley's Philosophical Writings*, ed. David M. Armstrong (London: Macmillan Co., Ltd., 1965), p. 70.

4 See CW.I.11, 40-41. Even in this fuller quotation, Emerson omits the first two stanzas and two of the final three, thus deemphasizing the notions of duty and man's subservience to God. For an analysis of the poem, see Stanley Fish, *The Living Temple: George Herbert and Catechizing* (Berkeley: University of California Press, 1978), pp. 85-88; and for its place in Emerson, F. O. Matthiessen, *American Renaissance: Art and Expression in the Age of Emerson and Whitman* (New York: Oxford University Press, 1941), pp. 107-08; and Packer, *Emerson's Fall*, p. 64. Coleridge treats the related sonnet "Sin" in *Biographia*, xix; II, 93-97. His misnaming the poem "The Bosom Sin" may have influenced Hawthorne in his similarly titled short story. Helen Vendler associates the two Herbert poems in *The Poetry of George Herbert* (Cambridge, Mass.: Harvard University Press, 1975), p. 180.

5 See, for example, "Dooms-day."

6 See Packer, *Emerson's Fall*, pp. 83-84; and, behind her, James M. Cox, "R. W. Emerson: The Circles of the Eye," in David Levin, ed., *Emerson: Prophecy, Metamorphosis, and Influence* (New York: Columbia University Press, 1975), p. 66; and Kenneth Burke, "I, Eye, Ay – Emerson's Early Essay 'Nature': Thoughts on the Machinery of Transcendence," in Myron Simon and Thornton H. Parsons, eds., *Transcendentalism and Its Legacy* (Ann Arbor: University of Michigan Press, 1966), pp. 19-20.

7 IV.i.264-99. The scene is, of course, central in the play, marking not only Richard's official transferral of power to Bolingbroke, but also the beginning of the self-knowledge that may compensate for his political incompetence. The imagery of the "banished king" that permeates the interlude between the two Orphic songs may allude in some more general way to Richard's situation; see CW.I.43-44.

8 Octavius Brooks Frothingham makes this claim in its most general form; *Transcendentalism in New England* (Gloucester, Mass.: Peter Smith, 1965), p. 108. For specific treatments of Emerson's relation to Puritanism, see Henry Bamford Parkes, *The Pragmatic Test: Essays on the History of Ideas* (San Francisco: The Colt Press, 1941), pp. 10-62; and Perry Miller, "From Edwards to Emerson," reprinted in *Errand into the Wilderness* (Cambridge, Mass.: Harvard University Press, 1956), pp. 184-203. For the limitations of this view, see note, pp. 214–15. For Emerson's earlier view, more akin to that of the Puritans, see the poem in JMN.IV.47-48.

9 Such agreement within disagreement is most clearly illustrated in the exchanges between Cotton and the Puritan elders, reprinted in David D. Hall, ed., *The Antinomian Controversy, 1636-1638: A Documentary History,* (Middletown, Conn.: Wesleyan University Press, 1968), pp. 43-151; see especially pp. 83-87.

10 Packer treats the scientific foundations of the Romantic concept of periodicity, *Emerson's Fall,* pp. 76-77. The very infrequency of "moments" in Emerson, however, makes one wonder if he is really less inspired than Wordsworth or only talking about something different.

11 The use of the house image here in a religious context recalls its earlier Kantian version, p. 30. The question is whether the implied comparison suggests that all idealisms, even Kant's, are as tepidly Neoplatonic as Herbert's, or that Herbert himself, like Paley in the lower argument, opens the door to more radical philosophical positions.

12 Packer treats brilliantly the related concepts of "coincidence," "axes," and "fittedness," *Emerson's Fall,* pp. 64, 67, 73-81.

13 Lines 42-44. For analyses of Emerson's use of the passage, see Burke, in Simon and Parsons, eds., *Transcendentalism,* pp. 19-20; and especially Packer, *Emerson's Fall,* pp. 53-54. On Emerson's general use of Milton, see Matthiessen, *American Renaissance,* pp. 103, 109; and Joel Porte, *Representative Man: Ralph Waldo Emerson in His Time* (New York: Oxford University Press, 1979), pp. 74-75 et passim. For an interesting reevaluation of the "Lycidas" passage, see Stanley Fish, "Interpreting the *Variorium,*" in *Is There a Text in This Class?: The Authority of Interpretive Communities* (Cambridge, Mass.: Harvard University Press, 1980), pp. 162-64.

14 The explanation has its counterpart in Puritan language theory as well, for, as Perry Miller has told us, on this point Swedenborg and John Cotton are the same person. Cotton would seem to argue, for example, that real goats exist primarily to teach us about the goatish hypocrisy of men. By the end of *Nature,* however, Emerson would insist that the chief virtue of hypocrisy is to teach us the reality of goats, and that for those who believe in the fact, the fabulous abstraction is unnecessary. For Cotton, see Perry Miller and Thomas H. Johnson, eds., *The Puritans,* rev. ed. (New York: Harper & Row Publishers, Inc., 1963), I, 314-15. Perry Miller's famous equation of Cotton and Swedenborg is in *The New England Mind: The Seventeenth Century* (Cambridge, Mass.: Harvard University Press, 1954), p. 213.

15 See especially Joel Porte, *Emerson and Thoreau: Transcendentalists in Conflict* (Middletown, Conn.: Wesleyan University Press, 1966), pp. 53, 61, 63-67. For praise of the passage's conservatism, see David Robinson, *Apostle of Culture: Emerson as Preacher and Lecturer* (Philadelphia: University of Pennsylvania Press, 1982), pp. 93-94.

16 For uses of "original" in the essay, see pp. 7, 19, 43; for "occult," see pp. 10, 20; for "radical," see pp. 17, 19, 26, 27; for "correspondence," see pp. 9, 18, 19, 29, 42, 45. "Relation," used at least twenty-seven times in the work, may be seen as one of Emerson's key terms and his epistemological point.

17 The passage reworks the claim a few pages before that "the foundations of man are not in matter, but in spirit" (p. 42). See also the opening claim in the "Lectures on the Times" that the times have "their root in an invisible spiritual reality" (CW.I.167).

18 Immanuel Kant, *Critique of Pure Reason,* trans. Norman Kemp Smith (New York: St. Martin's Press, 1965), pp. A673-74=B701-02, A681-82=B709-10.

19 It is this difference that makes Kant's project a scientific one, whereas Emerson's remains far more impressionistic – not epistemology in the narrow sense. For Kant's derivation of the Transcendental Ideas from propositional logic, see *Pure Reason*, pp. A303-05=B359-61, A321-32=B377-89. Modern commentators do not find this aspect of Kant's program especially convincing; see H. J. Paton, *Kant's Metaphysic of Experience: A Commentary on the First Half of the Kritik der reinen Vernunft* (New York: Humanities Press, Inc., 1976), II, 66-68; W. H. Walsh, *Kant's Criticism of Metaphysics* (Chicago: University of Chicago Press, 1976), pp. 174-76; and Lewis White Beck, *A Commentary on Kant's Critique of Practical Reason* (Chicago: University of Chicago Press, 1960), pp. 128-29.

20 For Emerson's use of the term in the essay, see pp. 13, 21, 22, 23, 31, 34 (4), 35 (3), 37 (4), 38, 42. The use of the term seems increasingly pejorative as the essay progresses: relatively neutral references to the dichotomy between "mind and matter" give way to treatment of "matter" alone as an inferior substance.

21 The objection is in part simply that Kant's distinction between the Aesthetic and the Analytic is unclear; time, space, self-consciousness, and causality all seem necessary to experience in about the same way. But to the extent that the epistemological priority of the "I think" establishes the absolute reality of the unknowable objectivity, the distinction is not merely one of Kant's architectonic eccentricities but is essential to his whole notion of realism. For an analysis of the problem – in language that strikingly echoes Emerson's own – see Jonathan Bennett, *Kant's Analytic* (New York: Cambridge University Press, 1966), pp. 103-07. For a similar use of the labyrinth image, see the journal passage that quotes from William Drummond's *Philosophical Questions*, probably by way of the *Edinburgh Review*. See JMN.I.376; and Porte, *Emerson and Thoreau*, pp. 57-58.

22 The revision whereby "self of self" becomes the more clearly divine "Supreme Being" suggests Emerson's intention to distance man from this power.

23 For the claim that "Spirit" is merely "highest idealism," see Stephen E. Whicher, *Freedom and Fate: An Inner Life of Ralph Waldo Emerson* (Philadelphia: University of Pennsylvania Press, 1953), p. 178.

24 For the claim that *Nature* is not the centerpiece of the career, see Leonard Neufeldt, *The House of Emerson* (Lincoln: University of Nebraska Press, 1982), p. 16. A similar attitude is implicit in all readings that emphasize the prophetic Emerson over the philosophical one.

25 JMN.IV.45. The passage is discussed on pp. 75-79.

26 The best analysis is contained in Perry Miller's headnotes to *The Transcendentalists: an Anthology* (Cambridge, Mass.: Harvard University Press, 1950), pp. 114-40, 157-246. See also William R. Hutchison, *The Transcendentalist Ministers: Church Reform in the New England Renaissance* (New Haven, Conn.: Yale University Press, 1959), pp. 52-97; and Philip F. Gura, *The Wisdom of Words: Language, Theology, and Literature in the New England Renaissance* (Middletown, Conn.: Wesleyan University Press, 1981), pp. 15-31; and, for a more biographical emphasis, Ralph L. Rusk, *The Life of Ralph Waldo Emerson* (New York: Columbia University Press, 1957), pp. 267-74; Allen, *Waldo Emerson*, pp. 316-24; Conrad Wright, *The Liberal Christians: Essays on American Unitarian*

History (Boston: Beacon Press, 1970), pp. 41-61; and Porte, *Representative Man,* pp. 91-104.

27 Emerson started preaching in East Lexington on Nov. 1, 1835; his last sermon there was on March 25, 1838. He resigned from his only official pastoral post, at the Second Church, in October 1832.

28 Wright studies this relation; see, *Liberal Christians,* pp. 42-51. For the relevant passages, see JMN.V.323-24, 334, 380, 398, 456, 463, 500, 502.

29 As Wright notes, after the psychological release of the "Address," Emerson tended to treat Frost more kindly in his journal references; see JMN.VII.73. Emerson invited Frost to meet Jones Very, one of his protégés, and sent him a presentation copy of *Essays: First Series* (Rusk, *Life,* p. 255; JMN.VII.546). See Wright, *Liberal Christians,* pp. 58-61.

30 On the early publication, see Rusk, *Life,* p. 97. On the salary problem, see L.I.267-68, and 267n. On Ware's advice, see L.I.272-73. Emerson himself compares their diseases, L.I.249. Ware died at the early age of thirty-nine, on Sept. 22, 1843. Emerson left the memorial service early, claiming a previous engagement, L.III.209 and n. For a positive reading of Emerson's relation to Ware, see Hutchison, *Transcendentalist Ministers,* p. 76; for one emphasizing the doctrinal and temperamental differences but the deep personal respect, see Robinson, *Apostle of Culture,* pp. 40-43, 126-28. The question largely involves how one reads Emerson's tone: it is possible, for example, to hear an element of condescension and parody in Emerson's supposed praise of Ware as *"le bon Henri."* For ambivalent comments on Ware in the journals, see JMN.III.125; V.47, 500; VIII.355.

31 The Ware in this passage is Henry Ware, Sr., the Hollis Professor of Divinity at Harvard College.

32 The characterization of Norton as the villain of the piece is Miller's in his *Transcendentalists* anthology, pp. 6-7, 158-59, 193 et passim. Most subsequent critics have repeated his account. For revisions that emphasize Norton's geniality and not his rage, see Hutchison, *Transcendentalist Ministers,* pp. 53-54; and Daniel Walker Howe, *The Unitarian Conscience: Harvard Moral Philosophy, 1805-1861* (Cambridge, Mass.: Harvard University Press, 1970), pp. 15-16.

33 "The New School in Literature and Religion," in Miller, *Transcendentalists,* pp. 193-96, especially p. 195.

34 On Ripley, see, for example, JMN.V.326, 380.

35 Porte, *Representative Man,* p. 98. See also Emerson's joking reference to Ripley's illness, JMN.V.503. After the "Address," Emerson's tone becomes even more ambiguous. "Dr R. prays for rain with great explicitness on Sunday & on Monday the showers fell. When I spoke of the speed with which his prayers were answered, the good man looked modest" (JMN.VII.49).

36 Porte, *Representative Man,* pp. 98-104.

37 Packer acknowledges the problem implicitly in recognizing that both the "Address" and "The American Scholar" concern the problem of imitation or belatedness, with Christ playing in the one the role of precursor that Shakespeare plays in the other (*Emerson's Fall,* p. 121).

38 Man's helplessness is emphasized by the use of the passive voice. Compare these formulations with Wordsworth's in his sonnet: "we lay waste" and "we have given our hearts away."

39 Although they would not agree with the Transcendentalists' demythification of the "historical Jesus," the Unitarians were themselves not very clear on the exact nature of Christ's divinity. For characteristic hedging on this point, see William Ellery Channing, "Unitarian Christianity," in *The Works of William E. Channing, D.D.*, 8th ed. (Boston: James Munroe and Company, 1848), III, 88-93. For an analysis of this uncertainty in Unitarian doctrine, see Hutchison, *Transcendentalist Ministers*, pp. 12-13.

40 For an account of German higher criticism in America, see Jerry W. Brown, *The Rise of Biblical Criticism in America, 1800-1870: The New England Scholars* (Middletown, Conn.: Wesleyan University Press, 1969).

41 Whicher sees the "Address" as a psychological turning point in Emerson's career, the "lapse of Uriel." Most subsequent critics, however much they challenge Whicher's particulars, have agreed that the conflict was essentially psychological, even oedipal.

42 Emerson's sermon was delivered twice, on Jan. 23, 1831, and a week later on January 31. For an analysis of its relation to Channing's piece, see YES, pp. xxvii-ix; Whicher, *Freedom and Fate*, pp. 5-7, 11; Wright, *Liberal Christians*, pp. 18, 39, 47; and Robinson, *Apostle of Culture*, pp. 76-77. On the importance of Channing's Dudleian lecture to Emerson, see JMN.II.237-42. For its influence on others, see Miller, *Transcendentalists*, p. 126; Channing is praised in general terms throughout the anthology.

43 *The Works*, III, 135. The presence of the terms "original" and "adaptation" suggests the extent to which – in Channing as in Emerson – an eighteenth-century education was sufficient to make the proto-Kantian point about the structure of the mind.

44 In the journal source for this passage, Hume is explicitly identified as "the skeptic" (JMN.III.214-15).

45 For a similar analysis of "negative" miracles, see Theodore Parker, "The Previous Questions between Mr. Andrews Norton and His Alumni . . . ," in Miller, *Transcendentalists*, p. 228. Hawthorne's account of Beatrice's mixture of poison and purity in "Rappaccini's Daughter" exists in part to examine this proposition. For a general review of these issues, with particular attention to Hawthorne, see Michael J. Colacurcio, "A Better Mode of Evidence – The Transcendental Problem of Faith and Spirit," *Emerson Society Quarterly* 54 (I Quarter 1969), 12-22.

46 Emerson's resignation took a number of stages. In June 1832 he first sent a letter suggesting changes in the administration of the Lord's Supper. He preached a sermon on this topic on Sept. 9, 1832. He sent in his official resignation letter two days later. The committee voted to accept his resignation on October 28. The journal entry is dated Oct. 1, 1832, and responds to an (anonymous) article by Carlyle on the Corn Law Rhymes.

47 There are two letters to Ware, one immediately after the "Address," on July 28, and a second (in response to Ware's sending him his own published rebuttal) on October 8. The first phrase comes from the second letter, the second from the first (L.II.167, 149-50). Whicher emphasizes the personal dimensions of the conflict; see *Freedom and Fate,* pp. 73-76. Yet it may be possible to distinguish two elements – a doctrinal assurance and an emotional irritation – and even to link these two to the two separate letters, the first calm, the second troubled. Porte suggests that even the angry second reply may not be so intense as we sometimes assume it to be: the famous phrase "chartered libertine" is not simply an outcry but is also a literary allusion, to *Henry V,* I.i.48. Fuller uses the same phrase to describe herself in a letter to Emerson, Mar. 10, 1849; see JMN.XI.503 and Porte, *Representative Man,* p. 219.

48 The question of historical Christianity had already been raised by Emerson, even in his published works; see *Nature* (CW.I.36).

49 For a general reading of the "Address" as developing from, and perhaps consonant with, Unitarian concerns, see Robinson, *Apostle of Culture,* pp. 123-37. This was, of course, the Calvinists' reading of the conflict between the Unitarians and the Transcendentalists; see the articles from the Princeton Theological Seminary and Brownson's response; in Miller, *Transcendentalists,* pp. 231-46.

50 For representative Unitarian discussions of this problem, see Channing's "The Moral Argument Against Calvinism" and his famous claim in "Unitarian Christianity" that the Calvinist God is a being "whom we cannot love if we would, and whom we ought not to love if we could"; in *The Works,* I, 217-41; III, 85.

51 CEC, p. 196. Although Perry Miller apologizes for telling his *Hamlet* without the prince, it is in fact significant that he needs to quote only one paragraph of the Divinity School "Address" to make his case.

52 On this distinction, see Antony Flew, in *The Encyclopedia of Philosophy,* ed. Paul Edwards (New York: Macmillan Co. and The Free Press, 1967), V, 347-53, especially p. 352. The central text is Hume's *An Enquiry concerning Human Understanding,* x-xi; ed. L. A. Selby-Bigge and P. H. Nidditch (Oxford: Clarendon Press, 1975), pp. 109-48. For an analysis, see David Fate Norton, *David Hume: Common-Sense Moralist, Sceptical Metaphysician* (Princeton, N.J.: Princeton University Press, 1982), pp. 295-304.

53 For less purely philosophical approaches, see the analyses of Ripley and Brownson collected by Miller. Here the argument is often that miracles as defended by Andrews Norton deny two qualities essential to human nature – academic freedom and democratic equality of thought. This focus, however, may be as much a result of Miller's interests as of the Transcendentalists he studies. See *Transcendentalists,* pp. 160-63, 205-09, 213-20 et passim. Emerson distinguishes between his interest in the logic of the argument and the more traditional objections to factuality and textual authority in JMN.V.478.

54 This philosophical position is called "occasionalism," the belief that the correspondence between physical activity and the mental life is accounted for by the moment-to-moment interposition of Divine authority. As explained by its chief proponent, Malebranche, it is similar in some aspects to Berkeleian idealism, a similarity Berkeley strenuously denied. For a general review, see Richard Taylor, *Metaphysics,* 2nd ed. (Englewood Cliffs, N.J.: Prentice-Hall, Inc.,

1974), pp. 17-19. Emerson would himself pull back from the theory, especially when he saw it all too graphically illustrated in the mysticism of Jones Very. For Very's belief that his ability to lift his arm was miraculous, see Edwin Gittleman, *Jones Very: The Effective Years, 1833-1840* (New York: Columbia University Press, 1967), p. 268. For Emerson's ambivalent response to Very's similar attitude toward washing his face, see JMN.VII.123, XIII.424, XIV.125; and W.VII.177.

55 In the passage quoted above from the sermon, however, Emerson makes clear that he agrees with Hume (YES, pp. 124-25; cf. JMN.III.214-15).

56 For Channing, see *The Works*, III, 111-13. The language throughout this paragraph recalls that of the noble doubt, especially in its emphasis on succession. See also p. 107, where the emphasis on "framing" recalls both Newton and Emerson's point in *Nature* about the structure of the mind.

57 See pp. 117-18. "Conviction" is, of course, a religious term identifying the presumptive saint's recognition of his hopeless condition. See Edmund S. Morgan, *Visible Saints: The History of a Puritan Idea* (Ithaca, N.Y.: Cornell University Press, 1965), pp. 68-69. Thus Emerson's claim in his earlier letter to Ware of the perfection of his "conviction" may not be innocent but an oblique reference to either the term's general religious implications or even Channing's specific use of it.

58 See also Emerson's famous dedication to eloquence, where in imitation of Channing's Dudleian lecture he wishes "to love Virtue for her own sake" (JMN.II.240). The quoted sentences are all that was omitted from my previous citation of the passage, p. 75. For the importance of the image of a candle to the sun, see Chapter 2, note 59.

59 Most critics accept Norton's centrality; for the argument that Ware is at least as important, see Robinson, *Apostle of Culture*, pp. 126-37. For Ware's sermon, see *The Works of Henry Ware, Jr.* (Boston: J. Munroe & Co., 1846-47), III, 26-39.

60 P. 37. As we have seen, this point was equally troublesome to Channing and to Unitarians in general.

61 P. 26 et passim. The last word of the sermon is "duty."

62 See, for example, pp. 28-30, 32-34.

63 The use of the oracular voice here may recall Emerson's own use of it in "Prospects." There are similar intellectual overlaps (perhaps even allusions) throughout the sermon. See especially the theory of the "conscious, active mind" which recalls "The American Scholar" (p. 30; CW.I.53, 61); and the claim that history is really about persons, an anticipation of Emerson's famous statement of his long-held belief that history is biography (p. 31; CW.II.6).

64 For a particularly fine review of these materials, see Robinson, *Apostle of Culture*, pp. 112-23. For Kant's similar argument that a prudential morality is redundant, see *Pure Reason*, p. A819=B847, and especially *Groundwork of the Metaphysic of Morals*, section II; in H. J. Paton's edition (New York: Harper & Row, Publishers, Inc., 1964), pp. 408-09. (Page references to the *Groundwork* traditionally cite the fourth volume of the Academy edition.)

65 The passage obviously recalls the one in *Nature* where, to defend against mean egotism, Emerson insists that the currents of Universal Being circulate through his personal transparency. For a general treatment of the lecture, see Robinson, *Apostle of Culture*, pp. 118-24.

66 For the contrasting claim that "devout motions of the soul" should be accepted even if they personalize the deity, see JMN.VII.26.

67 For the related (though apparently contradictory) claim that the ME is itself merely personal and instrumental, see JMN.V.321. For the claim that personality is ultimately "dangerous," see JMN.V.374.

68 Emerson used the concept of compensation to mean a number of not entirely consistent things. For this "highest" sense of compensation as self-fulfilling, see CW.II.70-72, and pp. 105-6, 110. For general analyses of the concept, see Whicher, *Freedom and Fate*, pp. 34-43; and Bishop, *Emerson on the Soul*, pp. 72-77.

69 See also the discussion of virtue in terms of the difference between being and seeming, JMN.V.282.

70 For a more extended explanation of the same point, with special emphasis on the resulting impersonality, see JMN.V.177.

71 See especially the journal entries labeled "Facts Are Tests," JMN.VII.28-33, 37. We can see the beginnings of this problem in the passage in *Nature* rejecting fables (CW.I.44; quoted above).

72 On belatedness and the related problem of creative reading, see Packer, *Emerson's Fall*, pp. 110-20. The formulation here is generally Bloomian, though Harold Bloom himself does not tend to read the oration in this way, and at times even claims that Emerson's uniqueness derives from the fact that he, like Milton, has no precursors and therefore no anxiety. See, for example, *A Map of Misreading* (New York: Oxford University Press, 1975), pp. 162-76.

73 The biblical source for Emerson's intimations of incorruption is, of course, I Cor. 15:53. There is, however, a difference between claiming with Paul that the change "must" or "shall have" happened and claiming with Emerson that it has.

74 Although the passage seems to deny the problem of influence, and therefore to invert the emphasis of "The American Scholar," the very fact that the denial alludes to that most influential of poets, Milton, may suggest that Emerson is in control of his ironies. It is at least interesting that the allusion is a late addition, added to the journal source. See JMN.V.469 and, for the original, *Paradise Lost*, I.16. For good analyses of the passage, see Packer, *Emerson's Fall*, p. 104; and especially Porte, *Representative Man*, pp. 157-58.

75 For the centrality of this passage to Emerson's later career, see Porte, *Representative Man*, pp. 150-54. See also Packer, *Emerson's Fall*, pp. 113-20; and William H. Gass, "Emerson and the Essay," *The Yale Review* 71 (1982), 336-43.

76 In *Nature*, of course, it was "religion and ethics" that so tyrannized over the world (CW.I.35).

77 For such an emphasis, see Bishop, *Emerson on the Soul*, pp. 87-92; Porte, *Representative Man*, pp. 118-20; and Mary Worden Edrich, "The Rhetoric of Apostasy," *Texas Studies in Literature and Language* 8 (1967), 547-60. All answer, implicitly or explicitly, Whicher's characterization of the language as mild, *Freedom and Fate*, p. 74.

78 Emerson's claim that the silence has not "yet" yielded explanation is not meant to anticipate a change in which such explanations will appear. For Bishop's recognition that the tone here is somewhat condescending, see *Emerson on the Soul*, p. 89.

79 Margaret D. Wilson has argued that Berkeley's sensuous language is a defense of the secondary qualities against the scientific realism of a post-Cartesian world. So in Emerson, the sensuous opening may not only tease the Unitarians for their coldness but also defend natural beauty as empirically (if not transcendentally) real. See Wilson, "The 'Phenomenalisms' of Berkeley and Kant," in Allen W. Wood, ed., *Self and Nature in Kant's Philosophy* (Ithaca, N.Y.: Cornell University Press, 1984), pp. 160-65. For the strikingly sensuous passage in Berkeley (which anticipates Emerson's in its poetic inappropriateness), see "First Dialogue"; Armstrong, p. 135. For a Kantian use of sacramental imagery, see *Pure Reason*, pp. A28-29; and Wilson in Wood, *Self and Nature*, pp. 166-67.

80 On this point, Bishop seems sensitive but wrong, a mark of the limits of a purely tonal reading of the argument; *Emerson on the Soul*, p. 89. For a related use of "constraint" in Emerson to indicate the natural functioning of the mind – here in terms of what Kant would call Reason – see EL.II.343. On Kantian constraint, see Beck, *A Commentary*, p. 112. For a similar use of the term in Coleridge to imply the givenness of external experience, see *The Philosophical Lectures*, ed. Kathleen Coburn (London: Pilot Press Limited, 1949), p. 372.

81 The tonal difference between the "Address" and the sermon "Summer," in some senses a source for the later essay, is representative. The presence of God in that sermon made natural beauty a proof of divine design. His absence here suggests that the source of the beauty – the adaptation of nature to the mind – is more narrowly epistemological. On the differences between the sermon and the address, see Porte, *Representative Man*, pp. 125-27; on "luxury" itself, see pp. 119, 338.

82 P. 90.

83 In his prize-winning undergraduate essay "The Present State of Ethical Philosophy," he outlined the situation in a clear though perfectly unoriginal way. Of the three topics central to modern moral philosophy, man's relation to God is better understood than his relations either to other men or to himself [in Edward Everett Hale, *Ralph Waldo Emerson* (Boston: Brown and Co., 1899), pp. 114-19]. The most important threat to our understanding of man's moral nature is Humean skepticism; the best answer to this threat, Price's and especially Reid's explanations of the moral faculty, generally defined as "an original principle of our nature, – an intuition by which we directly determine the merit or demerit of an action" (p. 116). For a more general treatment of Hume, see pp. 121-22; on Berkeley's visionary character and on Reid, p. 122; on Emerson's respect for Hume, p. 123; On Emerson's general approach to the moral sense, see Merrell R. Davis, "Emerson's 'Reason' and the Scottish Philosophers," *New England Quarterly* 17 (1944), 209-28. For a useful early formulation, see JMN.II.49-50. For a more general introduction to the moral-sense philosophy, in and out of literature, see D. Daiches Raphael, *The Moral Sense* (London: Oxford University Press, 1947); R. S. Crane, "Suggestions Toward a

Genealogy of the 'Man of Feeling,' " *ELH* 1 (1934), 205-30; and Ernest Tuveson's articles, "The Origins of the 'Moral Sense,' " *Huntington Library Quarterly* 11 (1948), 241-59; "The Importance of Shaftesbury," *ELH* 20 (1953), 267-99; and "Shaftesbury on the Not So Simple Plan of Human Nature," *Studies in English Literature, 1500-1900* 5 (1965), 403-34.

84 The basic distinction here is between the earlier sentimental moral sense of, say, Shaftesbury and Hutcheson and the common sense of, say, Reid and Dugald Stewart. The former is addressed to ethical issues; the latter to similar but distinct epistemological problems, largely deriving from Locke's problematic notion of "ideas." There may be an element of irony in Emerson's punning image of the moral sense as a scent. The rest of this passage is discussed on p. 38. For Reid's response to the "moral sense," see *Essays on the Active Powers of the Human Mind*, III.iii.6-8; (Cambridge, Mass.: MIT Press, 1969), pp. 231-58; and Raphael, *Moral Sense*, pp. 151-92. Emerson usually distinguishes between the two schools. For the distinction see the Bowdoin essay, Hale, *Emerson*, p. 122; for his occasional failure to make the distinction clear, see p. 112.

85 It is possible to see the transition from the lower to the higher argument in *Nature* as the shift from the genial Platonism of Shaftesbury and the moral sense school to the more narrowly epistemological concerns of Reid and finally Kant. For analyses of Shaftesbury's Platonism, see Ernst Cassirer's two books, *The Platonic Renaissance in England*, trans. James P. Pettegrove, (Austin: University of Texas Press, 1953), pp. 157-202; and *The Philosophy of the Enlightenment* (Princeton, N.J.: Princeton University Press, 1951), pp. 312-31; and in response, Stanley Grean, *Shaftesbury's Philosophy of Religion and Ethics: A Study in Enthusiasm* (Columbus: Ohio University Press, 1967), pp. 1-18.

86 The tangled phrase unraveled here is: "Reason, both speculative and practical, that is, philosophy and virtue" (p. 36).

87 Emerson revised his original "but the moment" in 1849 to read "but when" (CW.I.76, 295). Whatever his intention in so revising the passage, one of the obvious effects is to make clearer the syntactic parallel with the later claim of "when . . . then," p. 77.

88 An early journal entry, written before the two points came apart, clarifies their original identity. Emerson is complaining in 1834 of the church's trivialization of moral issues. His basic tactic is to distinguish between the constitution of man – that essence where morality lies – and the purely individual aspects of character, like common sense, which must inherently contradict the higher spiritual truth if virtue is to be anything special. "They have said in churches in this age 'Mere Morality'. O God they know thee not who speak contemptuously of all that is grand. It is the distinction of Christianity, that it is moral. All that is personal in it is nought. When any one comes who speaks with better insight into moral nature he will be the new gospel; miracle or not, inspired or uninspired, he will be the Christ" (JMN.IV.382-83). Although the mechanics of "insight into the moral nature" are uncertain, the last sentence suggests that Emerson is already halfway to the Divinity School "Address." Moreover, Emerson sees this morality as closely tied to an epistemology. "Excite the soul & it becomes suddenly virtuous. . . . Excite the soul, & the weather & the town & your condition in the world all disappear, the world itself loses its solidity, nothing remains but the soul & the Divine Presence in which it lives" (p. 383). This string of disappearances anticipates, both intellectually and syntactically, the moment two years later when, in a purely epistemological context, snakes and spiders will similarly vanish. In one sense, Emerson is even clearer in the journal passage than in the essay, referring directly to the Christic aspect later implied in the "well-pleased," God's traditional sign of approval. For the biblical source, see Matt. 3:17. On these passages more generally, see Packer, *Emerson's Fall,* pp. 124-25; and Michael J. Colacurcio's lecture "Pleasing God: The Anxious Context of the Divinity School 'Address,' " Princeton University, Mar. 28, 1983. The imperative construction followed by the conjunction "and" and a second independent clause (often with the verb inverted) is Emerson's other apocalyptic formulation. See, for example, the "Address," p. 78, and (almost) the sentence on vanishing at the end of *Nature* (CW.I.45).

89 Kant's famous statement – "it is impossible to conceive anything at all in the world, or even out of it, which can be taken as good without qualification, except only a *good will*" – is the opening to the *Groundwork*; p. 393. It is quoted in most accounts that treat Kant's morals, especially Francis Bowen, *Modern Philosophy from Descartes to Schopenhauer and Hartmann,* 6th ed. (New York: Charles Scribner's Sons, 1891), pp. 245-46. For the notion of privation, see Aristotle, *Metaphysics,* 1019b5-12, 1046a29-b28; (Ann Arbor: University of Michigan Press, 1960), pp. 105, 182-84. For the application of this concept to evil, see Plotinus, *Enneads,* I.8, III.2; and Augustine, *Enchiridion,* iii-v. On Kant's notion of will, see Beck, *A Commentary,* pp. 40-41, 176-203; and H. J. Paton, *The Categorical Imperative: A Study in Kant's Moral Philosophy* (Philadelphia: University of Pennsylvania Press, 1971), pp. 34-45.

90 The positive "wander" suggests the extent to which moral autonomy is more secure and God-centered than was epistemological idealism, where "wandering" was a mark of the theory's insufficiency.

91 Here Austin's notion of a speech act may be useful. Promises are always actions, statements that are also pledges to perform. But in the same way that performatives are oughts, Emerson seems to imply that oughts are performatives: the phrase "I ought" – like the more famous "I wed" or "I christen" – is itself an action. For this theory, see J. L. Austin, *How to Do Things with Words,* ed. J. O. Urmson and Marina Sbisa (Cambridge, Mass.: Harvard University Press, 1975), pp. 4-11.

92 The variety of Emersonian falls is the central focus of Packer's book, *Emerson's Fall;* oddly enough, however, she does not comment on this passage.

93 It must, however, be admitted that Kant is himself less clear on the possibility of intellectual intuitions in the practical realm, and seems to allow a constitutive value to the ideas earlier declared merely regulative.

94 This last sentence almost exactly inverts the last sentence of *Nature.*

95 For similar "spirit" language later in the essay, see pp. 87, 92.

96 It may make a difference that these concepts are discovered in a certain sequence: first "think," then "I," and finally "ought." But the more general point is that the concepts were never really separate or even separable, however much we talk about them as if they were.

97 It will not do to read into the "Address" the kind of specifically Kantian formulations we saw in *Nature;* nor can the address play second to *Nature's* first *Critique.* Kant's project in the second *Critique* is threefold: to determine logically what might be a universal motive for action; to prove that this logical law is indeed a practical motive; and to analyze those aspects of human knowledge that make the law a personal motive. The Divinity School "Address" agrees with Kant on the first point – that virtue must be defined as autonomous, an a priori. It may even agree with Kant on the second, and derive from the "I ought" a practical morality. It does not have anything to say on Kant's third and most troubling point. For Kant's threefold project, see Beck, *A Commentary,* pp. 68-69. Nevertheless it is important to recall that it is Kant who redefines virtue from an authoritarian or prudential code – "you ought" or even "thou shalt" – to a more self-evidencing or autonomous logical statement – "I ought." This move is not universally applauded. For modern attempts to define the practicability of Kant's morality, see Onora Nell, *Acting On Principle* (New York: Columbia University Press, 1975); Alan Donagan, *The Theory of Morality* (Chicago: University of Chicago Press, 1977), pp. 1-31; and Thomas Nagel, *The Possibility of Altruism* (Princeton, N.J.: Princeton University Press, 1970), especially pp. 11-17. In some respects, Nagel's book stands to Kant's moral theory as Strawson's *Bounds of Sense* stands to his epistemology: an attempt to identify (or translate) for the twentieth century the usable kernel of Kant's philosophy. For a post-Kantian critique of this position, see Alasdair MacIntyre, *A Short History of Ethics* (New York: The Macmillan Co., 1966), pp. 191-98; and his *After Virtue: A Study in Moral Theory* (Notre Dame: University of Notre Dame Press, 1981), especially pp. 42-59, 238-45. For a philosophically sophisticated history of this redefinition of morality, see Jeffrey Stout, *The Flight from Authority: Religion, Morality, and the Quest for Autonomy* (Notre Dame: University of Notre Dame Press, 1981), especially pp. 228-55.

98 Emerson's use of the term "consequence" (p. 84) implies a temporal progression from historical Christianity to moralism. But he is not really using history naively to deconstruct historical Christianity. Instead – as he wittily implies in his mixed metaphor, the "mind of Christ" – his argument is structural and his "consequence" is one of logic not of time.

99 "The Danger of an Unconverted Ministry" is a popular sermon delivered by Gilbert Tennent in 1740. The general complaint is, of course, much older. Mrs. Hutchinson's willingness to distinguish publicly between the inspired and unregenerate ministers was, in fact, one of the reasons the Boston establishment felt so strongly the need to drive her from the colony.

100 For the most famous use of the term, see Thomas Hooker's magisterial *The Application of Redemption* (1656).

101 Emerson would deliver his last sermon on Jan. 20, 1839. For the attack on linearity, see Emerson's poem "Uriel," l. 20. Whicher argues for the relation between the poem and the "Address"; see *Freedom and Fate,* pp. 74-76. Most subsequent critics have agreed. For the argument that Christ's timelessness is a mark of His divinity, see William Ellery Channing, "Evidences," in *The Works,* III, 121-22.

102 This claim reinforces, from a slightly different direction, Robinson's sense that Emerson's heterodoxy has been overstated. In my reading, however, Emerson says not that Unitarianism is right, but that, though irrelevant, it will not interfere with the real project. For the argument that Emerson's position grows out of a Unitarian sense of self-culture, see Robinson, *Apostle of Culture*, pp. 131-34 et passim.

4. THE REVISIONS OF SELF-RELIANCE

1 For versions of this claim, see Frederic Ives Carpenter, *Emerson Handbook* (New York: Hendricks House, Inc., 1953), p. 58; George E. Woodberry, *Ralph Waldo Emerson* (New York: The Macmillan Co., 1907), pp. 108-09; and O. W. Firkins, *Ralph Waldo Emerson* (Boston: Houghton Mifflin Company, 1915), pp. 173, 191. A distinction might be drawn between those who, emphasizing uncertainty, prefer the early energetic pieces (and certain troubled late works) and those who, favoring control, prefer the more settled later essays.

2 See JMN.II.242 and the discussion on p. 237.

3 CW.I.103. See Joel Porte, *Representative Man: Ralph Waldo Emerson in His Time* (New York: Oxford University Press, 1979), pp. 150-54; and William H. Gass, "Emerson and the Essay," *The Yale Review* 71 (1982), 336-43. The passage is discussed briefly on pp. 84–85.

4 For a general account of freedom in the essays, see Oliver Wendell Holmes, *Ralph Waldo Emerson* (1898; reprinted New York: Chelsea House, 1980), pp. 127-34; for a more theoretical account, see Gass, "Emerson." For Emerson's own comments on the role of structure, see for example, his claim that "the art of writing consists in putting two things together that are unlike and that belong together like a horse & cart" (JMN.VII.24). Even those critics who do assert Emerson's structural unity tend to find it in arguments for his organic form or his imagistic consistency. See, in addition to those critics of *Nature* previously mentioned, William J. Scheick, *The Slender Human Word: Emerson's Artistry in Prose* (Knoxville: University of Tennessee Press, 1978), especially pp. x, 148-49; and William K. Bottorff, "'Whatever Inly Rejoices Me': The Paradox of 'Self-Reliance,' " *ESQ* 18 (1972), 207-17. For more thematic approaches, see, in addition to Buell's article and book previously cited, Glen M. Johnson's works on Emerson's revisions: "Emerson's Craft of Revision: The Composition of *Essays* (1841)," *Studies in the American Renaissance* (1980), 51-72; and "Emerson on 'Making' In Literature: His Problem of Professionalism, 1836-1841," *Emerson Centenary Essays*, ed. Joel Myerson (Carbondale: Southern Illinois University Press, 1982), pp. 65-73. The standard work on Emerson's craft is Vivian C. Hopkins, *Spires of Form: A Study of Emerson's Aesthetic Theory* (Cambridge, Mass.: Harvard University Press, 1951). For the fullest nonthematic reading of Emerson's structures, see Julie Ellison, *Emerson's Romantic Style* (Princeton, N.J.: Princeton University Press, 1984), especially pp. 76-84.

5 L.II.194; CEC, p. 267. See also L.II.244-45, 282; CEC, pp. 291, 303. For a general review of Emerson's composition of the first series, see Joseph Slater's introduction to CW.II.xxiv-xxxiii. For Emerson's use of the notebooks in compiling the essays, see Linda Allardt's introduction to JMN.XII.xxv-viii. For more general treatments, see Ralph L. Rusk, *The Life of Ralph Waldo Emerson* (New York: Columbia University Press, 1957), pp. 278-85, and Gay Wilson

Allen, *Waldo Emerson: A Biography* (New York: Viking Press, 1981), pp. 369-81.

6 Most of Emerson's additions to the galleys involve new paragraphs added to the beginnings and endings of essays – perhaps an indication of his desire that the volume should work as a single whole. See CW.II.xxi-xxii.

7 In part, the argument against Emerson's structures rests upon a confusion of structure and conscious intention: to the extent that any progression can be described, any work will have a structure. For Emerson's own opinion, see JMN.VII.404-05. Scheick reads Emerson's complaint about "filling up the gaps" as a mark of his disinterest in structure (*Human Word*, p. 145). It seems just as plausible that, when we subtract Emerson's sense of the tediousness of revision, the statement marks his recognition of the need for transitions and development – of the necessity of structure and argument. Johnson makes a similar point about the inevitability of structure in "Emerson's Craft of Revision," p. 56.

8 The nineteenth-century proponents of such a shapelessness are, of course, Nietzsche and Kierkegaard. For Emerson's similarity to the latter, see Mary Edrich Redding, "Emerson's 'Instant Eternity': an Existential Approach," *American Transcendental Quarterly* 9 (1971), 43-52; Harold Fromm, "Emerson and Kierkegaard: The Problem of Historical Christianity," *Massachusetts Review* 9 (1968), 741-52; and Roland F. Lee, "Emerson Through Kierkegaard: Toward a Definition of Emerson's Theory of Communication," *ELH* 24 (1957), 229-48. Twentieth-century examples of more writerly styles of philosophy are, of course, legion.

9 For representative passages see JMN.I.63, III.98, IV.68, V.169, 280, 282-83, 336 et passim; and EL.II.186-88. The Orphic myth is, of course, CW.I.42. For a general review of Emerson's orphism, see R. A. Yoder, *Emerson and the Orphic Poet in America* (Berkeley: University of California Press, 1978), especially pp. xi-xvi, 3-30.

10 The most obvious source is Aristophanes's comic account of love in Plato's "Symposium," 189a-193d. See, in addition, Plutarch, *Moralia* (and Edward Emerson's note, W.I.417). Sacvan Bercovitch emphasizes Empedocles's influence in "The Philosophical Background to the Fable of Emerson's 'American Scholar,' " *Journal of the History of Ideas* 28 (1967), 123-28.

11 In general, references to the essays will identify the work by both title and the appropriate page in either CW.II (for the first series) or CW.III (for the second).

12 The parallel with the circulations of the Universal Being in the eyeball passage are obvious, especially in the sea/seen pun common to both. The notion of "one blood" is, of course, more generally biblical.

13 In abridging, I have left out only Emerson's examples of his general principles. For further clarification of his notion of mutual adaptation, see EL.II.12, 18. The passage is discussed in EL.II.4-6; and in Robert D. Richardson, Jr., "Emerson on History," *Emerson: Prospect and Retrospect*, ed. Joel Porte (Cambridge, Mass.: Harvard University Press, 1982), pp. 50-52.

14 Although Emerson continued to refer respectfully to Swedenborg throughout his career, especially in "The American Scholar" and "The Poet," he never again embraced him so fully as he had in the chapter on "Language." One can probably agree with Whicher, then, that the 1840s mark a gradual moving away from the theory of correspondences, a process climaxing in the rejection of Swedenborg's dogmatism in the essay in *Representative Men*. For an account of the split from the other side, see Sampson Reed's rejection of the pseudo-Swedenborgianism of the Transcendentalists in his "Preface" to his second edition of *Observations on the Growth of the Mind* (1838); reprinted in Perry Miller, ed., *The Transcendentalists: an Anthology* (Cambridge, Mass.: Harvard University Press, 1950), p. 205.

15 Usually he seems to claim only that things are explicable in relation to each other; see "Friendship," especially pp. 114-18. Occasionally, however, he relates intelligibility more directly to universality and claims that things are explicable only in relation to and so far as they contain the All; see, for example, the opening to "History," p. 3. Moreover it is at times unclear whether this intelligibility is an ontological property or a logical, even semantic, one—whether this is the way unity happens to be or what any "unity" inevitably is; see, for example, "Circles," "Spiritual Laws," or even the lecture on "Ethics," CW.II.184, 89; EL.II.146-47.

16 See also EL.II.155, and JMN.V.266.

17 See also "American Scholar," CW.I.54; and YES, p. 128.

18 See, for example, the conflation in "Prudence" of laws and lawfulness in the embattled phrase "the law,—any law," p. 134. See also the relation between laws and facts in "History" and "Circles," pp. 3, 179.

19 In addition to these passage from "Compensation," see the "self-executing" laws of "Spiritual Laws," and the "absolute law" of "The Over-Soul," pp. 79, 167.

20 For this argument, see Jonathan Bishop, *Emerson on the Soul* (Cambridge, Mass.: Harvard University Press, 1964), pp. 73-74.

21 The point is clearer (or at least less antagonistic) in its original form in EL.II.154, where Nemesis marks not the universal crack or the fatality of law but merely the unity of mind.

22 Emerson's list uses the term "nature" in all three ways and recalls the similar pun on the "nature of things" in "Spirit," CW.I.37.

23 Although most critics sense a logic in the ordering, extended arguments for unity of the first series are even rarer than those for the coherence of any one essay. See Slater, CW.II.xxx-xxxi, and Johnson, "Emerson's Craft of Revision."

24 It is often claimed that the uncertainties of language revealed in irony, puns, and jokes work primarily to undercut the very notion of validity, or indeed of any kind of metaphysics. Our inability to be certain about the source of irony is largely a function of our inadequate understanding of what we mean by authorial intention. Nevertheless some ironies seem so completely "constructed" that it is hard not to associate them with some conscious maker, or at least to read them as deconstructing a particular observation and not the whole language system itself. For a strong sense of Emerson's verbal wit, see Bishop, *Emerson on the Soul*, pp. 109-12. For a more sweepingly deconstructive notion of Emerson's irony, see B. L. Packer, *Emerson's Fall: A New Interpretation of the Major*

Essays (New York: Continuum, 1982), pp. 9-10, 168; behind her, Jonathan Culler, *Structuralist Poetics: Structuralism, Linguistics and the Study of Literature* (Ithaca, N.Y.: Cornell University Press, 1975), pp. 152-59; and, behind both, the various debates on whether jokes and puns are important (as Freud and Derrida think) or merely minor aberrations "parasitic" on more ordinary language usage (as Austin would have it). Jonathan Culler reviews much of this material in *On Deconstruction: Theory and Criticism after Structuralism* (Ithaca, N.Y.: Cornell University Press, 1982), pp. 110-34.

25 Once again, this emphasis begins with Whicher and is echoed in most subsequent criticism. For particularly forceful restatements, see Harold Bloom, *Figures of Capable Imagination* (New York: Seabury Press, 1976), pp. 52-59; and Gass, "Emerson," p. 348. For Packer, see *Emerson's Fall*, pp. 133-34; the characterization of the unsettled tone is Whicher's; see *Freedom and Fate: An Inner Life of Ralph Waldo Emerson* (Philadelphia: University of Pennsylvania Press, 1953), p. 94. Although one cannot deny these observations, one would at least want to remember that the change is not exactly a development; however "new" the tone, the essay itself dates from the same time as "Self-Reliance" – both written for the first volume of essays.

26 For representative references in Emerson, see JMN.I.178, V.436; EL.II.13, 147. The concept derives ultimately from Protagoras, though some of Emerson's references identify Aristotle as the source. For the place of the concept in Greek philosophy, see W. K. C. Guthrie, *The Sophists* [originally *A History of Greek Philosophy*, III, i] (Cambridge: Cambridge University Press, 1971), pp. 170-75, 183-88, 265-68. For the relation to the Pythagoreans, see Guthrie, *A History of Greek Philosophy* (Cambridge: Cambridge University Press, 1962-), I, 229-51; II, 483-88. See also Aristotle, *Metaphysics*, 1053a32-1053b4 (Ann Arbor: University of Michigan Press, 1960), pp. 203-04.

27 "Uriel," ll. 21-22. An early draft of the "Circles" motto makes this connection explicit; see JMN.IX.439-40.

28 See a similar claim in "Intellect," p. 194.

29 Emerson may here be punning on the similarity between "generation" and "generalization." He makes this pun explicit in the military imagery of the following pages, and especially the odd verb "outgeneralled," p. 183.

30 His basic point is clear, and the subjugation of world to the mind suggests that "natural world" here means "natural science." Yet, more generally, some ordering is going on. In adapting passages from the journals, he inverts the order of the paragraphs on literature, religion, and science, which appear as religion, science, and literature in the journals; see JMN.VII.362-63. For an overall account of the structure in terms of its argument, see Lawrence Buell, *Literary Transcendentalism: Style and Vision in the American Renaissance* (Ithaca, N.Y.: Cornell University Press, 1973), pp. 160-61; and David M. Wyatt, "Spelling Time: The Reader in Emerson's 'Circles,' " *American Literature* 48 (1976), 140-51.

31 See, for example, Whicher, *Freedom and Fate,* p. 97; Bishop, *Emerson on the Soul,* p. 203; and especially Porte, *Representative Man,* pp. 140-41.

32 One could, of course, argue that Emerson's increased ability to convey the emotional dimension of his intellectual position demonstrates his increased personal awareness of both extremes. Or, more subtly, that his failure to explain the reasons for the fluctuation – even to the extent of omitting the conjunction – suggests the feeling of fluctuation to be more important than the mechanics by which the change is effected. But the more fundamental point is that the admission, though striking, is not one on which Emerson spends much time, but only a brief moment in an argument whose intellectual thrust is elsewhere. The point was clearer before the two passages were joined; see JMN.VII.293, 362.

33 See the paragraph in "Spirit," CW.I.37, and the discussion on pp. 68–71.

34 On the extent to which Jesus is a minister of the Pure Reason, see JMN.V.273 and EL.II.90.

35 For Packer's revealing explications of the ironies, see *Emerson's Fall*, pp. 14-18; and "Uriel's Cloud: Emerson's Rhetoric," *Georgia Review* 31 (1977), 335-40.

36 See CW.I.35-36, 42, 45. There are, again, more general biblical overtones.

37 For a restatement of this position in the first series, see "History": "Who cares what the fact was, when we have made a constellation of it to hang in heaven an immortal sign?" (p. 6; cf. JMN.VII.33). The constellation passage in *Nature* is discussed on p. 32.

38 For another striking use of the notion of commensurability, see the lecture "The Protest," EL.III.98. See also EL.II.9 and CW.III.95, 123.

39 See Emerson's related notion of the omnipresence of the universe: "The true man in every act has the Universe at his back" (JMN.V.48).

40 See, for example, the loaded use throughout the essay of terms like "duration," "relation," and "principle." The most striking of these terms is "apprehension," used early in the essay to distinguish between past and present truth (p. 183). Though perhaps innocent, the term may recall Kant's famous "synthesis of apprehension," whereby the mind unifies sense impressions as a manifold. See especially Immanuel Kant, *Critique of Pure Reason,* trans. Norman Kemp Smith (New York: St. Martin's Press, 1965), pp. B157-65, B219; H. J. Paton, *Kant's Metaphysic of Experience: A Commentary on the First Half of the* Kritik der reinen Vernunft (New York: Humanities Press, Inc., 1976), I, 359-63. It is this principle that lies behind and permits the Analogies of Experience, of which the most important in this context is, of course, succession.

41 For this formulation of Kant's position, see W. H. Walsh, *Kant's Criticism of Metaphysics* (Chicago: University of Chicago Press, 1976), p. 131.

42 The Kantian emphasis on time reaffirms the extent to which the concept of "no Past" is entirely dependent on time. It may even explain Emerson's original conflation of Augustine's and God's circles. All work alike toward some notion of permanence – whether as substance, spirit, God, or Love. On Kant, see *Pure Reason*, pp. A182-89=B224-32; and Walsh, *Kant's Criticism*, pp. 129-35. On the particular question of time in the Analogies, see Walsh, *Kant's Criticism*, pp. 125-27. Most commentaries discuss the related notions of time, substance, and succession in the Analogies, often using Kant's specific terminology. See, for example, Francis Bowen, *Modern Philosophy from Descartes to Schopenhauer and Hartmann*, 6th ed. (New York: Charles Scribner's Sons, 1891), pp. 213-19, and

The Works of Orestes A. Brownson (Detroit: Thorndike Nourse, 1882), I, pp. 199-202. On the problems and possible sources of the opening image of God as a circle, see CW.II.253-54; and for more general studies of the image, Alexandre Koyré, *From the Closed World to the Infinite Universe* (Baltimore: Johns Hopkins University Press, 1957), pp. 8-22, 279 et passim; Karsten Harries, "The Infinite Sphere: Comments on the History of a Metaphor," *Journal of the History of Philosophy* 13 (1975), 5-15; and Robin Small, "Nietzsche and a Platonist Tradition of the Cosmos: Center Everywhere and Circumference Nowhere," *Journal of the History of Ideas* 44 (1983), 89-104.

43 See also the journal source for this second version of the statement, where the "but" still remains, JMN.VII.364. Evidently its omission in the essay is not accidental.

44 Contrast to this circularity the notion in "Intellect" that our curve is not complete, but merely an infinite parabola (p. 201).

45 For such uses of "circumscribe," compare "The Over-Soul" with "Circles," pp. 162, 184. For uses of "circumstance," see "Compensation," pp. 58, 60 et passim. For a fuller account of the way in which thought inevitably turns limiting, see JMN.V.481-82.

46 Emerson himself seems to claim as much in his reformulation of the idea in "The Over-Soul": "in ascending to this primary and aboriginal sentiment, we have come from our remote station on the circumference instantaneously to the centre of the world" (p. 164). For objections to Emerson's tone, see Whicher, *Freedom and Fate,* pp. 20-22; and Porte, *Representative Man,* p. 140.

47 Compare this formulation with its journal source, JMN.VII.395. The definition of "seeking," unlike the earlier passage on the "seeker," is written new for the essay.

48 The distinction between "eternal" and "sempiternal" is one Aristotle invented to distinguish his sense of the everlasting as always existing from Plato's sense of it as something actually apart from time. See *Physics,* 196b10, 203b30, 221b30. The concept is important in Kant: in the Analogies, for example, Kant argues not merely for the relative "duration" of objects, but for their sempiternity. See *Pure Reason,* pp. A182-89=B224-32; and, for analysis, Walsh, *Kant's Criticism,* pp. 134-35; and Jonathan Bennett, *Kant's Analytic* (New York: Cambridge University Press, 1966), pp. 182-84.

49 For some interesting concepts of self, often with explicit self-hyphenates, see JMN.II.192; III.142, 177, 192, 198, 290; IV.29, 240, 269, 309, 316, 364; V.34, 367, 433; VII.368, 483, 521; VIII.150.

50 This hostility almost becomes explicit in the lecture "Ethics," where self-trust is deduced from the unity of the universe. Although some of this lecture is incorporated into the later essays, especially "Self-Reliance" and "Spiritual Laws," Emerson eliminates both the general deduction of trust from cosmic unity and the specific attack on individuality, which he here calls "a man's own whim or conceit"; see EL.II.151-52.

51 At times he does not even take the world this seriously. See, for example, JMN.II.189-90: "What am I to the Universe, or, the Universe, what is it to me?" The parody of *Hamlet* may account for some, though not all, of his cavalier tone.

52 For a more sedate picture of this new man, see the sermon "The Genuine Man," in YES, pp. 180-90.

53 For a classic early statement of the bias of syntax, see Nietzsche's claim that "I am afraid we are not rid of God because we still have faith in grammar." See *Twilight of the Idols*, " 'Reason' in Philosophy," 5; in *The Portable Nietzsche*, ed. Walter Kaufmann (New York: Penguin Books, 1976), p. 483. See also James on "substance" in *Pragmatism: A New Name for Some Old Ways of Thinking [and] The Meaning of Truth: A Sequel to* Pragmatism (Cambridge, Mass.: Harvard University Press, 1978), pp. 45-47. Such discoveries of the tyranny of syntax do not demand a Benvenistian ontology of pronouns, but only suggest the limitations within which language works. Nevertheless even this limited critique is enough to suggest how Emerson's paradoxes might undermine more than social conventions. For a review of the traditional notions, see Bottorff, " 'Whatever Inly Rejoices Me,' " p. 207.

54 For discussion of this inelegant dualism, see pp. 81–82.

55 Emerson repeats this as one of "my proverbs," JMN.VI.197-98; see also JMN.V.304. In the essay "Compensation" the phrase is repeated, but here the crack is merely man's inability to get away with anything (CW.II.63). At the very least, one begins to wonder whether the "crack" Emerson imagines in *Nature* is not more a function of perception than of faulty structure. For other troubling formulations, see JMN.V.367, 433; L.II.384-85; EL.III.86-87; and various statements in "Intellect" and "Circles": for example, pp. 199, 182.

56 Emerson had advocated a program of general self-trust since at least 1823; see, for example, JMN.II.192 and especially III.198-200. The first use of the term itself in the journals is on Mar. 22, 1834 (JMN.IV.269). There may be an earlier use in the sermon "Trust Yourself," first delivered in 1830. See YES, pp. 109, 236-38, 267; and Kenneth Walter Cameron, *Emerson the Essayist* (Raleigh, N.C.: Thistle Press, 1945), I, 179-80. Bottorff helpfully reviews some of the major uses of the term; see " 'Whatever Inly Rejoices Me,' " p. 216. For representative general evaluations of the doctrine, see Carpenter, *Emerson Handbook*, pp. 192-94; Richard Colton Lyon, ed., *Santayana on America: Essays, Notes, and Letters on American Life, Literature, and Philosophy* (New York: Harcourt, Brace & World, Inc., 1968), pp. 43-44; and especially Kenneth Walter Cameron, *Emerson Among His Contemporaries: a Harvest of Estimates, Insights, and Anecdotes from the Victorian Literary World and an Index* (Hartford, Conn.: Transcendental Books, 1967), pp. 8, 9, 18, 26, 70, 172, 403.

57 The passage is given within quotation marks in the text and may indicate Emerson's quotation from Webster's *Dictionary*. Webster's definitions do not, however, include the key phrase "his own constitution." See CW.I.255. One might also want to compare the traditional phrase "crack of doom" with other "cracks" discussed above.

58 Such a principle of stabilization is, as we have seen, similar to Berkeley's use of God and James's of "moral holidays." This early journal passage – dated Sept. 27, 1830 – shows Emerson working out the implications of what he then called self-trust. In many respects, then, it stands like the list in the lecture series on the "Philosophy of History" as a clue to the various intellectual strands he saw in the doctrine.

59 Emerson is at this point making a number of parallel but not entirely consistent arguments. Self-trust is in part an injunction to religious humility: accept the traits that God has given. And it is in part a notion of beauty as particular: admire the unique against (or as part of) the universal. But at its most radical, the theory suggests that the particular is in some unintelligible way itself the true universal, and that the real problem rests less with attempts to universalize the particular than with attempts to know the unknowable.

60 The motif of the return of rejected thoughts is one of Emerson's most common points. For the more customary use of the argument as encouragement, see JMN.III.199, a continuation of the passage previously quoted. For a more theoretical use, see the first use of the term "self-reliance" in the journals, JMN.IV.269-70. Here the topic is "the principle of Self reliance," that is, not so much the ways it can be used, but what it means as a logical principle, one of the structures of the mind. See also JMN.V.367 and EL.III.87.

61 JMN.V.92. For a similar motif, see the injunction to "mortify the mind," JMN.II.113.

62 "The limits of self-reliance" (McGiffert's title); Houghton MS bMS Am 1280.215 (123). The sermon was delivered twice: July 31, 1831 and July 30, 1837. For a general history, see YES, p. 268, and the journal source, JMN.III.279. (Material quoted by permission of the Ralph Waldo Emerson Memorial Association and of the Houghton Library.)

63 Emerson uses the term "self-reliance" on p. 2 in an insert, which may date from the later revision in 1837 or may be a very early use of the term. See a similar problem in sermon 90, "Trust Yourself," YES, p. 109. The phrase that ends the quotation is as close as Emerson gets to an equation of self-reliance and God-reliance in the early works. See also W.XI.236, an 1854 lecture; and JMN.II.131, where self-reliance and reliance on God are associated but not equated.

64 The Latin tag became the motto to "Self-Reliance."

65 See Packer on fitting, Emerson's Fall, pp. 64, 67.

66 It is probably unwise to take this statement too literally as an indication of Emerson's progress on the essay itself. Emerson's "chapter" on self-reliance would be unfinished in the metaphoric sense long after the essay was published. At the very least, it is important to realize that the passage itself is used not in "Self-Reliance" but in "Circles."

67 Whatever our conclusion, we would want at least to remember that "redundancy" is itself a logical term: only in a strictly philosophical context does repetition carry with it any metaphysical significance.

68 Thus the passage really makes more sense in its journal form – where the echo of "if we are true" is explicit and intelligible – than in "Circles," where the tensions are exciting but the meaning uncertain. To note that in this sense Emerson does not perhaps revise enough is not, however, to undermine the more general claim that the essays are structured. For "structure" and "argument" in this context do not mean "consciously constructed," but only "having a shape of their own."

69 Although most critics mention the essay, there are relatively few extended treatments: see Bottorff, " 'Whatever Inly Rejoices Me' "; Packer, Emerson's

Fall, pp. 137-47; Scheick, *Human Word*, pp. 87-97; and Thomas P. Joswick, "The Conversion Drama of 'Self-Reliance': A Logological Study," *American Literature* 55 (1983), 507-24.

70 See, for example, Yvor Winters, *In Defense of Reason* (Denver: Alan Swallow, 1947), pp. 581-82; and Quentin Anderson, *The Imperial Self: An Essay in American Literary and Cultural History* (New York: Random House, 1971), pp. 26-33. Harold Bloom's praise for Emerson builds on essentially the same passages; see, for example, *Poetry and Repression: Revisionism from Blake to Stevens* (New Haven, Conn.: Yale University Press, 1976), pp. 240-42. The most explicit answers to the anti-social argument are Packer, *Emerson's Fall*, pp. 11-21; and Maurice Gonnaud, "Emerson and the Imperial Self: A European Critique," in David Levin, ed., *Emerson: Prophecy, Metamorphosis, and Influence* (New York: Columbia University Press, 1975), pp. 107-28. For other, more general attempts to show Emerson's social engagement, see Gonnaud, *Individu et Société dans l'oeuvre de Ralph Waldo Emerson* (Paris: Didier, 1964), passim; Leonard Neufeldt, *The House of Emerson* (Lincoln: University of Nebraska Press, 1982), pp. 73-140; Larzer Ziff, *Literary Democracy: The Declaration of Cultural Independence in America* (New York: Viking Press, 1981), pp. 13-46; and Carolyn Porter, *Seeing and Being: The Plight of the Participant Observer in Emerson, James, Adams, and Faulkner* (Middletown, Conn.: Wesleyan University Press, 1981), pp. 55-118. For the related argument that the dichotomy of self versus society is a false one in America, see Sacvan Bercovitch, *The Puritan Origins of the American Self* (New Haven, Conn.: Yale University Press, 1975), pp. 174-86.

71 For the most part, Whicher wages his war against "Self-Reliance" guerrilla style in the notes to his anthology. See, for example, *Selections from Ralph Waldo Emerson: An Organic Anthology* (Boston: Houghton Mifflin Company, 1957), p. 481; and *Freedom and Fate*, p. 50. For a similar, though basically positive, evaluation, see Alfred S. Reid, "Emerson's Prose Style: an Edge to Goodness," in Carl F. Strauch, ed., *Style in the American Renaissance: a Symposium*, (Hartford, Conn.: Transcendental Books, 1970), pp. 37-42.

72 Though some few passages from as early as 1832 are incorporated into the essay, in general the work is drawn from more recent entries, postdating the Phi Beta Kappa oration. "Self-Reliance" is thus as authentic a product of this difficult period of unsettlement as is the more accessibly tragic "Circles." Furthermore, most of the passages used are revised, some heavily, to neutralize the objectionable exuberance of the youthful claims – without, of course, totally denying the reassurance implicit in the doctrine. In many cases, the substantive changes are so great that only the original prose cadence remains. "Absolve you to yourself, and you shall have the suffrage of the world" does retain the rhythm of its early journal original – "Absolve yourself to the universe, &, as God liveth, you shall ray out light & heat, – absolute good." But the relation between man and the universe, and the quality of power resulting, is so altered as to make all talk about borrowing pointless. See CW.II.30 and JMN.IV.275. Although statistics are ultimately meaningless, one must remember that "Self-Reliance," though twice as long as "Circles," has only slightly more than half again as many source passages.

73 It is equally sobering to recall that one of the traditional objections to Kant is that the first *Critique* is a "patchwork." Part of the problem is that philosophy is too often narrowly defined as system, and Kantianism is reduced to its scientific, architectonic dimensions. For an answer to this objection, see subsequent looser approaches to philosophy in Kierkegaard and Nietzsche (to say nothing of the antisystematic reevaluations of Kant). Part of the problem, however, is the equation of the process of construction with its product. On this (now fairly common) distinction, see, for example, Kenneth Burke on Poe's description of the creative process in "The Principle of Composition," *Poetry* 99 (October 1961), 46-53; and Vladimir Nabokov's rejection of the "workshop" notion in his edition of *Eugene Onegin* (Princeton, N.J.: Princeton University Press, 1981), I, 15. Perhaps the most balanced approach is Packer's notion that the proverbial phrases of the essay are best interpreted as a multiplicity of voices, *Emerson's Fall*, p. 138.

74 Similar suggestions of catastrophe are implicit in the suicide that results from imitation and the deliverance that delivers not (pp. 27-28).

75 Emerson makes this distinction explicit later in the essay in his comparison of the primal "Intuition" to all other "tuitions," p. 37.

76 The key term here is, of course, "pre-established." For Emerson's knowledge of Leibniz in general, see JMN.I.202 and n. His sources seem in general indirect, largely from Stewart and de Staël.

77 For discussions of the essay's use of climaxes, see Bottorff, " 'Whatever Inly Rejoices Me,' " pp. 209-13; and Packer, *Emerson's Fall*, pp. 139-40.

78 This statement differs from the more direct prophecy of the Orphic Poet. There is no immediacy to the imperative, as the formal "thyself" suggests. Moreover the explanation that follows the colon – with its use of the distancing "that" – clarifies not the meaning of the injunction but only its cosmic necessity: it is less something that "we" do believe than something "people" must.

79 Throughout the essay, Emerson attempts to answer the most important historical objection to his theory, that true self-love would naturally include love for society. The general source for this theory is Shaftesbury. Indeed Shaftesbury may lie explicitly behind this paragraph. Ernest Tuveson – in "Shaftesbury on the Not So Simple Plan of Human Nature," *Studies in English Literature, 1500-1900* 5 (1965), 34 – summarizes Shaftesbury's notion of a "joint-stock Oeconomy" of the human species (p. 420). See *Characteristics*, VI.iv.2; ed. John M. Robertson (New York: Bobbs-Merrill, 1964), II, 292, 294. See also I, 285-93. It may make a difference that Shaftesbury's image is primarily horticultural and Emerson's primarily economic. For a similarly economic use of the term, see Carlyle, *Sartor Resartus*, II.ix; *The Works of Thomas Carlyle in Thirty Volumes*, centenary edition (New York: Charles Scribner's Sons, 1896-99), I, 152. For a more straightforward account of the conflict between man and society, see "The Protest," EL.III.89-96.

80 On this point see John Locke, *An Essay Concerning Human Understanding*, II.xxvii.11-26; ed. Alexander Campbell Fraser (1894; reprinted New York: Dover Books, 1959), I, 448-68, especially pp. 457, 461-62; and Edwards, *Original Sin*, IV.iii; in *The Works of Jonathan Edwards*, III, ed. Clyde A. Holbrook (New Haven: Yale University Press, 1970), pp. 402-05.

81 For a representative allusion to Lethe, see JMN.V.20; see also EL.II.85-86; JMN.V.33, VII.327; L.III.156; and CW.III.181n. For a similar association of self-reliance and Hades, see *The Letters of Margaret Fuller,* ed. Robert N. Hudspeth (Ithaca, N.Y.: Cornell University Press, 1983), II, 82-83. For a slightly different use of the image, see "The Protest," EL.III.88. The journal source for the passage focuses not on "consciousness," but on "publicity" (JMN.VII.66).

82 Emerson's general structural pattern, here and throughout the essay, seems to be to offer two paragraphs of examples followed by a third paragraph of summary and exhortation.

83 See also EL.II.151, where a formulation almost identical to that in the essay explains the nature not of nonconformity but of the unity of the universe.

84 For the most famous formulation of this notion of individualism, see Alexis de Tocqueville, *Democracy in America,* ed. J. P. Mayer (Garden City, N.Y.: Doubleday & Company, Inc., 1969), pp. 509-13, 525-28. More general forms of the doctrine can be traced back at least as far as Shaftesbury. See, for example, Shaftesbury's notion of social love, *Characteristics,* I, iv, 2.2.1; I, 308-12; and for commentary, Tuveson, "Plan"; David Fate Norton, *David Hume: Common-Sense Moralist, Sceptical Metaphysician* (Princeton, N.J.: Princeton University Press, 1982), pp. 33-43; and Norman Fiering, *Jonathan Edwards's Moral Thought and Its British Context* (Chapel Hill: The University of North Carolina Press for the Institute of Early American History and Culture, 1981), pp. 150-99.

85 In line with Packer's sense of the multiplicity of voices in the essay, it is wise to remember that, though the dramatized nature of the narrative voice is more obvious in "Circles" or "The Transcendentalist," "Self-Reliance" has in fact more internal dialogues than either of these more famously ironic essays.

86 For a representative distinction, see D. P. Walker, *Spiritual and Demonic Magic from Ficino to Campanella* (London: Warburg Institute, 1958), pp. 75-84. For classic statements, see Augustine, *City of God,* VIII.xv-xxiii; and Thomas Aquinas, *Summa Contra Gentiles,* III.civ-cx. Emerson's interest in the topic, a general legacy from Scott and Coleridge, dates at least from 1839 and the lecture on "Demonology" (EL.III.151-71; see especially pp. 166-70). One might also remark in Emerson's casual demonology his more characteristic conflation of being and doing.

87 Even the grammar is hypothetical and conditional: he does not write the word, but merely "would."

88 On the special significance of the lintel mezuzah, see Stanley Cavell, "An Emerson Mood," in *The Senses of Walden,* expanded ed. (San Francisco: North Point Press, 1981), pp. 154-60; and Packer, *Emerson's Fall,* p. 141. Both, however, want to place more emphasis on the content of the inscription than on its role as an action.

89 Individuating or identifiability is in fact one of the least puzzling of the philosophical questions associated with the problem of personal identity. Among the more important issues are reidentification, privileged access, responsibility, and immortality. Central to all is the problem of how something can change and yet remain the same thing – a paradox Emerson plays with in the notion of consistency, but one he does not treat especially seriously. For general introductions to the problem, see Terence Penelhum's article in *The*

Encyclopedia of Philosophy, ed. Paul Edwards (New York: Macmillan Co. and The Free Press, 1967), VI, 95-107; and the two companion anthologies: John Perry's set of historical essays, *Personal Identity* (Berkeley: University of California Press, 1975); and Amélie Oksenberg Rorty's collection of modern ones, *The Identities of Persons* (Berkeley: University of California Press, 1976).

90 Locke, of course, distinguishes between "man," a purely biological concept, and "person," which implies consciousness. Although Emerson does not seem to be making quite the same distinction, he does, like Locke, exclude consciousness from the notion of manhood. For Locke, see *Essay,* II.xxvii.21; I, 461-62.

91 Emerson recognizes this but obscures the point by breaking it in two, discussing the preacher's error on one page and the necessity for accepting religious dogmas on the next, under consistency (pp. 32-33).

92 Locke defines memory and the body as the two conditions necessary for personality. Bishop Butler (among others) attacks the notion that memory can prove personhood by showing that Locke's proof presupposes the notion of personality it means to demonstrate. Emerson could have known this famous argument either directly from Butler or in Reid's restatement of it. For Locke, see *Essay,* II.xxvii.11-11 [sic]; I, 448-52; for Butler, see "Of Personal Identity," published as the first appendix to *The Analogy of Religion* (1736); for Thomas Reid, see *Essays on the Intellectual Powers of Man,* III.iv, vi (Cambridge, Mass.: MIT Press, 1969), especially pp. 357-58. Perry reprints the relevant texts and includes modern articles by Quinton and Grice in favor and Shoemaker and Perry opposed, pp. 33-155.

93 Thus Emerson's point, though not itself in the contemporary mode of linguistic analysis, is perfectly compatible with that tradition as we inherit it from Saussure and Wittgenstein.

94 And in fact the paragraph concludes with not a course of action but the recognition of the epistemological identity of society and solitude: the great man who lives as a solitary within society represents less stoic self-control than an understanding of the true meaning of the two categories.

95 The complaint about Emerson's loudness is Whicher's, *Selections,* p. 481. My own claims about the essay's structure are to be taken very loosely. The essay divides most obviously into two sections–one of philosophical generalizations and the other of practical evidences or applications (pp. 44-51). My analysis focuses almost entirely on the former. Within the philosophical section, we can identify three basic strategies associated with three approximate subsections: an introductory critique of false notions of self (pp. 27-34); a new definition of self as non-referential (pp. 34-39); and a final section on the consequences of this new definition (pp. 39-44).

96 The joke here attacks what Austin refers to as Alice-in-Wonderland overprecision: the Caterpillar's claim that Alice's "I don't think that . . ." is a statement about herself. An even more exact echo is Noel Coward's response to the statement that life is for living: that it would be difficult to know what else one could do with it. For J. L. Austin, see *How to Do Things with Words,* ed. J. O. Urmson and Marina Sbisa (Cambridge, Mass.: Harvard University Press, 1975), p. 90.

97 See the similar statement in "The Over-Soul" that character teaches "over our head" (p. 169). For a general treatment of Emerson's notion of character, see Henry Nash Smith, "Emerson's Problem of Vocation," in Milton R. Konvitz and Stephen E. Whicher, eds., *Emerson: A Collection of Critical Essays* (Englewood Cliffs, N.J.: Prentice-Hall, Inc., 1962), pp. 66-67.

98 See also the notion throughout the *Essays: Second Series* of a mean or "average," especially in "Manners" (CW.III.72).

99 It is, of course, possible that Emerson is arguing a pragmatist or verificationist position – that an unmeasurable difference is no difference at all. It seems, however, a bad idea, at least for the moment, to associate Emerson with this problematic (and currently unpopular) position.

100 As with the word "epistemology" itself, the whole notion of "standing" may recall the Greek root, ἵστημι. For a more proximate source, see Luther's declaration that "Here I stand." For less successful readings of man's representativeness or correspondence, see pp. 28, 36.

101 For an emphasis on process in the essay, see Packer, *Emerson's Fall*, pp. 144-47.

102 There may be a joke buried in Emerson's use of the term "trustee" to personify the ground for universal reliance. Frequently a trustee is a negative authority, and recalls the jail image earlier in the essay.

103 Even the capitalized abstractions – Instinct, Intuition, and Spontaneity – are all familiar epistemological terms, used in fact by Kant.

104 The last sentence of this passage lies somewhere halfway between *Nature*'s claim that inspiration either appears or does not and the fluctuation between God and weed in "Circles" (CW.I.22, II.182).

105 IV.xi.5; II, 328-29. See also Berkeley, *The Principles of Human Knowledge* (PHK), I, §§ 29-33; *Berkeley's Philosophical Writings*, ed. David M. Armstrong (London: Macmillan Co., Ltd., 1965), pp. 72-74. For discussions of Locke, see Bennett, *Analytic*, pp. 20-21; Jonathan Bennett, *Locke, Berkeley, Hume: Central Themes* (Oxford: Clarendon Press, 1971), pp. 68-83; and J. L. Mackie, *Problems from Locke* (Oxford: Oxford University Press, 1976), pp. 37-71. For Berkeley, see George Pitcher, *Berkeley* (London: Routledge & Kegan Paul, 1977), pp. 106-09, 130-39; and, for modern versions, without reference to Locke or Berkeley, H. P. Grice, "The Causal Theory of Perception," *Aristotelian Society Supplement* 35 (1961), 121-52; and Pitcher, *A Theory of Perception* (Princeton, N.J.: Princeton University Press, 1971), pp. 43-59. [Note: Although all references to Locke cite Fraser's edition to profit from his annotation, I have checked the text with the more authoritative edition of Peter H. Nidditch (Oxford: Clarendon Press, 1975).]

106 In his critique of Locke, Leibniz himself does not object to the passage. For this significant absence, see *New Essays on Human Understanding*, IV.xi.5; trans. and ed. Peter Remnant and Jonathan Bennett (Cambridge: Cambridge University Press, 1981), pp. 443-44. In some senses the point is directed as much against Kant as against Locke. For although Kant derives the things-in-themselves from a logical and not an empirical necessity, he too tends to talk as if he held a causal theory of perception. See Bennett, *Analytic*, pp. 19-22.

107 For examples in Locke, see *Essay*, IV.ii.14; II, 186, 188. See also Leibniz, *New Essays*, IV.ii; pp. 373-75. Leibniz uses what I have called in Emerson the argument from indifference, p. 375. For a more neutral notion of conformity, see Emerson's own concept of "agreement," p. 34. In part, the apparent contradiction is only a function of the grammar, the difference between a purely descriptive plural (like "correspondences") and an implicitly metaphysical singular (like "correspondence"). At the very least, we would want to recall that the motif of a divine idea that we "represent" is inherently epistemological, suggesting only the method by which we re-present to the mind or reidentify for it some more truly eternal fact.

108 For Kant's most explicit treatment of this point, implicit throughout the first *Critique*, see pp. B422n-23n. For an explication, see Walsh, *Kant's Criticism*, pp. 176-83. More general explanations of Descartes's conflation are, of course, legion.

109 The incomplete punctuation and syntax are quoted exactly from Emerson. This sentence, in the lecture, leads directly to what would become the opening to "Self-Reliance."

110 In thus redefining the notion of Self, Emerson aligns himself with the Kantian attempt to demonstrate – contra most philosophers from Aristotle on – that soul is not a substance. See *Pure Reason*, pp. A348-51, B407; and for commentary, Jonathan Bennett, *Kant's Dialectic* (New York: Cambridge University Press, 1974), pp. 72-76.

111 These denials are not, however, a kind of inverted arrogance, for the passage implies the existence of an external authority: his book "should" so smell, and he "cannot" doubt.

112 The importance of this image is evident in the JMN index entry on "Roses," JMN.XII.451; see also JMN.VII.221, 223, 225-26. See also the source for the passage in the lectures, EL.III.283-84; the more general passage on the "untranslatability of life," JMN.VII.345-46; and the discussion of the rose in "Swedenborg," W.IV.143-44. There is more generally a tradition of rose imagery in philosophy. See, for example, Thomas Reid, *An Inquiry into the Human Mind*, II.iii; ed. Timothy Duggan (Chicago: University of Chicago Press, 1970), pp. 24-27; and *Intellectual Powers*, II.xvi; pp. 242-44.

113 The simplicity of soul is often taken as a mark of its substantiality. Here, however, Emerson does not find in that simplicity any essence at all. Kant, of course, redefines the tradition of the simplicity of the soul as he inherits it from Leibniz and more generally from the Church Fathers. See *Pure Reason*, pp. A351-61; and for commentary, Bennett, *Dialectic*, pp. 82-85.

114 My reading of these paragraphs agrees with Packer's (*Emerson's Fall*, pp. 144-47), though I feel she underestimates the importance of what Emerson rejects. Both her reading and mine react against the less ironic (and more disapproving) approach traditional at least since Whicher.

115 The passage is confusing. Part of it looks resolutely backward, finding justification in genuine acts "already" done or, more hypothetically, deducing from present firmness a previous right action. Part of it looks forward, appealing to the future and promising that the present scorn will "always" permit further indifference. But the real emphasis seems adamantly presentist: be it how it will (and, of course, how it was), do right now. Emerson immediately repeats this point – about what he calls the "cumulativeness" of character – in terms of honor (pp. 34-35).

116 For this common Puritan motif, see the debate between Cotton and the Elders summarized in *The Antinomian Controversy, 1636–1638: A Documentary History*, ed. David D. Hall (Middletown, Conn.: Wesleyan University Press, 1968), pp. 68, 104-05. A similar notion of an after-the-fact proof seems implicit in pragmatism, though William James denies this interpretation. See *Pragmatism*, pp. xxiii, 105.

117 Essentially Emerson seems to be equating virtue, duty, and working-and-being. For a similar move elsewhere, see "The Transcendentalist," where the self-existence of everything real is grounded in the self-existence of the Deity, CW.I.204.

118 For statements apparently hostile to such seeking earlier in the essay, see pp. 37, 38. The point evidently is that although too linear a search – seeking to pry or to interpose – is foolish, the process is itself necessary and inevitable.

119 Thus the "therefore" omitted earlier – in the phrase "I think, I am" (p. 38) – is absent not simply to maintain the integrity of the "I am" but to ensure the autonomy of the "I am" and the "I think" both.

120 Emerson himself uses the word, p. 47. For the structural relation between the sermons and the essays, see Buell, *Literary Transcendentalism*, pp. 102-39; David Robinson, *Apostle of Culture: Emerson as Preacher and Lecturer* (Philadelphia: University of Pennsylvania Press, 1982), pp. 48-50, 165-74; Porte, *Representative Man*, pp. 75-79; and especially Bottorff, " 'Whatever Inly Rejoices Me,' " pp. 213-16.

121 See also the return of "conspiracy," p. 41; and the neutral use of the term in the "Ode to Beauty" to mean simply "breathing together" (W.IX.90).

5. THE LIMITS OF EXPERIENCE

1 Emerson's sense of the essay's centrality is apparent throughout the work in his claims for a newfound maturity and honesty (CW.III.40, 47). For Stephen E. Whicher's praise, see *Freedom and Fate: An Inner Life of Ralph Waldo Emerson* (Philadelphia: University of Pennsylvania Press, 1953), pp. 111-22; and *Selections from Ralph Waldo Emerson: An Organic Anthology* (Boston: Houghton Mifflin Company, 1957), p. 253. Yet, at times, the essay is seen to succeed almost entirely through its new relativist tone. Whicher significantly calls the work "An Interim Report on an Experiment in Self-Reliance." This implicitly biographical focus can turn implicitly anti-intellectual, as in Gay Wilson Allen's claim that the essay is most interesing for its biographical insights; see *Waldo Emerson: A Biography* (New York: Viking Press, 1981), p. 430. At the very least, one would not want to overemphasize the chronological dimension of Emerson's growth. It is possible to see "Experience" as far removed in time from "Self-Reliance"; thus Whicher reads the statement that "I am not the novice I was fourteen, not yet seven years ago" as a reference to the earlier essay; *Freedom and Fate*, p. 111. Actually there was less than a year separating the publication of "Self-Reliance" and the important journal entries on Waldo's death. In fact, the earliest journal passages incorporated into the later essay occurred in 1838, while Emerson was still jotting down thoughts for "Self-Reliance": JMN.VII.79; see also JMN.VII.98, 270, 387, 418, 421, 508. For an analysis of the composition of the second series, see Allardt's introduction, JMN.XII.xxix-xxxi. See also B. L. Packer's wise reminder that the seven years and fourteen refer to the story of Jacob and Rachel, *Emerson's Fall: A New Interpretation of the Major Essays* (New York: Continuum, 1982), p. 177; and, behind it, JMN.V.489.

2 For the notion that Emerson translates his epistemology into literature, see Packer, *Emerson's Fall,* p. 162; for the claim that psychology and epistemology are two sides of the same coin, see Joel Porte, *Representative Man: Ralph Waldo Emerson in His Time* (New York: Oxford University Press, 1979), p. 183. For a more general argument about Wittgenstein's relation to epistemology, see David Pears, *Ludwig Wittgenstein* (New York: Viking Press, 1970), pp. 40-50; and P. M. S. Hacker, *Insight and Illusion: Wittgenstein on Philosophy and the Metaphysics of Experience* (New York: Oxford University Press, 1972), pp. 33-57. The basic point would be that all who try to explain reality in terms of the "logical limits of X" will be pursuing the same kind of (broadly "epistemological") project whatever they take as "X" – whether "thought," as did Kant, or "language," as did Wittgenstein.

3 The initial reception of the series was, in fact, better than the first, presumably a measure of the public's growing familiarity with what had previously seemed a radical mode of discourse. See, for example, Carlyle's opinion, CEC, pp. 369-71; and Fuller, *The Letters of Margaret Fuller,* ed. Robert N. Hudspeth (Ithaca, N.Y.: Cornell University Press, 1983), III, 243-44, 253. For representative modern readings, which prefer the first series, see Frederic Ives Carpenter, *Emerson Handbook* (New York: Hendricks House, Inc., 1953), p. 61; and O. W. Firkins, *Ralph Waldo Emerson* (Boston: Houghton Mifflin Company, 1915), p. 192. Carpenter remarks on the greater specificity of the second series, though Carlyle still finds the tone distressingly remote. For a more general review of the critical response, see Slater's introduction, CW.III.xxxii-xli.

4 Three of the essays – "Character," "Manners," and the second "Nature" – most likely derive directly from the 1839-40 lecture series on "The Times." Two more – "Gifts" and "New England Reformers" – are even more recent, one a *Dial* essay and the other an independent lecture added to the collection at the last minute. And the three essays largely written for the series draw on recent journal passages, reaching back less often than the first series to the journals of the 1830s. On the relation between the lecture series and the essays, see EL.III.335-45, CW.III.xlvii, and JMN.XII.xxix. On the other two revised essays, see CW.III.xxix, xxxi, xlviii, 284-87; and JMN.XII.xxxi.

5 It is important to recall that Emerson includes only the more general and theoretical of the lectures on "The Times." The more specific essays – "Introductory Lecture," "The Conservative," and "The Transcendentalist" – though published in *The Dial,* were not collected in book form until 1849. See CW.I.161-66. On the topical nature of the series, see Richard Lee Francis, "The Poet and Experience: *Essays: Second Series,*" in Joel Myerson, ed., *Emerson*

Centenary Essays (Carbondale: Southern Illinois University Press, 1982), pp. 93-94, 105-06.

6 Some passages also derive from "Politics," a fragment from the 1840 series on "The Present Age." Whicher argues that there are actually four layers: an 1837 emphasis on the One Mind; an optimistic emphasis from 1840 on the all-sufficiency of Character; some later revisions that qualify the optimism, shifting the focus from social influence to private consolation; and the final essay, whose second half is entirely new; see *Selections*, pp. 490-91.

7 For the source of this new opening, see the later "Politics" lecture, EL.III.240-41. Especially suggestive here is the revised notion of persons; see EL.II.70-71 and CW.III.118.

8 See the similar claim in "Character" that the longest list of good deeds seems very short (p. 61). In part, the notion is Anselm's that a finite man cannot pay an infinite debt. And in part, the notion is that magnanimity involves a kind of infinite regress, wherein the magnanimous man's generous response to payment itself creates a new debt.

9 See the related claim earlier in the paragraph that the only true use of a great man is to undercut previous exaggerations of the personal by showing that new forms of greatness can be achieved (p. 63).

10 Emerson had originally hoped to include a "Nature" in the first series as a companion piece to "Art" but had not been able to finish it in time. He did present in 1841 a transitional version as a lecture on "The Method of Nature." Here too the focus has shifted. Unlike the earlier "end" of nature, her "method" is unanalyzable, a "rushing stream [that] will not stop to be observed" (CW.I.124; see also pp. 126, 131). Self-accounting, though apparently equivalent to the vaunted self-absolution of "Self-Reliance," is now rejected as a vain pretense. Just as nature hastens without rendering account of herself, so if "he pretends to give account of himself to himself, . . . at the last, what has he to recite but the fact that there is a Life not to be described or known otherwise than by possession?" The only real form of self-description – that which we are "constrained by our constitution to take" from the platform of action – is entirely negative, one of self-accusation and self-denial (p. 127). For Emerson's original plans about "Nature," see L.II.387, and JMN.VII.374-75; see also CW.III.xxv-vi. For generally negative evaluations of the transitional lecture, see CW.I.117 and David Robinson, *"The Method of Nature* and Emerson's Period of Crisis," in Myerson, ed., *Centenary*, pp. 74-75. For a more favorable account, see Porte, *Representative Man*, pp. 163, 213. Robinson emphasizes the biographical over the intellectual elements of the piece, pp. 75-92.

11 For a fine reading of the opening paragraphs, with particular attention to the allusions to the Divinity School "Address" and to Bunyan, see Porte, *Representative Man*, pp. 199-203.

12 In fact, nature is here an enchantress. For a similar claim, see "Method," CW.I.131.

13 Emerson seems here teasingly to distinguish himself from the more literal naturalism of Thoreau, as he does earlier in his witty conflation of Bunyan's burden and the woodman's "knapsack."

14 For a similar notion of exaggeration, see the Divinity School "Address," CW.I.82.

15 For this surprisingly positive reading of fashion, see CW.III.75-87. For the simpler notion of fashion as social despotism, see EL.II.139.

16 See, for example, Porte, *Representative Man*, pp. 177-78; and Francis, "Poet," in Myerson, ed., *Centenary*, pp. 93-94.

17 After a short introduction, the essay divides roughly into three sections, defined by Emerson as treating the nature and functions of the Poet, or the man of Beauty (pp. 4-8); the means and materials he uses (pp. 8-14); and the general aspect of art in the present time (pp. 14-21). The essay then ends with a peroration about how the poet sought has not yet arrived (pp. 21-24). The passage outlining the sections is at the end of the introduction, p. 4. The outline is one of the few things that Emerson retains from the lecture form of the essay, EL.III.348. Its presence in a largely rewritten work may explain some of the structural inconsistencies in the essay. For the traditional account of Emerson's vocational crisis, see Smith, in Milton R. Konvitz and Stephen E. Whicher, eds., *Emerson: A Collection of Critical Essays* (Englewood Cliffs, N.J.: Prentice-Hall, Inc., 1962), pp. 60-71. Most subsequent critics have agreed with Smith. For a more recent account, see Merton M. Sealts, Jr.'s various statements on Emerson as scholar, especially "The American Scholar and Public Issues: The Case of Emerson," *Ariel* 7, iii (July 1976), 109-21; and "Emerson as Teacher," in Myerson, ed., *Centenary*, pp. 180-90. Although Smith does not mention the essay's role in Emerson's evolving sense of his vocation, Francis makes this amendment to Smith's general argument in "Poet," in *Centenary*, p. 94. In part, the new role of the Poet responds to Ripley's challenge that the old Emersonian role of the Scholar is embodied in Brook Farm, which community he felt Emerson morally obligated to join. For this exchange, see L.II.368-71 and JMN.VII.407-08. For an interpretation of the tensions, see Perry Miller, ed., *The Transcendentalists: an Anthology* (Cambridge, Mass.: Harvard University Press, 1950), pp. 464-65. More neutral accounts are given in James Elliot Cabot, *A Memoir of Ralph Waldo Emerson* (Boston: Houghton Mifflin and Company, 1887), II, 434-38; and Octavius Brooks Frothingham, *George Ripley* (Boston: Houghton Mifflin Company, 1899), pp. 307-18.

18 On the Romantic concept of the bard in general, see M. H. Abrams, *Natural Supernaturalism: Tradition and Revolution in Romantic Literature* (New York: W. W. Norton & Co., Inc., 1971), pp. 21-32. The concept of prophecy is central to the work of Harold Bloom; see especially *The Visionary Company: A Reading of English Romantic Poetry* (Garden City, N.Y.: Doubleday & Company, 1963), pp. xiii-xvi et passim. Most critics who emphasize Emerson's prophetic pose touch on the concept. See especially Packer, *Emerson's Fall*, pp. 179-97; and R. A. Yoder, *Emerson and the Orphic Poet in America* (Berkeley: University of California Press, 1978), pp. 89-105, 144-52. The passage in Coleridge is, of course, the thirteenth chapter of the *Biographia Literaria*; ed. James Engell and W. Jackson Bate (Princeton, N.J.: Princeton University Press, 1983), I, 295-306. For recent attempts to contextualize this theory of the imagination, see Thomas McFarland, *Originality and Imagination* (Baltimore: Johns Hopkins University Press, 1985), pp. 90-119; and especially Stanley Cavell, "Genteel Responses to Kant? In Emerson's 'Fate' and in Coleridge's *Biographia Literaria*," *Raritan* 3, ii (Fall 1983), 51-61. For a more traditional review of the influence, Frank T. Thompson, "Emerson's Indebtedness to Coleridge," *Studies in Philology* 23 (1926), 55-76. For an unfavorable comparison of "The Poet" to Coleridge, see David Porter, *Emerson and Literary Change* (Cambridge, Mass.: Harvard University Press, 1978), pp. 176-77.

19 Packer relates Swedenborgianism to the polysemous ambiguity of poetic language, *Emerson's Fall*, p. 190. But, as she herself admits, Emerson's tone on Swedenborg varied throughout this period. The Swedenborgian origin of the language theory is evident in the presence of "animal economy" as the first symbolic fact listed in the passage previously quoted.

20 The presence of the poetic, geometrical spider in the passage may similarly recall that spiders were among the vanished disagreeables, p. 11; cf. CW.I.45.

21 The editors of the CW have normalized the passage by choosing a variant from the 1876 edition: "the thought's independence of the symbol." I have reinstated the more awkward phrase, the one used in all four editions over which Emerson is known to have had full control. For a similarly awkward use of syntax, one not revised in even the late edition, see the question "Why should not . . . we participate the invention of nature?"; "Poet," p. 15.

22 For an analysis of the celebrated Swedenborgian doctrine of "Series and Degrees," see Inge Jonsson, *Emanuel Swedenborg* (New York: Twayne Publishers, 1971), pp. 71-77. It is most famously set forth in *The Economy of the Animal Kingdom*. Emerson refers to the concept in "Swedenborg," W.IV.105.

23 For a treatment of the essay in terms of this central ambiguity, see David Porter, *Emerson and Literary Change*, pp. 176-81. For a similarly troubling treatment of form in a more practical context, see "Politics," p. 121.

24 For earlier arguments on the necessity of publication, see especially "Intellect," CW.II.198-99.

25 On the concept of metamorphosis, here and elsewhere in Emerson, see Packer, *Emerson's Fall*, pp. 190-93; Robert D. Richardson, Jr., *Myth and Literature in the American Renaissance* (Bloomington: Indiana University Press, 1978), pp. 79-83; and the anthology ed. by David Levin, *Emerson: Prophecy, Metamorphosis, and Influence* (New York: Columbia University Press, 1975), especially Daniel B. Shea, "Emerson and the American Metamorphosis," pp. 38-53. The proto-evolutionary implications of metamorphosis, though undeniable, are often overstated. For a general overview of the issue, see Frederick William Conner, *Cosmic Optimism: A Study of the Interpretation of Evolution by American Poets from Emerson to Robinson* (Gainesville: University of Florida Press, 1949), pp. 37-66.

26 The range of responses to the essay is represented in the progression from Porte, who praises it as the culmination of the energy of the first series (*Representative Man*, p. 177); to Packer, who hears in its ironies "the affirmation of a second best" (*Emerson's Fall*, p. 179); to David Porter, who sees in the essay's subversive poetics Emerson's explanation for his own failure as poet (*Emerson* *and Literary Change*, pp. 176-80). My own view of the essay's weaknesses would lie somewhere between Packer's and Porter's.

27 For an account of identity in terms of "feeling like," see Thomas Nagel, *Mortal Questions* (Cambridge: Cambridge University Press, 1979), pp. 165-80.

28 Thus though my account looks like (and profits from) Whicher's, I would claim this one difference in our emphases. By focusing on the shifting tone, Whicher finds shape in Emerson's career; by focusing on the ideas, I do not. Although Emerson clearly comes to understand more fully the questions with which he began his philosophical career, the issues themselves remain sufficiently constant that it may be unwise to speak of this refinement as "growth" or "change." At the very least, it seems unfair to see the tonal progression from "Circles" through "Experience" to "Fate" as the characteristic shift: each of these pessimistic essays is published in a collection whose predominant tone is optimistic.

29 To this extent, Emerson does anticipate the modernist disorientation of an Eliot or a Beckett. And, in fact, the essay everywhere speaks the language of "ruins" and "fragments"; see pp. 44, 47. Thus even if Emerson speaks initially in clichés, he problematizes his apparently simplistic views through ironic repetition and redefinition.

30 Packer mentions both these similarities; *Emerson's Fall*, pp. 197-98.

31 In some senses, the pairing with "Character" is more interesting than that with "The Poet." For "Character" is all that remains of "Self-Reliance" and "The Over-Soul" in the second series.

32 See, for example, Packer, *Emerson's Fall*, p. 170; and especially Porte, *Representative Man*, pp. 182-83.

33 See, for example, "The Method of Nature," where our historical distance from the Puritans measures the way their inspiring piety "glides away from us day by day" (CW.I.135). See also "Poet," p. 15.

34 For images of surface and skating, see CW.II.131, 138; for the source in *The Prelude*, see Book I, ll. 425-63 and JMN.V.454. See also Packer's fine analysis, *Emerson's Fall*, pp. 102-09.

35 The image alludes also to the warts and wens of the Divinity School "Address" and the cicatrized wound of "Compensation." See EL.II.312; CW.I.83; CW.II.68.

36 Jonathan Bishop is especially good on the horizon image, though he seems not to see the importance of the recognition that the horizon too is a subjective phenomenon; see *Emerson on the Soul* (Cambridge, Mass.: Harvard University Press, 1964), pp. 34-35, 194, 197.

37 Many critics recognize this continuity; see, for example, Bishop, *Emerson on the Soul*, pp. 199-200; Packer, *Emerson's Fall*, p. 170; and Gayle L. Smith, "Style and Vision in 'Experience,' " *ESQ* 27 (1981), 85-86.

38 This claim is made most forcefully by Bishop, *Emerson on the Soul*, p. 193. For similar readings, see Porte, *Representative Man*, pp. 179-84; and Packer, *Emerson's Fall*, pp. 151-55.

39 For a modern formulation, see Ludwig Wittgenstein, *Tractatus Logico-Philosophicus* (London: Routledge & Kegan Paul, 1961), 6.431-4311.

40 For other uses of the image of the loaded dice, one of Emerson's favorites, see CW.I.25, II.60; W.VI.221; and JMN.V.124, VI.178, 215.

41 For a transitional image, see Emerson's claim in "The Poet" that language is vehicular, good "as ferries and horses are, for conveyance, not as farms and houses are, for homestead" (p. 20).

42 The passage recalls that in *Nature*, where the fields are the property of particular farmers whereas the horizon belongs to the integrating eye of the poet (CW.I.9).

43 For other interpretations of the term, see Whicher, who associates it with the more empirical "experiment" (*Freedom and Fate*, pp. 111-12); and Packer, who associates it with Hume (*Emerson's Fall*, pp. 157-59). Although agreeing with Packer that "experience" has a "technical meaning," I would insist that the source lies less in the empirical tradition, where the more representative term is "impression," than in Kant, where "experience" is almost literally the first word of the first *Critique*.

44 It is striking that in the eighteenth century the term "phenomenology" is defined as the "theory of illusions." Though the term is rarely used by Kant, his own definition of "phenomenon" broadened both this term and its relation to the "illusions" of the mind, the central topic of the Dialectic. Thus Emerson's essay may be a "phenomenology" in both the eighteenth-century and the modern, post-Hegelian sense.

45 See Packer, *Emerson's Fall*, p. 164. She seems, however, to think that this identity is merely characteristic of "temperament" and something that man can transcend.

46 See, for example, Cox's claim that the hubris of *Nature* is almost an implicit death sentence for Waldo; in Levin, *Emerson*, pp. 73-74. Similar charges of impersonality are implicit in Winters and Anderson. For the defenses, Edward Emerson's apologetic note is representative, W.III.304; see also pp. 302-03. It is suggestive that two of Emerson's most sensitive critics, Whicher and Porte, avoid the passage altogether.

47 The formulation here is Bishop's; see *Emerson on the Soul*, p. 198. Many sympathetic readings argue that Emerson simply misunderstood the depth of his grief, an explanation that both condescends and sidesteps the issue of the place of this personal revelation in his overall argument. Even those more subtle readers who argue that Emerson understood his emotions are faced with the problem of explaining why this tragedy was worse than previous ones. The result is almost always a fruitless, and unseemly, discrimination between corpses; see Bishop, *Emerson on the Soul*, p. 197, and Packer, *Emerson's Fall*, p. 169.

48 For the Cartesian source, see *Discourse on the Method*, IV; and *Principles of Philosophy*, I.xlv; in Elizabeth S. Haldane and G. R. T. Ross, eds., *The Philosophical Works of Descartes* (Cambridge: Cambridge University Press, 1968), I, 101, 237. For analyses, see Bernard Williams, *Descartes: The Project of Pure Enquiry* (Harmondsworth: Penguin Books, 1978), pp. 49-51, 73-76; and, more generally, Richard Rorty, *Philosophy and the Mirror of Nature* (Princeton, N.J.: Princeton University Press, 1979), pp. 54-69.

49 For this view, see Saul A. Kripke, *Naming and Necessity* (Cambridge, Mass.: Harvard University Press, 1980), pp. 152-53; and, in response, Rorty, *Mirror*, pp. 78-88.

50 On this point, see Packer, *Emerson's Fall*, p. 169.

51 For this fallacy, see Alfred North Whitehead, *Science and the Modern World* (New York: The Macmillan Co., 1967), pp. 51-58.

52 For Cavell's claim that Emerson, like Heidegger, is an epistemologist of moods, see "Thinking of Emerson," *New Literary History* 11 (1979), p. 168.

53 Richard Rorty has claimed, in a public lecture, that the image of beads on a string was in the late eighteenth and early nineteenth centuries a standard answer to Hume's denial of the self. Hume – it was argued – focused on the particulars of selfhood without seeing that the particulars presupposed a unifying concept, much as the beads of a necklace required an invisible string. I have found no source for this argument. For Emerson's use of the image elsewhere, see JMN.XIII.392; and Porte, *Representative Man*, p. 314.

54 For a related formulation, see "Character," p. 57.

55 The problem of "other minds" is largely a modern concern. For a roughly contemporary treatment, however, see the 1867 edition of John Stuart Mill, *An Examination of Sir William Hamilton's Philosophy*, ed. J. M. Robson (Toronto: University of Toronto Press, 1979), pp. 205-06n. Emerson would have had a discussion available to him in Thomas Reid; see, for example, *Essays on the Intellectual Powers of Man*, VI.v (Cambridge, Mass.: MIT Press, 1969), pp. 637-38.

56 For a similar account, see the famous passage in "The Poet," p. 6. The progression of the images suggests, once again, that Emerson's aesthetic theory is finally a function of his more pervasive epistemological one.

57 For discussions of succession earlier in Emerson, see "The Over-Soul," CW.II.160; and "Circles," CW.II.186. Most of the contemporary summaries of Kant refer at least in passing to this notion of succession; see, for example, Francis Bowen, *Modern Philosophy from Descartes to Schopenhauer and Hartmann,* 6th ed. (New York: Charles Scribner's Sons, 1891), pp. 216-18; and *The Works of Orestes A. Brownson* (Detroit: Thorndike Nourse, 1882), I, 196, 199.

58 Kant, *Pure Reason,* p. A193=B238. For a use of the loaded term "apprehension" in the context of a discussion on permanence and stability, see "Circles," CW.II.183.

59 Kant, *Pure Reason,* p. A189. For an analysis of this passage, see Jonathan Bennett, *Kant's Analytic* (New York: Cambridge University Press, 1966), pp. 223-29. It is customary in modern interpretations to prefer Kant's formulation in A to that in B.

60 There may be an implicit tension between the apparently positive notion of the "gaining party" and the more neutral "parti-colored" wheel of two sentences earlier (p. 34).

61 For positions somewhat between these two extremes, see "The Method of Nature," CW.I.123; and "Intellect," CW.II.201.

62 For this antiverificationist tone, which may also be antipragmatist, see Nagel, *Mortal Questions,* pp. ix-xii. One would want to remember, however, that "indifference" does not mean the same thing to Kant and James: transcendental indifference marks the extent to which the difference is indeterminable; pragmatic, the extent to which nothing depends on it. For a response to Nagel, see Richard Rorty, *Consequences of Pragmatism (Essays: 1972-1980)* (Minneapolis: University of Minnesota Press, 1982), pp. xxxi-vii.

63 In the reference to the drunkard, there may be here an implicit allusion to one of Emerson's favorite scenes, the prologue to *The Taming of the Shrew*.

64 Such a triumph over Waldo's death may seem cavalier. It is, however, better than the similar triumph in *Nature*, where Charles was reduced to a moral preceptor. Moreover the absences in the list implicitly admit that although many are still alive, one's father and brother are indeed dead.

65 Moreover, the pun on nature's "irresistible nature," by alluding to the more severe Calvinist doctrine of "irresistible grace," tempers the apparent determinism of the earlier sections. Similarly the claim that man must walk a "hair's breadth line" qualifies the earlier sense of temperament as an iron wire (pp. 38-39).

66 The passage rewrites an earlier statement in "Circles" (CW.II.189) to emphasize not endless generation but personal satisfaction.

67 To say that Emerson accepts surprise as given is not to say that world is real, or Sellars's "myth," but only that he thinks, with Quine, that at any given moment some, though not always the same, notions cannot be changed. For this debate in modern philosophy, see Wilfred Sellars, *Science, Perception, and Reality* (London: Routledge & Kegan Paul, 1963), pp. 127-96; and Willard Van Orman Quine, *From a Logical Point of View* (Cambridge, Mass.: Harvard University Press, 1980), pp. 42-46. Rorty treats these two views as complementary in *Mirror*, pp. 165-212.

68 This farewell to individuals at the end of the fifth section of the essay stands as roughly equivalent to the farewell to Charles at the end of the fifth chapter of *Nature*. In "Experience," however, Emerson is more fully in control of his rhetoric, and is clearer on the degree to which the point is logical and not autobiographical.

69 John Locke, *An Essay Concerning Human Understanding,* II.xxvii.11, 16; ed. Alexander Campbell Fraser (1894; reprinted New York: Dover Books, 1959), I, 449, 458. For analyses, see, in addition to the Perry and A. Rorty anthologies previously cited, J. L. Mackie, *Problems from Locke* (Oxford: Oxford University Press, 1976), pp. 173-203; and Antony Flew, "Locke and the Problem of Personal Identity," in C. B. Martin and D. M. Armstrong, eds., *Locke and Berkeley: A Collection of Critical Essays* (Garden City, N.Y.: Doubleday & Company, Inc., 1968), pp. 155-78.

70 For this formulation, see Terence Penelhum, "Personal Identity," *The Encyclopedia of Philosophy,* ed. Paul Edwards (New York: Macmillan Co. and The Free Press, 1967), VI, 97-98. He argues that the "hard" meaning of "could"– that there are actual psychological procedures that would induce John to recall the event–and the "soft"–that to John alone are these procedures appropriately applied–are both false. See also Flew, in Martin and Armstrong, *Locke and Berkeley,* pp. 160-63; and, behind both, Bishop Butler.

71 *Intellectual Powers*, III.iv; pp. 338-39.

72 *Intellectual Powers*, III.iv; pp. 340-41. The image of the lost limb, but not of the lost estate, comes from Locke, *Essay*, II.xxvii.11; I, 452. Emerson had, of course, known Reid since his Harvard days; see the Bowdoin essays, and Allen, *Waldo Emerson*, p. 44.

73 For the centrality of reidentification to the notion of personal identity, see Penelhum, *Encyclopedia of Philosophy*, VI, 95; and P. F. Strawson, *Individuals: An Essay in Descriptive Metaphysics* (Garden City, N.Y.: Doubleday & Company, 1963), pp. 19-27, 62-74. In part, the issue is merely a special case of the more general problem of memory and personhood.

74 *Philosophical Investigations*, trans. G. E. M. Anscombe (New York: Macmillan Publishing Co., Inc., 1968), § 265. (References to the *PI* traditionally cite section numbers for Part I and page numbers for Part II.) For treatments of this passage, see A. J. Ayer, "Can There Be a Private Language?" in George Pitcher, ed., *Wittgenstein: The Philosophical Investigations* (Notre Dame: University of Notre Dame Press, 1966), pp. 254-66; Anthony Kenny, *Wittgenstein* (Cambridge, Mass.: Harvard University Press, 1973), pp. 192-93; and Hacker, *Insight*, pp. 226, 236-37. For the Kantian dimensions of this point, see Bennett, *Analytic*, pp. 204-10.

75 For Hume's famous attack on the concept of self, see *A Treatise of Human Nature*, I.iv.6; ed. L. A. Selby-Bigge (Oxford: Clarendon Press, 1973), p. 252; see also the appendix; p. 634. It is suggestive that in the disorienting image of the mind as a theatre, which immediately follows his deconstruction of self, one mark of this evanescence is the way in which perceptions "glide away," just as at the beginning of "Experience"; see p. 253.

76 For Kant, see Jonathan Bennett's account of the "Cartesian basis," *Kant's Dialectic* (New York: Cambridge University Press, 1974), pp. 66-69; for Wittgenstein, see the articles by Alan Donagan and Anthony Kenny reprinted in Pitcher, ed., *Wittgenstein*, pp. 324-70.

77 See *PI*, §. 410; and Hacker, *Insight*, pp. 262-63.

78 Thus in the climax of the passage, we are told to leave off postponing and wishing and especially referring and, instead of asking "where," to do broad justice to that place wherever it is (p. 35).

79 For Kant, see *Pure Reason*, pp. A307=B363-64, and A361-66. This particular formulation is P. F. Strawson's, *The Bounds of Sense: An Essay on Kant's Critique of Pure Reason* (London: Methuen and Co., Ltd., 1966), pp. 37, 162-69.

80 The phrase is Bertrand Russell's. For its relevance to the modern, Wittgensteinian position, see Hacker, *Insight*, pp. 186, 213, 262. Wittgenstein's special (and changing) definition of "solipsism," of course, lies near the center of all accounts of his philosophy.

81 On Cartesianism and the essentially first-person status of mental concepts, see Colin McGinn, *The Character of Mind* (Oxford: Oxford University Press, 1982), pp. 6-7.

82 These distinctions are derived loosely from A. J. Ayer. See *The Concept of a Person* (New York: St. Martin's Press, 1964), p. 79; and Rorty's discussion of it in "Wittgenstein, Privileged Access, and Incommunicability," *American Philo-*

sophical Quarterly 7 (1970), 193. I have eliminated Ayer's fourth variety of unsharable.

83 For representative passages in Descartes, see *Principles of Philosophy*, I. xlvi, lxvii-xxii; I, 236, 247-50; and, for commentary, Williams, *Descartes,* pp. 82-86, 298; and Anthony Kenny, *Descartes: A Study of His Philosophy* (New York: Random House, 1968), pp. 121-25. For Locke, see *Essay*, II.vii.4-6; I, 161-63; and, for commentary, Flew in Martin and Armstrong, *Locke and Berkeley,* p. 178. For Kant, see *Pure Reason*, pp. B66-69, B152-59; and, for commentary, W. H. Walsh, *Kant's Criticism of Metaphysics* (Chicago: University of Chicago Press, 1976), pp. 187-89. Modern discussions grow out of Wittgenstein; see, for example, *PI*, §§ 246, 253, 271, 293, 304, 403-10; and, for commentary, Hacker, *Insight*, pp. 189-201, 246-77. For the argument that Locke differs significantly from Wittgenstein, see Hacker, *Insight*, pp. 224-31; for a similar distinction between Wittgenstein and Kant, see Bennett, *Analytic*, pp. 210-14. For a suggestive coupling of pain with other sensations, especially the smell of roses, see Reid, *Intellectual Powers*, II.xvi; pp. 242-51; see also II.xxii; p. 311.

84 For the argument that modern skepticism is parasitic on the notion of mind, see Rorty, *Mirror*, pp. 94-95n, 113-14, 139-40 et passim.

85 For the nineteenth-century objection against vibratiuncles, see Clarke; quoted in Miller, *Transcendentalists*, p. 48. The specific villain here is Hartley. More recently the criticism has focused on Gilbert Ryle and to some extent Wittgenstein himself. For commentary, see Rorty, *Mirror,* pp. 98-106.

86 See Williams, *Descartes,* pp. 81-85, 305-06.

87 For a similar argument about the thrust of Wittgenstein's point about other minds, see Norman Malcolm, "Knowledge of Other Minds," in Pitcher, ed., *Wittgenstein,* pp. 371-83. Critics have argued that Malcolm commits himself, and by extension Wittgenstein, to a problematic verificationism. For defenses, from two different directions, see Richard Rorty, "Verificationism and Transcendental Arguments," *Nous* 5 (1971), 3-14; and Saul A. Kripke, *Wittgenstein on Rules and Private Language* (Cambridge, Mass.: Harvard University Press, 1982), pp. 119-21.

88 Privileged access has the odd result of shutting the self off from objectivity, making it seem as if no observer's criteria could be mine. On this point in relation to Kant, see Bennett, *Dialectic*, pp. 100-02. The inevitable "insulation" that Bennett finds in Kant's position may help explain Emerson's insistence on the exclusivity of subjectivity. On the paradigmatic importance of the episodic to a definition of privacy, see Williams, *Descartes,* pp. 85, 298. By this account, "Experience" would be less Cavell's "epistemology" than a "phenomenology of moods." For the related point that moods are one sign of incorrigibility, see Rorty, *Mirror,* p. 81; and Flew in Martin and Armstrong, *Locke and Berkeley,* p. 177.

89 See *Intellectual Powers*, III.vii; pp. 371-76. For the passage in Hume to which Reid responds, see *Treatise*, I.iii; pp. 8-9.

90 For this argument see Kripke, *Wittgenstein*, pp. 129-45. The key texts here are *PI*, §§ 302, 403.

91 See *PI*, §§ 403-07. On this crucial "Expressive Thesis of Avowals," the heart of the argument against Wittgenstein's behaviorism, see Hacker, *Insight,* pp. 257-61; and Donagan in Pitcher, ed., *Wittgenstein,* pp. 324-32.

92 See *PI,* §§ 293, 271. Part of the problem here may be simply our lack of a full range of pain terms.

93 As Bennett explains, as a memory-independent check, people work no better than things; see *Analytic,* p. 212. In a passage strikingly similar to "Experience," Wittgenstein wonders if others' disbelief might not nevertheless prove sharability: perhaps the claim that "it's not so bad," though unsympathetic, is sufficient. Compare *PI,* § 310 with Emerson's claim that "it is not half so bad with them as they say" (CW.III.29).

94 There is, of course, a problem with the passage, for it is difficult here and elsewhere in Emerson to determine when the pronoun is merely personal and when it puns on the formal notion of the ME. Wittgenstein, of course, distinguishes between pain and grief; for the latter, see *PI,* pp. 174, 187.

95 For this crucial argument on the noncognitive thesis of avowals, see *PI,* § 246; and, for commentary, Hacker, *Insight,* pp. 251-56, 272-77. For the relation of this argument to Kant, see Bennett's implicit comparison, *Analytic,* pp. 109-11; and Walsh's explicit one, *Kant's Criticism,* p. 187.

96 For a modern formulation, see *PI,* §§ 304, 293.

97 To this extent, subjectiveness addresses the same paradox as that in "The Poet," where man was said simultaneously to be a symbol and to inhabit symbols, p. 12.

98 For J. L. Austin's notion of the "unhappy" aspects of modern discourse, see *How to Do Things with Words,* ed. J. O. Urmson and Marina Sbisa (Cambridge, Mass.: Harvard University Press, 1975), pp. 14-15 et passim. See also Hegel's notion of the "unhappy" (because divided) consciousness, *The Phenomenology of Mind,* B; trans. J. B. Baillie (New York: Harper & Row, Publishers, Inc., 1967), pp. 251-67. Emerson's interest in Hegel is uncertain before his visit to St. Louis in 1867.

99 For a useful review of the assault on the " 'idea' idea" – waged early by Arnaud and Reid, and more recently by Austin and Quine, who invents the self-reflexive term – see Rorty, *Mirror,* pp. 60-61n. The punctuation of Emerson's passage – with the dash before "objects" and the comma after – makes the status of the noun uncertain. Although the dash is present in most editions, Emerson's punctuation is erratic; so that the reading which sees "objects" as simply one particular on the list may in fact be right. See W.III.76; and for a similar problem with the verb "compose," CW.III.40.

100 For some other versions of this list, see CW.I.8, 44; and CW.III.12.

101 See Quine's claim that "in point of epistemological footing the physical objects and the gods differ only in degree not in kind"; *Logical,* p. 44.

102 See also p. 28.

103 See *Tractatus,* 5.632, and more generally 5.6-5.641. For commentary, see Hacker, *Insight,* pp. 67-81; Bennett, *Dialectic,* p. 69; and H. O. Mounce, *Wittgenstein's Tractatus: an Introduction* (Chicago: University of Chicago Press, 1981), pp. 88-92.

104 For famous misreadings, see Whicher, *Freedom and Fate,* pp. 120-22; and Bishop, *Emerson on the Soul,* pp. 200-02. Both assume that all idealisms are the

same, and all powerful selves a return to the original promise of *Nature*. Closer
to my own view is Michael Cowan's sense that Subjectiveness is in part a return
to the original Illusion, or Cox's that "Experience" depicts the fatal necessity of
self-reliance. See Michael Cowan, *City of the West: Emerson, America, and Urban
Metaphor* (New Haven, Conn.: Yale University Press, 1967), p. 120; and Cox in
Levin, ed., *Emerson*, p. 80. The use of the unusual adjective "crescive" may be
an allusion to *Henry V*, I.i.66. For Porte's association of another famous Emersonian phrase, "chartered libertine," with the same passage, see *Representative
Man*, p. 219.

105 Swedenborg discusses this issue in at least two works, *Heaven and Hell* and
Conjugal Love. On Swedenborg and Emerson see, in addition to Hotson's articles, Packer, *Emerson's Fall*, pp. 16-18. To my knowledge, however, no reader
had yet commented on this allusion in "Experience." See also W.IV.127-29.

106 For representative couplings of Kant and Swedenborg in Emerson, see
JMN.V.179, VIII.162. More generally, Emerson would just place Swedenborg
in a Kantian context as one of the prophets of the Reason over the Understanding; see, for example, "Religion," EL.II.92. On similar couplings in Coleridge,
see René Wellek, *Immanuel Kant in England, 1793-1838* (Princeton, N.J.: Princeton University Press, 1931), p. 308; and, more generally, Thomas McFarland,
Coleridge and the Pantheist Tradition (Oxford: Clarendon Press, 1969), pp.
283-86. Kant early tries to distinguish himself from Swedenborg in *Dreams of a
Spirit-Seer*. For Emerson's more customary attack on Swedenborg's symbolism,
see W.IV.121, 133-34.

107 Cf. pp. 38, 44.

108 This argument is merely a secular version of Anselm. For related approaches to the problem of infinites, see "Character" and "Gifts," pp. 61, 93,
95; and note 8 above.

109 See, for example, "The Over-Soul," CW.II.167; and the discussion on pp.
105-06. In part, he examines the linguistic unity of the word "life," the
discontinuity between the abstract noun and plural or possessive forms of it,
like "my" life or their "lives." In part, he reaffirms one last time the formal
unity of consciousness, the need for all experience potentially to be owned. And
in part, he admits the special status of certain sensations, whose self-affirming
nature is neither established objectively through criteria nor owned subjectively.
These three unities may not really be the same, and the second in fact seems to
deny the possibility of both the first and the third. On the problem of "life" as a
concept, and its relation to the equally problematic "mind," see McGinn, *Mind*,
pp. 12-14, 31. On the conflation of unities, see Wittgenstein's point that the
only thing the "I think" adds to the "I feel pain" is a protection against the
"neighborlessness" of solipsism; *PI*, §§ 398-410; and, for commentary, Hacker,
Insight, pp. 188-97, 209-14.

110 On Wittgenstein's notion of the purely formal character of the "I," see
especially *PI*, §§ 404, 410; on the distinction between grammatical and empirical, §§ 295, 458. For commentary see Kenny, *Wittgenstein*, p. 187; and Hacker,
Insight, pp. 203-09, 261-63. On the relation of this point to Kant's on the unity
of apperception, see Hacker, *Insight*, pp. 205-07, 268-72.

111 See Wittgenstein's definition of the experiential limits of logic: "So we cannot say in logic, 'The world has this in it, and this, but not that.' . . . We cannot think what we cannot think; so what we cannot think we cannot *say* either"; *Tractatus*, 5.61. For commentary, see Mounce, *Wittgenstein's Tractatus,* pp. 12-15, 22-34.

112 As with the earlier "great and crescive self," the tone here should not be ignored. Not only is this God an abstraction, but these rocks are quite literally "bleak." For Whicher's reading, which ignores the bleakness, see *Freedom and Fate,* p. 121; for Packer's equation of the bleak rocks and the sharp peaks, see *Emerson's Fall,* p. 177. Emerson's subsequent claim – that "that need makes in morals the capital virtue of self-trust" (p. 46) – seems simply wrong. The inevitability of privacy does not "make" self-trust inevitable: instead both are necessary (and good) because each is a self-evidencing category, carrying within itself its own proof.

113 For this Kantian formulation, see *Pure Reason,* p. A796=B824.

114 For this point, see *Tractatus,* especially 4.46-4661; and, for commentary Mounce, *Wittgenstein's Tractatus,* pp. 42-48; and Pears, *Wittgenstein,* pp. 75-92.

115 The use of the term "converse" alludes back to a similar use in the paragraph on Waldo (p. 29). See also p. 40, and the concept of "conversation" in the second "Nature," CW.III.110.

116 There is a suppressed pun in the final verb: not only do we not get what we think we do; but when we do get, we discover that getting is not an action, a doing.

117 Compare this notion of difference or discrepance with those of deferral, absence, and referred existence in the second "Nature," CW.III.111-12.

118 That Emerson alludes to the similarity between "success" and "succession" is evident in his use of the adverb "successively" earlier in the paragraph, p. 48.

119 The use of the loaded term "impression" makes explicit the allusion to Hume. For Hume's famous descent from his study, see *Treatise,* I.vii; pp. 264-70.

6. AFTER EPISTEMOLOGY

1 For a discussion of Emerson's later physical problems, see Gay Wilson Allen, *Waldo Emerson: A Biography* (New York: Viking Press, 1981), pp. 665-70.

2 The major later publications are *Representative Men* (1850), based on a lecture series of 1845-46; *English Traits* (1856); and *The Conduct of Life* (1860), based on a lecture series of 1851. The publications after 1870, which along with the poems and some earlier uncollected essays make up the last six volumes of the *Works,* are problematic: Emerson's interest (and even degree of participation) in their collection is debated. On this issue see Ralph L. Rusk, *The Life of Ralph Waldo Emerson* (New York: Columbia University Press, 1957), pp. 441-42 et passim; and especially Nancy Craig Simmons, "Man without a Shadow: The Life and Work of James Elliot Cabot, Emerson's Biographer and Literary Executor," Diss. Princeton University, 1980.

3 The essay is largely neglected in the scholarship. For notable exceptions, see the various appreciations by Harold Bloom, for example, in *A Map of Misreading* (New York: Oxford University Press, 1975), p. 175; and in David

Levin, ed., *Emerson: Prophecy, Metamorphosis, and Influence* (New York: Columbia University Press, 1975), p. 147. Linda Allardt, in her study of the construction of the second series, suggests that "Experience" and "Nominalist and Realist" developed as companion pieces, JMN.XII.xxxi. It is at least clear that "Experience" (originally entitled "Life") and "Nominalist and Realist" (originally called "Representative") are the only two essays in the second series not derived from previous lectures or essays. It is also probably significant that in the original outlines for the series, "Nominalist and Realist" was last; even in the final ordering, "Experience" and "Nominalist and Realist" occupy similar positions, as the second and penultimate essays. For O. W. Firkins's claim that the two essays are closely related, see *Ralph Waldo Emerson* (Boston: Houghton Mifflin Company, 1915), p. 195.

4 For these statements, see p. 137. For similar statements in "The American Scholar," see CW.I.55-58. For a fine account of the tensions in Emerson's theory of reading, see B. L. Packer, *Emerson's Fall: A New Interpretation of the Major Essays* (New York: Continuum, 1982), pp. 102-20.

5 The CW editors have chosen the variant from the (not especially reliable) 1876 edition, without explanation. That variant, by making the statement a question, inverts the meaning. My own text comes from the first edition, p. 248; see also W.III.227.

6 For a more positive account of magnetism, see "Character," pp. 53-54; and Packer, *Emerson's Fall*, p. 184. Such accounts refer back as far as Reason's momentary grasps of the sceptre in *Nature*, CW.I.43.

7 For "The Poet," see CW.III.6. See also "Experience," CW.III.31. As is evident in the reference to a "landscape-garden" in "The Poet," both passages may anticipate Emerson's eventual dismissal of Poe as the "jingle man," although the more explicit reference in "The Poet" is to Tennyson. See, for Tennyson, JMN.VII.471; and, for Poe, William Dean Howells, *Literary Friends and Acquaintance* (Bloomington: Indiana University Press, 1968), p. 58.

8 On the continuity of this image, see Joel Porte, "The Problem of Emerson," in Monroe Engel, ed., *Uses of Literature*, Harvard English Studies 4 (Cambridge, Mass.: Harvard University Press, 1973), p. 104. Porte also correctly identifies the "exorbitant" pun earlier in the same passage.

9 The Shakespearean phrase "beguile the time" has two meanings. In the more metaphoric meaning, "beguile" means merely "to charm so that time passes quickly"; see *Twelfth Night*, III.iii.41; and *Midsummer Night's Dream*, V.i.40-41, 374. The word can, however, more literally imply deceit, as in *Macbeth*, I.v.64-65. Emerson uses the term in both its neutral and ominous senses.

10 The paragraph combines two journal passages, JMN.IX.87, 40. That the linking of these two passages is not entirely consistent may say something about Emerson's techniques of revision. But at the very least, one must recognize that the more important of the two passages (and the longer) is also the older. Whatever Emerson means in yoking the two, it is not a simple case of ambivalence or changing his mind.

11 On the incarnation motif earlier in Emerson, see CW.II.164, 198-99; and pp. 104-05.

12 For references to corn in the earlier works, see CW.I.35, 76.

13 Although it might seem too much to find in this reference to games an anticipation of the high relativism of Wittgenstein, it at least looks toward the low relativism of Henry Adams. For this card metaphor, see *The Education of Henry Adams* (Cambridge, Mass.: Houghton Mifflin Company, 1961), p. 4. Adams, of course, both mentions Emerson openly and quotes him secretly; see pp. 27, 35, xxiv.

14 The allusion extends Emerson's original claim in *Nature* to grow like the corn and melons (CW.I.35). It anticipates Thoreau's desire in the first chapter of *Walden* to sit alone on a pumpkin rather than share a cushion; (Princeton, N.J.: Princeton University Press, 1971), p. 37, cf. p.64. Both images may look back to Carlyle's extended image of pumpkin-eating in "The Nigger Question"; see *The Works of Thomas Carlyle in Thirty Volumes*, centenary edition (New York: Charles Scribner's Sons, 1896-99), XXIX, 348-83; and Harold Bloom, *Agon: Towards a Theory of Revisionism* (New York: Oxford University Press, 1982), pp. 155-56.

15 The use of "consent" here probably alludes wittily to the theological notion most closely associated with Jonathan Edwards. See *The Nature of True Virtue* (Ann Arbor: University of Michigan Press, 1960), p. 3 et passim; and, for commentary, Perry Miller, *Jonathan Edwards* (New York: William Sloan Associates, 1949), pp. 240-43; and Norman Fiering, *Jonathan Edwards's Moral Thought and Its British Context* (Chapel Hill: The University of North Carolina Press for the Institute of Early American History and Culture, 1981), pp. 80-84, 112-15.

16 The time lag is less than it might appear. "Nominalist and Realist" is a late addition to the second series, compiled largely after February 1844. *Representative Men* was delivered as a lecture series in the winter of 1845-46. One would at least want to remember that "Nominalist and Realist" was originally called "Representative," JMN.XII.576-77.

17 The lecture series, reprinted in EL.I, dates from the early months of 1835 and contains none of the same figures. For the role of biography in the first series, see CW.II.6. This apparent preference for biography, in fact, really just introduces the later (and more important) idea that biography is merely personal and that all men have equal potential; see, for example, CW.II.174.

18 This difference is explicit in the introductory lectures to the two series. The early series on "Biography" examines the "tests" by which the great may be recognized, EL.I.424-25. *Representative Men* begins merely with a study of their "Uses." Compare also the more definite opening to Carlyle's similar work, *Heroes and Hero-worship*. Here the assertions of the reality of great men and the definition of "Universal History" as "the History of Great Men" recalls more Emerson's early statements in "Biography" and "History" than those in the later volume; see especially the first lecture; *The Works*, V, 1.

19 On the relation of rotation to great men, see JMN.VIII.430-31. Here Emerson makes it clear – as he does not when he inverts the passage in "Experience" (CW.III.32-33) – that rotation and succession are the same concept; and that what teaches him the Galilean truth of *pero si muove* is not planetary motion but the way in which his delight in Montaigne is superseded by that in other authors.

20 See especially pp. 6-7.

21 Similar objections might be raised to Swedenborg's presence as representative mystic. But Swedenborg has, of course, long been a figure in Emerson's pantheon, and the ambivalence of that essay announces his problematic status in a way that the admiring treatment of Montaigne does not.

22 Montaigne enters on p. 162 and exits on p. 170. Of the other representative men, only Goethe appears as late in his essay, and he stays through to the end. On this anomaly, see R. A. Yoder, *Emerson and the Orphic Poet in America* (Berkeley: University of California Press, 1978), pp. 67-68.

23 The reference is once again to the prologue of *The Taming of the Shrew*, a favorite of Emerson's. See also Stephen E. Whicher, *Freedom and Fate: An Inner Life of Ralph Waldo Emerson* (Philadelphia: University of Pennsylvania Press, 1953), p. 114.

24 See p. 155; and, for Herbert, lines 37-42:

> Whereas my birth and spirit rather took
> The way that takes the town,
> Thou didst betray me to a ling'ring book,
> And wrap me in a gown.
> I was entangled in the world of strife,
> Before I had the power to change my life.

For commentary see Edward Emerson's note, W.I.339; and Helen Vendler, *The Poetry of George Herbert* (Cambridge, Mass.: Harvard University Press, 1975), pp. 41-48. For Emerson's knowledge of these lines, see JMN.VIII.249, XII.369, 378. For a suggestive passage that may have influenced "Experience," see the earlier stanza on pain, especially ll. 25, 29-30:

> My flesh began unto my soul in pain.
>
> . . . .
>
> Sorrow was all my soul; I scarce beleeved,
> Till grief did tell me roundly that I lived.

25 In the characteristic Herbertian tag,

> Ah my dear God! though I am clean forgot,
> Let me not love thee, if I love thee not.

Although Emerson does not allude to this couplet in the essay, he clearly knew of it; see JMN.IV.255, VI.230, XIV.277.

A similar allusion overturns the later project to "secure those advantages which we can command." Refusing the "airy and unattainable," Emerson's skeptic declares, "Come, no chimeras! Let us go abroad; let us mix in affairs; let us learn and get and have and climb. 'Men are a sort of moving plants, and, like trees, receive a great part of their nourishment from the air. If they keep too much at home, they pine' " (p. 159). The mock-heroic rhetoric is inherently self-defeating, and the nourishment from air sharply qualifies his contempt for the airy. But more important, the uncharacteristic desire to go abroad lest he pine recalls the opening lines to one of Herbert's most famous poems, "The

Collar": "I struck the board, and cry'd, 'No more;/I will abroad.'/What, shall I ever sigh and pine?" As in the other poem, the narrator wildly overestimates his freedom, implicitly misunderstanding what a relation to God means and, after raging and reasoning throughout the poem, acquiesces immediately at the mere "thought" of God's call. Although there is in Emerson no explicit reference to the poem, it is very famous. The phrase "rope of sand," which Emerson regularly uses, is in the poem; and it seems as likely that Emerson knew it from there as from a later work like Butler's *Hudibras,* commonly thought the source. For representative uses, see CW.II.69, 236n.

26 For a related image see JMN.XIII.392; and Joel Porte's analysis in *Representative Man: Ralph Waldo Emerson in His Time* (New York: Oxford University Press, 1979), p. 314.

27 Illusion in this essay measures the difference between law and life and is not to be conflated with the felt illusion of "Experience," which marked simply the absence of objective criteria within the subjective realm.

28 The argument is generally Kantian, as is the language, especially the celestial imagery. Similarly the awkward "unbelief" derives as much from the German *Unglaube* as from the more normal English "disbelief" (p. 180).

29 For representative critical anger, see Whicher, *Freedom and Fate,* pp. 119-22; Jonathan Bishop, *Emerson on the Soul* (Cambridge, Mass.: Harvard University Press, 1964), p. 214; and Porte, *Representative Man,* p. 196. B. L. Packer reads the ending more positively as a leap into faith, *Emerson's Fall,* pp. 209-10.

30 Quine analyzes the relation between skepticism and belief in terms of the riddle of non-being, which he calls "Plato's beard," using the existence of Pegasus as example; see Willard Van Orman Quine, *From a Logical Point of View* (Cambridge, Mass.: Harvard University Press, 1980), pp. 1-4. The relevance of modern reference theory to Emerson's discussion suggests the extent to which "representative" may in Emerson be used as a philosophical term of art. At the very least, one would want to mark how Emerson's unbeliever who loves belief illustrates the paradox of Plato's beard. For a less theoretical history of skepticism, see Richard H. Popkin, *The History of Scepticism from Erasmus to Descartes,* rev. ed. (New York: Harper & Row, Publishers, Inc., 1968); and for the later tradition, David Fate Norton, *David Hume: Common-Sense Moralist, Sceptical Metaphysician* (Princeton, N.J.: Princeton University Press, 1982), pp. 241-90.

31 For this response, see Oliver Wendell Holmes, *Ralph Waldo Emerson* (1884; reprinted New York: Chelsea House, 1980), pp. 176-78. Modern readers frequently respond to this emphasis on fate and power; see, for example, Harold Bloom, *Figures of Capable Imagination* (New York: Seabury Press, 1976), pp. 60-63. For a response to Holmes's overemphasis on the early sections of the essay, see Edward Emerson's notes, W.VI.340-42. Emerson never really oversentimentalized nature: not in the second series, where she was, on the one hand, not a Buddhist and, on the other, downright bleak; nor even in *Nature,* where after an initial commodiousness she finally revealed her rending tigers and bears.

32 Fate is defined variously as: the laws of the world; the expense of ends to means; something whose "book" is the same as nature's; limitation; natural history; the meter of the growing man; facts not yet passed under the fire of thought; and causes that are unpenetrated (pp. 4, 8, 15, 20, 22, 23, 30, 31).

33 On this point, see Stanley Cavell, "Genteel Responses to Kant? In Emerson's 'Fate' and in Coleridge's *Biographia Literaria*," *Raritan* 3, ii (Fall 1983), 47-48. Much of what I say here is intended as a friendly amendment to Cavell's compelling analysis. Cavell is himself modifying earlier statements in *The Senses of Walden*, expanded ed. (San Francisco: North Point Press, 1981), pp. 94-97, 106-07n. For "condition" elsewhere in Emerson, see the Divinity School "Address" and "The Poet," CW.I.84, III.24.

34 For Kant's use of the term "condition," see *Critique of Pure Reason*, trans. Norman Kemp Smith (New York: St. Martin's Press, 1965), pp. A84-92= B116-24, A307=B364, A336-37=B393-94, and throughout the Antinomy of Pure Reason. It is on the relation between concepts and conditions that many philosophers find Kant most similar to modern philosophers, especially Wittgenstein; see, for example, Jonathan Bennett, *Kant's Analytic* (New York: Cambridge University Press, 1966), pp. 53-54; and Cavell, "Fate," p. 47.

35 Cavell emphasizes the importance of writing throughout his analyses of the American Renaissance – in terms of both Thoreau and Emerson. For this specific point, see "Fate," pp. 46-51; and, more generally, *Senses*, pp. xiv-xv, 3-35, 141-49.

36 It is perhaps this self-enclosed nature of language that has led modern philosophers to find it more fundamental than epistemology. Since philosophy of language is itself language, it to some extent speaks its own language. Epistemology, however, is also language, and thus its own peculiar problems are compounded with the problems of any linguistic discourse.

37 The second phrase, with its allusion to the possibility of penetrating causes, is of course not Kantian.

38 For Hegel's use of "annul" (*aufheben*), see *Logic*, being Part One of the *Encyclopaedia of the Philosophical Sciences*, § 96; trans. William Wallace (New York: Oxford University Press, 1975), p. 142. For "reconciliation" (*Versöhnung*), see *Ästhetik* (Frankfurt am Main: Europäische Verlagsanstalt, 1966), I, 520; II, 566-70. Charles Taylor discusses both in *Hegel* (Cambridge: Cambridge University Press, 1975), p. 119. Cavell notes explicitly the Hegelian aspects of Emerson's use of "annul" in "Fate," p. 50.

39 For Wittgenstein's similar point about the unsayable, see Ludwig Wittgenstein, *Tractatus Logico-Philosophicus* (London: Routledge & Kegan Paul, 1961), 7. A similar recognition lies behind Kant's general desire to deny knowledge to make room for faith (*Pure Reason*, p. B xxx).

40 For a related reading, see Bishop, *Emerson on the Soul*, pp. 209-10. The metaphor may also recall the distinction in Emerson whereby the early sense of knowledge as coming into the mind ("intuition") is replaced by the more social one of it going out ("ecstasy"). For "ecstasy" in the essay, see p. 41; on this distinction earlier in Emerson, see CW.I.80, 125; and II.37, 167, 195.

41 For the passage in "Circles," see CW.II.183-84. There is a similar allusion to the same passage earlier in the essay, p. 13.

42 Pp. 37, 46. For webs earlier in Emerson, see CW.II.163, 194, 199. A similar notion of relation informs Quine's holism; see especially W. V. Quine and J. S. Ullian, *The Web of Belief* (New York: Random House, 1978), pp. 9-19 et passim.

43 According to Cavell, the problem of fate is parasitic on our sense of alienation, just as that of skepticism is parasitic on our sense of an independent world; see "Fate," p. 46. Thus the real reason we cannot talk about the times, as Emerson complains at the beginning of the essay, is that we lack an external vantage point from which to view them: the times are what we now are. Our incorporation into the system we would analyze explains why the thought already contains the event, or, as in the opening, the dictation is irresistible (pp. 40, 3). Although the context is not narrowly epistemological, the point is the same as that in *Nature* wherein all man's questions were answered "already"; in both cases the apparent atemporality just measures the extent to which the conversation is really a monologue.

44 For the Platonic source, see *Phaedrus*, 246b-248b; in *Collected Dialogues of Plato*, ed. Edith Hamilton and Huntington Cairns (Princeton, N.J.: Princeton University Press, 1961), pp. 493-95. For an analysis of Emerson's horse imagery, largely in terms of the passage from "The Poet" (CW.III.13, cf. p. 16), see John Q. Anderson, "Emerson's 'Horses of Thought,' " *Emerson Society Quarterly* 5 (IV Quarter 1956), 1-2; and William J. Scheick, *The Slender Human Word: Emerson's Artistry in Prose* (Knoxville: University of Tennessee Press, 1978), pp. 107-08.

45 For the most telling criticism of this passage, echoed by subsequent critics, see Bishop, *Emerson on the Soul*, p. 211; also Bloom, *Figures*, pp. 62-63. For similar formulations earlier in the career, see "Spiritual Laws," CW.II.79; and "Politics," CW.III.124, cf. p. 122.

46 For a similarly pictorial approach, see *Nature*, CW.I.36; and the discussion on pp. 35, 41-2. For a similar notion of the pictorial status of propositions, see *Tractatus*, 2.1-2.225. For a modern reading of this aesthetic theory of truth as description, see Richard Rorty, *Consequences of Pragmatism (Essays: 1972-1980)* (Minneapolis: University of Minnesota Press, 1982), p. 12.

Index

279